Marketing for Tourism

"You booked us a holiday abroad during the summer. Could you tell us, please, where we went?"

(Reproduced by kind permission of Punch)

Marketing for Tourism

J C Holloway · R V Plant

SECOND EDITION

PITMAN
PUBLISHING

PITMAN PUBLISHING
128 Long Acre, London WC2E 9AN

A Division of Longman Group Limited

© J C Holloway and R V Plant 1992

Second edition first published in Great Britain 1992
Reprinted 1993

British Library Cataloguing in Publication Data
A catalogue record for this book is available from the
British Library.

ISBN 0-273-03844-3

Typeset by Avocet Typesetters, Bicester, Oxon
Printed and bound in Great Britain

Contents

Preface

PART 1

1 **The marketing perspective 1**
What is marketing? 4
A historical overview 5
Some issues in travel and tourism
marketing 5
Marketing as a field of study 7
Constraints in marketing 7
Categories of marketing 9
The nature of tourism services 10

2 **Marketing planning 13**
What is marketing planning? 13
Planning for what? 13
Setting objectives 14
The business environment 15
SWOT analysis 17
Strategic planning 20
Forecasting 22
Setting the marketing budget 25
Organising for effective marketing 26
The marketing mix 28
Controlling the marketing plan 29

3 **Marketing research and its applications
   in tourism 30**
What is marketing research? 30
Why marketing research? 30
What information do we need? 31
The Marketing Information System 31
Qualitative versus quantitative research
methods 45
Econometric models 46
The effectiveness of research 47

4 **The tourist market 49**
Understanding needs and wants 49
Sociological groups 52

The psychology of the consumer 53
Applying consumer theory to tourism
marketing 55
Segmentation in travel and tourism
marketing 55
Other lessons from Maslow 57
Decision-making for the travel
purchase 59
Market segmentation as a guide to
marketing planning 60

5 **Tourism product policy 62**
What is product policy? 62
Differentiating the product 63
The product mix 69
The product life cycle 70
Launching a new product 73
Why do products fail? 74
Screening the product 75

6 **Pricing the product 79**
The economics of price 79
Pricing to meet objectives 81
Internal influences on pricing 82
Pricing and the product mix 84
Price's role in the tourism marketing mix 85
Other influences on price 86
Developing a price policy 87
Strategic and tactical pricing 91
Discounting tactics 93

7 **Marketing communications 96**
The communications process 96
Determining the promotions mix 96
The communications budget 99
The message objectives 100
Designing the message 103
Successful communications 105
Personal selling 105
The sales sequence 107
Travel agency design 110

8 The distribution system 117
Channel choice 117
Selecting the channel 119
Intensive versus selective distribution 120
The agency relationship and its distribution implications 121
Availability and suitability of distributors 122
The travel agent as distributive system 123
Co-operative distribution systems 124
Building links with the retail agent 127
The role of the sales representative 130
The management of the sales representative 132
Inventory control 133
Future directions 136

9 Tourism advertising 138
Expenditure 138
Advertising agencies 139
Advertising effectiveness 139
Media choice 140
Competition 141
Timing of the campaign 142
Who advertises? 143
Cost justification 143
Door-to-door distribution 145
Posters 145
Planning advertising 146

10 The travel brochure 148
The role of the travel brochure 148
The need for accuracy 148
Further regulatory requirements 149
Style and layout 149
Brochure covers 150
Design and print 150
Segmentation of the market 153
Evolution problems 154
Successful brochures 155
Getting the brochure to the prospective customer 156
The booking process 156
Brochures in a video age? 157

11 Sales promotion for travel and tourism 159
The nature of sales promotion 159
The techniques of sales promotion 160
Planning the sales promotion 162
Evaluating the impact of promotion 165

Exhibitions 166
Making presentations 168

12 Direct marketing: theory and practice 171
What is direct marketing? 171
Direct sell holidays: the case of Tjaereborg 173
Problems in the expansion of direct marketing 174
Gardeners' Delight: a success story in direct marketing 174
Off the page selling: the case of Jules Verne 176
Direct contact and direct mail 176
Using databases 177
Direct marketing for destinations: the case of the Tunisian National Tourist Office 178
Some guidelines for good direct mail letters 178

13 Public relations and its use in the tourism industry 184
PR: its definition, characteristics and role 184
The organisation of public relations 186
The Public Relations Officer 187
Mounting a PR campaign 187
Gaining publicity 187
Press relations 188
The travel agents' educational visit 194
Handling unfavourable publicity 197
Evaluating campaign results 198

14 Marketing control 200
Control in the marketing process 200
Performance control 201
Quality control 203
Financial control 204
Efficiency control 204
Strategic control 205

PART 2 CASE STUDIES

1 The marketing of a tourist attraction: Mr Bowler's Business, Bath 209
Background 209
Staffing 210
Operating evaluation 210
The marketing plan 211
Public relations 213

2 **The launch of a special event: Garden Festival Wales, Ebbw Vale 1992 216**
Background to the study 216
The product 217
Marketing strategy 217
Summary 219

3 **Marketing for market dominance in retail travel: Bakers Dolphin Travel 222**
Background 222
The problem 222
Company policy 223
Product policy 223
Organising for marketing effectiveness 224
Niche marketing strategy 225
Summary 226

4 **Marketing management in the public sector: sustainable tourism and the case of Konstanz, Germany 228**
Background 228
Strategies 230

5 **Study of an award-winning advertising campaign: The London Zoo 232**
Background 232
Objectives of the 1990 campaign 232
Advertising strategy 233

Research methodology 234
Evaluation of the campaign 234
Conclusion 234

6 **Promoting short breaks: the case of Best Western Hotels 237**
Background 237
The campaign for the short break market 237
Media planning in 1991 238
Evaluation 240

7 **Co-operative marketing of river tourism: boating holidays in the Anjou region, France 241**
Background 241
Fluvial tourism marketing 241
The promotional campaign of Mayenne Navigation 243

Appendix 1 Sources of tourism research data 244
Appendix 2 Proof-reading marks 246

References 247

Bibliography 248

Index 251

Preface

This book is written with one important premise – that the principles behind the marketing of tourism are little different from general principles of marketing. The aim of this text is therefore to help bridge the gap between general principles and actual marketing practice.

A manager who plans to work in the travel and tourism industry needs a basic understanding of general marketing philosophy and principles in order to market a product effectively, whether that product be an aircraft seat, a holiday resort, a guided tour or a bed and breakfast establishment. It is enlightening to note how recent marketing posts for large tourism firms are increasingly advertised; experience in tourism is described as 'useful, but not essential', while evidence is sought of experience in other forms of marketing, especially in the field of Fast Moving Consumer Goods (FMCG). The reason for this is not only because marketing requires a common approach regardless of industry; it is also because the FMCG business has applied the marketing philosophy much earlier than the travel business, and has established a lead in strategic marketing practice. Small businesses – and the travel industry is still made up largely of small units – generally remain unaware of marketing principles, tending to equate marketing with the sales function. However, larger corporations, especially in transport, hotels and tour operations, borrow liberally from American marketing expertise and have been quicker to recognise the need for more professionalism in management generally, and in marketing in particular. The success of such companies in responding to the needs of their clients is self-evident.

But there is another side to the coin. The marketing of *services*, of which tourism is one, does call for a different approach than is required in the marketing of goods: a different marketing mix, different distribution systems, a different emphasis on sales and customer servicing. Tourism is a people industry, in which the product is inseparable from the staff who deliver it, be they waiters, tour guides, travel agents or coach drivers. Each member of the industry has a marketing function to perform in their dealings with the public, and it is therefore vital that they acquire and put into use the practical skills of marketing.

It has been said that selling tourism is selling dreams, but all too often, for the consumer, those dreams turn into nightmares because of a lack of consumer orientation in the travel companies' management philosophy.

This book is designed to be read by those starting out their careers in the tourism industry. It is directed particularly at students on BTEC National and Higher National Diploma courses and first degree courses in which tourism marketing is studied, but it will also be a useful text for those studying marketing on professional courses such as HCIMA, CIT and ILAM. It can usefully be read by those without formal tourism or business qualifications who are working, or planning to work, in tourism marketing.

Marketing for Tourism is designed to lay the groundwork for an understanding of marketing principles, and to reveal how these principles are applied in marketing generally and in the travel and tourism industry in particular. This knowledge will provide the basis for further study of specific aspects of marketing, such as marketing research, international marketing, and advertising, which cannot be covered fully in a basic textbook of this nature. This text will, however, replace those texts, many of them excellent in their field, which are written to provide an introduction to marketing but suffer either from being too goods-orientated or too strongly directed towards the American reader.

Practical (and factual) illustrations are given throughout of how marketing theory is implemented in the travel and tourism industry.

It was for these reasons that the authors – one an academic with 15 years experience in the tourism business, the other a practitioner with wide experience in travel and consultancy work – came together to provide a textbook which would be comprehensive, simple to understand and closely related to how marketing is carried out in the 'real world'. It is our hope that through this text, students who will form the future backbone of the tourism business will have the knowledge and tools to enable them to survive in the increasingly competitive world in which they are proposing to make their careers.

Chris Holloway · Ron Plant

Part 1

1 The marketing perspective

After studying this chapter, you should be able to:

- understand the basic philosophy of marketing
- differentiate between production and marketing orientation
- appreciate the need for marketing in the present travel and tourism business environment
- recognise the constraints under which marketing is conducted
- understand the nature of travel and tourism as a product and be aware of issues affecting its marketing

'What's this marketing all about, then?'*

There's probably more talk about marketing today than at any previous time in business. It is the term managers like to use to show that their company is modern, dynamic and forward-thinking. But the fact remains that marketing in the true sense of the word is all too seldom applied in the business world, and still less in the travel and tourism industry. Of course, there are some tourism organisations, both in the public and private sectors, which have wholeheartedly adopted the marketing philosophy, and can be counted among the most effective marketing organisations in Britain; but these remain the exception rather than the rule, and good marketing practice is still rare among the smaller travel companies.

There are a number of reasons for this failure to come to terms with marketing. One is the inherent conservatism of our society, our suspicion of new ideas and reluctance to change old, well-tried ways of doing things. Another is a very real ignorance of what marketing is all about – a result of our tendency to believe that the best way of learning business is to recruit staff straight from school and 'train them up' in the ways of the company. Under this system, methods of business operation tend to perpetuate themselves, and innovation, where it exists,

depends upon the 'gut feel' of the proprietor rather than on skilled analysis of the market. Small companies believe that marketing is something that can only be undertaken by large corporations and is too expensive to be considered within the small firm. The tourism industry itself is a very young one, and only now is it beginning to come to grips with modern business practice. This has also played a part in inhibiting the development of modern marketing techniques.

This book will attempt to show that marketing is not just a 'flavour of the month' jargon term, but a business philosophy that should underline our whole approach to the running of a company. Marketing is not 'something done by the marketing department' alone; its philosophy should permeate every department. All too often, a company which declares itself to be marketing-orientated is in fact product-orientated; it is concerned principally with finding ways to make use of surplus capacity rather than with tackling the question of what the customer really wants. We see this regularly in the travel business, in the process known as 'consolidation', whereby package tour charter flights with low load factors are merged or withdrawn, necessitating passengers switching flights, airports or even distinations. The belief, widely held in the travel industry, that low price is the key to success has

* a local authority official on his appointment as Tourism Marketing Officer for the District

resulted in inconvenience, discomfort and dissatisfaction among the travelling public. One example of product-orientation in travel is the case of a major city bus company which used its buses for sightseeing on Sundays only, because that was the only day on which the company had spare capacity. Unfortunately, in this instance passenger demand was for mid-week and Saturday excursions, so the product was a failure.

In other areas of business, our competitors abroad have learned to apply the marketing philosophy very successfully, and have gained a competitive edge over many British goods and services as a result. We will need to learn the lesson for ourselves.

Let us start by defining the term and taking a look at marketing in the wider context before going on to see its relevance to the travel and tourism industry.

What is marketing?

Perhaps the best way of describing what marketing *is* is to show what it *is not*. One of the authors recently accompanied his daughter shopping for a new bikini. After a fruitless search through countless shops for a top and bottom that would fit her, she tried the branch of a well-known department store. The saleswoman was polite and helpful, but after the umpteenth bikini had been unsuccessfully tried on, she cried in exasperation, 'I just don't know what's happening these days; people don't seem to fit our clothes any longer!'

As a postscript to this story, for years in the United States it has been possible to buy the tops and bottoms of bikinis separately, a marketing-orientated solution which is gradually being adopted in Britain. Could the clothing manufacturers have discovered that our changing social habits were leading to new body shapes? Exercise, dieting and health foods are all likely to have lasting implications for the average shape and weight of our bodies, which will in turn affect the demand for clothes.

Too many people equate marketing with selling, as if the terms were synonymous. Even a travel trade paper has carried an article on travel marketing which defined it as selling – a point quickly picked up in the correspondence which followed in subsequent weeks! Others have defined it as a more sophisticated form of advertising. Actually, both selling and advertising are functions of marketing, which is an all-embracing term to indicate the direction and thrust of a firm's policies and strategies.

Marketing is about anticipating demand, recognising it, stimulating it and finally satisfying it. It is understanding what can be sold, to whom, when, where and in what quantities. There are literally dozens of acceptable definitions of marketing, but this is the definition offered by the Chartered Institute of Marketing:

'Marketing is the management function which organises and directs all those business activities involved in assessing customer needs and converting customer purchasing power into effective demand for a specific product or service, and in moving that product or service to the final consumer or user so as to achieve the profit target or other objective set by the company or other organisation.'

The definition has three important implications:

1 It is a *management* function within the company.
2 It underlies, and provides the framework for, all the activities which a business undertakes.
3 It places the emphasis on customers' needs as the starting point for the business's operations.

As Theodore Levitt expressed it, while 'selling focuses on the needs of the seller, marketing focuses on the needs of the buyer'[1]. Marketing is about finding out what the customer wants first, and then producing the product to fit those needs (a 'market-orientated' approach) as opposed to producing the product or service and then seeing to whom it can be sold (a 'product-orientated' approach).

Clearly, a marketing-orientated company is one in which the philosophy of marketing pervades the entire organisation. If decisions at board level are production-orientated, or the Chief Executive is unsympathetic to the marketing philosophy, the marketing manager's task becomes impossible. Equally, marketing cannot function effectively if other departments are inefficient. If the company's costs are high, or inadequate control over product quality results in poor value for money, no amount of 'marketing' will make the company a success. The customer's needs will remain unsatisfied, however well advertised or hard sold the product is.

A historical overview

It has taken a long time for British companies to wake up to this need. In the past, we didn't need to market our products; our colonies around the world created a ready demand for our manufactured goods. However, with independence, these countries turned to production of their own goods, or bought from our competitors. For too long we traded in the belief that what was British was best; meanwhile, our quality deteriorated, we failed to match our competitors on delivery dates and our after-sales service weakened. Workers lost confidence in their companies' management, and lost pride in their own performance. In consequence, our share of world markets in almost every commodity became smaller and our nation less wealthy compared with our competitors. At the same time, the introduction of mass production methods meant that we needed to sell more goods, in order to take advantage of the benefits of economies of scale by reducing the unit cost of our products. Our declining markets meant higher costs compared with those of other countries, making it still harder to sell our goods.

At first, our response was to sell harder. This failed, so we attempted to undercut our competitors on price, selling inferior products cheaply. This failed to take into account the customers' preference for quality and reliability, and again sales were lost.

While some major industries learnt the lesson in the early post-war years, it was only in the late 1960s and 1970s that industry started to apply the marketing concept – some 50 years later than the USA. This process accelerated in the '80s, with emphasis on design and quality coming to the fore. Firms discovered that it was better to tailor their products to the specific needs of one market, rather than to try to produce products that would meet everyone's needs. We learned to appreciate that people don't buy products, but the *benefits* which those products offer. This encouraged companies to research specific needs and how to satisfy them. Above all, companies came to understand that marketing is a dynamic concept; people's needs change over time, requiring companies to recognise and respond to those changes. The successful company today cannot guarantee that its products will continue to be in demand in the future.

Some issues in travel and tourism marketing

The early post-war years saw the birth of modern tourism as an industry. Initially, this too was sales-led and product-orientated. The spectacular growth of package holidays in the 1960s was generated by the ideas of entrepreneurs who saw opportunities to create holidays making use of spare airline capacity that had resulted from the introduction of new technology aircraft. Linked with low cost accommodation in the newly-emerging Spanish resorts and benefiting from favourable exchange rates, they were able to offer exciting holidays in the sun for less than 'dreary' holidays at home.

'. . . holidays making use of spare airline capacity . . .'

Because of the success of the venture, there were enormous pressures to increase the supply of accommodation, and repeatedly hotels failed to be built on time. Unfamiliar food gave rise to complaints, and aircraft reliability and safety gave cause for considerable concern. Then marketing experts began to arrive, questioning underlying assumptions.

It was said that in order to sell holidays, one had to overcome three essential fears:

- Fear of flying.
- Fear of foreign food.
- Fear of foreigners.

The early marketers in overseas holidays set about providing reassurance and undertook research as a prerequisite for marketing action.

Fear of flying

In a decade where such importance is attached to safety, it seems inconceivable that risks should have been taken with people's lives for commercial gain, yet effectively this was done. Elderly aircraft were being pressed into service to the limits of their capabilities. Due to restrictive pricing policies promoted by state airlines, and backed by bilateral agreements, unsuitable airports were being used (especially the notorious Perpignan in the French Pyrenees). Poor on-board layouts were uncomfortable and resulted in dangers from loose cabin baggage. Even the government added to individuals' uncertainty by insisting that aircraft used for trooping flights should have seats facing rearward to increase survival probability in the event of a forced or bad landing. When holiday passengers enquired about the reasons for this bizarre configuration, the answer hardly added to their confidence!

From the original concept of cheap redundant aircraft availability, it soon became apparent that much greater gains could be achieved by purchasing newer technology which would not only show operational economies through higher utilisation and better load factors, but would also create an aura of customer confidence that would build business levels for those associated with the new standards of holidays.

Fear of foreign food

Foreign foods presented different problems. At a time when British eating habits were much less adventurous than they are today, many of the normal Mediterranean ingredients were reviled as 'greasy', or 'foreign rubbish'. Even the ways of presentation and service were misunderstood, with different traditions, such as serving meat and vegetables separately, and the time taken over mealtimes, much criticised. Hoteliers complained of doing their best under the constraint of tight budgets. They probably complained even louder than the holidaymakers about the awkwardness of customers and the levels of food waste. A little research into methods soon paid off. Catering experts were dispatched, who advised hoteliers how to spend less on ingredients and yet achieve greater satisfaction through changes in cooking methods, presentation and service. As labour became more expensive, many hotels introduced buffets, enabling holidaymakers to choose for themselves. Though ingredient costs have risen as a result, the savings in service and in wasted food have balanced the cost, and the result is a much better answer for the majority.

Fear of foreigners

Fear of foreigners is really an insoluble problem if taken literally, for it would remove one of the main incentives for travel – to meet and understand others better. It arose in part from unreliability in the provision of accommodation, together with a misunderstanding of local customs and habits. In the 1970s, the large British travel companies decided that the only way of overcoming this barrier was to control totally the overseas accommodation and services. They invested heavily in properties built to their own specification, managed by themselves or their nominees. They introduced expertise that had not previously been available locally and raised standards substantially. Probably the most salutary changes in attitudes were created by the need of tour operators to comply with the Trades Description Act (1968) which meant that the days of careless overbooking were over. Positive moves were made by tour operators to create even greater consumer confidence by offering substantial cash compensation if failure to provide accommodation occurred. The follow-through was that the tour operators' contracts with hoteliers provided that in the event of such failures, the punitive compensation was deductable directly from the hotelier.

On a personal level, the role of the resort representative was changed from merely being an arrival/departure escort and seller of excursions to being a uniformed staff member dedicated to assisting customers to get the most out of their holidays.

Now the quality of the product of major companies should no longer be in question, any more than a sweater from Marks and Spencer. However, unfortunately price has continued to bedevil buying attitudes and too many expect higher standards than they pay for. The result is a continuing concern among consumers about the standards offered.

Marketing as a field of study

While marketing as a field of serious study in the UK goes back to the 1950s, it has now become an essential ingredient of any business course, at all levels up to post-graduate level. While the body of knowledge forming a marketing syllabus has been refined to nationally agreed standards, no one individual who has studied marketing can be expected to be an expert in all facets of the discipline. Marketing tasks are extremely diverse, requiring the application of both management and craft skills. The ability to sell effectively, to put together an effective advertisement, to create an eye-catching and attractive window display, to conduct research interviews successfully are all skills which are as important in their own way as the assiduous research, planning, recording and analysis that we associate with the management function of marketing.

It will be apparent that the strengths of the larger organisation include the ability to employ several marketing staff, who can offer widely differing talents within the sphere of marketing. Certainly, good marketing will always call for an element of entrepreneurial flair, but if our view of marketing is limited to the extrovert, dynamic salesperson who catches the headlines we are in danger of overlooking the less visible qualities of good marketing; the ability to interpret statistical data and draw rational conclusions, to demonstrate understanding of tourist needs and behaviour patterns. 'Flair' on its own is no longer enough.

Anyone who is planning to enter marketing because of its glamorous image should obtain a copy of the official *Digest of Statistics* (published by HMSO), and should recognise that the ability to analyse the demographic and social trends revealed by this publication is an essential cornerstone of their career.

Constraints in marketing

Good marketing forms the basis of the so-called 'growth economy', to which the industrialised world is committed. However, it is not without its critics, both on economic and social grounds. Economically, it is criticised for its wasteful use of resources. Huge amounts of money are spent on advertising products which are almost identical to other products, in an attempt to persuade consumers that they are unique, or better in some way than their competitors. Products are designed to date before their normal life span, in order to increase sales of more recent models, while consumer goods are designed with parts that will wear out within a given time so that the entire product will require replacing. Social critics point to the emphasis marketers place on material values by playing on consumer emotions in order to build an acquisitive society where wants, rather than needs, are manipulated, and where the consumer is led to believe that the possession of more and more goods and services is the key to a happy and successful life. As one critic put it, marketers first persuade you that you have a problem and then tell you they can help you to solve it!

Defending their role, marketers argue that in creating growth, they are helping to create employment and wealth; that our failure to compete against foreign products will lead to our becoming an impoverished country without political power or influence, our way of life dominated by our more successful neighbours.

This is not the place for a full discussion of these issues, but some understanding of the arguments and counter-arguments is important, because marketers will need to be aware of the pressures they face in their work. It is also important that those who intend to work in the marketing field believe in their work, and in the products they are selling. This is both a moral issue and a practical one; no salesperson is likely to perform to maximum efficiency if they do not believe in the product they are selling. If we are obliged to sell products about which we are cynical, we denigrate both ourselves and our society.

In this respect, we are fortunate that the product under consideration is tourism. Most of those involved in the tourism business can genuinely believe that the product they are selling is beneficial to their clients, whether holidays are being sold to relieve stress, to aid health or to provide clients with a novel or cultural experience. But those with the responsibility of selling tourism must take care to sell the products which will satisfy their clients' needs; it is not enough for the travel agent to sell whatever holidays will generate the most profits. Agents have a moral responsibility towards their clients – and incidentally, by satisfying them, the agents ensure that they will return to book with their company another year. And that is what marketing is all about.

This is not to say that tourism marketers will not face some serious soul-searching. A destination which is popular will achieve a level of demand which threatens the very attractiveness it offers. This is the paradox of mass tourism – it can become a victim of its own success. Anyone who has visited a popular seaside resort, such as Clovelly or Polperro, in the height of the summer season will be aware of the problems of congestion and pollution caused by the influx of huge numbers of tourists. Should the industry continue to promote such destinations with impunity? What should the marketing role of a local tourist officer be in such a situation?

In fact, contrary to popular opinion, marketing is not just concerned with selling more; it is also about regulating demand. This applies particularly where the supply of a product is finite. In the case of the congested summer seaside resort the tourist officer's role may be to *counter-market* the destination in the summer, and to try to switch demand to the shoulder season or off-season; to attempt to select market segments to increase the average spend (by focusing on staying visitors, rather than day trippers, for example); to maintain the quality of the product at present levels of consumption. The management of marketing is about the management of demand, and a marketing manager's role can be to demarket, to stabilise demand levels. The British Tourist Authority's more recent marketing plans include the aims of spreading tourist traffic geographically and seasonally as a means of relieving the pressure of high demand for popular British tourist destinations. Just as a popular theatre show will be packed to capacity throughout its run and unable to expand to satisfy the total level of demand it is experiencing, so a facility such as Heathrow Airport has a finite capacity, both short- and long-term, which calls for demand management. In such a situation, marketing may be restricted to attempts to improve levels of existing service, rather than trying to accommodate all those wishing to use the service.

A growing concern with 'eco-tourism', or 'green' tourism, is causing many organisations, both public and private, to place conservation issues above marketing considerations. Conservation and commercialism must be balanced, and *sustainable tourism* should become an integral part of any tourism planning in the future.

Since tourism is a product which is purchased in advance of its consumption and must be *described* rather than *demonstrated* to consumers, many opportunities arise for unethical practice in the industry. The product may be oversold, or services promised that are not fulfilled. However, the days when brochures deliberately set out to mislead are now largely gone, killed by a combination of statutory legislation and internal 'policing' in the industry. ABTA's (the Association of British Travel Agents) Codes of

Conduct for travel agencies and tour operators, and their guidelines for booking conditions, have substantially reduced the possibility for misleading the public. Constraints are also exercised by the media, always anxious to exploit any evidence of malpractice in the industry, and by organisations such as the Consumers' Association, publishers of *Holiday Which?* Carriers, too, have their own watchdogs – the Air Transport Users' Committee in Britain, and on a global scale the International Airline Passengers' Association. Such organisations have been set up to safeguard the interests of the travelling public.

However, as companies grow, they generally seek for themselves a more professional standard of conduct and, therefore, are more sensitive about their public image. A company seeking long-term survival cannot afford to ignore its critics, or have too high a level of complaint from its customers. Newer and smaller companies may be less concerned, but should the industry itself not take effective action to police their activities, the consumer movement will call for more legislation to protect the public.

Categories of marketing

If you look back at the definition of marketing given earlier in the chapter, you will see that the aim of an organisation's marketing is to achieve a profit *or other objective*. This distinction is important, since it clarifies the fact that marketing embraces the activities of all kinds of other organisations besides businesses.

Social marketing

Even within the commercial sphere, not all organisations will have profit as their objective. The British Tourist Authority, for example, has no direct profit objective, its goal being to generate tourism to Britain, hence stimulating the economy, employment and the profits of private tourist enterprises. In the same way other organisations providing non-commercial services, such as educational institutions, have to communicate their 'product' to their 'customers'

– in the case of colleges, their students. Ideas, too, will require communicating. Churches, charity organisations and political lobbies all aim to satisfy certain needs, and the employment of effective communications techniques will help them to do so. (Has your eye ever been caught by one of those punchy slogans on the noticeboard outside your local church, for example?) Present concern about the pollution of our environment has led to the formation of a strong ecology movement, whose aim is to market an idea to opinion leaders such as MPs and journalists, as well as to the general public. This concept of 'social marketing' is a relatively recent one, and brings home the point that organisations of all types can apply good marketing practice to their activities.

Consumer and industrial marketing

At this point, it will be helpful to clarify what we mean by the term *product*. In marketing terms, the word encompasses not only tangible goods, but anything which can be offered to someone to satisfy their needs or wants, including services.

Products are sold to two kinds of buyer; those who buy for their own consumption, and those who buy on behalf of others. The term 'consumer marketing' is used to describe the practice of marketing to the former category, and 'industrial marketing' to the latter. Just as manufacturing industries buy raw materials to convert into finished products for their customers and retail shops buy stock to sell to their customers, so in the travel world there are many forms of industrial buyer. Many large companies whose staff are engaged in frequent business travel will employ travel managers, whose task it is to arrange all the business travel of the company employees. Business conferences may be organised by professional firms of conference organisers, rather than by firms whose employees actually attend the conference. Hotels, airlines, and other travel companies will be eager to solicit business from these industrial buyers.

Home and export marketing

Finally, we need to draw a distinction between marketing products in the home (or domestic) market, and marketing them abroad to foreign markets. Export marketing, or international marketing, is a specialised field of marketing which will have to take into account different legal systems and business climates, different cultures affecting buyer behaviour, and the problems associated with transporting products abroad. Tourism, again, is substantially concerned with export marketing. British Airways has to sell the concept of flying British to Americans in competition with American carriers; the British Tourist Authority must market Britain as a destination to travellers in dozens of countries around the world, in competition with other tourist destinations; while in-coming tour operators must learn the needs of visitors from different countries and how to cater for them.

We can now bring all these forms of marketing together in a diagram (see Fig. 1.1).

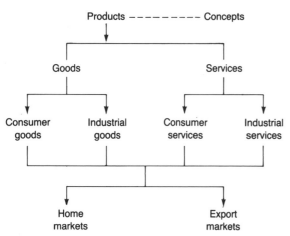

Fig. 1.1. Categories of product marketing

The nature of tourism services

Since we are dealing throughout this book with a service industry, it will be as well to look at the nature of services at this point, in order to understand how their marketing needs, and those of tourism in particular, differ from those of goods.

1 Services are by their nature *intangible*. They

cannot be inspected or sampled in advance of their purchase, therefore an element of *risk* is involved on the part of the purchaser. This is a critically important aspect of the transaction. From one perspective, this makes marketing services much easier; none of the usual problems of physical distribution are encountered, and there is no question of having to store the product in warehouses prior to its delivery to the customer. However, intangible products have many drawbacks. The fact that travel agents, for example, do not have to purchase the products before selling them to clients reduces both their commitment to the sale and their loyalty to particular brands. In place of a distribution system, the travel industry must deal with a *reservations system*, which is simply a method of matching demand with supply. The problems inherent in this form of distribution will be discussed in Chapter 8.

Tourism marketers must attempt to overcome the drawbacks posed by an intangible product, and there are a number of imaginative ways in which this has been achieved in practice. The development of video cassettes, which produce a more faithful (and more favourable) image of the holiday product than can be obtained with a holiday brochure, is one way in which travel can be effectively communicated to consumers. Another idea, introduced briefly during the rapid growth era of the 1960s before oil price rises sent air fares rocketing, was low price 'trial flights' to a destination, whereby unsold charter air seats were made available to the public at very low fares to enable prospective purchasers of package holidays to 'sample' the destinations and the experience of flying. Sometimes the fare charged (as low as £1) would be refunded against the later purchase of a holiday. In the 1990s, Britannia Airways have experimented with low price short flights to help prospective passengers overcome their fear of flying. Following the Gulf War in 1991, British Airways held a free flights lottery to stimulate air travel after people's fear of flying due to terrorist threats hit airlines worldwide.

2 The second problem is *heterogeneity*. If one buys a tangible product – say, a dining room table or a television set – mass production methods can go a long way to ensuring that each article

produced is homogeneous, that is, standardised, with each unit sharing identical characteristics. With good quality control 'lemons' occur very infrequently, and the customer can be assured of a product of a certain uniformity and quality. This is not the case with a service. Although the package tour concept, with its combination of flight, hotel room and transfer, has gone a long way to help the standardisation of the travel product, there are elements of the product over which the 'manufacturer', i.e. the tour operator, can have no control. A holiday taken in a week of continuous rainfall is a totally different product from one taken in glorious sunshine. Although the operator might offer you the consolation of an insurance against bad weather, he cannot *guarantee* you good weather. At the same time, a consumer buying a service such as tourism is buying a range of services provided by individuals, and these too are difficult to control. Hotel waiters who have had a tiff with their partners the previous evening will not render the same friendly service at breakfast that they had offered at dinner the day before. The resort representative facing redundancy due to a takeover of his or her company by a rival is unlikely to treat clients with the same consideration as usual. While good quality control procedures can help to reduce extreme variations in performance, they cannot overcome the human problems inherent in the performance of tourism services.

3 The tourism product is a highly *perishable* one. If the TV set in the showroom is not sold today, it can be sold tomorrow; if necessary, at a reduced price. Or it can be stored and offered at a later date. But an airline seat or hotel room not sold today is lost forever. This fact is of great importance for marketing, particularly when determining pricing. The heavy discounts on rooms sold after 6 pm and the 'standby' fares offered by airlines to fill empty seats reflect this need to off-load products before their sale potential is lost. The problem is compounded by the fact that the travel industry suffers from *time-variable demand*. Often, holiday demand is concentrated in peak summer months such as July and August, and short trips are more likely to be taken at weekends than weekdays. Business

travellers wish to fly from Heathrow at a time convenient to *them*, say between 10 am and noon, whereas airports and airlines prefer to offer a balanced service around the clock to maximise the use of their resources. Once again, pricing strategies can help spread demand by offering substantial reductions during periods of low demand, but this does not totally solve the problem.

4 The question of *inseparability*: services are highly personalised, the product being the outcome of the performance of the seller. The simplest way to demonstrate this is again to take our television set as an example. If we see an advertisement for a particular brand of TV that we want to buy, at a price which is highly competitive against those of other stores, we are likely to visit the shop. If we find that the salesperson selling the TV is unkempt and disinterested, this alone is unlikely to dissuade us from making the purchase; price and brand reputation have already predetermined our actions. However, transpose the same scenario to a restaurant or hotel and our reaction will be very different. Whatever the quality of the food, however attractive the decor, service is so much an integral part of the product that it would be unlikely that we should be prepared to purchase from a poor representative. The travel agent who sells us our holiday, the airline steward/ess who caters to our needs en route, the resort representative who greets us on arrival, the hotel's front office receptionist – all are elements in the product we are purchasing, and their social skills in dealing with us are an essential part of the product. It is for this reason that training becomes so vital for the successful marketing of travel and tourism.

The very fact that the product is a composite of several services leads to further problems associated with product development. In a package holiday, customers expect to receive levels of quality which are broadly comparable; whatever quality holiday they may have bought – high, medium or 'budget' – they will expect the component parts of that holiday to be of equivalent standard. Therefore, if the tourist is booked at a premium-priced hotel and takes an optional excursion associated with that holiday, he or she will justifiably feel cheated if the coach providing the service is dirty or in poor mechanical condition. This 'law of tourism harmony' is an aspect of product development that must always be borne in mind when planning products in the travel field.

These issues will have helped to demonstrate that, while basic principles of marketing apply to all products, in practice there are special considerations to take into account when marketing tourism. It is the very peculiarity of tourism that makes it such a problematic, and at the same time fascinating, product to create and sell.

Questions, tasks and issues for discussion

1 'In a way, a tourist organisation is not involved in marketing, because marketing *per se* supposes you've got control of the product, and that you can change it'
Frank Kelly *former Director of marketing, BTA*

To what extend do you agree with this statement?
Given the position of a public sector tourist board, can it ever be completely marketing-orientated?

2 How far do you think the mass market operators of package holidays have successfully overcome the 'three fears' (of flying, foreign food and foreigners) identified in this chapter? If changes have occurred, how far do you think this can be ascribed to good marketing practice, rather than other factors?

3 Identify one major company in the travel industry which provides a good example of the market-orientated approach, and list the factors which support this view.

4 What are the 'skills' of marketing? How effectively do you think these skills are actually used in (a) travel agencies and (b) tour operators?

Exercise

Museums are changing from their traditional role of providing exhibits for inspection at a distance and under glass, to centres of interpretation and experience for their visitors. Visit a local museum, and undertake research which will indicate:

• to what extent the museum is catering for this new approach
• what could further be achieved.

Your research should be based on talks to museum staff – curators, guards, guides – and to members of the general public visiting the attraction. Use semi-structured interviews, aided by tape recorders to record the discussions. Also spend time observing the attraction and its exhibits, noting such features as signs, descriptive boards or literature, interactive opportunities for visitors, etc. Is there an education officer or department responsible for educational visits? How well does the museum meet the different needs for interpretation among its varied visitors – adults, children, foreign tourists, and so on?

Write a brief report indicating what has been achieved, how well this has been implemented, and what remains to be done to improve customer satisfaction.

2 Marketing planning

After studying this chapter, you should be able to:

- explain the planning function and its role within marketing
- understand the elements of a marketing plan and how to construct it
- recognise how uncontrollable factors affect the planning process
- employ SWOT analysis as the foundation for a marketing plan
- describe simple forecasting methods and understand their role in the planning process
- list organisational systems for marketing, and evaluate their suitability for different marketing conditions
- list the elements of the marketing mix, and understand their role in the marketing plan

What is marketing planning?

All tourism organisations, however small and whether consciously or not, engage in marketing activity. The local travel agent, for example, has to make decisions about which services to offer, which brochures to rack and how they will be displayed. The choice of brochures, level of service, type of decor and furnishings, all reflect the market segment the agent has decided to cater for and the ways in which the needs of that market will be met. Advertising the products; drawing attention to special opportunities; perhaps providing free coach travel to the local airport as an incentive to book with that agent; checking past records to see who the regular clients are, and undertaking mail shots with details of holidays that may appeal to them are all examples of marketing activity. There is, however, an important distinction between so-called 'seat of the pants' marketing, where decisions are taken on the spur of the moment, and a carefully thought out and co-ordinated approach to marketing. This latter process is known as the marketing planning process, and it will be described in this chapter.

Expressed simply, planning is designed to link an organisation's goals and resources to its marketing opportunities, and in doing so to make the best use of its resources. Clearly then, we must first know what our goals and resources are, as well as what opportunities exist for us to exploit. If a market is growing fast, as was the case with foreign holidays from the 1960s to the mid-1980s, opportunities may be comparatively simple to identify, and in these circumstances even relatively inefficient and poorly managed companies may be able to survive and prosper. But the marketing environment is subject to constant change and if demand stabilises or falls (as happened in the case of package holidays in the early 1990s), the failure to develop a strategic marketing plan which responds to that change may result in the collapse of less efficiently managed organisations. Planning is simply a means of survival in a competitive and quickly changing environment.

Planning for what?

Planning is needed to meet short-term and long-term objectives. At its most basic, short-term planning is required simply in order to identify where the company is now, and where it will be next week, or next month. Managers need to be able to judge their cash flow position, since without knowing how much money will be flowing into a company, it will not be possible to predict whether funds will be adequate to pay the organisation's running costs, such as salaries. The marketing plan determines what needs to be sold in a given period, at a given price, and how this is to be achieved, in order to meet operating costs.

Beyond this, the company must plan to achieve its longer-term objectives. This could mean finding additional sources of capital for future investment. No banker is likely to look favourably at a request for further funds unless the organisation's aims and strategies are clearly defined. The marketing plan is, of course, only one aspect of a company's overall planning, and as such must be co-ordinated with the financial plans, organisational plans, purchasing plans and other aspects of the organisation's total business activity. Marketing is simply a tool by which an organisation achieves its objectives, by identifying new product and market opportunities, evaluating them and taking action to develop them. In diagrammatic form, a company's Marketing Action Plan will look like that shown in Fig. 2.1.

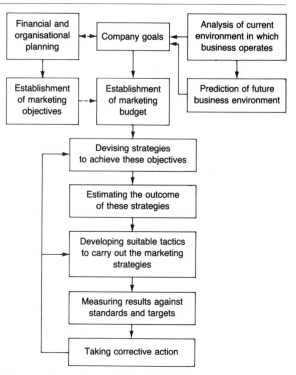

Fig. 2.1 A marketing action plan

Setting objectives

Typical objectives likely to be sought by the company will include:

*   achieving a certain level of sales growth within a given period of time
*   increasing the profitability of the organisation by a given percentage within an agreed time scale
*   obtaining a given percentage share of the market within a given period of time (new product), or increasing current market share by x% within the period (existing product)
*   reducing business risk by diversifying the product range
*   obtaining a measured increase in the return on capital employed by the company.

The marketing plan will be designed to achieve one or more of these objectives by the use of a selected choice of strategies.

There is a danger in trying to achieve too many objectives simultaneously within a marketing plan, since this can result in conflicting strategies. If asked, most managers would declare their aims would be to satisfy all of the objectives listed above; but, as tour operators and other travel firms have learned to their cost, the achievement of increases in market share, or a policy of long-term growth may be at the expense of short-term profits.

A marketing manager is faced with many alternative strategies from which to choose when drawing up a marketing plan. To achieve an increase in the return on capital invested, for example, the tour operator might choose to raise prices, to find ways of reducing costs, to seek higher productivity from present resources, to push for increased sales to present markets served, or to introduce products to new markets. Which of these is adopted will depend upon an analysis of the current market situation in which the business is operating. A major company such as Owners Abroad, for example, which has several operating divisions – among them Falcon Holidays, Twenties, Small World and Flairfares – may set quite distinct objectives, involving different strategic plans, for each of these divisions.

The business environment

In drawing up a marketing plan, a balance must be struck between establishing rigid bureaucratic guidelines and a dependency upon entrepreneurial 'flair'. Any plan has to be flexible, to take into account changing circumstances. If a company sticks too rigidly to its pre-established plans, it stands in danger of missing new opportunities which arise in the course of the plan's implementation. The collapse of a specialist tour operator in mid-season, for instance, will allow another operator to move into a new market or a new geographical area which may have been considered and rejected earlier. At the same time, any company which chooses to ignore its plans will be in danger of heading off in a number of different directions, disrupting the organisation's overall planning and possibly over-stretching its resources.

A business has within its power the ability to change any aspect of its internal operations as it sees fit. However, it operates within an environment over which it has little, if any, control.

This environment comprises the political, legal, economic, geographical and cultural framework in which all businesses operate. It is subject to continual change and the business, if it is to survive, must learn to adapt to these changes. An understanding of the current business environment is an essential prerequisite for planning. We can demonstrate this by taking the example of a typical mass market tour operator. Figure 2.2. illustrates the range of influences on the operator.

The operator needs to understand first the nature and scope of the *competition* which it faces from other tour operating companies. How easy is it for new companies to enter the market? Who are the company's main competitors? What share

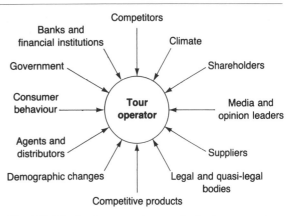

Fig. 2.2. The business environment of a tour operator

of the market do they possess? And what are their marketing strategies? In some countries, entry to the market may be controlled by government legislation, a *political* constraint, but in most countries a relatively free market exists, in which, subject to satisfying certain criteria, any company can enter and trade. There will, however, be *legal* considerations to take into account; licences may have to be obtained and restrictions on night flights may inhibit 24-hour operations.

One important factor in tourism, over which companies have no control, is that of *weather*. A poor early summer in Britain will lead to an increase in late demand for holidays abroad (as happened in 1991), while a mild winter followed by a promisingly warm spring will lead people to plan to take their holidays at home in Britain.

A *cultural* factor is changing fashion. While it is true that businesses can sometimes manipulate fashion (the great fashion houses in the clothes trade provide ample evidence of this), overdevelopment, such as occurred in Benidorm in Spain or Honolulu in Hawaii, can make resorts appear less attractive to some holiday markets, while still attracting the more gregarious visitors. There are a great many complex factors at work which will make one country or resort more fashionable than another, and marketing planners have to be sensitive to such changes in consumer demand resulting from changing taste.

Above all, *economic* influences are at work which will affect demand for the company's products. The business must be aware of the extent to which its suppliers dictate the prices at which accommodation, air seats and other travel facilities are offered. A sudden late demand for foreign holidays will have the effect of pushing up prices as many operators try to purchase extra arrangements at short notice. Operators negotiating for hotel rooms in Majorca, whatever share they may enjoy in the British market, will find themselves competing with German, Dutch, Swedish and other operators who may be prepared to pay higher prices, or have greater bargaining power, driving up prices for British operators.

Operators must be aware, too, of the *elasticity of demand* for their product; that is, the extent to which a change in price of the holidays leads to a change in demand from consumers. A product such as a package tour, which is not clearly differentiated from products of other tour operators, is very price-sensitive, and price reductions will lead to substantial expansion in the total demand for holidays, as well as attracting holidaymakers away from other operators. Similarly, any price increase not also affecting competitors can lead to a dramatic fall in the company's market share.

Consumer demand for holidays is also determined by the *substitutability* of the package tour, not just against other forms of holiday, but also against other goods and services, such as a new television set or a three piece suite for the living room. Economists use the term *cross-elasticity of demand* to describe this highly important factor (and one too readily overlooked by many in the travel industry). In recent years, the annual holiday has become a habit for millions of Britons, who have in many cases been willing to sacrifice purchases of consumer goods in order to continue to take their annual holiday in the sun during periods of recession. However, if prices of these foreign holidays are driven up at a significantly faster rate than other goods and services (due, for example, to changes in exchange rates between, or inflation rates within, the two countries), then consumers may switch their spending patterns. A holidaymaker may decide to stay at home working in the garden, spending the money on a greenhouse (especially if the summer is good) rather than taking the traditional fortnight in the sun.

Finally, we must recognise that holiday demand can also be affected by the demand for goods 'in fashion' which compete for leisure money. Video recorders and home computers both represent a considerable outlay for the consumer, who may sacrifice holidays in order to 'join the crowd' in buying the new product on the market.

In addition to the factors we have cited here, a host of other factors can affect the company's business objectives. Demographic changes – a rise or fall in population, a decline in a particular age group, even changes in traditional marriage patterns – must be understood, and taken into account when planning for long-term objectives, while the need to take into account shareholders' demands to sustain satisfactory dividends must also figure in the company's short-term marketing plans.

Requirements imposed by finance houses and banks, as conditions for loans, will have to be considered. The national trade body, ABTA (the Association of British Travel Agents), imposes its own standards on its members as we have seen in Chapter 1, while the Office of Fair Trading will press for conditions which improve the consumers' interests, such as insisting on brochures showing all-inclusive prices, instead of listing airport taxes and other ancillary costs separately. Environmental lobbyists, or MPs, may be pressing for reductions in the number of night flights, or for greater use of less popular airports. Even the media exercise influence over the business practices of the travel trade (think of the influence of programmes such as the BBC's *Holiday, Holiday Outings,* or *The Travel Show* and ITV's *Wish You were Here,* for example).

In short, the business environment is made up of a huge complex of public and private institutions and individuals, each of which may impose constraints on the way in which the marketing manager functions.

The tour operators, in fact, are in a particularly vulnerable position, since they can be affected both by changes in the environment of their customers and changes in the countries in which they operate. They may be operating to a region suddenly beset by political unrest as happened in Yugoslavia in 1991, where the safety of their clients can no longer be assured. Industrial strife, such as an Air Traffic Controllers' strike will also hit tour operators badly. A destination country may change the value of its currency, impose a higher airport tax on departing passengers, or increase VAT, all of which will substantially affect the operators' prices and/or reduce demand to that destination. For this reason, they must be prepared to react quickly to amend their marketing plans.

SWOT analysis

This analysis of the business environment which we have just described is a necessary first step in systematically appraising the present position of the company and identifying its problems, prior to determining objectives for the coming year. Whether the company is preparing a feasibility study for a new product launch, or merely assessing the current market situation in order to prepare a new marketing plan, it must be aware of:

- the economic, political, legal, socio-cultural and technological events which currently affect or could have a bearing on company operations and performance
- the current shape of the markets served by the company, including their size, growth, and trends; product ranges on offer and prices charged in each market; channels through which the products are distributed; and ways in which product knowledge is communicated to the consumers and distributors
- the nature of the competition, including size of each competitor, share of the market they hold, their reputation, marketing methods, strengths and weaknesses
- full details of the company's own market share, sales, profitability, and patterns of trading.

This review is often undertaken using a technique known as SWOT analysis; that is, the identification of *strengths* and *weaknesses* in the business, the *opportunities* presented by the trading environment and any *threats* faced by the

company. This information provides the basis for further action. Let us look at a typical SWOT analysis for a travel agent planning to open a new branch in a suburban town.

Strengths

These have to be seen from the perspective of the customer, not the company. For example, the fact that the internal size of the office will be large enough to accommodate a separate office for the manager is of little concern to the customers. On the other hand, if the company has an established reputation in the region, and is already known in the area for its reliability or service, this will be a distinct advantage in early trading. Convenience of location is extremely important for customers, so a new agency opening in the heart of a new shopping precinct, perhaps adjacent to a popular chain store, has a clear strength. The attraction of a new shop front and smart modern decor with comfortable seating will be another plus in the company's efforts to win customers from the competition.

Weaknesses

One difficulty always facing an agent opening a new office is that of finding sales staff of the right calibre. If in addition it is planned to open in the London area, where employment is relatively high and good staff at affordable salaries more difficult to come by, the problem is compounded. At the same time, competitive agencies in the area may have well-established, competent staff, popular with their customers, which will make it difficult to attract business to the new location. Perhaps the shop fronts onto a street with a traffic barrier, requiring customers to use an unattractive underpass in order to reach the agency from across the road. This would be a serious weakness in attracting passing trade. So would inadequate or expensive parking facilities.

Opportunities

Perhaps a new housing estate is being built in the vicinity? Or a new industrial development, with potential for business travel? A new department store is planned to open in the near future? This kind of opportunity needs to be not only recognised but acted upon. Marketing tactics should take advantage of the opportunity, such as directing a mail shot to all residents on the new estate.

Threats

By the same token, major companies in the area may be laying off staff or planning to close; the agency manager or one of the sales staff is planning to quit in order to open up an agency in competition. Perhaps present traffic patterns are to change as a result of road improvements in the area. There are always threats in any business; but if they are recognised and tackled early enough, they can be overcome and perhaps even turned into opportunities. Similarly, weaknesses can sometimes be turned into opportunities: the Mississipi delta is noted for its rather unpleasant mudbanks, but shops in the area make a feature of souvenir bags of mud, sold at $1.49 a bag!

At this point it might be helpful to introduce a case study of an actual SWOT analysis undertaken in an independent travel agency in the suburbs of a town in South East England, together with the resulting new marketing plan. Let us call the agency 'Go-Right Travel'.

SWOT analysis of Go-Right Travel Ltd

Strengths
- convenient – this agency is on a major intersection close to the centre of a major shopping centre
- secure – known by customers to be owned and run by a local family who have traded in the town for many years
- full service – any travel facility is available, including rail, coach and theatre tickets
- helpful staff – they seem to have been everywhere and go out of their way to help. 'Some have been there as long as I can remember'
- wide choice – 'they seem to stock brochures for every holiday company I have ever heard of'.

Weaknesses
- location – Thomas Cook and British Airways both

have even better sites close to Marks and Spencer and the Army & Navy Stores
- salaries – following recent increases by the major multiples, our own salaries no longer match up, though we do look after our staff better as individuals and attempt to help them more with their own discounted holidays, etc.
- we never seem to get the same coverage as our competitors in the local newspaper
- our staff come in their own clothes and don't look as smart as the competitors who have uniforms
- the shop faces south and west, making it very hot in summer, and resulting in uncomfortable working conditions for staff when they are under the greatest pressure, probably affecting their performance too
- we don't accept credit cards on our own account

Opportunities
- it is believed that the local 'free sheet' newspaper might be willing to run a joint promotion on a 'payment by results' basis as a readers' offer
- the assistant manager has just taken up golf and joined the local golf club
- Prestel/Viewdata use seems to be improving our sales performance but we have only one set
- additional commissions have been offered by a variety of principals, dependent upon increased sales in most instances.

Threats
- there are too many competitors in the town, including a former coach excursion operator, and branches of Thomas Cook, British Airways and Lunn Poly
- staff costs represent over 60 per cent of our total outgoings and are rising faster than turnover in percentage terms
- later booking patterns seem to involve more staff time per booking but often for less reward
- major retail groups are increasingly offering substantial cash discounts to customers, often nearly as much as we earn on the booking.

Resultant marketing plan

Product
Realistically what we sell to the customer is no different from what our competitors offer. Our only advantage is related to service, i.e. the way we sell. We must therefore ensure that our product knowledge, customer

care and quality control are above criticism. An additional sum should be devoted to training in the coming year.

Strict control must be exercised over which brochures are allowed to be displayed in the shop to ensure that we never offer any companies' products about which we have any doubts whatsoever. A preferred operator policy is to be evolved.

We shall continue to offer a full service in respect of all travel products, and will emphasise this in all promotion. Theatre tickets are the only item which carry a booking fee (an excessive one which is not controlled by us, and for which we receive much unfair criticism), and as these are not strictly speaking travel products, we shall cease offering this service. Coach and rail ticket sales will be directed to designated desks to ensure that holiday clients are not kept waiting to a point where they seek other travel agents.

All travel tickets will be issued in envelopes or travel wallets. Plastic 'tote' bags will be issued with all holiday tickets for holiday use. Luggage labels will be issued when appropriate. All will carry our name and house style, as subliminal reminders of us throughout the customers' holiday.

Recruitment will be restricted to mature, well-travelled staff to enhance our feeling of authority. They are more likely to be loyal and less likely to be affected by cash benefits alone.

In future uniforms will be worn by all counter staff.

Price
We cannot match the buying power of major retail competitors and will not become involved in discounting, even if it loses us some sales.

Sales are to be directed towards those companies that pay us best commission levels, when there is a choice of similar alternatives of equal quality standards.

Sources of lower than tariff air fares are to be investigated in order to offer keener prices.

Positive attempts are to be made to 'sell' customers the advantages of paying a little more for their holidays rather than always seeking the lowest possible price, e.g. the greater likelihood of satisfaction deriving from better quality hotels.

Place
Our shop windows are too large and take up more floor space than necessary. Changing over to a more open layout will allow a much needed additional brochure rack to be installed.

An air conditioner is to be installed to provide a better climate for staff and customers in summer.

An agreement is to be sought with the local free sheet newspaper whereby we can co-operate in 'Readers' Club' travel promotions throughout the year.

Promotion
An agreement is to be sought with the major credit card companies whereby we agree to accept their cards and they undertake a joint promotion with us in this neighbourhood, by mailing out a special offer to cardholders to announce this agreement, thus bringing in additional sales.

A series of wintertime travel talks to be offered to local clubs and societies, together with individual suggestions for group travel suited to their needs, e.g. golf club.

A travel supplement to be set up featuring the travel agency and carrying advertisements from a variety of travel principals, to be distributed by door to door methods throughout the district. This is intended especially to reach those who do not currently use our services.

A series of tactical 'late booking' advertisements to be planned for the established local newspaper for the Easter to end-July period.

Personal contacts to be established with the staff of both the free sheet and the local newspaper, and regular stories, with photographs, to be submitted to them on anything newsworthy undertaken by agency staff or (with their permission) by customers.

A direct mail letter to be sent out in October to invite established customers to a travel 'extravaganza' at a local banqueting suite, with a modest entry fee both to help meet costs and to avoid 'no-shows'.

The marketing plan devised above will introduce readers to many of the issues discussed in later chapters of this book, dealing as it does with proposals for product policy, pricing decisions and communications with the customers. Above all, it introduces the idea that even the small travel agent can embark on a process of formal marketing planning, rather than taking *ad hoc* decisions. It also leads us to consider issues of strategic planning in travel which will now be examined below.

Strategic planning

Once a company has evaluated its marketing position it has, broadly speaking, three directions in which it can move, strategically.

1 Low price leadership

If a company is big and powerful enough to undercut its rivals on price, it may choose this strategy as the basis for its consumer appeal. Price reductions are achieved through cost reductions resulting from volume throughput or economies of scale.

Large companies can benefit from economies of scale, with companies such as Thomson Holidays in the UK and TUI in Germany being able to negotiate very low prices. However, large companies will often suffer from diseconomies of scale, in that as organisations become larger, so they become more difficult to manage. This can result in problems of impersonality for their customers and difficulties in communicating effectively between staff within the organisation.

Because large tour operators carry large numbers of clients, this can preclude them from dealing with the many small family run hotels and guesthouses at the destinations they serve, whereas a small tour operator may be able to negotiate to fill such small hotels at even lower prices than those offered by the major operators.

2 Product differentiation

As an alternative to price leadership, another company may choose to specialise in certain kinds of products which are not provided by their competitors. It may also opt to focus on quality, justifying a higher price than the large competitors by offering improved value. This will require a heavy emphasis on quality control to ensure standards are maintained. One tour operator differentiates products by emphasising the all-inclusive nature of the package, in which entertainments, excursions and child-minding services are all included in the basic price of the holidays.

In cases where prices are broadly similar, as on certain airline routes where price control is in force, attempts to differentiate products become even more important, since price competition is ruled out. One airline's Boeing 747 is very like any other's, making it necessary to find other means of differentiation than that of the basic product. One airline might stress on-time reliability, another its safety record ('our multimillion-mile pilots . . .') while yet another will seek to create an atmosphere of relaxed informality on board.

. . . **another will seek to create an atmosphere of relaxed informality on board.**

3 Market focus

In this strategy, the decision is taken to concentrate on one or more specific markets (this market segmentation approach will be discussed in greater depth in Chapter 4). By catering for individual markets in this way, and adapting products to meet the precise needs of those markets, the company reduces the competition it faces and becomes, in effect, a 'big fish in a small pond'. Within these markets, the company can develop a policy of either cost leadership or product differentiation.

In this way, a company can avoid the danger of trying to do all things well but excelling in none. A marketing manager must always ask himself, 'Why should my customers buy my products rather than those of my competitors?' Unless he can provide a sound answer to that question, the success of the product will remain in doubt.

As the operators in particular have moved more and more to mass market, low price strategies, so smaller operators have turned to specialisation, whether by geographical region, type of activity or market served.

Travel agencies, too, can develop their marketing strategies along similar lines – indeed, many smaller agencies will need to in order to survive, as the marketplace becomes increasingly dominated by a handful of large travel chains. The smaller agency may opt to provide old-fashioned, high quality service, or offer specific kinds of product knowledge, such as an in-depth knowledge of cruising and different cruise lines. Alternatively, the agency may choose to deal only with customers from one sector of the market for holidays, or specialise in business house travel.

A popular exercise for marketing managers, now being adopted by travel companies, is to produce a product-positioning map, revealing the customers' image of existing companies competing in certain fields. This can be very helpful both to a company already operating in the market, or one contemplating launching a new product. A survey is conducted among a random sample of holidaymakers, who are asked a series of questions designed to provide an image of the various companies. This image can then be plotted on a matrix. One specialist operator undertook such a study, in which the image of nine competitive operators was mapped along a two-dimensional matrix, as illustrated in Fig. 2.3.

This exercise clearly reveals a gap in the market for mass market, culture-orientated long-haul holidays, which a new programme might be designed to fill. However, a word of warning is necessary in this exercise; it is possible that the product gap exists precisely because there is no demand for the product. Further research is needed to find out if this is the case, or whether it is simply that the competition has not yet seen the marketing opportunities.

Where a company offers a range of products, each with its own market strengths, it is helpful to analyse this portfolio of products using a tool developed by the Boston Consultancy Group (BCG). The BCG Growth-Share Matrix enables the company to compare the performance of each of its products, allowing the company to identify what planning decisions must be made for each.

A typical BCG Matrix is shown in Fig. 2.4. The eight circles represent the current sizes and market positions of each product marketed by a

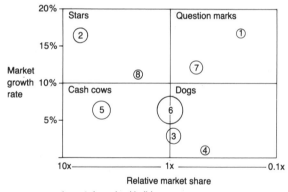

key: 1 Long haul holidays
2 Young people's holidays
3 Lakes and mountains holidays
4 Coaching holidays
5 Holidays for the elderly
6 Summer sun holidays
7 Winter sports holidays
8 Winter sun holidays

Fig. 2.4 BCG growth-share matrix applied to a major tour operator's package tour programme

hypothetical tour operator. The size of each circle is proportional to the amount of revenue that the product range generates, while location in the matrix indicates the growth rate and share of the market compared to its leading competitor.

The vertical axis shows the rate of growth of

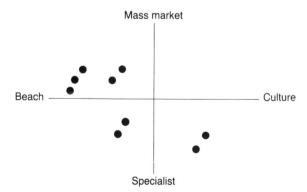

Fig. 2.3 Product-positioning map, showing perceived image of long-haul holidays offered by nine companies

the market in which the product is sold, while the horizontal axis represents the market share of the product compared with its major competitor. A market share of 0.1 would indicate that the company has only one tenth of the market share of its leading rival, while a figure of 10 would reveal it has ten times its rival's share.

The matrix is divided into four cells. If the company had a product which is both a leader in the market and that market is expanding rapidly, the product is termed a *star*, since it offers the prospect of stable profitability (although not necessarily high profitability, since the company may be forced to defend itself against intense competition for such a lucrative market).

Question marks offer the promise of success, since they are trading in high growth markets, and here the company's objective will be to seek a greater share of the market for such products.

Cash cows identify products which have a large market share, but in a declining or low growth market. Their benefit is that they can often prove highly profitable in terms of cash flow to cover the company's operating expenses, since competition will be less fierce, and hence marketing costs lower.

Finally, *dogs* are weak both in market share and growth rate, and unless the company has some expectation of gaining greater market share or of seeing an expansion in the market growth, it will gain little from pumping additional resources into marketing the product.

Planning for each of these products will therefore entail policies of either building up the product to increase market share or sales, fighting to hold the present market share, milking the product for its immediate cash returns, or retreating from the market altogether. If, in the situation explored here, the tour operator sees itself in danger of losing market share to its rivals, it can choose to increase its sales effort, to improve the product in some way, or to find ways of reducing its prices to make it more competitive. These are vital marketing decisions which will form the linch-pin of the marketing plan.

Forecasting

As well as measuring where it is at the moment, a company must also determine where it is going, and where it will be at any given point in the future, following the execution of the marketing plan. A forecast is prepared to reflect the anticipated results, with projected sales, profitability and cash flow. In turn, the forecast will influence future marketing plans. If sales are forecasted to fall by 10 per cent in the following year, due, for example, to a fall in visitors to the UK, it will be the marketing department's task to consider ways in which the shortfall can be made up through new product development, increased promotional activity or whatever other means the department can devise.

Unfortunately, forecasting is a notoriously unreliable science. The sheer number of different factors which influence the flow of international tourism makes it difficult to create an economic model that will permit accurate forecasts to be made. The volatile nature of tourism means that unforeseen events can overtake projected forecasts (particularly those longer than one year into the future). In 1991, for example, the combined impact of the recession and the Gulf War in January threw all projected sales out.

Marketing plans will usually include short-term forecasts (between three and six months) and medium-term to longer term forecasts of expected performance. The former can make use of simple statistical principles to project sales, and will be useful in making day-to-day tactical marketing decisions (reduction of prices for late bookings of package holidays is a typical example). Longer forecasts will tend to be more subjective, drawing on a wider selection of forecasting techniques, and will be used as an aid in strategic marketing decisions, such as new product development. The long-term forecast will help to pinpoint changing trends in travel, enabling a company to take advance action if one particular destination appears to be in decline, so that a new product can be developed to fill the gap.

Public sector bodies in tourism tend to take forecasting more seriously than the private sector, and forecasts are used to underpin government or local authority development policies in order to aid regional development and employment opportunities. Meanwhile, in the private sector, demand for overseas holidays throughout the 1980s was seriously overestimated, leading to massive overcapacity (although to some extent this was accounted for by the desire of the largest companies to achieve greater market share). Forecasting for the most part remains a process of 'educated guesswork' among travel companies, few of which employ methods that go beyond simple statistical extrapolation of existing trends.

If forecasting is to be of any value, it must be undertaken systematically, and be made subject to continual revision in the light of changing circumstances. Even allowing for typical margins of error that occur with most forecasts, the process is deemed an improvement over the 'gut feel' method of operation employed by most travel firms. Not all the methods discussed here will be appropriate for small firms, since they can be expensive and time-consuming to introduce, but the simpler ones are easy to incorporate into marketing plans of any company, whatever its size.

Demand

Obviously, the basis of any forecast will be the measurement of existing market demand – how many holidays, visits, or whatever the organisation presently sells. This can be relatively easily refined by breaking the figures down by geographical region or market sector. Estimates must then be made of the total market for the product sold, and the proportion of that market the company expects to attract.

Let us take the example of a tour operator who deals exclusively in medium-prices holidays from one particular regional airport. In order to forecast demand, the operator must know, or estimate;

- the number of people living in the catchment area of the airport, i.e. within a reasonable travelling time compared with other airports that could be used
- the proportion of these likely to take package holidays abroad

- how many of these are likely to take a holiday at the price, and to the destinations, provided for in the company's programme.

There is of course a trade-off to be estimated here, as to the willingness of consumers to pay more for the convenience of a nearby departure point compared with the low-priced package tours available from, say, Gatwick or Luton airports. This figure will represent the served market. The company must finally determine:

- the proportion of those willing to buy the company's packages compared with those of competitors offering flights to the same destinations from the same airport.

This final figure will represent the sales potential for holidays.

Sales

Forecasting should be taken at three levels:

1 Environmental forecasts, which take into account the uncontrollable factors – economic, political, etc. – which affect travel generally. This will integrate economic growth forecasts, expectations of changes in exchange rates, growth in leisure time and discretionary incomes, the propensity to spend discretionary income on holidays, and comparative studies of inflation rates in different countries. We can refer to such forecasts as *macro-studies*.
2 Industry forecasts, which take into account levels of competition and profitability in the travel industry, legislation affecting the industry, and other factors within the business but outside the control of the company.
3 Company forecasts, in which the firm projects its own expectations of sales based on controllable and uncontrollable factors operating within the company.

All forecasts will be prepared on the basis of an assumed set of circumstances. However, it is also helpful to include forecasts which examine performance based on the most pessimistic view of future events and the most optimistic view. This will allow for a mid-range of the 'most likely' result, as demonstrated in Fig. 2.5.

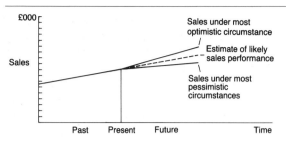

Fig. 2.5 Forecast of future performance based on the marketing plan

Trends in sales

Most short to medium term forecasts are based on the use of statistical methods to extrapolate trends from sales occurring in the past. Time series analysis, which smooths out the effects of seasonal or cyclical variation in sales, will be commonly used to project travel sales. Sales may be projected either as a linear trend (as in Fig. 2.5) or as an exponential trend, in which sales are expected to multiply at a constant rate, giving a steady upward curve.

More complicated forecasting methods will take into account a variety of variables to build economic models which are beyond the means of most travel firms, who tend to fall back on 'assumptive forecasting', that is, forecasts developed through a process of making assumptions of what people think will happen. If these assumptions are based on one person's expectations, they are unlikely to provide a great degree of accuracy, but if they are refined through a process of integrating many individual views within and outside the company, their accuracy will be improved. Interviews with a cross-section of senior staff within the firm, coupled with trade opinions, the views of sales staff closest to the market, and views of the travel 'pontiffs' can all help to refine forecasts. It should be remembered, though, that sales staff will be inclined to conservatism in their projections if their sales targets are to be tied to forecasts.

Refinements on assumptive forecasting include the *Delphi* forecast, which ask for independent assessments to be made by senior staff, with justifications for their figures. Staff are then shown the forecasts of their colleagues, and asked to refine their own forecasts on the basis of this new knowledge. In this way a more considered view is obtained.

Intention to Buy surveys, such as those carried out by the English Tourist Board, are helpful as indicators for short term trends. Random surveys ask such questions as:

'How likely are you to take a holiday abroad this year?'

definitely	very likely	quite likely	quite unlikely	very unlikely	definitely not
☐	☐	☐	☐	☐	☐

New products

Earlier in the chapter, reference was made to the greater use of forecasting within the public sector. Many of these forecasts can also be helpful to private sector companies undertaking feasibility studies for the introduction of new products. Let us take a hypothetical example of how a forecast of future tourism flows can assist the planning for new hotels in a region.

Let us say a region currently welcomes some 1.5 million staying visitors a year, and forecasts suggest that this will increase to about three million over the next five years. What hotel provision is needed to cater for this influx? The planners will need to know:

• average length of stay of tourists
• the proportion of visitors staying in hotels
• the distribution of visitors over the months of the year
• average hotel occupancy anticipated.

These figures may have to be refined to take into account different rates of increase between business and holiday visitors, different average lengths of stay between these two markets, etc., but for simplicity's sake, let us use the following figures:

average length of stay: 14 nights
60% of visitors stay in the four months of summer
50% of visitors stay in hotels
50% of visitors require double rooms, 50% single rooms
planned high season occupancy rate will be 90%.

The increase in visitors of 1.5m will require 1.5 × 14 nights = 21 million bed nights. Assuming that accommodation will be planned to satisfy average demand over the peak period, i.e. 15% over each of the four summer months, this would require 3 150 000 bed nights if everyone stayed at hotels (15% × 21 M). But only 50% stay in hotels, therefore we need 1 575 000 bed nights. At an average of 30.5 days in the month, the daily bed night increase required will be:

$$\frac{1\,575\,000}{30.5} = \text{approx. } 51\,640$$

If occupancy of these rooms is to be planned at 90%, we shall require 10% more rooms, i.e. 56 804 rooms. Assuming room demand is for 50% doubles, every 100 visitors will require 75 rooms. The region will therefore require another 42 603 rooms within the next five years.

It must be recognised that forecasts are dynamic in nature. If an organisation merely extrapolates its existing sales, rather than planning to achieve a certain level of sales, the result may be a decline in sales growth due to the greater marketing activity of its competitors. Forecasts must be based on what the organisation expects to happen as a result of its marketing plan, as well as what is expected to happen as a result of changes in the environment within which the company operates.

Setting the marketing budget

The establishment of an overall budget for marketing will be part of the corporate financial planning process, but should represent the outcome of negotiation between the head of the marketing department and other planning executives. These budgets are generally based on estimates of sales revenue and cash flow for the coming year, and introduce a measure of control over cash flow expenditure during the year. The budget determines both the resourcing of the department (including staff) and promotional expenditure.

How this figure is to be calculated is one of the most difficult decisions in corporate planning.

Often, budgets are determined, particularly in the case of smaller companies, by no more sophisticated methods than some arbitrary decision on 'what the company can afford'. Alternatively, a rule of thumb is applied, such as the allocation of some percentage of the previous year's revenue, or a percentage of next year's expected revenue. However, in both these cases, what the company is suggesting in effect is that the marketing budget should be the *outcome* of sales, rather than determining what those sales should be.

In other instances, companies attempt to estimate what their main competitors are spending on promotion, and match this sum. It is by no means clear why a competitor should be judged better at determining what should be spent on promotion, but in any case, a rival firm is likely to have very different resources and objectives, which will require different budgetary considerations.

A more logical approach to budget setting is an attempt to relate that budget to the objectives that the company intends to achieve. If, for example, the objective is to increase the company's market share by, say, two per cent, it is the marketing manager's responsibility to estimate what needs to be spent, and how, in order to achieve this. While it is never easy to forecast revenue based on a given expenditure, this approach is certainly more scientific than the kind of guesswork which usually takes place in travel companies, and it has the advantage of forcing the marketing manager to consider the relationship between expenditure and sales, through the appraisal of alternative promotional strategies.

One other important consideration is the need to recognise the relationship between profits, as opposed to sales, and the promotional budget. An airline could be expecting to sell 65% of its capacity in the coming year with its present marketing strategies. Assuming its prices are set to enable the airline to break even with a load factor of 60%, this will enable it to make an operating profit on the other 5% sold. However, airlines have very high fixed costs, so that the cost of carrying another 10 or 20% is very small – a few extra meals, a little extra fuel. If an extra market can be attracted, this would represent almost pure profit, and the company would be justified in spending a very considerable proportion of the profit on marketing to attract those other customers, provided it could be reassured tht it would not dilute sales to present customers as a result.

Organising for effective marketing

No marketing plan will be effective unless the organisation is equipped to achieve its objectives. In marketing terms, this means that the company as a whole develops a marketing-orientated approach, with staff sharing common aims and the will to achieve those aims.

Marketing is not just 'something which the marketing department does'. Its philosophy should permeate the whole organisation. Many companies pay lip-service to marketing, but remain production-orientated, concerned principally with finding ways to make use of surplus capacity rather than tackling the question of what the customer *really* wants.

At board level in large companies, it is common for marketing to be thought of in terms of sales and promotion activities, rather than the guiding philosophy of the company. Clashes occur between the marketing department and its operations staff, or financial controllers: how often does a company, faced with a decline in sales, take measures to cut back marketing expenditure instead of expanding it? A chief executive who is sympathetic to the marketing concept can play a major role in co-ordinating a common set of marketing goals for the company.

Within the marketing department itself, staff must be equipped to function effectively. This means effective organisation of staff. Many small travel companies, of course, must function with very few staff, and marketing, such as it is, will be undertaken by the proprietor or managing director as a part of the general duties of management. While this has the advantage of reducing problems of communication, it does not in itself guarantee more effective marketing. Larger organisations, however, will be likely to employ specialist staff with marketing responsibility, and will have to decide how best to

organise this staff for the achievement of their aims.

There are four ways in which a marketing department can be organised:

- by marketing function
- by geographic region
- by product and brand
- by markets served.

We will go on to look at each of these in turn.

Functional organisation

Perhaps the most traditional way of organising a department is to give staff individual responsibility for one or more of the marketing functions. Marketing entails a great many functions, and in an organisation such as a major tour operator, we may find the marketing organisation chart looking like that in Fig. 2.6

Fig. 2.6 Possible organisation of a tour operator's marketing department

This form of organisation has the advantage that each functional manager can concentrate on one specific area of marketing expertise, under the overall control of a single marketing manager or director who co-ordinates and controls their activities.

Some functionally organised departments are split, with sales and marketing each having independent executives. This arrangement does seem to run counter to the concept of sales as a function of marketing, but it has worked successfully in companies such as Thomson Holidays, and can function well enough if there is good communication, co-operation and goodwill between the respective managers.

Figure 2.7 provides an example of how a major overseas holiday company has been organised (it should be noted that all such organisations are

(a)

Director of Sales

- Client Relations Manager
  - 3 Specialist Managers
    - 4 Supervisors Staff
- Sales Manager
  - 4 Senior and Regional Managers
    - 10 Area Managers
      - Representatives
- Systems Manager
  - 4 Senior Managers
    - Managers Supervisors Programmers

(b)

Director of Marketing

- Summer Sun Manager
  - 4 Product Managers
    - 4 Assistants
- Winter Sun Manager
  - 2 Product Managers
    - 2 Assistants
- Specialist Products Manager
  - 3 Product Managers
    - 3 Assistants
- Programme Co-ordination Manager
  - 3 Specialists
    - 4 Assistants
- Brochure Production Manager
  - Photo Librarian

Fig. 2.7 The organisation of a major overseas holiday company

subject to frequent change, and this chart represents only the shape of the section at a given point in time).

Geographic organisation

Companies with very large national or international markets may prefer to organise their marketing functions by geographic area. This is particularly useful where the nature of those markets differs greatly, as for example in the case with many travel firms selling to both home (domestic) and overseas (export) markets.

A company such as Tjaereborg, which sells its holidays in a number of European countries, will necessarily undertake some, if not all, of its marketing functions separately, with different marketing staff in each country. Hotel chains take a number of different approaches to the problem, in some cases directing most of their marketing effort from a corporate marketing headquarters in the parent company's head office, with only local sales functions in the hands of marketing

staff in each individual hotel, while in other cases chains have decentralised their marketing responsibilities by country or region. The latter arrangement allows a greater measure of response to local market conditions, although naturally it loses some of the benefits of economies of scale and requires larger numbers of staff.

According to market conditions, objectives are also likely to vary considerably from one country to another, requiring distinct marketing plans to be developed in each region, although these may be co-ordinated through head office. Regional organisation of this kind can, of course, be further sub-divided along functional lines as described earlier.

Product/brand organisation

Where a company produces a variety of different products or brands, it can prove advantageous to provide separate marketing expertise for each. This is apparent in the organisation chart of a major holiday company illustrated in Fig. 2.7, in which separate marketing staff are responsible for distinct package holiday programmes. In a large hotel, the Banqueting Manager is often made responsible for the marketing of catering functions which exclude accommodation services, while the Sales Manager is responsible for convention and tour sales, and the Front Office Manager for individual transient sales (mail, telephone and personal) and all reservations.

Where companies market their products under quite distinct brand names, the marketing may be organised quite separately for each brand. A company such as the Rank Organisation, which owns such diverse businesses as Butlin's, Shearings National and Haven Warner, may find it beneficial to appoint separate marketing staff for each business, as long as it is intended to retain distinct identities for the brands. Again, the functional breakdown within the marketing departments is possible.

In practice, product managers often have less autonomy than do marketing managers, but they can control strategies for the marketing of their own product lines, and therefore can react quickly to changes in demand or other circumstances affecting their markets.

Market organisation

Finally, instead of brand or product divisions, it is possible to organise marketing according to the markets served. Hotels, for instance, may separate marketing by business and leisure guests, since the nature of demand is clearly different in each case, and the strategies designed to attract guests will also differ in each case. This can be further organised according to functional or geographical divisions of responsibility.

It is important to recognise that there are no right or wrong ways to structure marketing departments. Each firm must develop the structure that meets its needs best, and this can often only be assessed in the long-term after experimentation. Needs will change over time, too, so that what works best for a company today will not necessarily suffice as the company grows, or diversifies its product range.

The marketing mix

The concept of the marketing mix is one of the most important in marketing. It determines how the marketing budget is allocated, forms the foundation of the marketing plan's strategy, and provides the marketing manager with the techniques to optimise budgetary expenditure.

The marketing mix is defined by Kotler[1] as:

> 'The mixture of controllable marketing variables that the firm uses to pursue the sought level of sales in the target market.'

These variables are numerous, but can be conveniently grouped together into four categories, popularly known as the four P's – *product, price, place and promotion*. Figure 2.8 lists these in more detail.

It can be seen that the variety of ways in which a marketing manager can decide to distribute the budget between these variables is almost infinite. Furthermore, expenditure on some variables can be changed at very short notice, (promotion, price) while others (new product development,

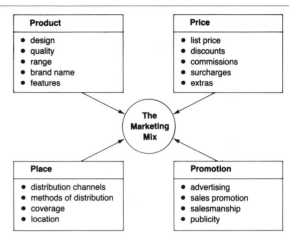

Fig. 2.8 The marketing mix variables

channels of distribution) are likely to take much longer to alter.

Once again using our hypothetical tour operator as an example, let us think through a set of possible strategies which the marketing manager may adopt as the basis for a new marketing plan.

1 Within the *product* category, the manager may choose to focus on two new destinations to be added to the summer sun programme, and to change some of the hotels used currently in the programme in order to provide a better overall standard of product and push the programme up-market slightly. For the winter programme, two hotels owned by the company in Fuengirola are to be marketed in holiday packages for the elderly, and all holiday packages henceforth are to include a cocktail welcome party on the first night.

2 Under *pricing*, the operator will offer a no surcharge guarantee for all holidays booked and paid for prior to 30 April, agree new extended payment terms for holidays in a new credit scheme, and introduce (for the first time) reductions of 30% for children on all holidays booked for the first week of September onwards.

3 Under the category of *place*, the operator decides to encourage more direct sell, setting a target of 20% direct bookings for next summer's packages, while simultaneously providing extra support for key agents. Agency sales calls are to be reduced, and the company's representatives

will no longer call on agents providing less than ten bookings in any one year.

4 Finally, under *promotion*, the operator allocates £1.5m from the budget to be spent on selective television and national press advertising campaigns, and introduces a co-operative advertising scheme with travel agents, whereby it is agreed to pay 50% towards the cost of joint advertising in local papers. Two hundred selected agents are to be taken on educational study trips to the company's recently launched destinations, and 20 travel writers and journalists will be invited on another educational visit to the company's resorts in Southern Spain.

These ideas are designed only to indicate the diversity of decisions facing an operator when drawing up a marketing plan for the year. In practice, a much wider range of decisions will have to be made, outlining both the strategy to be adopted and the tactics that will be employed to help achieve the plan's objectives. These issues will be examined at greater length in subsequent chapters.

Controlling the marketing plan

Any plan which a company introduces must be subject to control. The marketing plan must, therefore, be clear in it objectives, with each objective quantified and measurable. Control will be required over budget expenditure, and the performance of each element in the plan should be continually monitored to ensure the plan is on target. Any deviations from the plan will require action to improve performance, or to consider alternative means of reaching objectives.

Ways in which control is exercised over a firm's marketing activities will be detailed in the final chapter of this book, and therefore will not need to be further examined in this chapter. However, it should be stressed above all that a marketing plan is dynamic by nature; it is not a set of bureaucratic rules to be followed faithfully for the duration of the plan, but rather a fluid set of guidelines for action that will require constant updating in the light of changing circumstances.

Questions, tasks and issues for discussion

1 List the objectives which a travel agent might incorporate into its marketing plan. Explain how the choice of more than one objective could create a conflict in marketing strategy.

2 Using the diagram in Fig. 2.2, prepare a paper for discussion on the ways in which these factors can influence the marketing operations of a tour operator.

3 Suggest some of the ways a travel agent might 'differentiate' its product, or corporate identity, from those of its competitors.

4 Draft another two-dimensional matrix like that in Fig. 2.3, using different variables of your own choice, which a hotel might use to discover marketing gaps.

Exercise

You have been employed as research assistant for a local tourist attraction (you may choose an appropriate attraction near to you). Your manager has asked you to carry out a SWOT analysis of the attraction as a prelude to the new marketing plan she is developing. Undertake the research (using both primary and secondary research methods – see Chapter 3) and write a memorandum to your manager containing your SWOT analysis, and any suggestions you feel to be relevant and which will help your manager in her plans for the coming year.

3 Marketing research and its applications in tourism

After studying this chapter, you should be able to:

- understand the need for research in an organisation
- describe a Marketing Information System and its elements
- plan a simple research programme, construct questionnaires and carry out surveys
- explain and evaluate different methods of gathering research information

What is marketing research?

Marketing research is the planned, systematic collection, collation and analysis of data designed to help the management of an organisation to reach decisions and to monitor the results of those decisions once taken. It embraces all forms of research undertaken to help the marketing of products, including product research, price research, distribution research, publicity research and consumer research. However, research into consumers and their patterns of behaviour is more commonly referred to as *market research* to distinguish it from the more all-embracing term of marketing research.

Research is designed to help an organisation to understand the nature of the marketplace in which it operates, including understanding its suppliers, wholesalers, retailers, competitors and customers.

Research can be *descriptive*, that is, it can help us to find out factual data about what is happening in the marketplace; or it can be *analytical*, attempting to explain the relationship between variables – for example, to find out why these things are happening. Both kinds of information have their place in the process of management decision-making. While in the past, much of the research commissioned by the travel and tourism industry has tended to concentrate on gathering descriptive data – who goes where, when; market shares of the major companies; total sales in each category of travel – in recent years there has been a greater interest in, and awareness of, explanatory research which will tell companies why these statistics are as they are.

Why marketing research?

One potential danger of focusing on the four P's in marketing is that these omit a key element of the marketing role, on which every other marketing activity depends; the function of research. Unless we know what our customers want, we cannot be certain that the products we produce will appeal to them. If our sales are falling off, we have to know whether this is the result of a general economic malaise affecting all products, a problem specifically affecting the travel and tourism industry, or the result of clients switching their purchases to other travel products. In each case, we should have to devise a different marketing plan to respond to the challenge. Intelligence gathering is therefore a crucial precedent to planning.

Research has a place in the management of any company, however small. The belief, held by many independent travel agents and other small companies, that marketing research is a luxury only affordable by the larger travel corporations, is a dangerous fallacy. True, only the larger companies are likely to be able to buy in the expertise provided by research consultants, to commission, for instance, a survey of trends in travel purchasing. Summaries of such research are, however, often published in a variety of media available at your local library, a specialist library such as that of the English Tourist Board, or even from time to time in the trade press. Keeping up with these reports should be a part of the responsibilities of any travel manager who calls himself a professional.

In the larger companies, formal intelligence gathering techniques become essential for two reasons. First, by its very nature the larger company has less opportunity for face to face contact with its customers; its feedback on changing consumer tastes and preferences has to be planned. Secondly, large businesses involve greater financial investment, which in turn means greater risk. Think of the investment an airline must make today to re-equip its fleet, with some aircraft costing in excess of $100 million each. Consider the investment a hotel chain is making, when purchasing a new property in central London. Even a tour operator developing a new resort must invest substantial time, effort and money in doing so. Marketing research cannot guarantee success; but it does help to reduce risk and offer better prospects of success.

What information do we need?

All organisations, regardless of size, need to know where they stand in the business environment. In the case of existing products, they need to know how many of each product they are selling; how sales are performing over time, and the forecast for future sales; how their products compare with those of the competitors, and the respective shares of the market held by their own company and their competitors. If a principal or tour operator is involved, they must monitor their distribution strategy, to determine what quantities of their products are being sold by each retailer and which of their retailing outlets are performing best.

All companies need to know the effectiveness of their advertising and promotion campaigns. They should also know the profitability and contribution to overheads which each product makes. They must fully understand the customer: who buys what, when, where and why.

Where new products are planned, the company must research the market opportunities, test new product concepts on these markets, find the right appeals to attract attention, test market the product wherever possible, forecast sales and monitor sales performance against forecasts, as described in Chapter 5, dealing with new product development.

The Marketing Information System

Research should form the basis of an on-going system for gathering intelligence about the company, its products and its markets. Often, such intelligence is gathered informally and subconsciously by managers in the course of their everyday duties, by observing, listening to discussions, talking to colleagues in the industry, and reading trade or other journals and papers. Valuable as this process is, it should be supported by more formal procedures carried out in a systematic and scientific way. Establishing a Marketing Information System (MIS) ensures that the company has a system for the regular planned collection, analysis and presentation of data.

Designing an MIS requires a company to undertake two tasks:

- To consider the decisions that its management has to take.
- To determine what information is needed to make these decisions.

Obviously, the availability of finance influences the kinds of information that can be obtained. Here, the company must realistically judge what proportion of its profits, or reserves, it should set aside for research, separating the costs of its annual research from any special *ad hoc* research needs which may arise from time to time (such as a feasibility study to judge the merits of taking over another company).

Since the MIS is designed to ensure that the company has a regular flow of information to monitor its markets and marketing effectiveness, a proportion of the annual budget should be allocated for this purpose, while exceptional research needs, such as those dictated by a decision to expand, will require a topping up of funds, either from reserves or even by way of a loan.

Let's take the case of a small regional chain of travel agents, considering setting up or purchasing a new branch in the region. The location of the branch will be critical for its chances of success, and a feasibility study will have to be undertaken to decide whether expansion in the region is the correct decision, and which of the available sites will stand the best chance of success. While a full-scale survey will be beyond the means of all but the largest chains, some research data can be bought in at moderate cost while substantial fieldwork can be undertaken by a branch manager at the expense only of time and effort.

Figure 3.1 details the setting up of an MIS and it shows that there are four distinct ways in which information can be obtained in an MIS:

1 Through the use of internal records, that is, the use of recorded data already available within the firm;
2 By identifying and selecting suitable data available externally;
3 By undertaking or commissioning new research, e.g. tests in 'laboratory' conditions;
4 By carrying out observations or surveys.

We will go on to look at each of these methods of research in the sections that follow.

Internal records

The gathering of information from existing records, whether from within or outside the firm, is known as *secondary research*. In some ways it is the easiest method of gathering data, since much of the data is already available to the firm and only needs to be collated and analysed. It is

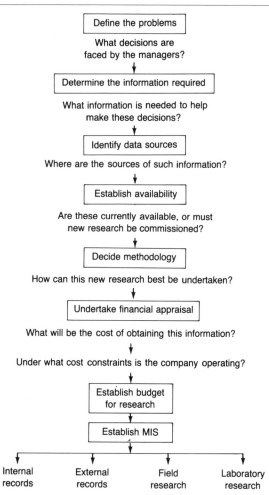

Fig. 3.1 **Procedures for setting up a marketing information system**

also relatively inexpensive to set up internal information systems to collect material as needed.

To take one example, travel agents have a huge range of data on tap. Sales records will advise them which products they are selling and in what quantities. This information, plus that provided by their principals, will enable them to break down sales by company. Some judgement can be made about future sales by comparing forward sales with bookings achieved during the comparable period in the previous year, or with any earlier period of trading, to give a clear picture of trends in sales over time. They can compute the average revenue per booking, average commission received for each type of travel product sold, and average sales achieved by each member of the counter staff. A complete profile of customers can be built up – total numbers, breakdown by week of booking or week of departure (enabling the agent to judge whether and to what extent bookings are being made later in the year than formerly), breakdown by area of residence and by type of holiday preferred. How such data can be used in the marketing of the agency is shown in Table 3.1.

Table 3.1 Travel agency data and their marketing applications

Data	Marketing application
Sales and revenue records	develop promotional campaigns to achieve targets set by selected principals for bonus commissions
	negotiate with principals for joint promotions
	decide which brochures to rack and where
Average commission achieved	decide to drop a product range or give it extra promotion
Bookings/revenue per member of staff	set revenue targets for each member of staff
	determine bonus payments for performance
	ascertain sales training needs
Customer profiles	establish mailing lists for special offers
	devise direct mail campaigns to previous customers, or to catchment areas from which high numbers of bookings are being achieved

Principals will be continually gathering information of this type both formally and through informal feedback through their personal contacts. For example, sales representatives will continually monitor data on clients and distributors, and provide regular reports to their sales managers which will be integrated into the information system.

With the advent of computers into the travel industry on a wide basis, it has now become a comparatively simple matter to produce data for management decision-making at regular intervals, whether daily, weekly or monthly according to need. The danger of overload must be recognised, however; a manager's time has not expanded to keep pace with the increased flow of information, and therefore data must be selected and presented in a form which is easily assimilated if it is to be useful.

External records

An enormous amount of data is available to the travel company from existing records. These data can be classified in two ways.

1 We can distinguish between information specifically related to travel and tourism, and information which is more general in nature but nevertheless provides a useful insight into patterns of travel and tourism. For example, statistics produced by the government to show the growth of paid holidays over the past 20 years have been an important factor in the increase in package tours. If the trend towards more holiday entitlement continues over the next 20 years, this fact will be important in estimating the growth of the holiday and leisure business.

2 Information which is available freely as a matter of public record, and available on subscription.

Public

Appendix 1 at the end of this book provides a list of sources of data, most of which are freely available for consultation in public libraries, or in libraries accessible to the public, such as those of colleges and universities which include the study of leisure and tourism in their curricula. Two further libraries should also be mentioned here:
(a) The British Tourist Authority library
   Thames Tower
   Blacks Road
   London W6 9EL
(b) The Civil Aviation Authority library
   45–59 Kingsway
   London WC2B 6TE

Many of these libraries will also have bibliographies of tourism to consult. Several of these have been published in recent years, of which the most comprehensive is probably Jeanne Gay's three-volume *Travel and Tourism Bibliography and Resource Handbook*, published by Travel and Tourism Press, California. However, bibliographies tend to date quickly, and any search of public records must include a study of the most recent data published, which may not yet appear in the listing of any bibliography.

Publications of ABTA, the BTA itself, the BAA, the CAA, the Bus and Coach Council and annual reports of major travel enterprises such as airlines, hotel chains and tour operators, all contain valuable statistical information. One unexpected source is the Department of Employment, which publishes the 'International Passenger Survey', which includes information on UK residents travelling abroad and the purpose of their visits defined by destination area. Further material can be discovered in the travel trade press, and academic journals such as *Tourism Management, Annals of Tourism Research*, and the EIU's *International Tourism Quarterly*.

Travel statistics are sometimes brought together in a very useful compendium, such as will be found in the *Keynote Reports* and *Market Assessment Reports*, the *Travel and Tourism Analyst*, the ETB's *Insights* and the Tourism Society's *Tourism Industry*. The BTA/ETB research library is probably the best place to start one's search, particularly for data dealing with domestic and in-coming tourists to Britain.

Information about the advertising spend of major companies in the industry can be found by consulting MEAL (Marketing Expenditure Analysis Ltd), which is also available in many public libraries.

Subscriptions

A company with adequate financial resources can choose between commissioning its own specific research, or subscribing to an on-going 'syndicated' survey of consumers which includes information about the pattern of holidays or travel taken.

General surveys of consumer habits of purchasing are conducted by a variety of companies, and use different methods related to scale, speed of reporting and other criteria.

Regular reports by STATS MR provide useful information on the tourism industry and market, based on a national survey.

A similar survey is undertaken by the AGB Home audit. Here, a massive 11 000 households are recruited each quarter and the respondents are also requested to complete further questionnaires at three monthly intervals until the year end. The 24 000 respondents who indicate that they travel abroad are asked to complete a special questionnaire on travel habits.

Perhaps the best known survey is the UK Tourism Survey (UKTS) commissioned by the Tourist Boards. The report (and those of UKTS's predecessor, the British Tourism Survey) is based on in-depth research into the holiday travel of British people undertaken in the past year, comparing this with previous years. In addition to the annual report each March, subscribers now receive copies of monthly survey results which give valuable travel data.

The English Tourist Board, in addition to its joint sponsorship of the UKTS, carries out an 'intention to purchase' survey at the beginning of spring, which offers useful data for short-term forecasting of patterns of overseas and domestic holidaytaking among British tourists.

Because of the comprehensive and extensive nature of these surveys, the subscriptions are expensive, and only the largest companies are likely to be able to subscribe regularly. Advertising agents often subscribe to aid their own campaign planning in a variety of fields, and the travel companies using the larger advertising agencies can obtain the benefits of this knowledge through this source.

More specific services are offered by such bodies as TATR (Travel and Tourism Research), who report regularly upon travel agencies and their attitudes to travel products, as well as their readership of the travel media. Other marketing research bodies provide services such as newspaper cuttings.

One word of warning about the use of published statistics: do not automatically apply general findings to specific situations. Figures which indicate a growth of overseas package holidays may conceal the fact that there is a marked decline to one country at the expense of a growth to another. In the same way, a rise in visitors to the UK will not necessarily mean that there has been an increase of tourism to Northumbria, nor will statistics relevant to the West Country necessarily relate to tourism in Bristol or Bath. There is, in fact, an acute shortage of data dealing with specific locations, making it necessary to use more general data about travel patterns, but unless this can be supported with specific evidence relating to a town or region, findings will be very questionable.

Primary research

If the knowledge required by the organisation is not available through a search of secondary material, it is necessary to undertake primary research, that is, information obtained directly from the market. There are two principal ways in which this is carried out: by asking people questions, and by observing their behaviour systematically.

'. . . by observing their behaviour systematically . . .'

Such research can be undertaken by research organisations on commission, but can be extremely costly. However, for the smaller company, simple quantitative research can be undertaken 'in-house', providing it is scienti-fically and systematically carried out. It is better to leave more qualitative methods to the experts.

Full-scale national surveys of the market will cost tens of thousands of pounds, well beyond the means of all but the largest travel firms; but some of the data may be already obtainable through organisations such as AGB, and it is as well to shop around to find the lowest cost at which one can acquire the information. At the other end of the scale, a local survey of a travel agent's market is unlikely to be available through secondary research, but could be undertaken by the firm itself. Questionnaires designed to find out, for example, whether existing customers would continue to use the agency if it were to move location, or whether clients would purchase charter flights to Greece if these were available from the local airport though at a higher cost than from London, are relatively straight-forward 'number-crunching' exercises which, if carefully planned and executed, can yield useful information. Researchers do need to be conscious, however, of the fact that what people *say* they will do and what they *actually* do are not always the same thing!

Let us take a slightly more sophisticated example of primary research which an agent might undertake. A travel agent currently offers free transport to the local airport for all local package tour bookings, as an inducement to book. The agent wants to know how far this incentive is reponsible for:

(a) keeping existing clients from going to competitors, and
(b) attracting clients away from other agencies.

The agent may also want to know whether some other incentive might give greater market satisfaction, without adding to costs, or how much business they stand to lose if they withdraw the present offer. While a question-naire could be sent out to present customers, this will be no help in reaching competitors' clients, so some form of random survey of people in the 'catchment area' will need to be undertaken. This could be done by talking to people in the streets or interviewing them in their homes. Both methods have advantages and drawbacks. Home interviews are more difficult to arrange and more costly in time to conduct, but are likely to result in less refusals (if carefully managed) and, as more time is taken to consider the questions, responses are likely to be more accurate. Home interviews also allow the interviewer more time to draw out respondents on their opinions and attitudes towards travel generally, leading to more rewarding data; this does call for more interviewing skills, however. At the same time, the collation and analysis of information gained in this way is more complex than responses to simple questions in the street survey. Street surveys can be carried out quite quickly whereas a home survey will take time to organise and conduct, delaying action, which may be crucial.

In short, there are a great many factors which have to be taken into account in deciding which methods to adopt. We will go on to look at the design of a piece of research, and then consider the different ways in which research can be conducted.

The elements of a research project

The following steps are necessary in planning a research programme:

1 Definition of the problem and the objectives

The organisation must be quite clear about its intentions – clear about what it hopes to achieve as a result of its research. This may seem an obvious point, but a surprising amount of questionnaires carry questions which don't actually throw light on the problem under investigation, but have been incorporated because 'it would be nice to know what the market feels about the issue'. Responses therefore may end up being unused.

Knowledge acquired through this step leads to the formation of the Market Research Brief, as a basis for action.

2 Identification of sources of information

At this point the aim is to find out what, if anything, is known about the problem already. There is little point in paying good money for research which has already been undertaken by someone else, if one can get hold of this. However, a great deal of research which might be relevant will have been carried out by rival commercial organisations, and would not be accessible. How much will the organisation's existing records help in solving the problem? Where else might the information be found?

3 Develop the research plan

Depending upon the information available in step 2, the main stage of research may now be planned, or it may be thought necessary to conduct some *exploratory* research first, as a guide in developing a more detailed plan.

For instance, let us assume that a company is interested in developing a low price multi-centre programme of package tours to the United States, using Greyhound bus for overland travel between the centres. While statistics on the use of Greyhound by British travellers will be available, attitudes towards travel by coach over long distances may be less well understood. As a prelude to knowing what questions to ask in a full scale survey, it may be helpful first to conduct a *panel interview* to explore attitudes towards coach travel and to holidays in the USA. The use of this technique will be explained more fully later in the chapter.

4 Research design and methodology

The detailed plan for research can now be prepared. If this is to incorporate a survey, which is the customary means by which facts will be collected, the plan will include:

- selection of respondents – who is to be interviewed, the total size of the sample and how they will be chosen
- the form in which the survey will be conducted (personal interviews, mailed questionnaires, etc.)
- the design of the questionnaire to be used
- the organisation of the fieldwork, including recruitment, training and briefing interviewers
- establishment of the time schedule, and overall budget for the research.

Once these matters have been agreed, it is imperative to 'pilot test' the questionnaire, by trying it out on a handful of respondents selected at random. There will invariably be changes that must be made to the questions and the pilot will pick these up. It will also give an idea of the average time taken to carry out one interview. This will help in planning the schedule of interviews.

Once the questionnaire has been refined to a point where the research supervisor is satisfied that the questions and structure are right, the research can be implemented. Survey data are collected and collated. Today this is normally done by computer, rather than by hand, making it comparatively easy to 'cross-tabulate', i.e. compare responses to any two or more variables in the questionnaire. We could, for example, discover how many **females over 18 years of age** went **overseas** for their holiday last year, and spent **over £500 per person** for their holiday. Here we are examining four variables, females, adults, those who went abroad, and those spending more than £500. This process is known as 'analysis', and calls for skills to select what is relevant, and interpret correctly what the data reveal, so that the correct conclusions can be drawn, and recommendations for action can be made.

The results of the survey are presented in the form of a report, which will incorporate the following elements:

- the title, date, company name, and name of organisation contracted to undertake the research
- the brief: terms of reference, acknowledgements, and statement of objectives
- a detailed statement of the methodology: methods used, reasons for their selection, and details of how the sample of respondents was drawn, number of interviews conducted, how the fieldwork was undertaken, etc.
- the findings of the survey
- conclusions and recommendations for action
- appendices: these should contain the bulk of the statistical information gathered (full tables of results, etc.) and a copy of any questionnaire used.

We will now look in a little more detail at the ways in which surveys can be conducted.

The survey

Surveys are generally the best means of collecting descriptive information, and will invariably make use of a questionnaire; that is, a series of questions which will be put to respondents designed to help provide answers to the problems the organisation is investigating. The survey can be conducted in many different ways, as we shall see, but regardless of survey method, the procedure must be scientific. This requires that every possible effort is made to avoid or reduce bias in the response. It will usually be impossible to interview all the possible respondents in whom the company is interested, therefore those that are interviewed (the 'sample') must accurately reflect the general views of the total population, or 'universe' (the total number of people in the category in which we are interested). Thus, if we are proposing to solicit the views of British tourists to Spain on some issue, we need firstly to have some idea of the total size of the universe, and must then choose a representative sample of that universe having regard to demographics.

Our first task is then to determine *who* is to be interviewed. Are we interested in the views only of British holidaymakers, or of all British visitors to Spain, including business and VFR visitors? Are we interested only in the opinions of those who take package holidays, or also of those on independent holiday arrangements, or staying in second homes? Is it only the views of adults that we seek and, if so, do we interview only those over 16, over 18 or over 21? If we intend to include business travellers in the survey, are we interested only in the views of those who use the service, or also of those who buy the service (many secretaries make the arrangements for their bosses)? If our interest is in those who travel regularly, how will we define regularity for the purposes of the survey?

Our next problem is the size of the sample we will select. Large samples provide more accurate results than small ones, but the increase in accuracy becomes less and less significant as the sampling size is increased. As long as scientific methods of selection have been employed to get the views of 56 million people in Britain, we need no more than some 2000 respondents to obtain views accurately reflecting the population's views on general matters to within 95% probability; that is, we have only a 5% chance of being wrong in our findings. Interestingly, Sunday newspapers generally use 1000 respondents for opinion polls. The sample of 2000 respondents, giving a 5% margin of error, is sufficiently accurate for most purposes, where the question is one of a general nature. The additional cost of interviewing enough people to raise the level of accuracy is generally not justified, since we would have to increase the number of respondents four-fold to improve the level of accuracy from 5% chance of being wrong to only 2.5%.

Scientific procedures are crucial if this level of accuracy is to be retained. A *probability sample* of the universe must be selected. In the case of a simple random sample, this means selecting respondents in a scientifically random way so that each has one chance only, and an equal chance, of being selected. Other acceptable systems of scientific selection include *stratified random sampling*, in which the universe is divided into mutually exclusive groups (such as age ranges), in which the proportion of the total in each group is known, with random samples then drawn from each group in the same ratio as exists in the universe. A third method is known as *cluster sampling*, in which, for example, samples are taken by area of residence, again in the same proportion as the ratio of residents in the universe, and again with each respondent having an equal opportunity to be selected once only.

Major research companies employ sophisticated techniques to ensure that the samples are truly representative. In a national survey they will define how many respondents are to be chosen, and will ensure that the numbers in each category, i.e. age, sex, socio-economic status, domicile, correspond with the standards they have defined from previous work.

In order to correct any imbalances, a process known as *weighting* is employed, whereby a computer automatically adjusts the results to equate to the standards already set down, e.g. if the sample was correct in all aspects except the breakdown of respondents by social class, the views of the under-represented sectors may be given additional weight in the final analysis by increasing the relevant answers in proportion to the under-representation detected.

Having said that a 2000 person sample is enough for general questions, it must be emphasised that many questions are much more specific and require different techniques. It is very expensive indeed to establish the views of a minority group.

Example It has been suggested that we need to establish whether apartment holidays to Spain marketed by major package holiday companies are seen by customers to be satisfactory.

Stage 1: 2000 respondents
Have you booked a holiday in the past year?
NO 65%   YES 35%

Stage 2: 700 respondents
Was it an independent or a package holiday?
INDEPENDENT 40%   PACKAGE 60%

Stage 3: 420 respondents
Did you go to Spain?
NO 70%   YES 30%

Stage 4: 126 respondents
Did you stay in an apartment?
NO 80%   YES 20%

Result: 25 relevant respondents

Whether 25 people who contribute useful information is adequate will depend upon the nature of the questions to be asked. Given a possibility that the market research firm charges £2 per interviewee, it can be seen that the costing will be as follows:

2000 × £2 = £4000
25 useful respondents
= £160 per usable respondent

It obviously involves going to a great deal of trouble to ensure scientific accuracy, and this is one of the factors in the high costs of such research. Because of this, firms sometimes undertake surveys using convenience samples, such as stopping every tenth person in the street to ask their opinion. While this may help to throw light on the problem, the results cannot be subject to statistical tests and there must always be some doubt about degrees of accuracy achieved. It must be remembered that the test of any survey is that the results are both *valid* and *reliable*.

Validity means that the survey proves what it sets out to prove, and reliability means that if the survey were to be conducted with another sample of respondents, exactly the same results would be achieved (within the limits of probability established).

Let us take the example of a survey of visitors to a seaside resort. An interviewer could be assigned to stand on a particular street corner and question every *n*th person who passed by. This *convenience sample* will have a number of inherent biases. Many visitors to the resort not passing these points will have no opportunity for selection, and the flow of visitors will be greater at certain times of the day and certain days of the week than at others (although this factor can be weighted to obtain more accurate results). It is also possible that other overt or covert biases will emerge. Passers-by with more time on their hands will be more likely to stop to answer questions than those who are busy, and there is a strong temptation for interviewers to approach those who look friendly, or are from the same age group, sex or social background. Ethnic minorities may be ignored, and those visitors who cannot speak sufficient English to be interviewed will be rejected. By the use of good interviewer training, by weighting responses, and perhaps by supporting the survey with other forms of research, such as hotel occupancy surveys and car park observation (licence plates reveal some very interesting statistics about visitor origins!), bias will be reduced, though never entirely eliminated. This is likely to be the most realistic approach to research for many small companies, such as the travel agent anxious for information about the local market. By instructing interviewers to deliberately choose a cross-section of respondents according to age, sex, group size, etc. (known as *quota sampling*) a wider range of opinions will be obtained, although not necessarily a more accurate one.

While the street interview is the most common form of interview, surveys can be carried out in a number of other ways. Telephone interviews are becoming more popular, and as the number of subscribers to telephones in Britain comes closer to 100 per cent, so this form of interview becomes more statistically significant. However, phones are increasingly being used by commercial firms to make 'cold calls' (i.e. unsolicited efforts to sell) and there is a growing resistance among consumers to what is seen as an invasion of privacy, which will result in further biases as refusals grow. However, the telephone interview does reduce cost, especially if a national survey is being undertaken – a phone call is a lot cheaper than sending an interviewer to remote corners of the British Isles! Telephone interviews can, of course, also be carried out far more quickly.

Home interviews are best for longer questionnaires, for asking those questions which require some forethought or probing from the interviewer, and for open questions calling for opinions and attitudes. Once again, households must be selected scientifically, so that each has an equal opportunity for selection, and it may be necessary for interviewers to make several calls in order to find the householder at home. This delays the completion of the survey. Possible bias emerges through the closer relationship which is established between an interviewer and respondent in a longer, home interview, with respondents sometimes giving answers which it is thought the interviewer will want to hear, if the respondent finds the interviewer sympathetic.

The cheapest type of survey of all, dispensing entirely with the interviewer, is the mailed questionnaire. This means, however, that response rates are usually lower (although the inclusion of a stamped addressed envelope for the reply will boost responses) and replies are more likely to be attracted from those with an interest in the survey – the research may produce a higher level of people who have taken holidays abroad than those who have not, since they may be more interested in the questions. Respondents also have the opportunity to read their questionnaire through before answering the questions, and what they read later in the paper may prejudice the way they respond to the earlier questions. With this system, there can be no absolute certainty that the person selected for the interview has in fact filled out the questionnaire, or has given much thought to the questions.

Questionnaires may also be distributed to

passengers on aircraft in flight, or on coaches, given to visitors leaving a tourist attraction with the request that they be mailed back, or left in hotel rooms to be handed in at the front desk on leaving. Each of these approaches has its own advantages and drawbacks. However, where the opportunity is given to have passengers complete a questionnaire on the flight home, the method has significant benefits over others. To start with, one is dealing with a captive audience representing 100 per cent of the universe. Passengers have their experiences fresh in their minds, and they also have time on their hands during the flight, so seldom object to filling in a questionnaire. Response rates will therefore be unusually high, especially if cabin staff on board collect questionnaires. Staff can also clarify any uncertainties about the completion of the questionnaire. Tour operators such as Thomsons make good use of this opportunity to monitor satisfaction, and thus to affect quality control.

When used to its full extent, this technique brings many benefits. Not only can the operators monitor the true level of any difficulties experienced with hotels or resorts, but they can also monitor satisfaction levels in respect of any aspect of the holiday, such as flights used. It is known that when airlines find that their 'ratings' relative to other competitors are slipping, they will take steps to improve service levels in order to impress the tour operator and to secure future business. This process has had a significant effect upon the quality of service given by the major independent charter airlines used for package tours.

Questionnaire design

Good questionnaire design in itself is a well-developed skill, since even the way a question is phrased can bias the response. Questions must be expressed in as neutral a manner as possible, must be unambiguous and written in a language which is simple enough to be understood by respondents of all levels of intelligence. However, expressing a question neutrally is surprisingly difficult. Take the following two examples:

(a) *Do you think that the Spanish Government should allow people to drink alcohol on the beach?*

(b) *Do you think that the Spanish Government should forbid people to drink alcohol on the beach?*

Tests have shown that substituting the word 'forbid' for 'allow' suggests a greater level of control which results in respondents being less willing to answer in the affirmative to question (b).

A transport authority questioned respondents' attitudes towards special bus lanes during rush hours by asking:

Are you in favour of giving special priority to buses in the rush hour?

Sixty-two per cent of those responding agreed that they were in favour. However, in a later questionnaire, the question was rephrased to read:

Are you in favour of giving special priority to buses in the rush hour, or should cars have just as much priority?

The number of those in favour now dropped to 40%.

The designers of questionnaires must also avoid questions that are:

- vague
- ambiguous
- contain double negatives
- set impossible tests of respondents' memory
- lead respondents to reply in a particular way

There follow some examples of questions that would need to be avoided, or rephrased, to make them acceptable.

1 *On your last trip abroad, how much did you spend on average per day in the bar of your hotel?*
- this is a memory test, even if the respondent travelled abroad as recently as this year. A fair question to those returning from an overseas trip, or on the last day of their trip, but even here, at best the interviewer will get only an educated guess.

2 *Do you care enough about the family to ensure that they always carry enough insurance while on holiday?*
- a loaded question. Who can reply no?

3 *How do the clothes you wear on holiday compare with those that you wear at home?*
- vague. What is the question getting at? It will

tend to encourage equally vague responses such as 'not at all', or 'very well', unless the interviewer has the opportunity to explain the question.

4 *What are your views about arbitrary surcharges for ITX packages?*
 - even if directed to members of the travel trade, the question makes a dangerous assumption about knowledge of technical expressions. Avoid all use of technical expressions, unless it is essential to include them, in which case an explanation of the term should be added. Respondents hate to admit their ignorance!

5 *How did you find the travel agent you booked with?*
 - ambiguous. You may get responses such as 'I looked him up in the yellow pages' coupled with other responses such as 'very friendly and helpful'!

6 *Would you prefer not to travel in a non-smoking flight?*
 - Help! What does it mean? The respondent will have to think too long to work it out.

7 *What do you think of the colour and taste of the ice-cream you have just bought?*
 - you are asking two questions in one. Respondents' views about colour may differ from their opinions about the taste.

As far as possible, for simplicity in collating and classifying information, closed-end questions should be used in questionnaires. These are questions in which the respondent is asked to pick from one of several responses possible, or the question is phrased so that the interviewer can check responses from a choice of possible replies. Closed-end questions vary from the simple dichotomous question calling for a 'yes/no' reply to checklists of responses such as the following:

How many times have you travelled abroad on a holiday of four nights or more in the past year?

once	1
twice	2
three or more times	3
none	4

Using this form of question, rating scales can be employed to obtain respondents' views about attributes:

What was your opinion of the food served in the hotel?

Excellent	1
Good	2
Fair	3
Poor	4
Very poor	5

With questions of this nature, it is important that there is an equal balance between 'positive' rankings and 'negative' rankings, otherwise the overall result will indicate a skewing to one side or the other. It is not uncommon to find tour operator questionnaires which ask respondents to choose from the following categories:

Excellent
Good
Fair
Poor

This provides two positive responses, one 'neutral' and one negative. The result will make it appear that the product is slightly better than might be the case in a more objective set of choices. Usually, five choices are provided in scales such as these, but on occasion as many as seven, or even nine have been used to provide 'fine tuning' of responses.

Views can also be solicited by the use of a simple scale from 1 to 10 to rate respondents' opinions of a product:

What was your opinion of the service you received while at the hotel?
(Give a mark from 1 to 10, with a maximum of 10 points if you thought it really outstanding, and a minimum of 1 point if you thought it very poor.)

In this way, an average grade for service can be more easily assessed. Similarly, the use of a **Likert Scale** will solicit respondents' extent of agreement to a statement:

French hotels generally offer better food than do British hotels.

1	2	3	4	5
strongly disagree	disagree	neither disagree nor agree	agree	strongly agree

It is a useful tactic to vary the polarity of the scales where several questions of this type are used, so that sometimes 'strongly agree' appears on the left side of the scale, and sometimes 'strongly disagree' appears. This prevents the phenomenon of respondents checking automatically all one column if they generally have a favourable or unfavourable view of the product, causing them to think before responding.

Yet another technique is the **Guilford Constant-Sum Scale** which requires the respondent to apportion 10 marks between two attributes or variables, as in the following question. Since the technique is quite complex, it will require careful explanation to make certain that every respondent understands it.

In the following question, you are asked to divide 10 marks between the two resorts shown, for each of the attributes shown in the left hand column. For example, if you were asked about the quality of the food in each resort, and felt that the food in Corfu was much better than the food in Majorca, you might allocate 8 marks to Corfu and 2 to Majorca for this attribute. If you thought the food to be equally good in both resorts, you would allocate 5 marks to each.

attribute	Corfu	Majorca
sunny and warm	——	——
good beaches	——	——
good resorts for young children	——	——
inexpensive as a holiday destination	——	——

Questionnaires should always be constructed so that initial questions are broad in scope (*'Did you have a holiday last year?'*) and gradually become more specific as the interview progresses (*'In what kind of accommodation did you stay while on holiday?'* . . . *'What were your views of the entertainment provided at the hotel?'*) Questions of a personal nature, such as age range, occupation, salary etc., are best left to the end of the questionnaire. Since it is seldom necessary to know respondents' exact ages, this question is best asked within a range, as follows:

15–24	1
25–34	2
35–44	3
45–54	4
55–64	5
65 or over	6
No response	7

In all such scales, make sure that each category is mutually exclusive. It is a common mistake to overlap categories (e.g. age range 25–35, 35–45 etc).

Whether the questionnaire is to be filled in by the respondent or by the interviewer, clear instructions should be given on how to fill it in, and its completion should be designed to be as simple and rapid as possible. For example, instructions should be issued to circle the number corresponding to the respondents' choice:

Where did you buy your ticket? (circle your answer)

direct from the airline	1
from a travel agent	2
from a ticket machine	3
from some other source	4
don't know/can't remember	5

This will greatly simplify transposing the answers to the computer for processing.

In some cases, open-ended questions will be unavoidable, although the completely unstructured question should be rare in a questionnaire, since it becomes difficult to categorise answers in a form which will enable them to be processed. A question such as 'What do you think of British Airways?', for example, will result in answers in so many different categories that they become unmanageable. The question would be better rephrased to ask separately about respondents' opinions of the airline's service, food, reliability, etc.

The use of semi-structured questions such as the sentence completion question may make answers easier to classify:

When I enter a travel agency, the first thing that I look for is . . .

Figure 3.2 provides an extract from a questionnaire which will indicate how precoding simplifies the processing of information in order to enter it on the computer. With the growth of moderately priced personal computers and survey software such as SNAP, collation and cross-tabulation of survey material has become easier and within the reach of the smaller company.

Interviewer: Follow instructions and read questions exactly as shown

COLUMN

Interviewer number   1,2

Date | 8 | 2 | 3–8
     Day   Month   Year

Day of the week: (circle)	Monday	1	
	Tuesday	2	
	Wednesday	3	
	Thursday	4	
	Friday	5	
	Saturday	6	
	Sunday	7	9
Weather:	Sunny	1	
	Cloudy/Fog	2	
	Changeable	3	
	Rain/snow	4	10

QUESTIONS

A WHERE IS YOUR HOME?

Dorset	1 1	W.Mid/H.ofE.	1 7	
(name town or village:)		E.Mid/E.Anglia	1 8	
_____		Wales	1 9	
Hampshire	1 2	North + NW	2 0	
London	1 3	Scotland	2 1	
Other WCTB	1 4	N. Ireland	2 2	
Other STB	1 5	Other Europe	2 3	
SEETB	1 6	Non Europe	2 4	11,12

If respondent gives answer to A giving codes 1 1–1 6, ask questions B1 and B2. If an answer code 1 7–2 4 was given, circle 2 for B1 and B2

B1 HAVE YOU COME FROM THERE TODAY?

     Yes   1
     No   2   13

B2 ARE YOU RETURNING THERE TODAY?
     Yes   1
     No   2   14

If respondent answers 'Yes' to both B1 and B2, circle:

  and go directly to E   0/0/0/0   15–18

Otherwise ask:

C WHAT IS THE TOTAL LENGTH OF YOUR HOLIDAY OR STAY AWAY FROM HOME?

Days   15–17
     (enter 3 digits, eg 3 days = 003)

D WHAT PLACE ARE YOU STAYING AT?

Weymouth/Osmington/Portland	1	
Lulworth area	2	
Dorchester/Warmwell/Mid + W.Dorset	3	
Wareham/Wool/Bovington area	4	
Swanage/Corfe Castle area	5	
Poole/Wimborne	6	
Bournemouth	7	
Christchurch/New Forest	8	
Other	9	18

E WHAT FORM OF TRANSPORT HAVE YOU USED TO GET HERE TODAY?

Train + bus/taxi	1	
Regular bus/coach	2	
Coach tour/excursion	3	
Minibus	4	
Car: own/firm's/friend's	5	
Car: hired	6	
Motor cycle/bicycle	7	
Other	8	19

F1 IS THIS YOUR FIRST VISIT TO BOVINGTON TANK MUSEUM?

Yes	1 0	20,21
No	2	20

If respondent answers 'No' to F1, ask:

F2 HOW MANY TIMES HAVE YOU BEEN BEFORE?

Once	1	
Twice	2	
3–5 times	3	
Frequently	4	
Stationed here	5	21

If respondent answered question E with an answer coded 1, 2, 3 or 4:

     circle: 0   22

If respondent answered question E with an answer coded 5, 6, 7 or 8:

     ask:

G WHAT WAS THE JOURNEY HERE LIKE?
   (Interviewer: explain this question if necessary)

Been to Bovington before	1	
Easy/well signposted all way	2	
Easy to find the camp, but museum not well signposted	3	
Difficult/poor signposting	4	
Other	5	22

H WHAT SORT OF GROUP ARE YOU WITH TODAY?

Alone	1	
With family	2	
With friends	3	
With family and friends	4	
Organised party	5	23
(state type:) _____		

_____

If respondent has been to the Tank Museum before, ie answered 'No' to question F1:

circle: 0   24

If respondent is on first visit to the Museum, ie answered 'Yes' to question F1:

ask:

I HOW DID YOU COME TO HEAR ABOUT THE TANK MUSEUM?

Stationed here	1	
Just passing/saw signposts	2	
With organised party itinerary	3	
Military contacts	4	
Tank restoration/specialism	5	
Heard from friends/family	6	
Leaflet in accommodation	7	
Saw or heard other publicity	8	
(specify:) _____		
Can't remember/other	9	24

J HOW MUCH TIME HAVE YOU SPENT HERE TODAY?

less than 30 minutes	1	
30 minutes – less than 1 hour	2	
1 hour – less than 1½ hours	3	
1½ hours – less than 2 hours	4	
2 hours or more	5	25

K HAVE YOU ANY SPECIAL VIEWS ON THE OPENING TIMES?

No special view, times satisfactory	1	
Should stay open at lunch time	2	
Should open earlier in the morning	3	
Earlier morning and lunch time	4	
Should stay open later	5	
Open later and lunch time	6	
Other	7	26

L IF A CHARGE WERE TO BE MADE FOR ENTRY, HOW MUCH WOULD YOU CONSIDER REASONABLE, FOR ADULTS, CHILDREN, AND SENIOR CITIZENS?

(Interviewer: circle one in each column)

	Adults	Children	Senior Citizens	
Free/nominal	1	1	1	
Around 25p	2	2	2	
Around 50p	3	3	3	
Around £1.00	4	4	4	
Around £1.50 +	5	5	5	27–29

(Interviewer: now conclude interview and thank respondent for help and co-operation)

Estimate number of people of different age groups in respondent's group (Enter numbers in appropriate boxes as TWO digits)

	Males	Columns	Females	Columns
under 11 years		30,31		42,43
11–15 years		32,33		44,45
16–24 years		34,35		46,47
25–44 years		36,37		48,49
45–64 years		38,39		50,51
65 + years		40,41		52,53

Number of questionnaire (enter two digits)

54,55

END

(Source: Bournemouth Polytechnic)
Fig. 3.2 Bovington Tank Museum visitors' survey

Observation

Whatever the strengths of scientific surveys, they have their limitations. Other techniques, such as observation, play a useful role in supporting evidence gained through the use of questionnaires. However, if observation is to be taken seriously as a research method, it must be conducted no less scientifically. This requires two things: the use of scientific procedure in conducting an orderly and sustained programme of investigation, and the ability of the observer to 'distance' himself from the event observed in order to record material in a dispassionate and professional manner. This second requirement is difficult for the untrained researcher, since attitudes and behaviour are moulded by our life experiences, and it is hard to step outside them. For this reason, most observation research is used at an exploratory stage in the research programme, and is carried out by professional researchers with psychological training.

We should not fail to recognise, however, that much useful material can still be gathered by the layman through a process of careful observation; from the travel agent who observes certain patterns of behaviour in clients who enter the shop and select brochures from the racks, to airline managers who listen to the way check-ins are handled at airports and observe the behaviour of passengers waiting for their flights. The essential thing to remember is that one is doing more than 'gathering impressions'. Patterns of behaviour are being recorded in detail, through the use of field notes or a tape recorder, and over extended periods of time.

A very high proportion of what is observed is likely to prove of little use, so that the process is both tedious and wasteful. The technique is nonetheless particularly valuable when researching competitors' products. The hotelier wishing to know more about competitors and how they handle conference enquiries might call the hotels in question, taking the role of a conference organiser, to see how the enquiry is handled; or sit in the lobby of a hotel to listen to the comments of guests or observe how front office staff handle incoming guests. One American hotelier (evidently little recognised by his staff!) made it a practice to stay as a guest in his hotels to check the levels of service provided. He would ask the lift operator or hotel porter to recommend a good place to eat (usually he was directed to somewhere other than the hotel's own restaurant!), and in this way discover how the sales training of staff could be improved and where it needed improvement.

On the whole, the technique is best used for generating hypotheses about situations, but it will improve the researchers' knowledge about what sort of questions need to be included in questionnaires.

Experimentation

Experiments usually conjure up an image of a laboratory, and indeed many tests are carried out under laboratory conditions which can be useful in travel and tourism research. Such research includes testing the effectiveness of different advertisements on a cross-section of consumers.

Many forms of experimentation can be carried out away from the laboratory, however. An agent who switches brochures around in their racks to see how this affects their selection is conducting a 'controlled experiment'. Airlines test different seats on their aircraft to see which proves most comfortable for their passengers, and a tour operator might experiment with the use of different excursions on different departures to see if these changes affect customer sales and satisfaction. The technique is useful in helping to establish whether there is a *causal relationship* between two variables, i.e. that a change in one variable produces a change in another. As well as demonstrating the cause and effect, the objective will be to offer an explanation for it, too.

Qualitative versus quantitative research methods

At the beginning of this chapter, mention was made of the distinction between qualitative and quantitative research. Much of what has been discussed up to this point can be described as quantitative in nature, and involves research which is concerned with gathering statistics to describe what is happening. In this, it is answering questions such as who?, where?, when?, and how? Answers to these questions are usually sought through the use of questionnaires. However, there are serious weaknesses with the use of the questionnaire. Their statistical significance is dependent upon their being answered honestly and accurately, but we have no way of knowing whether this is the case. Nor is the survey useful in helping to answer questions dealing with the Why? of travel. Let us say, for example, that we are interested in knowing why people travel by ferry rather than by air to the south of France. People may not actually know their real motives, or they may be reluctant to reveal them. Some will not want to admit to fear of flying, or being unable to afford to fly. Even if respondents aim to be totally honest, they may themselves have little understanding of their underlying motivation; motives can be extremely complex, and result from a great many different factors, while the questionnaire may only bring out the more obvious ones.

Qualitative techniques such as in-depth motivation research come into use for this purpose, and involve less structured interviews in which the purpose is to get the respondent to talk freely about the issue. This may call for interviews lasting two or three hours at a time, and clearly these cannot be carried out on the same scale as a 10-minute street interview. They will need to be conducted by skilled researchers, and this will greatly add to the time and cost of the exercise. They are intensely valuable, though, in probing beneath the surface responses generated in structured surveys.

One such technique widely used in market research is the *panel interview*, in which around six to eight consumers are invited to meet in informal surroundings to discuss a product or topic under research, under the guidance and direction of a skilled interviewer. Through the process of group dynamics, people's deeper feelings about issues are explored, with answers from one participant triggering off comments from other members of the panel. The material is generally tape-recorded for future analysis and, as exploratory research, can be helpful in guiding the direction of future research needed.

Other forms of qualitative research include *projective tests*, where respondents are asked to project themselves into another person's role. Examples of projective tests include *picture completion* wherein respondents are shown a cartoon or illustration in which one character is making a statement; they are then asked to complete the illustration by stating what they think the second character may be replying. The *Thematic Apperception Test (TAT)* employs a picture depicting a story and respondents are asked to identify what they believe is going on in the picture. Respondents are able in this way to project what they think as if these responses were a third person's views.

The beauty of research methodology is that there are so many ways in which research can be conducted, and researchers constantly seek new ways in which to secure evidence. One innovatory piece of research carried out by Thomson Holidays will illustrate this. Thomson were interested in finding out what image consumers had of the company, and how this image compared with that of other tour companies. To do this they used a form of projective technique, asking respondents to imagine that well-known tour companies had come alive as real people. In this way, Thomson discovered that the company projected an image of the solid, reliable family man, while Enterprise Holidays was personified as the rising young executive and Thomas Cook the pernickety, bossy squire. Such knowledge can be enormously beneficial in planning the company's promotional strategy and knowing what strengths to build on.

Research today is characterised by a growing interest in such techniques, with researchers always on the look out for innovative approaches. A museum in the United States, planning to find out which exhibits were the most popular, chose to support surveys by measuring the patterns of wear on the carpets in the museum and the noseprints on the glass cases surrounding the exhibits. Both measures gave a good indication of the levels of popularity of different exhibits.

Although, as has been made clear, many qualitative techniques do not lend themselves to tests of statistical probability, they will often throw light on issues which the more common forms of research technique cannot resolve; they should, therefore, be a part of the repertoire of any market research department.

Econometric models

A model consists of a set of variables and their interrelationship which reflect real life experience. By identifying how variables move in sympathy with one another, models can be helpful in predicting the future. Their use in travel and tourism research and forecasting is still limited, although they are being developed at a macro level to predict tourism trends by research organisations such as the EIU. This organisation has shown how fluctuating exchange rates and rates of inflation affect flows of international tourism.[1] Research of this kind is essential for public sector planning, and can also be extremely useful in forecasting future sales in the travel business. Models can be constructed on a smaller scale to show the effect of advertising spend on sales, and how this relationship is affected by other factors such as competitors' spend and changes in discretionary income.

Since there are so many variables affecting travel behaviour, the construction of a model to predict changes in the market for tourism is a complex and expensive process, but it is one which is being continually refined and improved.

The effectiveness of research

While some firms in the travel industry, and virtually all organisations in public sector tourism, undertake some form of marketing research, there are still many smaller companies which make no allowance for research in their annual budget, seeing it as inaccurate and an expensive use of resources which can be better channelled into other forms of marketing expenditure. This is shortsighted at best and, at worst, can be catastrophic if managers continue to commit major expenditure to new product development with insufficient background knowledge. Even today, too many small hotels are being bought, and small travel agencies opened, based purely on the 'gut feel' of their proprietors.

Research is never an exact science, but it can reduce the margins of error to which hunches alone are subject. The feasibility study is an essential prerequisite to any new project, whether the launch of a new company, the introduction of a new logo or the development of a new product. Above all, the success of research will be based on three things:

1 Sufficient resources must be allocated to the project to do the job properly, both in terms of time and money. Good research does take time to do, and managers wanting research results 'yesterday', or allocating only a fraction of the necessary funds, will force the methodology to be skimped and the end result to be of questionable value.

2 Managers should be willing to believe the results of the research when they become available, even if they conflict with the management's own preconceived views.

3 The results should be used. All too frequently, research is commissioned in order to avoid taking an immediate decision. Expensively commissioned research is then left to gather dust in a bottom drawer instead of being used to enable managers to make better decisions on the future direction of the company's strategy.

Questions, tasks and issues for discussion

1 Working in small groups, plan an observation exercise which might provide useful qualitative data for a local travel agent.

2 Obtain a questionnaire (preferably one that is used in the travel and tourism industry) and analyse its question construction, suggesting any ways in which you feel it could be improved. What additional questions could be asked that would give the company valuable information not provided by the present questions?

3 Discuss how you would plan a survey to obtain a market profile of visitors to your nearest tourism resort. Using a plan of the resort, identify the points most suitable for conducting street interviews and explain the reasons for your choice.

4 What sources of data exist on the number and profile of visitors to your town or region? What gaps in knowledge about the market exist, and what weakneses are there in the available data?

Exercise

You are given the task of carrying out a programme of research into your own travel and tourism or leisure course, with the aim of finding ways in which its content or structure could be improved. Produce a report for your Course Tutor which explains the methods you would plan to use and your reasons for choosing them.

Include in the report a short comment on the constraints under which the course is operating. Sum up by analysing the extent to which you believe the course is 'marketing-orientated', and what areas should become more orientated towards meeting the needs of students and/or employers.

4 The tourist market

After studying this chapter, you should be able to:

- understand consumer needs and wants, and the distinction between them
- appreciate the factors affecting consumer motivation and demand
- understand basic principles of psychology and sociology, as they relate to the buying process
- apply behavioural theory to the marketing of travel and tourism services
- understand market segmentation and its uses in the marketing plan

We speak of an individual customer for our products as a 'consumer', but in referring to consumers in aggregate, or groups of consumers, we use the term 'market'. A *market* can be described as *a defined group of consumers for a particular product or range of products*. Exactly how that market is defined is of crucial importance for our understanding of consumer behaviour, since it will shape the marketing response we make to our consumers' wants and needs.

Tourists are consumers who purchase a number of diverse travel and tourism services. If those in the industry have a clearer understanding of why their products are in demand, they will not only be able to tailor their products more closely to the needs of their clients, but will also be better able to select the advertising and sales messages used to inform and persuade those clients to buy the products.

Curiously, most research expenditure in the travel industry has tended to focus on what tourists buy, when they buy it, where they buy it and how they buy it; vital enough information, to be sure, but these bare facts tell us little about *why* the client purchases the product. Why, for instance, do certain tourists choose to holiday in Florida rather than Greece – what variables are at work here apart from cost? Why do they choose to travel with British Airways rather than, say, Lufthansa? Why do they buy an independent inclusive tour rather than a group tour, and

why have they taken the trouble to go direct to the airline to book, rather than through a local travel agency? These questions are not only of academic interest when striving for an understanding of tourist behaviour; their answers can be enormously helpful in the preparation of marketing plans.

Understanding needs and wants

As elsewhere in this book, our aim will be to understand basic principles, while relating these to the context of tourism. We shall start by looking at consumer needs and wants, and learning to understand how these arise.

As consumers, we often talk about our 'needing' a new television set, a new dress, or a holiday. Do we in fact really *need* these things, or are we merely expressing a desire for more goods and services? We live in a society orientated to increasing material consumption. We compare our success as a nation against that of other nations in terms of Gross National Product (GNP), a measure of material wealth; and we are therefore encouraged to discover new wants, or 'needs', as soon as existing ones are satisfied. One result of this is that it becomes increasingly difficult to distinguish between wants and needs.

We must first determine what is meant by a

need. People have certain physiological needs that are basic to survival; the need to eat, to drink, to sleep, to keep warm, and to reproduce, are all essential for the survival of the human race. However, for our psychological well-being, we also have other needs which require satisfaction; the need to give and receive affection, the need for self-esteem, for recognition of our abilities by others, for status and respect. There is also in mankind a fundamental drive for competence, a desire to master the environment, and to gain understanding for its own sake. Abraham Maslow[1] has conveniently categorised these needs into a hierarchy (Fig. 4.1), theorising that the more basic needs have to be satisfied before our interest will focus on higher level needs. Until we are fed and sheltered satisfactorily (and 'satisfactorily' means according to the needs of our cultural group) we are unlikely to give much thought to self-esteem or 'mastering our environment'.

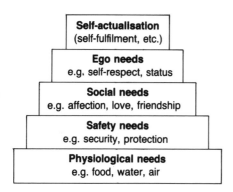

Fig. 4.1 Maslow's hierarchy of needs

The way we perceive our needs is built up of a complex interrelationship of beliefs and attitudes which arise out of our knowledge and opinions. Let us take the purchase of a car, for instance. At its basic level, a car provides us with transportation, and our choice is based partly on economic considerations. It is more *convenient* to use a car than public transport, we look for a car that is *cheap to run*, *reliable in operation*, with *easy access* to maintenance and servicing, *roomy* enough for ourselves and our luggage. But we may also seek to satisfy certain psychological needs in the purchase of our car. The design of

a particular model may appeal to us, either for aesthetic reasons or because its fast, sporty shape will be envied by others, gaining us *status*. Different colours appeal for similar reasons, and we may choose a bigger car to demonstrate our wealth to others. Conversely, we may choose a small, more fuel-efficient car as a demonstration of our attempt to be more ecologically frugal. Our choice of car, as with our choice of so many other goods and services we buy, reflects the way we see ourselves, – our perception of the kind of people we are.

It is not the role of this book to moralise about individual lifestyles. Our aim is only to bring the reader's attention to the impulses that shape consumer motivation. It is sufficient at this point to emphasise that there is a very complex set of motives influencing most of the products we buy, and that this is true of holidays as much as other products.

The variables affecting human needs

All of us have the same basic physiological needs. But how is it that in various countries and regions, different needs arise, leading to different patterns of demand? Why is the American satisfied with 'convenience' food, to be served quickly and accompanied by a glass of iced water, while the French consider the meal the most important event of the day, to be lingered over and enjoyed? Why is the demand for personal computers and video recorders in Britain among the highest in the world? Why is the sale of toothpaste so relatively small in France compared with other western nations?

Variables affecting the demand for goods and services may be conveniently divided into two categories: *demographic* variables, which are broadly population statistics, and *psychographic* variables, which are concerned with our patterns of lifetyle and personality.

Demographic variables

Population statistics include the numbers of people living in a country or region, and the component make-up of that population – the proportion in different age ranges, the marital status, proportion of those with children, number unemployed, and so on. Marketers will be interested to know not only the present statistics of the population, but also the changing trends taking place in the population.

If the number of young people is declining, for instance, while the number of those of retiring age is increasing, this will have important implications for tour operators who are specialising in holidays for the older traveller and those concerned with young people's holidays. If a company produces shirts, it would obviously be helpful to know the proportion of males in the population taking a size 15″ collar, and whether demand for larger collar and shirt sizes is increasing – due perhaps to the population eating better, or doing more sedentary jobs without exercise.

'. . . to know whether demand for larger collar sizes is increasing . . .'

If, in addition, we know something about the disposable income of these groupings (i.e. the amount of money these families are left with to buy goods and services after their regular commitment to mortgages, insurance, taxes and other essential household expenses have been paid), this will further aim our marketing planning. It is known that in Britain, for example, two groups with substantial discretionary income are young single people and 'empty nesters' – those aged about 40+ whose children have

grown up and left home, and who may have two earners in the family at the peak of their earning potential. It is also a characteristic of our changing population that the numbers of young people are declining, due to lower birth rates, while the numbers of those in middle age are increasing, due partly to better health care. We are likely to see much more attention focus on marketing new goods and services to the middle aged instead of the young over the next decade.

Psychographic variables

Simply counting heads in this way unfortunately tells us little about the motivation of individuals within these groups. How many will prefer coloured shirts to white ones? How important to young people is it to buy clothes made from natural fibres (cotton, linen, wool) rather than artificial materials? To answer questions such as these, we need to know much more about the cultural climate of a country and the psychological needs of its population.

Countries and regions develop their own unique cultures and values, which are learned rather than instinctive. Thus the British seek a greater measure of privacy in their lives than do Americans, leading to a greater demand for products like garden fencing. The British Tourist Authority, as part of its marketing research undertaken abroad, regularly monitors differing consumer needs of tourists from those destinations which provide substantial tourist demand in Britain. They have found, for example, that the Germans love beauty and art, appreciate their environment, are obsessed with physical well-being; their tourists demand accommodation with private facilities, accommodation that is clean and simple, and offers fresh food with large helpings in the restaurant. They enjoy family-run accommodation and a 'local atmosphere'. Knowledge such as this will be much more helpful in determining the basis for a hotel's marketing plan designed to attract German tourists.

Regional differences within countries are also often pronounced. Although changing, the demand for health foods in Britain is still greater in the South than the North, while products such as mushy peas, popular in the North of England, are hard to sell in Southern England. Although Americans share a common culture that is quite distinctive from that of the British, there are huge differences in culture and lifestyle between those residing in the North and South, and between those in the East and the mid-West. US marketers have long been aware of the need to treat domestic markets as consisting of up to nine distinctive 'market regions' when drawing up marketing plans.

Within national and regional groups, we can further distinguish a number of minority cultural groupings. *Ethnic* groups are those with differing racial, cultural or religious characteristics. Immigration from Britain's former colonies and elsewhere has led to concentrated populations of West Indians, Pakistanis, Poles, Chinese and other ethnic groups in Britain's major cities, which in turn has given rise to demand for specialist food, clothing and other products (including long haul air travel to the maternal countries!). In Germany, specialist travel agencies have sprung up to cater for the huge foreign travel demand created by the 'gastarbeiter' – guest workers from countries such as Turkey and Yugoslavia – who return home periodically for their holidays. Since German reunification, the flood of Eastern Europeans entering the country may well give rise to further opportunities to specialise in the future. In the USA, New York counts among its population a high proportion of Jews, who have marked preferences for travel – weekend breaks in the Catskill mountains, and holidays in Miami Beach, for example. In turn, this has led to hotel proprietors learning to cater for the particular needs of these markets, by providing Kosher food, and traditional Jewish dishes, such as 'lox and bagels'.

Social class continues to play an important role in all societies, whether capitalist or communist, although its importance is so often thought to be declining. Class is usually defined in terms of occupation of the head of household, although this variable alone can be misleading.

The system of social grading most commonly employed among marketers divides occupations into six categories, known as socio-economic groupings, as illustrated below:

Socio-economic groupings

A   Higher managerial, administrative or professional

B   Middle managerial, administrative or professional

C1   Supervisory or clerical, junior managerial

C2   Skilled manual workers

D   Semi-skilled and unskilled manual workers

E   Pensioners, unemployed, casual or lowest grade workers.

In this categorisation, ABC1 are broadly defined as middle class, while C2 and D categories are working class. E groups, as a catch-all, are less easily defined in terms of social class, but represent those at the lowest level of subsistence in society.

Between these groups, norms, values and patterns of consumer behaviour are distinctive, to an extent not explained by purchasing power alone. In fact, it would not necessarily be the case that those in the ABC1 categories have more discretionary income than do C2D categories. Many skilled manual workers today have more discretionary income to spend than those in traditional 'white collar' jobs, especially when taking into consideration the added burden of expenditure upon middle class consumers on items such as private schooling for their children, private health insurance, etc. Of equal importance for those providing leisure services is the relative amounts of leisure time available for short breaks or holidays. Many managers and professionals are obliged to take work home and can give less time to relaxation than can the 'nine-to-five' manual worker, who today may enjoy as much as four to five weeks' holiday each year.

Sociological groups

We have shown that consumers can be divided into a number of cultural groupings according to nationality, racial origin, or other forms of common background. There are two further groups to be discussed here, of which marketers must be aware.

Peer groups

The first of these is the *peer group*. This is defined as the group with which an individual is most closely associated in his or her life. Such groups include fellow students, colleagues and work-mates, friends and relations or close neighbours, and there is a strong tendency for individuals to conform to the norms and values of their peer groups. The latter therefore exercise considerable influence on the buying decisions of individuals within them. We have only to remember the pressures to conform on us in matters of dress or hairstyle in our last years of school to realise how great this pressure can sometimes be! The desire to emulate the purchasing patterns of our neighbours is proverbial – 'keeping up with the Jones's'.

Reference groups

In addition to these groups with which we as individuals are most closely associated, there are others with which we would *choose* to associate ourselves, either because we admire them or simply because we would like to emulate their lifestyle. These *reference groups*, as they are known, exercise strong influences on aggregate patterns of consumer demand. Members of the Royal Family, for instance, are trend setters, introducing fashions in hairstyles or clothing, as are film, TV and pop stars. Members of the so-called 'jet set' which surround prominent personalities are widely admired by the general populace, who copy their way of life, and purchase goods and services which are (or are thought to be) purchased by these 'innovators'. When products receive the personal endorsement of members of the reference group (film stars advertising soap or perfume, for example) huge increases in sales may follow. Many marketers for this reason are keen to see links established between their products and prominent people in society.

This desire to emulate those in an esteemed position in society gives rise to the phenomenon of the 'trickle effect', whereby products originally purchased by élite members of a society are adopted by those further down the hierarchy.

Many products once thought of as 'up-market' gradually trickle down the social scale, while those at the top of the social scale are continually seeking new products and services to distinguish themselves from the mass consumers. Articles such as filofaxes, cafetières and Austrian blinds spring to mind as examples of the trickle down effect, which holds true equally for tourism. Consider, for example, the way in which resorts such as St Tropez have over the years been transformed from holiday centres for the jet set to popular resorts for the mass market tourist.

Earlier, we made clear that social class is not simply a factor of occupation or income. It is, rather, a compendium of norms and values to the extent that a marketer's real concern is less with social class than with lifestyle; the ways in which social groups choose to live. Those following a 'bohemian' or unconventional lifestyle may be drawn from different social classes, but select the products and services they buy on the basis of their peer or reference groups. A good example of such groups is provided by those following what has become known as the 'alternative lifestyle', where products demanded include wholefoods, natural fabrics for clothes (handwoven rather than machine made), with fashions often following ethnic styles and designs, minimal use of cosmetics, and simple 'folk' furniture. It is interesting to note that in spite of the growing influence of this group in buying behaviour, little is known of their habits in holidays and travel. However, many new forms of tour have sprung up to cater for the special interest tourist by this market. One example of this is 'Cycling for Softies', a small specialist company providing independent cycling holidays in France coupled with comfortable accommodation in typical traditional hotels.

The psychology of the consumer

Up to now we have dealt with patterns of consumer behaviour in aggregate. For a thorough understanding of consumers, we must also know how they act and react as individuals.

Various models have been suggested by researchers of human behaviour, who are in general agreement that the number of, and interrelationship between, variables affecting product choice is extremely complex. In this chapter we can do no more than provide an introduction to consumer choice and outline some of the factors as a prelude to understanding how marketing can aid product choice.

Many models have been developed, of various levels of sophistication, to show how consumers react to stimuli. Howard and Sheth, for example, have argued that consumers can be classified as being in one of three stages of behaviour: an initial extensive problem-solving stage, where they have little knowledge about products or brands, and are seeking information from a wide range of sources; a stage of more limited problem-solving, where decisions have narrowed and information seeking has become more directed; and routinised behaviour, where buying has become based largely on habit and previous satisfaction with the product.[2]

Buyers choose products which they perceive as having the best potential to satisfy their needs. Buyers choosing a dietary product as an aid to slimming will be motivated by a product that offers some combination of low calories, nutrition, taste and value for money. They learn about such products partly through experience with the same or similar products in the past, and partly by seeking information. Information is sometimes sought actively (as when the buyer has an immediate need), or passively (where the buyer may be responsive to information and stores it away for future use). Sources of the buyer's information may be the commercial world or their social environment. The commercial world produces messages about products which act as stimuli – for example, advertisements which describe a product's quality, price, availability, service, and its distinctive qualities against its competitors. Social sources of information include word of mouth recommendation from friends or family, or objective articles about the product in newspapers or periodicals. A number of variables which we have discussed earlier mediate the effect of these stimuli. Our social class, personality, culture and group influences, as well as economic influences such as our financial means, pressure of time and the importance of the purchase, all interact with our internal state to affect our decision-making. Internally, individual decisions are based on the way we perceive and learn about new products. Research has shown that our perception of products is highly selective. We tend to 'screen out' information which is too simple or too familiar (hence boring), or too complex to take in, while we are more receptive to information to which we are predisposed. If, for example, we are thinking about a holiday, we become more aware of holiday advertisements. However, our perception of informatioin is also biased: we tend to distort information to suit our own frame of reference. Many continentals who have never visited Britain quite genuinely believe that the country is veiled in permanent rain and fog. Such preconceptions form a formidable problem for the BTA, but they can be modified by strong stimuli, such as the personal experience and recommendation of a member of the family or a friend.

Learning theory

One of the simplest models of the theory of how we learn is shown in Fig. 4.2. The model suggests that our individual needs give rise to a drive

Fig. 4.2

which we take action to satisfy. If our action does indeed result in satisfying the need, we tend to repeat the experience, leading to the development of habit formation and customer loyalty to particular brands. In the same way, we tend to generalise from past experience of a product, so that the satisfaction we receive, for example, by taking a cruise will lead us to take another cruise, or another type of holiday with the same company. However, Howard and Sheth have shown that constant repeat purchase of the same product leads to monotony and a search for a new product or brand, with the consumer once again returning to extensive problem-solving activity. An awareness of this phenomenon is useful to marketers attempting to switch loyal users of rival products to their own company's products.

The interaction of stimulus and exogenous variables results in buyers responding in a number of ways. First, their attention to new products may be achieved. Secondly, they become aware of the product, either broadly, or to an extent that they will recall and recognise it again in the future, or acquire a deeper knowledge of the product's benefits. Thirdly, consumers may form the intention to purchase the product at some future time. Finally, they will engage in overt purchasing behaviour – that is, they will purchase a particular quantity of the product at a particular time, through particular distributive outlets and at a particular price.

This hierarchical pattern of response is well known to marketers as AIDA – Attention, Interest, Desire and Action – representing four stages of response by consumers to a product. The marketing strategy is aimed at achieving one or more of these consumer responses. This will be discussed in greater depth in Chapter 9.

Applying consumer theory to tourism marketing

We have necessarily taken a number of pages to explain the fundamentals of consumer theory. Some of you may have found the theory rather heavy going and academic! But theory only has value when it is applied, so we now turn to examining ways in which our understanding of consumer behaviour can help the practice of marketing, and of marketing tourism specifically.

Although *individual* behaviour has been shown to be complex, it is possible to identify patterns of generalised group behaviour among consumers sharing common characteristics. Marketers have long recognised that few organisations are powerful enough to aim their products at the consumer in general. The cost of such a strategy is huge, and, particularly if the company is engaged in selling to international markets, such a 'shotgun' approach which fails to accurately target the markets for which products are aimed, does not make effective use of resources.

In very few cases are the products of one organisation attractive to all consumers in the marketplace. It therefore makes good sense to target the products to specific types of consumer, for which the product offers specific benefits, thereby making it more distinctive from its competitors: adopting, as marketers refer to it, a 'rifle' approach. This approach is also known as *market segmentation*, the basis of which is that the company first determines the market or markets it will serve, and then develops its products to serve the needs of those markets. This 'concentrated marketing' strategy reflects a marketing-orientated approach to business that is fundamental in planning.

A market segment can be defined as:

> a subgroup of the total consumer market whose members share common characteristics relevant to the purchase or use of a product.

The value of market segmentation is that the subgroup is also reachable through advertising messages aimed exclusively at them. Let us now look at some of the ways in which markets can be segmented in the travel and tourism industry.

Segmentation in travel and tourism marketing

Markets can be segmented in many different ways. If we go back to our earlier description of the variables affecting the demand for goods and services, we can start by segmenting our customers according to these criteria.

We could, for instance, decide to cater for groups of holidaymakers according to their age, their social class, or their regional distribution. Let us assume that we have decided to become specialists in developing package holidays for customers living in a particular region of Britain. We might feature, as benefits for this group, the convenience of local airport departures, free transport to the airport and/or free parking at the airport. While we would be carrying smaller numbers of clients than the large mass-market operators, and would not therefore gain the same economies of scale, many consumers will be satisfied to pay slightly higher prices for the convenience of a local departure and the additional benefits offered. We could stress that we are a local company supporting the economy of the region, and be active in local community events, so that local residents tend to think of our company first when planning their holidays.

Other tour companies have specialised by age. The success of companies such as The Club (formerly Club 18–30), who focus on the provision of youth holidays, and Saga Holidays, who specialise in holidays for older clients, reflects the success of concentrated marketing strategies. In-coming tour operators have specialised in handling groups of tourists from specific countries, such as Japan, the USA or Israel. They make it their business to know, and cater for, the needs of nationals from these countries. In the USA, certain tour operators have aimed to capture the black ethnic market (by, for example, establishing tours to West Africa for black Americans curious about their roots).

Just as with demographic segmentation, so can we segment by psychographic variables. Some companies have developed specialist villa holidays catering for young professionals (the so-called 'yuppies'), while other organisations have packaged tours for those with specific lifestyles. Research by the Irish Tourist Board has found that holidays in Ireland tend to meet the needs of those seeking to know and understand themselves better – a 'self-actualisation' need in Maslow's terms. This knowledge can be used by those promoting holidays to Ireland, by their emphasising Ireland as a destination for self-reflection and tranquility. Stanley Plog[3] in the United States has found that tourists can be categorised broadly as either psychocentrics or allocentrics. The former are self-inhibited, nervous and lack the desire for adventure, preferring well-packaged routine holidays in popular tourist destinations, mainly of the 'sun, sand, sea' variety. Conversely, the latter are more outgoing, have varied interests and are keen to explore new places and find new things to do. Such tourists are more likely to travel independently.

This model in itself is no doubt too simplistic. Most of us have some mix of these characteristics, and it is a noticeable fact that many mass tourists

to popular destinations, who would fall into the psychocentric category, gain confidence after a number of trips abroad, and become more adventurous. They may hire a car, for instance, and drive to areas less frequented by tourists, during their routine package holiday. Nevertheless, the model is helpful in thinking about the facilities we should provide to meet these differing needs.

Yet another way of segmenting our markets is according to the benefits the product offers. In many cases, different benefits appeal to different markets, and this can be seen in the case of a hotel which attracts both business people and holidaymakers. Sometimes both markets are attracted at the same time (as with London hotels, although weekend visitors are more likely to be leisure clients), while in other cases different markets are attracted at different times of the year. Seaside hotels may find that they are attracting a more up-market clientele, pehaps from an older age bracket, during the shoulder season than in the peak summer season.

Some hotels, particularly in country towns, will have to cater for different guests, based on whether their visitors are 'transient' (stopping only overnight while touring) or 'terminal' (using the hotel as a base for touring). Hotels in US cities (and some other countries) have recognised the need among day trippers and shoppers for a base in the city to rest, leave their purchases or take a bath, and hoteliers have hired rooms by the hour for this market, thus finding a new way to use the product.

Major hotel chains have identified a steady rise in the number of business women to whom they are catering, and have responded by providing facilities to meet their needs, including more feminine decor, cosmetic mirrors, hairdryers and other benefits. In some cases floors in large hotels have been experimentally restricted for the use of females only, to enhance the security of single female travellers. The development of motels in America was a direct marketing response to an identified need. Transient tourists required easy check-in and check-out facilities, minimal service or public rooms but convenient parking and low prices. The motel meets all these needs.

Major tour operators might be thought at first to be largely undifferentiated in their market segmentation. In fact, their products have in some cases become highly differentiated, even if less specialised than with small companies. To take advantage of the many different needs of their national market, they offer a huge range of different resorts, the convenience of local airports, holidays of different lengths, a wide range of hotels and prices, and catering arrangements varying from self-service to half board and full board.

Volume segmentation

There is one other form of market segmentation to which we must make reference, that of *volume segmentation*. This distinguishes between light and heavy users of the product (or loyal, repeat purchasers compared with occasional or infrequent purchasers). Hotel companies offer discounted rates, and other benefits, to regular purchasers such as companies booking employees regularly, or airlines who have contracts for crew accommodation. In some countries, loyal users of certain airlines may benefit from 'frequent flyer' programmes – once members exceed a certain annual mileage of travel with the airline, they are rewarded with a free trip for themselves, or their partners. While this strategy has proved highly successful in building brand loyalty, it has also suffered from an unforeseen drawback – all recipients tend to cash in their vouchers at the same time, and the resultant decline in cash tickets creates cash flow problems for the airlines!

Other lessons from Maslow

It will by now be appreciated that an understanding of consumer needs is critical for successful marketing. It might be helpful at this point to summarise consumers' travel and tourism needs and relate these to the Maslow hierarchy discussed earlier.

Motivation for travel and tourism can be categorised as follows:

- holiday travel
- business travel
- health travel
- visiting friends and relatives (VFR)
- religious travel
- travel for economic benefit (e.g. shopping)
- travel for educational purposes (study tours, etc.)
- sports and activities travel (participation or observation).

In fact, we can summarise all of these activities under five basic needs: *physical, cultural, interpersonal, status and prestige,* and *commercial.* Although there will be some overlap of motives between these categories, it will be useful to see how these needs are met by tourism facilities or destinations, and how they relate to levels of need in Maslow's hierarchy.

The demand for business travel is quite different from that for leisure travel, since it is by nature less 'discretionary', that is, less a matter of personal choice. Business people travel because of the demands of their business. As a result, such travel is less price-sensitive, since the company rather than the individual will be footing the bills. Business people tend to make frequent short-duration trips, which are generally taken mid-week rather than at weekends, and travel is not subject to seasonal fluctuations. Travel decisions often have to be taken at short notice, so that they need regular scheduled flights available and a fast and convenient reservations service.

At a basic physiological level, travel can sometimes be essential for health as in the case of travelling overseas for complex surgery, or the need to travel to warm, dry climates to recover from illnesses such as asthma and tuberculosis. These are then survival-related needs. Many people in stressful occupations also need a break from the mental or physical strain of their work to avoid a breakdown in health, and this 'cathartic' travel is no less necessary for survival. Even business travel, usually only thought of in terms of economic need, may be required for the survival of the organisation in the face of overseas competition. However, we must also recognise that quite a lot of business travel is in fact taken for prestige purposes – the requirement for first class travel and top price hotels, for instance –

while conference travel may be ascribed to competence needs.

Many people fail to travel, due to real or imagined fears; the fear of flying, or fear of being attacked. In these cases, the failure to travel is again related to basic safety needs of survival. In these cases, the marketer's responsibility is to overcome such fear, for example, by the National Tourist Office mounting a campaign to reassure visitors of the safety of their country, or bringing pressure on the government to provide protection for tourists, while airlines have to take steps to educate their clients about air safety. British Airways, for example, have run flights designed for those with a psychological fear of flying.

Our social needs for loving and belonging are often met through package holiday programmes, since many tourists find group tours an excellent way to make new friends or seek romance. Cruises fulfil this function well, and also provide a recognised outlet for those recently bereaved, who need a change of environment to escape their distress. A desire to appear attractive to others is achieved by gaining a suntan. Similarly, by visiting little known and distant tourist destinations, tourists are able to gain prestige in the eyes of their friends who are less travelled. Cultural travel provides opportunities for self-actualisation; the process of achieving or fulfilling one's potential.

These examples will be sufficient to show that travel satisfies many physical, social and psychological needs. They will also have shown us that travel motivation can be both *general* and *specific*. We experience the general drive to get away from our present environment, to escape from routine and seek new and different experiences, while at the same time we demonstrate individual motivations to see specific destinations and undertake specific activities while on holiday.

Some of the ways in which tourist needs for physical and cultural experiences are met are shown in Table 4.1. It is important to appreciate, however, that tourists seek to satisfy not one *single* need but a number of quite distinct needs simultaneously. The most successful products are those which respond best to this 'bundle of

needs' within a given market segment. As Pearce says,

> It is not the specific qualities of a destination and its attractions which motivate, but the broad suitability of the destination to fulfil particular psychological needs[4].

Table 4.1 Tourist needs and the marketing response

Need	Response
1 Physical	
Rest and relaxation	Beach holidays
	Lakes and mountains
Action and adventure	Trekking
	Ponytrekking
	Skiing
	Canoeing
	Sailing
	Safari parks
Health	Gentle walking trails
	Spas
	Health farms
2 Cultural	
Educational	Lecture cruises
	Study tours
Historical/Archeological	Tours of war sites
	Birthplace museums
	Nile cruises
	Ironbridge Gorge
Political	Kremlin tours
	Tours of UN
	Houses of Parliament
Scientific/Technical	NASA space centre
	Big Pit mining museum
	Car assembly plant
	Hollywood film studio
Arts	Music festivals
	Theatre visits
	Folk dance shows
	Craft or painting holidays
Religion	Mecca
	Lourdes
	'Retreats'
	Oberammergau
Commercial	Shops/restaurants
	Conference facilities
	Freeports
	Craft centres
	Wine/beer fairs

It is perhaps significant that, in a Gallup poll taken in 1983, it was found that if one looked at the countries in Europe to which British tourists aspired to travel, and if differences in cost were ignored, Switzerland, France and Germany were listed as the three favourite destinations, with Spain lying only fourth. Clearly, the bundle of benefits provided by the first three countries was greater than that provided by Britain's then premier package holiday destination.

Having now discussed consumer needs for travel, we can examine one other important aspect of consumer behaviour, that of decision-making.

Decision-making for the travel purchase

Studies of the decision-making process are becoming more common in tourism research. *How* decisions are taken, as well as when they are taken, are important factors in helping to understand the consumer purchase.

We discussed earlier the process by which consumers are influenced in product decisions, in models such as AIDA. The process is further complicated by the degree of risk inherent in the purchase. Obviously, deciding whether to buy a new bar of chocolate involves minimal risk, whereas deciding where to take the annual holiday involves substantial expenditure and a high degree of uncertainty. The consumer often lacks sufficient experience on which to base a decision. Experience is a key element in the learning process, and gaining objective information about new destinations is not easy. For this reason, word of mouth recommendation plays a very significant role in encouraging decisions.

Risk can be reduced in several ways. Familiarity gives confidence and results in the regular repeat purchase of a product; hence the tendency among more conservative holidaymakers to return to their traditional seaside resort year after year, or to buy another holiday from the same tour operator (brand loyalty). Risk can also be reduced by lowering our expectation of the product. However, consumers tend to idealise their major purchases, so this is rarely practical in the case of travel purchases. Nevertheless, there is great danger of overselling a travel experience, because of the frame of mind in which holiday purchasers are making their decision.

A third way of reducing risk is to maximise knowledge, seeking as much information about the product and selecting the 'best' choice from a wide selection of alternatives. An individual's personality plays a role here, as certain types of people tend to optimise their choice, while others, especially those with authoritarian personalities, consider fewer alternatives and are more easily satisfied. Advance booking is a characteristic of the search for security, reflecting not only the desire to make the booking of one's choice, but also the need to gather and consider information about the product well in advance. The tendency to book later in the UK is not only the result of expectation of bargains, but also reflects the increased sophistication of the British travelling public, who have become more familiar with overseas destinations.

In consuming a product, risk is reduced by searching for familiarity. However, tourism by its nature involves some novelty. Hence the common tourist problem of how to balance the need for adventure and new experiences with the need for familiarity and reassurance.

Studies of American tourists show that this problem is resolved in a number of different ways. First time US visitors abroad may venture into the border towns of Mexico, where they are close to the 'perceived safety' of their home country and culture. US visitors to Europe frequently make the UK their first stop, as the two countries share a common language and culture. Perceived security may also be increased by travelling to the foreign country by one's own national airline, and by staying in hotel chains operated or owned by a travel company from the home country.

In the case of British tourists, Jersey has successfully promoted the island as a 'bit of France that is British', while Gibraltar has been marketed as 'so British, so Mediterranean', effectively combining the appeal of security and familiarity with that of a warm climate in a foreign destination.

The package tour is the marketer's response to the need for familiarity. Tourists travel to mass tourist destinations where they will be in company with others from their own culture, where many locals will be conversant with their language, and where it may be possible to buy familiar food and drinks, but where there is also scope to sample new foods and different ways of life. The guided tour, particularly when led by a guide from the home country, gives psychological security, while the guide acts as 'culture-broker' but also caters to the tourists' social needs by acting as a catalyst in getting members of the group to know one another.

Family group decision-making

Where decisions have to be made together, rather than individually, it is important to understand who participates in the decision, and the degree of influence each member of the group exercises. In family travel, how far is the choice of where to go, and when to go, made by the heads of the household, or is it a joint decision by all members of the household? Recent evidence suggests that women play a much more important role than was formerly thought in the process of deciding the family holidays. An IPC magazine survey undertaken in 1984 found that nearly twice as many women as men played the major role in influencing the holiday choice, while women were also found to be mainly responsible for the planning and organising of holidays. What has to be borne in mind when marketing travel is that, where joint decisions must be made, the parties involved may have different needs and objectives; consequently different messages may have to be directed to women and men. The typical travel brochure, with its pretty bikini-clad models on the cover, appears to be aimed at males, but is also appealing to the fantasy in women which encourages them to believe that just possibly the holiday will make them become more like the model. This is illustrated by research carried out at one travel agency, following the launch by Panorama Holidays of a brochure featuring a tasteful photograph of a slim, bronzed girl wading into the sea clad only in a wrap tied nonchalantly around her waist.

Most staff took the view that it was a male-orientated brochure, while only one declared, 'I know that I couldn't be like that; but how I wish I could'. While there are obvious attractions in using glamour, there is also the danger of giving offence. Overseas camping and caravanning holidays, which are designed to appeal to the family market, will feature children and their parents on the cover of brochures as an appeal to *all* the decision-makers in this type of holiday.

Market segmentation as a guide to marketing planning

It may be helpful to close our discussion of consumer behaviour by instancing one campaign in which demand for different kinds of holidays has been identified according to the needs of different markets. The Heart of England Tourist Board[5] identifies its existing or potential markets as follows:

1 **Domestic long holidays**
   General interest, independent tourists
   Group inclusive tour traffic
   Activity holiday tourists (tuition, family recreation)
   Waterways holidays
2 **Domestic short breaks**
   General interest, independent tourists
   Group general interest packages
   Special interest/activity events/special attractions
3 **Overseas visitors**
   Independent
   Inclusive tour groups
   Individual inclusive tours

While this type of classification is useful in planning a marketing campaign, in itself it tells us little about the characteristics of the markets which the products are designed to attract, apart from distinguishing between foreign and domestic tourists. For example, special interest programmes might include angling holidays. What are the characteristics of anglers, and how would they best be attracted to the region? From which regions are they likely to come? Would they be likely to travel individually, or will they bring their families? Are anglers drawn evenly from all age groups and social classes, or can we focus on particular age groups? What facilities do such tourists seek – self-catering, small intimate family-run accommodation, or larger hotels with all facilities? How price-sensitive is the market?

These are the kinds of question to which we shall need answers before planning our programme. Such answers would also help us to pinpoint our advertising expenditure more effectively, in selecting the right media and text to appeal to these tourists.

Questions, tasks and issues for discussion

1 Examine and analyse:
   (a) the factors which led to your own choice of a recent holiday, and
   (b) your ambition to visit any destination in the world.
   What are the motivations behind these choices, and how were they influenced?

2 It is known that travel agents have comparatively little effect in influencing their clients' choice of holiday. Why do you think this is?

3 Design a holiday which will appeal to an alternative lifestyle market segment, and suggest ways in which the product might be promoted to the market.

4 What evidence is there that the 'trickle-down effect' operates in travel? Is the process desirable from a marketing point of view, and if not can it be arrested?
   In the role of a tourist officer for a resort which is going down-market, suggest how a reversal of this trend might be made possible in the marketing plan.

5 Describe some of the ways by which tourists achieve a satisfactory compromise between their desire for novelty and adventure, and their need for security and familiarity.

Exercise

You have recently taken up a position in the research and development unit in the marketing department of a large UK tour operator. Research carried out by the unit has shown a significant market gap for holidays for the, broadly defined, 'middle-aged' – the 35–55 year-old group.

You are required to carry out further research on this market, to identify the type of holidays this age band demands, following which you are to devise a programme of holidays aimed at this particular age group. You may further segment the market in any way you think fit.

Working in small groups, construct a questionnaire and carry out a survey of people in this age group. Use the results to plan an itinerary which will identify:

- the destination (country, resort)
- the type of accommodation to be used
- the package arrangements (independent or group? Escorted? What meal arrangements? What activities to be included? Any special considerations?).

Produce a mock-up of a brochure for the programme. Detailed copy and costings are not required.

Your team will be required to make a presentation to an audience of independent travel agents who specialise in unusual holidays, outlining the programme and the reasons why it has been selected.

5 Tourism product policy

After studying this chapter, you should be able to:

- define product policy and understand its importance in the marketing plan
- explain how products are differentiated
- understand the role and importance of branding in the marketing mix
- describe the product life cycle, and the actions necessary to launch a new product and revitalise a flagging one
- understand the concepts of product benefits and added value

What is product policy?

Getting the product right is the single most important activity of marketing. If the product isn't what the market wants, no amount of price adjustment, dependable delivery or brilliant promotion will encourage consumers to buy it – or at least, not more than once, and very few companies produce products which are 'once-in-a-lifetime' buys. On the other hand, if the product produced does satisfy the consumer, the purchase is likely to be repeated, and the purchaser may go on to buy other products offered by the same company, and to recommend that company's products to other consumers – three very strong reasons why a company must make sure the product is right for the market at which it is aimed.

As we indicated in Chapter 1, a product is defined as anything that is offered to a market to satisfy a want or need. The term therefore includes tangible goods, services, people, places, organisations or ideas.

The tourism product is really quite a complex one, since it can comprise a place (the holiday destination), a service (a tour operator's package, incorporating the temporary use of an airline seat, hotel room and sometimes other facilities) and, on occasion, certain tangible products such as free flight bags, or a complimentary bottle of duty free spirits to encourage booking.

When consumers buy products, they are buying *features*, of a perceived standard of *quality and style* which reflects the product's design. The product's image and value may be further enhanced through the use of a *brand name*, which acts as a cue, helping the consumer to identify a product as of a particular standard. Further enhancement may result from the product's *packaging*, which both protects the product and increases its attractiveness. The brand may also be indicative of reliable *delivery and after sales service*. Such characteristics are features of any product. Let us now, by way of example, look at the features of a package holiday.

Let us say Mr and Mrs Jones are looking for a two week beach holiday abroad. They have two young children of eight and five accompanying them. They aren't too concerned where they go, as long as it's fairly hot, and the price fits their budget. But in fact they are looking for a complex bundle of features to fit their needs, some of which may not even be spelled out when they book the holiday, since they will presume they are included anyway (but if absent this would constitute grounds for reasonable complaint). Table 5.1 provides a summary of what the Jones family may be expecting. The list is not necessarily exhaustive, and could be expanded into greater detail, but it is sufficient to demonstrate the complexity of the product being purchased, and the range of needs it is designed to satisfy. Almost inevitably, there will be some conflict between these needs, such as between cost and quality, or between the different needs of each member of the family (what Mrs Jones finds attractive hotel decor may not appeal to her husband, while the children's idea of entertainment will differ from their parents'). Consumer decisions invariably require some compromise.

Table 5.1 The composition of a package holiday product

Product segment	Features
1 Destination	not too distant in flying time, clean, sandy beaches, reasonable certainty of sunshine, lively entertainment at night, good shops, reasonable prices, interesting excursions, friendly locals, safe to walk about, English widely spoken.
2 Originating airport	convenient local airport, car parking, not too congested, duty frees available.
3 Airline	flights at convenient time, reliable, good safety record, thoughtful, polite service, modern type of aircraft.
4 Coach transfers	clean, modern coaches, reliable, competent and friendly driver and courier.
5 Hotel	location: accessible to beach, shops, etc., staff trustworthy, English speaking, competent, friendly; facilities: well maintained, attractive decor, quiet at night, adequate public rooms, swimming pool, child care service, bar with good range of drinks at moderate prices, adequate size bedroom with balcony, sea view, comfortable beds, phone, colour TV, adequate cupboard space, wood (not wire) hangers, shower, toilet, shaver point, good lighting for make-up; restaurant/meals: good food, well cooked, served hot, adequate portions, good variety and choice, pleasant atmosphere, comfortable seating, flexible meal hours, fast, polite and friendly service.
6 Resort representatives	knowledgeable, competent, friendly, reliable, accessible.
7 Tour operator	price reflects good value for money, secure, reliable, offers guarantees, extras.
8 Travel agent	convenient, competent, reliable, friendly, pleasant 'shopping atmosphere', extra services provided (e.g. discounts, free transfers to airport, free insurance).
9 Miscellaneous	companionable fellow travellers with common interests; 'expectation': widening of general knowledge and interests, pleasant memories of experience.

In fact, the needs listed in Table 5.1 are not 'core needs' at all, but rather *second level* needs. Core needs are those which give rise to the demand for the holiday in the first place, as discussed in Chapter 4. Both Mr and Mrs Jones may be expressing a need to get away from the work environment, or Mrs Jones may be seeking a break from the responsibility of caring for her children 24 hours a day, from cooking and from housework, and may be looking to make new friends and widen her social contacts. Underlying needs of fitness, status, adventure and romance may all be implicit in the demand for this particular holiday.

Differentiating the product

It is important to recognise at this point that what consumers are demanding are not products, or even features of products, but the *benefits* these products offer. What is sought is the satisfaction of needs; or, as Theodore Levitt puts it, 'purchasing agents don't buy quarter inch drills; they buy quarter inch holes'. Our needs are very diverse, and the greater number of needs that can be satisfied through the purchase of one product, the more attractive that product becomes to the consumer.

It is this essential role of marketing, to *produce added benefits*, which enables the marketer to distinguish one product from another. The marketer must ask himself, 'if the product which I am supplying offers no appreciable benefits beyond those offered by my competitor, why shouldn't my customers buy my competitors' products?'

The need to invest distinctive benefits in a product gives rise to the concept of the *Unique Selling Proposition*, or USP. This is the feature or features in a product which offer unique benefits not found in those of its competitors. There are a number of holiday companies specialising in the organisation of package tours aimed at the young (18–30) travel market. While the product offered is similar in many respects, companies focusing on this market segment seek ways to differentiate their product from others. Thus for example, Twenties emphasised that their hotels are used exclusively by their customers, while some young people's companies may hint at the possibility of romantic or sexual adventure.

Companies will distinguish products in a wide variety of ways. Some may provide added features at an inclusive price, others may choose to emphasise the *reliability* of the product on offer. Quality is an important attribute of many products, and not only premium-priced products. Japanese car manufacturers have established a wonderful international reputation for their products by the application of careful quality control in their manufacturing process, ensuring better finish and reliability than most of their rivals throughout the price range. In the travel industry, certain airlines have chosen to identify their product with reliability ('multi-million mile pilots', 'on-time arrivals'), and Thomson Holidays have chosen to stress the careful process of checking foreign resorts and hotels to reduce complaints and improve customer satisfaction.

At the opposite extreme, companies have also tried to distinguish their product by making it cheaper than their rivals', with their marketing emphasis on the reduction of production costs and/or low promotional expenditure. This will reduce unit profits, but the resultant increase in volume demand created by the attraction of low price can be sufficient inducement to adopt such a policy in order to establish a leading market share. The 'pile it high, sell it cheap' philosophy that was at one time the principle of Tesco Supermarkets has been taken up by a great many British companies, sometimes at the expense of quality control. The travel industry, too, has fallen victim to the belief that low price is the key to success; and over time, the belief becomes a self-fulfilling prophecy, since if companies promote low price, their customers will come to believe the message and demand low price. However, they are not necessarily willing to forego the other attributes they seek, such as reliability and quality, with the result that overall satisfaction falls.

Tour operators will concede that they receive a higher ratio of complaints on, and their customers often have higher expectations of, their cheapest holidays! It must be remembered that price is only one aspect of a product, and countries such as Germany, Sweden and Switzerland, which suffer from high labour costs, have nevertheless successfully marketed products on the basis of value for money and high quality. Their success in export sales, at the expense of cheaper British products, is all too apparent, while British products that *have* gained an international reputation – Jaguar and Rolls Royce cars, Pringle knitwear, Royal Doulton china, Tiptree jams – have done so on the basis of reliability and quality.

It is significant that in the late '80s Tesco itself changed its marketing approach, no longer relying on the old 'pile it high, sell it cheap' concept.

Good design, or 'style', can also form the basis of product differentiation. This is perhaps more readily appreciated in physical products, and the success of companies such as Gucci clothing and accessories, Bang and Olufsen hi-fi, Braun consumer durables or Olivetti office equipment spring readily to mind as examples of companies where style is closely associated with both distinctiveness and quality. Good design provides three important aids to the consumer: it represents the *perceived* value of the product, it enables the company to create a 'personality' for its products, and by judicious periodical alterations in styling, it creates demand through creating the desire for replacement with more fashionable new styles.

Style also has a role to play in travel, both in terms of the physical features of the travel product and the image which certain companies have generated. The design and decor of hotels, ships and aircraft provide opportunities for companies to personalise their products, as well as periodically to update them. Alternatively, some hotels and carriers have actually played on the nostalgia of travellers, with the Orient Express perhaps being the outstanding example of 'style' in travel design.

Style can be a two-edged sword, however. Hotels are as subject as other products to the vagaries of fashion, and must allow within their marketing plans for frequent refurbishing and new themes to attract their customers.

The creation of a particular image or 'personality' for a company or its products is a particularly astute form of marketing, especially in those companies in which physical design can play no part. In this case, the marketer aims to create an 'aura' for the product, distinguishing it from its competitors in sometimes indefinable ways. Companies such as Serenissima Travel, which features cultural long-haul tours, are offering a product which is perceived as distinct from competitors, even though they may be selling the same destination and accommodation. In the airline industry, during the 1960s and before deregulation, when differentiation under IATA regulations was virtually excluded, nonetheless certain airlines were able to develop distinct 'personalities'. Eagle Airlines created an entirely new market between New York and Bermuda, for example, by developing an image of a friendly, easy-going airline quite distinctive from other airlines serving the route. A similar style was evident in Freddie Laker's brief foray into 'Skytrain' and is apparent in Richard Branson's Virgin Airways – helped, no doubt, by the ebullient personalities of their respective Chairmen, but not dependent upon that alone. Certain hotels are renowned for their atmosphere – the Algonquin and Plaza in New York, Brown's and Claridges in London – giving them a unique quality that cannot be captured by their competitors. A history or tradition is obviously helpful in creating this atmosphere. Marketing managers must never forget that their customers are buying experiences, and the atmosphere of a hotel, cruise ship or destination is a major contribution to overall tourist satisfaction.

Branding

Giving a product a brand name is not only a useful way of differentiating it from others but also a means of adding perceived value. This has implications for the price that can be charged for the product and the profit margins attainable on each unit sold.

A brand may be defined as a 'name, sign, symbol or design, or combination of these, intended to identify the products of an organisation and distinguish them from those of competitors'. This name, symbol or combination is referred to as a 'logotype', or *logo* for short. The design of the logo may be registered as a trademark, legally protecting the company's right to use it exclusively in the home country and overseas. Registration also makes it an offence for competitors to copy the design too closely – and conversely, to be acceptable for registration, a

Fig. 5.1 Some examples of logos in use in the travel and tourism industry

design must be sufficiently distinctive from others already registered.

Branding a product is one of the oldest marketing techniques, but has become a potent tool of marketing in the twentieth century. Virtually anything can be branded, from matches (Swan Vestas) to petrol (Shell Oil) and turkeys (Bernard Matthews has been a notable success story). Service industries have also become aware of the benefits of branding, and brand names have become household names in tourism. One has only to think of aircraft livery, the funnel colours of shipping companies, such familiar logos as those sported by Holiday Inn, American Express or Thomas Cook, to realise the extent to which branding has become important to the industry. Figure 5.1 offers some common examples of branding in travel and tourism.

The benefits of branding

Ascribing a brand name or symbol to a product offers a marketer a number of advantages:

1 It helps to identify a particular product and distinguish it from competitors, as we have described.

2 It becomes associated with the particular benefits offered by the product, acting as a 'cue' to purchasers in their decision-making. In particular, it indicates to purchasers what level of quality they can expect, since a range of products marketed under the same brand name will carry similar expectations of quality standard (and for this reason it is essential that companies branding their products exercise very strong control over the quality of their production).

3 Where the product is intangible, such as is the case with tourism products, since it cannot be seen or sampled in advance, the purchase of a branded product helps consumers to *avoid risk*. If they are satisfied with the brand purchase, they are likely to repeat the purchase and, over time, to become regular purchasers of the brand. Repeat purchase becomes instinctive and habitual over time, at which point we can describe the customer as being 'brand loyal'. Some travel companies are already dependent upon brand loyalty. Cruise companies such as P & O, for example, claim that as many as 60 per cent of

their customers are regular repeat purchasers, and it is also becoming a feature of the mass market tour operators, although the continuing emphasis on price tends to undermine efforts to build brand loyalty.

Branding becomes a key tool in market segmentation strategy. Associating a brand with a particular segment of the market can help to expand a company's market share at a time when the total market for a product is saturated. As one example of this in the field of tangible products, consider the range of different washing powders (arguably one of the most homogeneous products available) offered by Procter and Gamble or Unilever in their attempt to widen their respective companies' market shares.

Major tour operators such as Thomson Holidays and Owners Abroad regularly develop new brand names for their products as part of their marketing segmentation strategy. Thomson's use of the 'Skytours' brand, for instance, distances that programme aimed at the cheaper end of the market from the broader, more up-market programme sold under the Thomson banner.

Finally, use of a brand name enables companies to employ a technique known as 'brand stretching' – the introduction of new products into an existing range under the same brand name. In the Fast Moving Consumer Goods (FMCG) market, this is a critical factor in the launch of new products by companies such as Heinz or Campbells. Well-established travel brands such as Thomson or Cosmos could be stretched to include new ranges of holidays such as seat only flight programmes (e.g. Thomson 'Airfares' and Cosmos 'Travjet'), or cruises, enabling them to gain immediate credibility in the market, as well as willingness on the part of the travel agents to deal with the new products. 'Big name' brands become increasingly important as the competition intensifies to get brochures displayed on travel agency racks.

Branding decisions

If a company decides to introduce a brand, it can do so in a number of ways. It can introduce a 'blanket', or family brand name, as is the case with Heinz; or, as with Procter & Gamble, it can introduce different brand names for each product it manufactures. There are examples of each of these approaches in travel. Accor Hotels trade under a range of company names (Sofitel, Novotel, Mercure, Ibis, Formule 1), while Forte may choose to project a family image with some properties, differentiate with other products (Forte Crest Hotels, Forte Posthouse Hotels, Forte Heritage Inns, Forte Grand Hotels and The Exclusive Portfolio). Scheduled airlines may run charter off-shoots under different brand names (Lutfhansa: Condor, Iberia: Aviaco).

A new brand name may be chosen if an existing brand is too closely associated with a particular type of product, making it difficult to stretch and encompass new concepts. Companies such as Yugotours, Olympic, Austrotours or Paris Travel, whose original choice of name reflected the policy of specialisation in specific travel destinations, would find it difficult to introduce new destinations under the same brand name (although some have tried to do so), whereas a company with a more universal brand name, such as Global or Cosmos, would be less restricted.

In first developing a brand, the objectives of the brand need to be carefully thought out. A brand is not just a means of drawing attention to the product: it should stand for something. It must act as a cue to the product characteristics, including the product's quality. Is it to be low, medium or premium quality? Is it to offer the economic appeal of 'value for money', or the more emotional appeal of high price for a status product? Think of the diverse messages associated with clothing labels such as Harrods, C & A and St Michael to realise the immense power of brands to communicate effective messages about product characteristics.

Branding provides the opportunity for a company to enhance its corporate image, because how the consumers feel about a brand reflects their feeling about the company. Companies such as Shell use their brand names as a means of enhancing the corporate image, and this is reflected in travel companies such as Swissair, Cunard and Hilton Hotels.

Repositioning a brand: the case of Thomson Holidays

However successful a company may be, from time to time it becomes necessary to recognise that the market (or those parts of the total market that are currently believed to offer profit potential) is changing. A company may then decide that it has to change its established image in order to benefit from the future potential.

This can be shown by the example of one tour operator, well-known for the reliability of its middle-market package holidays based on charter flights, which launched a programme of world-wide holidays based on scheduled air services. The company's airport representative at Heathrow, whose role was to ensure that their travellers received every help before departure, made a practice of identifying clients in the check-in queues; armed with a clipboard, she would proffer help to those so identified. However, she found that though she was able to identify the company's clients by name and destination, many did not use the company's labels, and moreover flatly rejected the representative's help. They did not want to be identified as 'package tourists', preferring to be seen as sophisticated world travellers on the international airlines with which they travelled. In this case, the company's image was the wrong one for the holiday and the type of holidaymaker it attracted.

By the beginning of 1991, companies were grasping that the so-called mass market for package holidays was declining. The future was clearly for lower numbers of higher priced holidays, offering higher levels of satisfaction.

At the beginning of the '90s, Thomson Holidays was firmly established as the market leader, with some 35 per cent of the package holiday market. It offered the widest range of holidays from the UK, having built its reputation on the package holiday market (largely to Spain) over the previous three decades. Consumers associated Thomson with mainstream beach holidays to the Mediterranean. While they recognised the company's reputation for such intangibles as reliability and good value for money, their ignorance of the full range of holiday opportunities meant that Thomson was often excluded from their 'shopping list' when they were seeking information on a more sophisticated far away holiday.

Thomson's response was to set its advertising agency a challenging brief: without in any way diminishing the perceived values of quality and reliability, the agency was asked to stretch customers' perceptions of the type of holidays available from Thomsons, not just in terms of destinations but also in respect of more unusual types of holidays, especially those featuring activities. The target age group was broad – between 20 and 65 years.

Three special holidays were chosen to be featured on advertising hoardings and in prestigious full colour double-page spreads in the *TV Times* and the weekend colour supplements of the quality newspapers. In each there was a 'throw-away' headline, apparently torn out of a package tour brochure, but contrasting a boring normality with an exciting illustration:

Flights are met by a Thomson Rep
Pictured was a hot air balloon hovering in the sunset over a Kenyan safari park, which featured in Thomson's safari programmes.

Your rep will make sure that everything runs smoothly
Pictured was a graphic photograph of white water rafting. The logic behind this was that lakes and mountains holidays were seen by many as somewhat unexciting, picturesque walking holidays, whereas more adventurous activities were also available.

All rooms have a sea view
A beautiful Turkish island cruising yacht was pictured against a background of an idyllic unspoilt Mediterranean bay. Unexpectedly, this type of sophisticated cruising holiday was also featured in Thomson's programme.
The award-winning advertisements were designed to lift the Thomson brand and to inject into it what was described as 'a more relevant image for today's holiday market'. It proved to be one of the most inspired campaigns of 1991.

Brand sponsorship

When a firm decides to introduce a new brand, it has several options open to it. It may choose to develop and use a brand exclusively for itself, or it can manufacture the brand of another organisation under licence. This applies equally to a service product. Thomas Cook, for example, buys in holidays of Jules Verne to China.

A third alternative is to franchise a brand. In this situation, the company owning the brand allows others to sell the product, with certain preconditions attached – such as the obligation to purchase raw materials exclusively from the supplying company, or the obligation to pay a proportion of the earnings to the franchiser (royalty payments). Franchising offers the benefits of rapid expansion for a brand, and the security, for consumers, of consistent and recognised standards of quality. To be effective, though, the brand must be well established in the market before it is launched as a franchised product. Fast food firms in particular have expanded rapidly with the use of franchises, so that companies such as Kentucky Fried Chicken and Macdonalds Hamburgers have become household names world-wide. In the travel industry, Holiday Inns and Hilton International are just two hotel chains which have benefited from the use of franchising, and other sectors of the travel industry are just beginning to experiment with the technique. Franchising as a distributive technique is discussed further in Chapter 8.

What makes a good brand name?

A number of guidelines have been drawn up by marketing theorists for the development of a good brand name. Since a critical function of the brand name is to obtain immediate recognition for both the product and its attributes, the name or symbol has to communicate these attributes with appropriate imagery. Names must be easy to pronounce and remember, as well as helping to convey the product's benefits. Symbols should be distinctive, their design and colour supporting the product concept.

Although corporate names, often associated

with the founder (Thomson, Hilton) remain popular brand names, words conveying the nature of the product or having pleasant associations (Sunair, Serenissima) help to reinforce the benefits in the purchaser's mind. 'Catchy' brand names (Britrail) retain the parent organisation's name but reduce it to a more easily memorised 'logo'.

It is important, particularly in such an international field as travel, that brand names are registerable in all the countries in which the company can expect to operate, and that these names are both easy to pronounce and to remember by those speaking foreign languages. Words need to be screened to ensure they don't project a different association in other languages – the French may be hard put if they were to try to market their popular soft drink 'Pschitt' in Great Britain! There are companies which will help international brand name choice by screening new product names in advance and singling out any judged unsuitable for any reason – a wise precaution.

The simplicity of a word or illustration will enhance recall and recognition. This is important in the travel industry, where the brand may have to be displayed on a fast moving object such as an aircraft or coach.

Finally, one must remember that there are always examples of companies that have managed to break all the rules and have nevertheless succeeded. Who would have imagined that Kawasaki or Mitsubishi could become household words in Britain? Or that Tjaereborg could be successful in selling package holidays to the British? These companies have succeeded in establishing a reputation through the quality of their products alone; but this is not to deny that their marketing task might have been easier had they been marketing their products under names such as Honda or Touropa.

A brand will enhance the corporate identify of an organisation so that product and company become inseparable in the minds of the consumers. But to gain maximum impact, it must be used in all areas of the company's marketing; on stationery, brochures, representatives' uniforms, shopfront, literature racks and in promotional aids such as flight bags, carrier bags or other 'give-away' material. This represents the 'total marketing' approach so essential in modern marketing.

The product mix

Few companies produce a single product. Companies are therefore faced with making marketing decisions on the *mix* of products which they propose to offer to their customers. The product mix comprises the range of different *product lines* the company produces (called the 'product width'), together with the number of variants offered within each product line (the 'product depth'). A white goods manufacturer such as Hoover, for example, will have to decide on the range of products it will manufacture – washing machines, dryers, vacuum cleaners, toasters, etc. – as well as what options will be made available in each product; different motors, designs, capacities, colours, and so on.

Such decisions have implications for the whole marketing mix. Different products may be targeted at different market segments, for example, requiring different advertising and promotional strategies. Some products may be marketed in an intensively competitive environment, with consequent implications for pricing, and profit margins. Some, because of technical complexity or other factors, will need exceptional sales back-up, while others may be suitable for self-selection, affecting distribution strategies.

In the manufacturing process, a critical factor is to what extent existing resources – machinery, skilled labour etc. – can be used in making diverse products. If a machine has spare capacity and can be used in the manufacture of a new product line, this may make all the difference as to whether it will prove profitable for the company to make the new line. For each product line, the manager must be knowledgeable about the market; who is buying the product and why, how competitive it is against those of rival organisations, what market share the product enjoys, the level of sales achieved, and the contribution it makes to overall revenue and profits. Such knowledge will enable further decisions to be made about new products – should existing products be strengthened or extended, should some options be withdrawn, should new product lines be introduced and should such products be consistent with the existing product range, or would it be better for the company to diversify into entirely new lines?

Just as with any other business, a travel or tourism business must also decide its product width and depth. A large mass market operator has to make a number of critical marketing decisions.

Although at first glance one might be inclined to think that a tour operating programme is a single product line, in fact the nature of package holidays makes them quite distinctive, appealing to different market segments and satisfying different needs. For this reason, a company may organise its products into separate divisions, under separate product managers, producing separate brochures, and even operating these holidays under different brand names. Thomson, in addition to operating its winter and summer sun programmes, offers long-haul holidays, lakes and mountains holidays, programmes for the mature traveller ('Young at Heart') and the young 'Young and Lively') as well as holiday programmes under separate brand names ('Horizon' and 'OSL'), and even some brands operated as quite distinct divisions from the mainstream company, with a unique distribution system (Portland Holidays). Within each of these programmes, decisions must be made on product depth: what holiday length to offer (3, 7, 10, or 14 days?); from which airports to operate; to which destinations and airports; how will the price of each product be determined in order to achieve the overall target profitability for the company?

Sometimes, as we have seen with branding, lines can be 'stretched' to encompass new market segments. Such decisions may be taken if the current market is experiencing slow growth, or the company finds itself increasingly under attack from the competition. A company at the bottom end of the market may find profits squeezed, and attempt to reposition its products further up the market to allow a greater margin of profit; or a company which has focused on the upper end

of the market may choose to widen its appeal by reaching a larger market, capitalising on its reputation for quality in the top-market field. Such policies carry the inherent danger that the public image of the company and its markets may become confused, causing it to lose its niche and original marketing strengths. Some shopping companies, for example, in their attempt to widen their appeal to reach new mass markets for cruising, downgraded the product, thereby losing the confidence of their loyal original customers. It is interesting to note that this lesson was learnt and the experience acted upon. P & O, in taking over Princess Cruises, retained both the distinctive names and separate marketing activities for the two companies, who drew their clientele from discrete markets, while Cunard, in purchasing the former Norwegian ships Vistafjord and Sagafjord, retained distinctive marketing policies for the two ships although absorbing them into the Cunard shipping division.

The product life cycle

Although the exact duration of a product's life cycle cannot be forecast, all products exhibit characteristic life cycles, which can be illustrated graphically, as in Fig. 5.2.

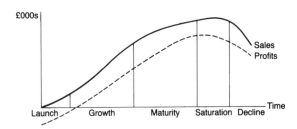

Fig. 5.2 The product life cycle

The 'S' curve of this graph indicates that typically a product will experience slow initial sales after launch, while it is still comparatively unknown, with accelerating sales as it becomes better known and its reputation is established. Steady growth is then achieved until almost all the consumers likely to buy the product have done so, at which point sales even out. The product also faces increasing competition as its sales expand, so that at saturation point it may be fighting harder to retain its existing share of a stagnant market. If newer products are seen as better than the existing one, sales will decline. At this point the company must take some action, either to restore the fortunes of the product or to kill it off.

This theoretical model holds true for all products, including tourism. A destination will gradually become known to tourists, who are initially attracted in small numbers. As it becomes more popular, and exploited by other carriers and tour operators, sales will rise rapidly; perhaps a different market is attracted. The uniqueness of the resort is lost, and it becomes another mass market destination, appealing to a more down-market holidaymaker. The expansion of hotels and other facilities at the resort may lead to a surplus of supply over demand; for example, tourism promoters in Majorca now believe that the town must reduce its bedstock by 50 000 beds to ensure enough occupancy to maintain the quality of service provided. Neglect or over-development can lead to despoliation of the resort. Eventually, the resort may decline to a point where tourism is no longer significant and other industries may be encouraged into the region, or the local authority decides to take action to improve the appeal of the destination again.

Of course, each product has its unique life cycle. In some cases, this pattern of growth-maturity-decline may be quite rapid (skateboards, novelty items) while in others, the product can sell at saturation level for a very long period (Oxo). It is also important to recognise that brands are subject to similar life cycle stages, although generally of a shorter duration. Clearly, the marketing manager must be aware of what stage in the life cycle the brand, as well as the product, as reached. As competition increases, brand life cycles tend to shorten, requiring the introduction of new marketing strategies designed either to increase sales or to kill off one brand to make way for a new one.

Forecasting product life cycles, and when a product is about to move into a new stage, is clearly no easy matter, although the danger signals heralding a decline are clear enough – declining sales or market share, especially in relation to one particular brand or product in the product line. There is evidence to show that when life cycle forecasting is attempted, it can prove surprisingly accurate. More generally, however, an understanding of the relationship between a product and its life cycle enables marketing managers to plan their campaigns more effectively, and to be in a better position to judge product sales and profit potential.

As can be seen from Fig. 5.2, as profits rise and fall at different stages of the life cycle the extent to which a particular product will contribute to overall profit objectives of the firm can be anticipated, based on its position in the life cycle. At the launch stage, the marketing costs associated with a new product will be substantial, as the company tries to bring the new product to the attention of its market. Only as sales accelerate will these costs be recovered and the company start making a profit. Highest profit-ability is generally achieved at the maturity stage, with profits falling back thereafter as sales decline. However, by careful manipulation it may be possible to maintain high profit levels at advanced stages, by reducing advertising expenditure and allowing the product to 'live on its reputation'. This is known as 'milking a cash cow', and as long as loyal customers continue to purchase the product, it may be worth the company's while to continue to produce it.

The value in understanding the nature of the product life cycle is in its relationship with marketing strategy. It will alert the company to the need for positive action at the so-called 'threshold point', where some change to strategy will be essential if the product is to continue. But beyond this, the marketing mix will be different for every stage of the life cycle.

First of all, the type of consumer purchasing the product may be different when a new product is introduced, compared with those purchasing the product at a later stage in the cycle. This fact enables a company to use a market segmentation approach based on 'lifestyle'. Early buyers of a new product are frequently experimenters, willing to take chances for the novelty or status of being in possession of a little-known product.

This market segment will generally have more disposable income, and will be more 'value-conscious' than 'price-sensitive'. The product image will be based on its uniqueness, and its appeal to status or curiosity. Advertising and promotion will be aimed at communicating this message to a specific market, using the most suitable channels and giving potential consumers maximum information about the product's benefits. Prices at this point may be relatively high. The system of distribution may be fairly selective, since it may be difficult for the company to support, or gain acceptability from, a wide selection of distributive outlets.

Once the product is well established, and has achieved a wide market through a process of emulation, competitors will have introduced their own version of the product into the market. Faced with a growing choice of products, the consumer may become confused and uncertain about which to select. The marketer's role then becomes one of persuading and constantly reminding consumers about the product's benefits, ensuring convenience of purchase by maximising distributive outlets, manipulating price to keep the product competitive and reinforcing the brand image associated with the product.

Finally, as sales peak and falter, the company has to look at the relative merits of revitalising the product, allowing it to decline slowly, or killing it off and planning a replacement.

Revitalising a product

There are many different ways in which a company can rejuvenate its product, and the method it will choose will depend on the reason or reasons for the product's initial decline. If this occurred because of the introduction of a new competitive product with additional benefits, the company might choose to add similar benefits to its own product, to add new but different benefits, or to reduce the present price and emphasise its value for money – perhaps trying to reach a new, more price-sensitive market in doing so. If on the other hand in the company's view the competitive product is not superior to its own, the decision may be taken merely to

increase advertising spend, or to introduce a sales promotion to regain market share. Marketing is about selecting strategies which are either designed to counteract threats, or to take advantage of opportunities in the marketplace. If you remember the 'four Ps' of marketing, you will realise that the action a firm can take is limited to one of four areas: it can alter the **product**, the **price**, the **promotional** campaign, or the **place** (where and how the product can be bought). Let us take an example below.

Maddington Hall

Maddington Hall is a stately home open to the public between Easter and the end of October each year. It is not a major visitor attraction, but has the appeal of a smaller home·which has been in the hands of the present family for over three hundred years. It has historical connections with the Civil War, and prior to that was the home of a leading member of Queen Elizabeth I's court. There are also links with the USA, through the settling of some members of the family in New Jersey at the beginning of the eighteenth century.

During the '80s, the house persistently attracted over 20 000 visitors a year, but in more recent years figures have slumped:

Admissions to Maddington Hall, 1983–91

1983	27 300 (peak year)
1984	27 120
1985	26 580
1986	20 084
1987	21 312
1988	22 033
1989	22 441
1990	18 256
1991	18 002

The decline in 1986, and the sharp downturn in 1990 and 1991, were attributed to the fall-off in American visitors to Britain in those years. The combination of recession, the Gulf War and poor spring weather in Britain held domestic visits down in 1991. Moreover, there has not been a compensating increase in visitors from EC countries, especially Germany, in spite of a steady increase in European visitors to Britain. Nor was there any evidence of a pick-up in the domestic market in 1991 during the period of good weather in August, traditionally the time of most visits.

Management faces the following choices. It can spend more money on advertising; but income from the house is barely enough to pay for upkeep and running costs, and the budget for promotion is very low. Because of the diversity of the market, it would be unrealistic to be able to advertise directly to overseas visitors, and much of the budget is spent on publishing a leaflet which is left in hotels and other places frequented by visitors. Attempts to interest coach operators and tour operators to include the house in packages have been unsuccessful, as the hall is not seen by the trade as sufficiently famous or interesting in itself to attract a market.

It could lower the entry price, but it is believed that this would result in a fall in revenue, as the increase in numbers attracted would be insufficient to make up for lost revenue. It could even increase the price, if it is believed that the added revenue will more than off-set the fall in visitors.

It could also consider ways in which the product could be made more attractive to a wider market. For example, it could seek additional revenue by becoming more commercial – adding tea-rooms, souvenir shops or other revenue-producing facilities, or staging events such as the recreation of civil war battles or jousting tournaments, to attract larger crowds on specific days of the year. If willing, the owner could arrange to preside over candle-lit dinners for exclusive groups of visitors who would be willing to pay handsomely for the privilege of meeting him and his family (particularly if titled). Some of these activities would need considerable capital expenditure, requiring a bank loan or other means of raising funds. Management would have to consider carefully whether this expense would result in a big enough jump in attendance to ensure profitability.

Finally, ways could be considered of improving the distribution – for example, by identifying specialist tour operators abroad who may be interested in marketing the attraction, or by joining a consortium of other attractions in the region, or a group of stately homes to produce a joint leaflet reaching a wider audience.

Whatever decision is made, it needs to be carefully thought through and researched. Each choice would need to be considered on its own merits, just as in the case of the launch of a new product.

Launching a new product

Launching a new product, be it aircraft, ferry route, hotel or tour package, is the riskiest undertaking in marketing. The statistical failure rate of new products is daunting, but the likelihood of product failure can be reduced (though never totally removed) by following a process of careful screening.

But first, we should be quite clear about what is meant by a 'new product'. Improvements to an existing product can render that product so new as to make it be seen by prospective purchasers as a genuinely new product. Similarly, if an existing product is launched to a new market unfamiliar with it, that product is also, to all intents and purposes, a new product. This can best be illustrated in Fig. 5.3.

		Market	
		existing	new
Product	new	introduce new product to present market	launch of new product to new market
	existing	modification to existing product for present market	reposition present product to attract new market

Fig. 5.3 New products

Clearly, the least risk is taken by the company which chooses to modify an existing product to make it more attractive to the present market – by adding additional benefits, for instance. If the product is losing its appeal to the present market, it may be feasible to 'reposition' the product, that is, to direct its appeal to a different market segment – or to sell the product overseas instead of to domestic consumers. This may also call for changing the concept of the product to make it more appealing to a new type of consumer. A third alternative is to develop a genuinely new product (or new brand) to be sold to one's present consumers. The appeal of this is that if the company has an established reputation, the likelihood is that present satisfied customers will be prepared to give the new product a trial also. Finally, the company can choose to introduce a genuinely new product to a new market segment – a double risk, but one where research may show significant profit potential in the long run and hence make the gamble worth taking.

It is difficult to determine exactly when a product can be termed genuinely 'new'. Most products we buy are advances and modifications of existing products, but every now and again a concept is so original and different from any other product on the market that it can be defined as totally new. The ball-point pen, although a modification of existing writing instruments, used technology so totally distinct from anything employed before that it must be accepted as unique, as must the photocopier or the folding bicycle. In travel and tourism, Concorde offered a totally new concept in air travel, and the motel was distinctive enough from the traditional hotel to be termed a new product. Billy Butlin, looking in the 1930s for a way of keeping seaside visitors entertained in all weathers, introduced the concept of the holiday camp, which was unlike any existing form of holiday at the time.

Market gaps

The aim with any new product is to find the 'market gap' – a product opportunity with a ready market which has not yet been tapped. Again, this is derived from taking a market-orientated approach to new product development, in which the first step is to see what new products, or modifications of existing products, are wanted by consumers. The high cost of labour in Scandinavian hotels was resulting in prohibitively high prices for hotel food; the solution was to introduce self-service breakfasts which, although a break from the traditional service expected in hotels, proved to be very popular with hotel guests because it both reduced prices and offered a comprehensive choice of quantity and menu selection. The Sea Goddess cruise ships incorporated an intriguing drop-down stern which converted the ship, when anchored, into a floating base from which

passengers could swim or windsurf – a marketing breakthrough to reach a new type of clientele for cruising. Luxury coaches have been converted to appeal to business executives, by altering the layout of seats and making it possible to hold meetings round a table while travelling.

All these concepts are based on modifying existing products, but in doing so, making them sufficiently distinctive to offer substantial advantages over existing products and filling wants, whether expressed or unexpressed, of consumers. But the launch of each of these products should be more than a hit-or-miss gamble based on some executive's hunch. It should be the end result of a process of new product development which is carefully structured at each stage of its development.

Why do products fail?

Before looking at the process of new product development, we need to ask ourselves why so many products fail. It is not enough to say that this is simply the outcome of too much competition. Products have succeeded in exceptionally competitive markets, while others have failed despite having no serious competition. Again, explanation for the failure must lie within one of the four Ps.

If the product is not really new – if it is only an attempt to emulate existing products on the market, offering no appreciable advantages over what is currently available – it stands a poor chance of success. It may be that the competition in the marketplace is already too great to give the new product much scope for success; but oversupply in itself does not threaten a new product. When Holiday Inns announced plans to build a new hotel in Liverpool in the 1970s, hoteliers poured scorn on the idea; the city was already over-supplied with hotel rooms, and present hotels were achieving poor occupancy levels. But the hotel chain had correctly identified its market. The existing business clients of hotels in the city were dissatisfied with the facilities available, but their business required them to be in the city. When they were offered a more modern hotel, with the facilities they preferred, there was a rapid switch to the new hotel and away from the more traditional hotels, some of which were soon forced to close.

This is a simple illustration of the fact that there is more than one kind of demand. In fact, four distinct kinds of demand can be listed:

1 Existing demand – the demand which results from inadequate supply of the products the consumers want;
2 Displacement demand – the demand resulting from the dissatisfaction experience by current consumers;
3 Created demand – the demand which marketers can develop, which results from wants that are latent and unrecognised by consumers, but can be awakened and promoted by effective marketing;
4 Future demand – the demand that will arise naturally in the future as a result of demographic or other changes in the population.

Projection on the future sales potential of the new product should take into account all four of these demands.

The product must also be sold at the right price. What is a 'right price' for a product must clearly depend on many different factors, which are discussed at length in Chapter 6. Suffice to say at this point that the price must be right in relation to other, competitive products, providing an adequate level of profit for the company while remaining within the range which the market can bear.

While no amount of promotion will sell a poor product, the promotion must be adequate to accomplish its task. Unless consumers are made aware of the product, no matter how good it is it will not be bought. That means that the choice of medium must be appropriate for the market segment at which the product is aimed; Forte's classical concert weekends are better advertised in *The Gramophone* than the *Golfer's Weekly*, for instance.

Lastly, it is no good creating demand for a product, if the consumer cannot buy the product easily. This means having the support of travel agents who are prepared to rack your brochure and sell the product, or else some equally effective form of distribution on which one can rely for sales. It also means effective briefing of agents. Many travel sales have been lost through inadequate briefing of retailers on new products and their benefits.

Screening the product

The process of screening new products is illustrated in Fig. 5.4. Let us look at each of these steps in turn.

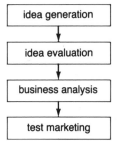

Fig. 5.4 Screening the new product

Ideas can be generated from many sources, both within and outside the company. Most typically, an idea for a new product is generated by a company executive, and may then be discussed between a group of executives responsible for new product development. However, other employees further down the ladder can also make significant contributions to new product development if encouraged, and this needs to go further than the usual suggestion box. The sales force in particular are in touch with dealers or customers, and can feed back to management many useful ideas for product improvements, based on either what competitors are offering or on what customers and dealers are saying is needed. Regular reviews should be undertaken in retail outlets to ensure that the company's products are remaining competitive with others on the market. In larger companies, departmental heads can encourage individual staff to suggest improvements to products, or new product ideas, based on their separate spheres of knowledge.

Each of these ideas should be carefully evaluated, so that those whose advantages seem less clear-cut are screened out from the alternatives put forward. This is most easily attained by drawing up a checklist of the strengths and weaknesses of each idea. The market at which the product is to be aimed must be identified, a listing of the benefits of the product over existing products drawn up, and suggestions made on the price that could be charged for the product.

Once the most promising new ideas have been refined, they need to be tested for business viability. An estimate must be made of sales potential, based on the market expected to buy the product, the profit potential, and the cash flow, so that management has a clear picture of how long it will take before the new product starts to realise a profit. Research will be undertaken at this stage to test public reaction to the concept. If this is positive, the programme can move on to the final stage, where the product is made in limited quantities for test marketing.

In the case of tangible goods, test marketing has usually meant selling the product in one region of the UK to see if estimated potential sales are realised. If the projections on sales are met, then a full scale launch is undertaken.

In the case of travel, test marketing is less easily undertaken. Aircraft cannot be produced for test marketing, and hotels cannot be built with the ability to be withdrawn if they are unsuccessful. Nevertheless, there are ways of reducing risk by testing product concepts, and some innovatory ideas have been used to overcome this problem in travel. Hotels, for example, have been able to test proposed new room decor by having a few rooms redecorated in existing properties and having guests pass comments on the appeal of the decor. There is also scope for introducing new package tours on a limited scale to test the market, before committing the full resources of a company to mass marketing a new destination. However, in general it has to be recognised that launching a travel product entails much greater risk than is the case for other products, and for this reason alone it is essential that much greater care is taken to follow the earlier screening processes outlined above.

The new tourism product: the case of Rosemoor
Those who associate tourism with the glamour of foreign travel can overlook opportunities closer to home. A search of market research reports will often provide the key to such opportunities. One such report was produced in 1990 by the BTA, and identified garden visiting as one of the fastest growing sectors of home tourism:

> The good weather last year helped to boost visits by 12%. Stapely Water Gardens in Cheshire alone increased their number of visitors by 27% to more than 1.2 million, overtaking London's Kew Gardens . . . this compares with an overall increase of 4% in visitors at all types of attractions in the United Kingdom.

These facts have been recognised by many with an interest in this form of attraction. In North Wales, which boasts many magnificent gardens, an important publicity booklet promotes the natural features of Gwynnedd to visitors, including the many public and private gardens open to visitors; attendance has risen sharply in recent years.

The Royal Horticultural Society were undoubtedly aware of the increase in interest in gardens, following increased attendances at their old established centre at Wisley. They had already determined to admit members only on Sundays, due to the pressure of increased attendance. They were aware that the West Country was the catchment area of many of their members, and when in 1988 they were offered the remarkable garden at Rosemoor that had been Lady Anne Palmer's greatest work, they decided to open

Fig. 5.5 Rosemoor House

their first regional centre – primarily to serve the needs of their members.

A major plan was conceived, and work commenced in 1989, to add an entirely new area of gardens covering some 40 acres of farmland, just across the road from Lady Anne's original 8-acre garden near Torrington, Devon. An underpass was built to link the two parts, and a visitor centre constructed, complete with garden centre, restaurant and retail facilities.

While the Society predicted some modest increase on the 19 000 who had visited the smaller area during their first year in 1989, and had planned car parking and restaurant facilities in line with these predictions, they could not have envisaged the enormous success of the new venture. The severe storms in January that year put back the opening until June, but within three days of opening an overflow car park had to be pressed into service. The restaurant built to cope with 20 to 30 visitors a day was actually catering for 375 by the fifth day. Continued success during the balance of the season led to the Society deciding to keep the gardens open until December, rather than closing in October as originally planned. By the closing date, 49 000 had visited, far in excess of the Society's optimistic forecast of 29 000, and of these, only 13 000 were members.

Evidence that this is not a freak experience is provided by estimates for 1991, which at the time of writing stand at 89 000 visits. On some days in the year, as many as 1000 visitors arrived, in spite of there being no public encouragement to visit, and the only coaches being admitted being those chartered by gardening groups or societies. The rise in admissions income has been matched by the increased spend at the garden centre, restaurant and retail outlet.

This success has not been a question of chance. Rosemoor is marked by a level of quality which is apparent throughout the development. This is most evident in the architectural design of the visitor centre, but can be seen more subtly in the choice of high quality and unusual plants set in inspired garden layouts that demonstrate horticultural theories being put into practice. For local members, there are short courses in gardening techniques, given by a team led by the curator, Christopher Bailes. Interest in the unusual plants leads visitors to buy in the garden centre before leaving.

Recognising such trends and coping with them is one of the challenges for those working in the tourism industry, in all its forms. Rosemoor is attracting visitors to neighbourhood restaurants and providers of accommodation, whether hotels, country cottages or bed and breakfast establishments. A nearby visitor attraction, Mill Lodge, has benefited by an increase in passing trade, while Rosemoor has a reciprocal agreement with the Dartington Glass factory in Torrington, signposting each other's attraction. Perhaps Rosemoor's major challenge is to cope with success; maintenance is already a challenge, and the original plans to create new areas of interest in order to relieve wear and tear on the older and smaller garden are fast being superceded by the need to cater for the much larger visitor flows which are causing pressures throughout the site.

Questions, tasks and issues for discussion

1 In 1986, Weymouth tourist office publicised the blowing up of its obsolete bandstand as a special event for visitors. What other innovatory ways of creating tourist products can you think of?

2 What examples can you provide of travel or tourism companies that have developed products with distinct 'personalities'? How important has this been for the success of the company?

3 The value of a slogan to promote a town for tourism is revealed by the success of such examples as Bradford's 'a surprising place', South Tyneside's 'Catherine Cookson Country' and 'Glasgow's Miles Better'.

Suggest a slogan for a town in your own locality which attracts tourists, or has the potential to do so.

4 Collect what are, in your view, good logos of four travel companies, and write

brief notes for a presentation at which you will explain why you consider each effective, and what its image aims to project. What role does colour play in this?

5 Some large tour companies operate divisions under distinct brand names which are marketed quite separately from the parent company. What are the relative marketing advantages and disadvantages of this practice?

Exercise

Following the work undertaken in Chapter 4, in which you planned a programme of package holidays for the 35–55 year-old age group, you have now been asked by your manager, Rosemary Andrews, to make comments on the best manner of 'test marketing' these holidays before they are fully launched on the marketplace.

Write a memorandum to Ms Andrews, suggesting how the holidays might be screened and tested before introducing them to the market.

6 Pricing the product

After studying this chapter, you should be able to:

- understand the factors affecting demand for products at different prices
- explain basic economic principles of price demand
- understand how pricing can be used as a tool to achieve marketing objectives
- explain how costs affect price, and the significance of marginal costing in travel and tourism marketing
- recognise that price is only one factor influencing the demand for travel
- list key pricing policies
- know how to use strategic and tactical pricing as elements in the marketing plan

What determines the price of a product? Price is as much a tool of marketing as promotion, and plays a critical role in the marketing mix. The price of a product should be seen not only as the outcome of market forces. A marketing manager will be aware that price says something to the consumer about the nature of the product, and by manipulating price in combination with product quality and the promotional messages, sales can be orientated to a new market, or market share can be increased at the expense of competitors.

In order to understand how to use price as a tool, we need to have a clear picture of how customers interpret product prices. Here, the concept of the 'fair price' is paramount. Buyers judge whether a product is fairly priced by asking themselves whether it represents value for money. Unfortunately, however, all consumers do not share the same view about what represents value for money, because, even assuming that we have the same disposable income, we establish different priorities for what we purchase, and attach different values to the benefits products offer.

Many people are bemused by the willingness of avid collectors to pay huge sums of money for works of art. Others will go heavily into debt in order to pay for a car or a house they covet, while still others treasure the ambition to experience a world cruise, and may well 'blow' an inheritance on such a luxury.

In the late '80s, a room little bigger than a broom cupboard in Knightsbridge, London, was sold for £35 000; its appeal – its proximity to Harrods as a *pied-à-terre*. Two collectors, trying to outbid one another for a unique 'collectible', can drive auction prices to incredible heights, simply because it is one of a kind, or is the only one remaining in private hands. Following the decision of the United States to reclassify the work of the potter Hans Coper as sculpture rather than craft, prices of his work rose from around £6000 to around £40 000 at subsequent auctions – yet the quality of the work remained unchanged! Clearly, the meaning of value is complex, as indicated by examples such as this.

The economics of price

Price and demand

From these examples of non-tourism products, what will have become clear is that price has little to do with cost, and far more to do with what customers are prepared to pay for a product. In a market where the product is unique, or without satisfactory substitute, or where the product is manufactured by a company which enjoys a monopoly or near monopoly, price will be set high. A luxury item, the purchase of which offers the owner prestige, will also command a high price. A flight on Concorde, or a round the world cruise, are two examples; and significantly, the top price suites and deluxe cabins are often the first to be sold on RTW (round the world) cruises, due to both their prestige and uniqueness.

However, it is more customary for travel products to be sold in highly competititve environments, where price is constrained by the substitutability of the product by other, similar, products. To understand the interplay between price and demand, we need to know something about how the *individual* responds to products at different prices, as well as how *aggregate* demand (the sum of all individual demand) is determined.

Individual demand

Individual consumers make judgements about products based, as we have seen, partly on price. Price acts as a guide to *quality*, and where consumers have the means to make comparisons with other products, price must be perceived as neither too dear nor too cheap. If the price lies outside an acceptable range, customers will either reject the product outright, or will seek much more *information* before committing themselves to a purchase. This can be demonstrated in Fig. 6.1.

information about the product to be convinced that it offers value for money.

If customers are unable to examine the product in advance of purchase, as is the case with many tourism services, judgements about value for money are equally difficult to make. For example, overseas package campsite holidays, combining long-distance express coach transport with tent, mobile home or chalet accommodation, attract many buyers due to their low prices. Where the customers are first-time travellers abroad, have no prior knowledge of site, resort or nature of the programme, and have no clear way of establishing an acceptable price range, they may find their expectations are not met. Full information must be given in advance to customers, either through the medium of the brochure, or through the advice offered by the travel agent. Since many of these products are sold direct to the public, the information conveyed by the brochure alone may be inadequate to gain an accurate and objective picture of the product.

Aggregate demand

The aggregate demand for a product is the demand resulting from the total of each individual consumer's demand patterns, and these will constantly change according to the price and market circumstances, such as availability, convenience of purchase, and competition level. The extent to which a change in price alone will affect a change in total demand is known as the *price elasticity of demand*, and is illustrated in diagrams A and B in Fig. 6.2.

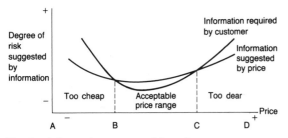

Fig. 6.1 Information conveyed by price

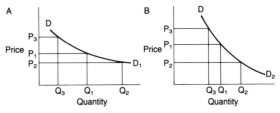

Fig. 6.2 Price elasticity of demand

If the price of our holiday lies within the sectors AB or CD, customers will require much more

In diagram A, Q_1 represents the number of products (e.g. package holidays offered by a particular company to a specific destination) sold at the price of P_1. Now let us assume that the company finds itself able to reduce the price of these holidays to P_2, as a result of better negotiations with airlines and hotels. More holidaymakers now want to buy these packages, so the number of holidays sold rises to Q_2. If the revenue achieved by these extra sales exceeds the revenue lost by the reduction in price, we say that demand is relatively *elastic*. By the same token, an equivalent increase in price, from P_1 to P_3, will cause sales to drop off substantially to Q_3.

A different picture is presented by diagram B. Here, Q_1 represents the number of units sold at a price of P_1, where price is not the major consideration in the purchase; say, club class seats in airlines operating on a major business route such as Frankfurt to London. In this case, if the price falls to P_2, sales will still only increase to Q_2, since business travellers for the most part have to travel to a particular destination, and are unlikely to be influenced to travel there more frequently, or to switch from other routes. If the gap between economy and club class fares narrows, it may cause a few holiday travellers to switch to the higher class, but such changes will be few and the increase in revenue achieved by the extra seats sold may be less than the revenue lost by reducing the seat prices. Equally, should the airlines on the route increase the fares to P_3, business travellers will be unlikely to cancel their journeys. Only a very substantial increase may cause a company to look at other means of travel or to reduce the number of trips their staff make. The quantity of seats sold drops, therefore, to only Q_3. We can say that demand is relatively *inelastic* for this product, and this will be reflected in the fairly steep demand curve shown in D_1D_2. However, demand patterns will be very different if the route is deregulated, and each airline has the freedom to set its own price. In such a competitive market, the business traveller may well switch to an alternative carrier, unless the airline charging the higher price can convince its customers that the extra expense is worth paying for – for example, by offering more convenient flight times, schedule reliability or superior in-flight service. Price decisions are always subject to the extent to which customers can find an acceptable *substitute* for the product. Low prices to

Maastricht in Holland, or to Luxembourg, could tempt some travellers to fly there instead, and continue their journey by road or rail into Germany.

In setting prices, the company will want to know what levels of demand it is likely to experience at different prices. For a new product this is hard to gauge. The two most common methods of assessing demand are:

1 asking potential customers what they would be willing to pay for the service, and
2 test marketing the product at different prices in different regions.

The difficulty with the first method is that what people say they will do does not always translate into actual behaviour when the product is launched, while with method 2, it is difficult to control all the factors apart from price which will influence consumer decisions in different areas. With a major item of expenditure such as tourism, it is possible that consumers from other areas may take advantage of the low prices in other regions. German tourists, for example, have discovered that they can make substantial savings on their package tours abroad by booking them and joining them in Britain.

Pricing to meet objectives

As with other elements in the marketing mix, pricing should be treated as a tool to achieve one's marketing objectives. If the target market has been clearly identified, and a decision taken about where the product is to be positioned, pricing bands will become easier to determine.

Looking back to our introduction to strategic marketing, you will recall that companies can adopt one of three broad marketing objectives. they can attempt to lead the field by keeping prices down; or they can adopt a strategy of 'niche marketing' by differentiating their product from the market leaders or by selecting a particular market segment to which they will aim their appeal. A company with a substantial hold on a market may seek to maximise its profits by finding ways to reduce costs while maintaining or moderately increasing prices; or it may seek to increase still further its share of the market by cutting prices in line with its reduced costs. Companies with a more tenuous hold in the market will then either be forced to price low in order to survive, or to attempt still further to differentiate their product – for example, by using price as an indicator of quality.

As we have seen, below or above a certain price range there will be no demand for the product. But within the range, there will be some scope for flexibility to adjust prices, within three 'concept bands'.

1 Premium pricing

Here the decision is taken to set prices above market price, either to reflect the image of quality or the unique status of the product. The product may be new, or it may have features not shared by its competitors, or the company itself may enjoy such a strong reputation that the 'brand image' alone is sufficient to merit a premium price. This is known as 'value added'.

2 Value for money pricing

Here the intention is to charge medium prices for the product, and emphasise that it represents excellent value for money at this price. Marks & Spencer have traded very successfully using this policy, which enables a company to achieve good levels of profit on the basis of an established reputation.

3 'Cheap value' pricing

The objective here is to undercut the competition, and price is used as a trigger to purchase immediately. Unit profits are low, but satisfactory overall profits are achieved through high turnover. Low prices will often be introduced by a company seeking to gain rapid expansion in the market, or a toehold in a new market.

It must be stressed that any of these policies may be seen as 'fair pricing' policies, notwithstanding the criticism sometimes directed at companies achieving higher than average profits. Market orientation seeks to ensure that the customer is satisfied with the product at the price paid. A fair price can be defined as one which the customer is happy to pay while the company achieves a satisfactory level of profit. Thus a premium pricing policy is acceptable providing that the customer receives the benefits appropriate to the price. Only where companies are able to force up prices against the consumers' will, such as in the case of monopolies, can it be said that fair pricing is inoperative.

Internal influences on pricing

In the long run, a commercial organisation will only continue to produce a product if it can realise a profit; but profit can be defined in a number of ways.

Gross profit is the price of the product less the direct costs of its production. For a travel agent, the figure represents the difference between the price paid for travel services and the price charged to the consumer, i.e. the commission received on the holidays and travel services sold. These commissions will usually range between 7% and 10% (slightly higher in a few instances where incentive commissions are agreed with principals. This may add another 2½ to 5% to the income received by the agent). The cost of a package tour to a tour operator is the price he or she must pay to airlines, hotels and other organisations offering the services which are included in the package, i.e. the 'raw materials' cost. To these costs must be added the 'overheads' which the company must meet – the costs involved in running the company, including administrative costs (office rent and business charges, light and heat, telephones, etc), salaries, and marketing costs (advertising, distribution, reservations, brochure production, etc.), plus any other miscellaneous expenses incurred in running the business. These costs are deducted from the gross profits to ascertain the net profits.

Accounting practice dictates that total costs are divided between *variable costs* (VC), that is, costs that vary with the amount of products made, and *fixed costs* (FC), which are relatively difficult to change in the short-term, and will accrue regardless of the amount of products made. The cost of renting an office and cleaning it cannot be changed in the short-term regardless of how many, or how few, of its products the company succeeds in selling.

The Marketing Manager will need to know at what point in sales 'break-even point' is achieved; that is, where total costs exactly equal the total revenue received from sales; it will then be possible to establish how this breakeven point will be affected by charging different prices for the product. This will tell him how many more holidays (or other products) must be sold at a lower price in order to recover costs.

Let us take an example of a theme park or tourist attraction which is considering three different pricing possibilities as its basic entry price: £2.50, £3.00 and £3.50. In Fig. 6.3, the lines VC and FC represent respectively the variable costs and the fixed costs associated with running the project. In a venture such as this, fixed costs represent a very high proportion of total costs, since the major expenditure is in the capital outlay to construct the attraction and to staff it. Variable costs will be a small element, and will include some staff costs (seasonal part-time labour), catering, and energy costs (power for amusement rides, etc.), plus some additional maintenance costs associated with the added wear and tear resulting from larger crowds. diagrammatically, the breakeven chart tells the marketing staff how many customers they must attract at each level of price in order to cover their costs.

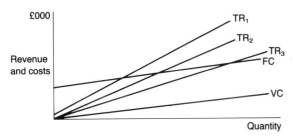

Fig. 6.3 Breakeven chart

TR_1, TR_2 and TR_3 represent the total revenue received at entry charges of £3.50, £3.00 and £2.50 respectively. Presenting the diagram in this form tells us not only where the breakeven points

occur, but also what *contribution* the revenue will make to the fixed costs at each pricing level, should sales fail to break-even. If sales fall below the breakeven point, and as long as the variable costs are covered, the income received will still make a useful contribution to the on-going costs of the project, which will have to be paid regardless of the number of visitors.

Recognising the importance of contribution has been a significant development in pricing policy in the travel industry. British Rail, for example, has high fixed costs in maintaining its track and signalling equipment, as well as in capital expenditure on rolling stock. Apart from peak routes and periods such as the rush hour, much of this rolling stock would lie idle, unless low priced off-peak excursion fares were introduced. These fares easily cover the small element of variable cost involved in operating the equipment (extra power, maintenance) and make a significant contribution to the high capital costs of running a railway. Another example is provided by the educational institutions who make student accommodation available for out-of-term holiday use. Students are away from universities and colleges for up to 20 weeks in the year and many of these weeks coincide with peak holiday periods. This, coupled with the fact that many educational institutions are situated in geographically attractive regions of the country, means that the colleges have found it worthwhile to sell their accommodation at 'marginal costs' little above variable cost, to avoid closing down during the holidays. They have gone on to promote their public rooms for meetings and conferences, thus increasing the demand for such accommodation during the holiday periods.

Costs establish the floor price below which a company would be unprepared to consider selling its products. But simply ascertaining costs and adding a 'mark-up' of some arbitrary percentage to determine the selling price does not represent a marketing approach to pricing, since it ignores the dynamics of the marketplace – what competitors are charging, the elasticity of demand for the product and what the market will bear. It also fails to take into account that price actually influences cost through its effect on the volume of sales. Low prices stimulate demand leading to high turnover, which provides increased negotiating power with suppliers, enabling tour operators, for instance, to drive costs down by promising very large purchases. If the proposed selling price appears too high against competitors' prices, an appraisal of the costs is needed. Can costs be shaved? Might it be possible, for example, to adopt a new distribution system such as direct sell, to reduce costs and make the product competitive in price?

One further complication in costing is the allocation of fixed costs to a product. Some acceptable means has to be found to apportion the fixed costs of a company to each product and range of products in a manner which can be judged fair. An airline may divide its costs by the routes served, in proportion to the passenger ton kilometres flown, or based on the anticipated revenue for a given route. No single system of cost allocation is perfect, however, and it is not uncommon for a lower level of fixed costs to be assigned to new products launched, in order to give them a better chance to achieve quick profitability in the market.

Pricing and the product mix

It is important that the price set for a product is right not only in itself, but in relation to the other products marketed by the company. If the product appears cheap by comparison with others in the range, consumers may switch their purchasing patterns and sales overall will fall; or equally, the market may view the cheaper product with suspicion, unless a satisfactory explanation is given for the price differentials. As most travel products are increasingly viewed as homogeneous, a low priced holiday in, say, Greece will divert holidaymakers from Spain, unless Spanish holiday benefits are promoted very heavily.

However, with many travel products it is common to find that each product in the range faces entirely different market conditions. An airline may experience significant competition both in price and service on one route, while enjoying market leadership on another. Airlines are generally reluctant to allow authorised routes to lapse, allowing competitors to step in (and market patterns can change very swiftly, as has been apparent on routes to the Middle East during the early '90s), and instead may be willing to cross-subsidise a loss-making route with profits made on more successful routes, provided that a satisfctory overall level of profitability can be achieved in the year.

Let us take a hypothetical example of cross-subsidies, using the services of Britainair, a British carrier with three routes. Let us assume that the marketing plan for the airline calls for targeted profits of not less than seven per cent overall. This could be achieved by balancing the profit levels on all routes as follows:

Route A is a recently awarded route which faces intense competition from other airlines who are well-established in the market, and who are themselves cutting prices in efforts to increase their market shares. Britainair is anxious to get a toehold in the market and gain a 10 per cent share of what is thought to be a potentially lucrative route.

On **route B**, the airline is already well-established, and shares the route with two other carriers, with roughly equal market shares. While market share is stable, and profits satisfactory, the route is not growing and load factors, while adequate, could

'. . . the market may view the cheaper product with suspicion . . .'

be healthier. All three airlines are anxious to discourage any new entrants to this market.

Route C is one on which Britainair is the market leader. There is strong flag loyalty from the major market segment, and the company enjoys an excellent reputation in the market.

The marketing plan for the coming year suggests the following price structure:

Sales	Average unit price per seat (£)	Total revenue per route (£)	Target profit % at average prices	Target profit (£)
Route A: 50 000	90	4 500 000	3	135 000
Route B: 250 000	110	25 500 000	5	1 375 000
Route C: 200 000	100	20 000 000	11	2 200 000
Total Revenue, all routes:		52 000 000		
Total Target Profit Overall:				3 710 000
Total Target Profit (%):				7.13

Such cross-subsidies would be considered appropriate only in the comparatively short-term, to achieve strictly short-term objectives. In the long-term, each product will normally be expected to become profitable in its own right (although in the case of certain airline routes which serve the needs of the community, the public sector may provide grants to keep otherwise unprofitable routes in operation). However, it is not uncommon for companies which are horizontally or vertically integrated to accept lower than normal profits when 'selling' or transferring their products to other divisions within the company. This practice, known as 'transfer pricing' or 'shadow pricing', could be employed, for example, where a tour operator owns its own airline, and the aircraft are 'leased' to the tour operator at an artificially low price to enable the operator to compete at a time when cut-throat competition is restricting profits generally. It should be added that the leading tour operators owning their own airlines deny that this practice occurs within their own sphere of operations. However, it is generally accepted that profits on sales of duty-free goods on board cross channel ferry services are substantial enough to enable the ferry operators to sell tickets

for their services at much lower prices than would otherwise be possible. In effect, the ferry companies are attracting passengers with low prices in order to recoup profits overall through the sale of on-board goods and services – a situation which will be radically affected if, as planned, the EC withdraws duty-free rights among member countries after 1998.

Price's role in the tourism marketing mix

Pricing, as we have already emphasised, is only one tool in the marketing mix, and pricing decisions must be determined in relationship with all the other elements of the mix. The impression is gathering strength within the travel industry that price is the *sole* criterion of importance to the consumer, or that other elements are relatively insignificant. While it is true that brand images (with a handful of notable exceptions) have not played a big role in tourism marketing up until the present, this is not to say that symbolic values in travel products are any less important than in other industries, and 'futures' forecasters such as the Henley Centre are suggesting that as discretionary income rises, the symbolic and emotional values attached to brand names will increase[1].

All too often, however, travel companies have chosen to ignore the creation of added value in their marketing plans, and have concentrated exclusively on the promotion of price. The major tour operators in particular have used low price as a means of increasing their market shares, at the expense of profit levels. There can be little doubt that this policy was highly successful during the 1980s, although this may have had as much to do with the publicity that resulted from the price wars between operators, causing consumers to become conscious of price rather than value. Over-optimistic sales projections led to heavy discounts to 'dump' unsold seats through late bookings, encouraging consumers both to shop around for the best bargains and to book later. It is likely that increasing disposable income and other favourable factors such as exchange rates would have led to substantial increases in the number of package tours sold during the '80s, even had discounting not been introduced.

The 1990s, however, present a very different scenario, with volume sales less likely to be attained, and with lower volumes but high prices the goal of most companies.

Other influences on price

Earlier, we explored some of the factors affecting price decisions over which the company will have very little control. Chief of these are:

- The economic health of the country (or region). It is notable that at the time of the depression in the 1970s, unemployment was less of a problem in London and the South East than in the North and Midlands, and consequently travel bookings from the former areas were less affected. On the other hand, at the beginning of the '90s the slump in the South East proved to be severe, while the situation in the North remained relatively unchanged.
- The elasticity of demand for travel and tourism products
- Levels of competition faced by individual companies and substitutability between competing products
- The nature of the target market, which will determine what kind of holiday or other travel products they will buy and at what price.

There will also be ethical considerations to be taken into account. A company concerned about its public image will wish to reassure its public that it is not making excessive profits, even assuming it is in a position to do so without challenge from the Monopolies and Mergers Commission. It would also be short-sighted of companies to attempt to introduce swinging price increases at a time when the political climate favours price restraint, even were the market able to bear such increases.

Legal constraints

Under certain conditions there may even be *legal* constraints affecting price decisions. In the past, prices in Britain have at times been subject to government control, as a means to constrain inflation, while legislation still exists to affect pricing tactics in a number of ways. In the hotel industry, for instance, the Tourism (Sleeping Accommodation Price Display) Order (1977) requires hotels with four or more letting rooms to display room prices at reception, and the Price Marking (Food and Drink on Premises) Order (1979) enforces similar requirements for the display of food and drink prices where they can be seen by customers before entering. The Price Marking (Bargain Offers) Order (1979) requires any money-off offers to be genuine reductions on original prices.

Codes of practice

Additionally, there are a number of organisations, quasi-governmental and industrial, that exercise some influence on pricing policies and strategies, which marketing managers must bear in mind. Many of these exercise control through Codes of Practice which companies are either obliged, or strongly advised, to follow if they are to be accepted as professionals. The IBA (Independent Broadcasting Authority) has its own code relating to advertising, to which reference is made in Chapter 9. The Chartered Institute of Marketing, the professional body representing marketing staff in all sectors of industry (which, incidentally, has its own travel and tourism sector, CIMTIG – The Chartered Institute of Marketing Travel Industry Group) has its own Code of Conduct, and ABTA itself enforces Codes of Conduct for both Tour Operators and Travel Agents. The Tour Operators' Code, for example, requires under Section 4.1 (viii) that brochures carry full details of the total price of products, or a means of arriving at the price, with a clear statement of the services which are included within the price, the date on which brochure prices were calculated and the conditions under which prices can be amended. Clear directions on surcharges and how these can be imposed must be given, and in the event such surcharges are imposed, a detailed explanation of the reasons for the surcharge must be provided to customers. Airport and seaport taxes must be integrated into the price of all European holidays.

The Office of Fair Trading now prohibits the imposition of resale price maintenance on travel agents, who are at liberty to discount their own commission to reduce the price if they wish to do so. Agents are permitted to charge fees for services they render, but such fees must be determined individually, not 'in collusion' by ABTA, under OFT rules. Bodies such as the Air Transport Users' Committee, who are the watch-dogs concerned with the protection of passengers, closely monitor air fares and will react strongly where they find evidence of price anomalies (this could mean concern with low prices, too, if these are seen as evidence of 'predatory pricing' – prices set below cost, designed to drive a competitor out of business). The National Consumers' Council, Consumers' Association and, indeed, the media themselves, all play a role in publicising prices thought to be out of line with the achievement of normal business profits.

Developing a price policy

Policies are plans for the future direction of the business. A company's price policy therefore appears in the marketing plan as an indication of the company's objectives in setting prices.

In some cases, price policy may be no more than a reaction to market forces or the result of a failure to plan, but good marketing implies a more positive approach to considerations of price, and the development of an active plan to influence the market through price. These policies will now be examined.

Profit maximisation

This is a commonly stated objective which combines charging what the market will bear with attempts to reduce costs. One difficulty associated with the policy is to know exactly what any market *will* bear, and the problems inherent in constant price adjustment cause many companies to settle for a policy of 'satisfactory'

rather than maximum profits. There is also the danger in maximising profits that the firm will attract unwelcome competition; by keeping profits moderate, and prices low, this may deter opportunist firms from entering the market.

There is another argument against the reduction of costs to their minimum. A hotel, for example, could adopt a strategy of employing casual labour in season and closing down out of season, as a means of maximising profits. This may still be true even after assessing the marginal contribution of staying open throughout the year, which we have discussed earlier. However, there is a *social* cost in hiring and firing indiscriminately in areas of already high unemployment. Such jobs will attract the less committed casual workers, and a hotel which relies so much on providing good service may find it hard to attract the qualified staff necessary for the achievement of this. Customers who are disappointed do not re-book, and the long-term effects may be to actually reduce profits.

Target Return on Investment (ROI)

A common practice is to measure the amount of profits achieved each year as a proportion of the total capital invested in the company. This can be helpful, since comparisons can then be made with the profit potential if the capital were invested in other forms of business. Many small tourism businesses do not achieve the same level of profit which might be possible through other investments (indeed, higher returns could generally be achieved simply by investing capital in building society accounts!) and it has to be assumed that profit is not the only motive in setting up a tourism business. Many small business people are content to achieve low returns on their invested capital for the privilege of working for themselves, or running their own businesses. This has always been the case with proprietors of small hotels and guest houses, which are frequently family-run concerns, while proprietors of travel agencies and others in the travel industry enjoy the opportunities for cheap travel offered by their jobs. Larger companies tend to measure success purely in economic terms.

It should be recognised that in the case of some sectors of the travel business, capital appreciation on assets is as important as operating profit. Hotels in London, for instance, saw the scarcity of building land in the city centre lead to huge rises in the value of their property during the 1980s, far exceeding any operating profit they were achieving.

Finally, ROI is not a good measure of travel agency success, since the actual cost of setting up an agency is quite small, involving as it does no investment in stock. The cost of purchase of a well-established travel agency will include a large element of 'goodwill', based on the assumption that present customers of the agency will continue to trade there after the change in ownership.

Pricing for market share

Many companies will set their prices at a level designed to ensure that they will achieve a certain share of the market. This, disparagingly known in the industry as 'playing the numbers game', generally calls for price restraint, especially in the early stages of the PLC (product life cycle), where the aim is market *penetration* (as opposed to market *expansion* in later stages of the PLC). However, if it is the intention to deliberately curb profits in the early stages of the PLC in order to achieve a given market share, there must be the underlying objective of achieving a good profit level in the longer term, since there would be little point in becoming locked into a long-term price war without some evidence of ultimate benefit to the company.

Falling profitability in the tour operating business has resulted from the combined objectives of major companies to restrain prices to build market share. This has had the effect of driving some middle-sized and small companies out of business, but the substantial growth achieved by the market leaders has led to potentially large turnover and profits. The major operator, at the time of writing, had built up a market share of 35 per cent, with the top three, Thomson Holidays, Owners Abroad and Airtours, together accounting for some 70 per cent of the mass package holiday market abroad.

For this policy to succeed, the product itself must be elastic in demand, and costs per unit must fall as 'production' increases (as they do in the case of tour operations, where lower prices can be negotiated if more customers are guaranteed to the suppliers). Additionally, the product should anticipate a long life cycle (expansion of leisure time and discretionary income suggests that holidays and travel will enjoy a long-term growth curve). Any company embarking on such a policy also needs, of course, to be in a very strong financial position to survive the price war which will ensue.

Although instances are much rarer, the reader should be aware that on occasions a company may set prices in order to decrease its share of the market. Such a policy will be followed if the company estimates that it will become more profitable with a lower share of the market, since it can charge a higher price to its customers (relatively inelastic demand), but it could also be introduced if the firm in question is concerned that its market share has grown to a point where its dominant position in the market might cause it to come under the scrutiny of the Monopolies and Mergers Commission. By divesting itself of some of its market share before an investigation is launched, the company may lessen the threat of such an investigation.

Pricing for market share becomes a key policy where the company is operating in a saturated market, since the best way in which the company can increase sales is to take business away from the competition. Most travel products still offer considerable potential for increases in markets, but a few offer very small prospects for growth. For example, the transport of military personnel and their dependants on leave is a static or declining market now that the armed forces are being reduced in number. Special price offers to this market will attract business from competitors, although there may also be some scope to increase the frequency of use, i.e. get existing consumers to travel more often.

Increasing turnover

It is important to note the distinction between pricing policies which aim to increase turnover, and those aiming to increase market share. Certainly, turnover is easier to measure than market share, but using turnover as a yardstick for success may disguise the fact that a company's actual share of the market is falling. If, for example, demand for overseas flights increases dramatically, an airline could experience a three per cent growth in its traffic although its total market share might have fallen by ten per cent or more, suggesting that its management has not maximised its opportunities. Concern with turnover can also overlook a decline in profitability.

Readers are reminded that turnover may be increased in one of four ways:

* by getting more people to buy the product
* by getting present purchasers to buy it more frequently
* by finding new uses for the product
* by increasing the price of the product.

A large country hotel may attract more visitors by improving its facilities without an increase in price, and promoting this improvement in the main regions where its current market is generated. It might encourage its summer guests to return for a three-day winter break, with special package prices available to guests who book while on their summer holidays. It could also choose to market its facilities to conference users, with new meeting rooms and improved catering, at a commensurately higher price. It could make more cost-effective use of its public space by sub-contracting retail shopping space in its lobbies, with a percentage of the revenue accruing to the hotel turnover. Recently, hotels have further innovated by offering off-season occupancy on a time-share basis. All these are strategies which will help the hotel achieve its price policy, which is to price to increase the operating turnover of the hotel.

Price restraint

Sometimes companies will take the decision to maintain or lower prices simply in order to retain existing markets. This could be a response to falling sales generally, or even a goodwill gesture at a time when the government is actively seeking price restraint to control inflation. This will normally be a short-term policy designed to meet current market conditions.

Meeting competitors' prices

On the face of it, this is an attractive policy for consumers, since it reassures them that they will not find the product more cheaply by shopping around. Although the outstanding example of this is to be found outside the travel industry, in the John Lewis Partnership's guarantee 'we are never knowingly undersold', the policy has been used by Thomas Cook in their 'price promise' which offered to refund the difference in price on package tours which could be bought more cheaply elsewhere.

If a policy such as this is adopted by more than one leading competitor, a price war can develop, with smaller companies adopting 'survival pricing' to remain in business. Without sufficient reserves, they will be driven out of business as in the case of severe market share pricing policies. If this results in a handful of major companies forming an oligopoly or cartel to dominate the market, this will be against the consumer's long-term interests, since new companies will find it difficult to get established in the market, and the larger companies may force up prices and profits. This in turn can lead to the formation of new market gaps for cheaper holidays.

Short-term profit maximisation

Often known as 'skimming the cream', this policy calls for the setting of high prices at the launch stage, with a progressive lowering of price as the product becomes better established, and progresses through the life cycle. Reducing prices to boost sales is an alternative to innovating the product to rejuvenate it when sales falter, as discussed in Chapter 5. This is illustrated in Fig. 6.4.

The policy takes advantage of the fact that most products are in high demand in the early stage of the life cycle when they are novel or unique, or when supplies are limited. A new museum with exhibits that will attract many tourists, such as the Jorvik Centre in York, or a theme park with

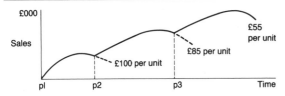

Fig. 6.4 Skimming the cream

exciting new rides, will both be limited in their ability to expand sales when popularity peaks. Longer opening hours may be one possibility, but if the event is very popular, long queues will form. Demand can be managed by setting very high prices initially to cream off those prepared to meet them, gradually reducing the price to meet different market segments' price elasticities.

If there is no problem with supply, the object will be to obtain the highest level of sales possible in the post launch period, at the highest price. This will call for a large promotional spend at the launch stage to make the market aware of the new product as quickly as possible and influence them to buy it.

The particular value of this policy is that it provides a high inflow of funds to the company when the marketing costs are highest. As high prices in travel will increase the revenue earned by travel agents, this will also encourage the distributors' support. If the product also anticipates a very short life cycle, as is the case with event tourism such as the Olympic Games, where costs of organising and marketing the programme must be recovered quickly, this is a sensible policy to pursue. Care must be taken, however, not to antagonise regular markets for short-term benefits. All too often hotel prices have been increased very substantially during events such as World Fairs, and if accommodation thereby becomes unavailable or overpriced to the regular markets, there may be a consumer reaction; loyal customers may go elsewhere.

Premium pricing

In this policy, the intention is to price high in the long term, using price as an indication of quality, or symbolic value, as with the case of high status holidays. Here one is dealing with a highly inelastic market demand, but the product must deliver what it promises. Its scarcity value may be a major part of its appeal, therefore such products in travel are more likely to be developed by small specialist firms. The package tour sold largely to the American market, comprising a visit to a stately home, with dinner hosted by its titled owners, is one example of such a product which has both scarcity and prestige value.

While all the above policies involve active decisions to influence markets through price, some companies will adopt passive price policies, of which three can be identified:

Following price leadership

Sometimes referred to as 'going rate pricing', this policy is adopted by those who feel their products are insufficiently distinguishable from their leading competitors'. Prices are set based on what the competitors charge.

A drawback to the policy is that prices cannot be established or marketed until the competitors' decision on price has been publicised. Small seaside hotels and guest houses traditionally wait to see what shape prices are taking before determining their own for the coming season, while many tour operators in Britain wait for the launch of the major companies' brochures to see the prices charged before going to print with their own brochures. This policy obviously inhibits forward sales.

Price agreements

The concept of a 'cartel', a group of companies coming together in order to set uniform prices, is now rare, and indeed in Britain − virtually without exception − it is illegal. The OFT have made it clear that fixed price agreements cannot be imposed on travel agents for package tours, nor is ABTA permitted to agree uniform fees for the services provided by agents. Distributors are therefore required to determine their own pricing policy, which allows them to discount inclusive holidays by some proportion of their commission if they so choose.

Tourism, however, is an international product, and may be subject to other regulations. Until recently, price regulation in the air transport industry represented one of the very few examples of an officially sanctioned cartel, with prices agreed through the International Air Transport Association (IATA). The growth of deregulation of air transport, first in North America and more recently in Europe, has significantly reduced the effectiveness of the air price cartel, although on many routes to the developing world price regulation is still in force. However, in other areas of tourism within the UK, the OFT will investigate any suspected cases of price collusion.

Cost-plus pricing

This is the simplest mechanism of all for pricing decisions. The company establishes its costs for a particular product, allocates some share of overhead costs to production plus a percentage mark-up for profits, and this then becomes the selling price. Clearly, this takes little account of market forces, and while costs do have to be covered in the long run, policies have to respond more to changing market conditions and 'what the market will bear', as we discussed earlier in this chapter.

However, the concept of *marginal costing*, which attempts to identify the cost of one more unit of a product, is an important one in cost-plus pricing, since it offers the marketing manager a flexible tool for pricing. We earlier examined the concept of 'contribution' to fixed costs, in which the variable cost of one more unit is ascertained. In the case of, say, an airline ticket to the USA, the additional cost of carrying one more passenger is extremely small: an added meal, a minute addition to fuel and equally minuscule costs for ticket issuance, etc. Therefore, once breakeven point is achieved it becomes very attractive to price the 'marginal seat' (any remaining seats over the number that have to be sold to break even) at a price which will attract market demand from those unwilling to pay regular fares. Scheduled carriers introduce such fares as 'stand-by' to fill these last remaining seats, and tour operators originally introduced

'seat only' sales on charter flights to achieve the same purpose.

It makes good sense for all companies to predetermine their pricing policies, but in fact of those that do, most tend to be the larger corporations, where the marketing concept is treated more seriously. One study on pricing policy found that smaller units (hotels with up to 24 beds) for the most part either had no policy or one in which they simply followed price leadership. Hotels up to 200 beds in size tended to use cost-plus pricing, with some emphasis on the achievement of target profits, while only in the largest hotels was price used as an active marketing tool, with an emphasis on Return on Investment[2]. The idea that pricing policy is linked through marketing plans to the achievement of organisational objectives is still to receive widespread application in the travel and tourism industry.

Price policies have many important implications for other areas of the marketing mix. The price determined for a product will influence the decision on whether 'push' or 'pull' strategies are more appropriate to use, with promotional tactics developed to support one or other approach. A decision to price for rapid penetration in a new market will call for the widest possible distribution of the product, while the decision to 'skim the cream' will suggest that a more select distribution system would be appropriate.

We will now turn to the ways in which pricing policies are implemented as part of the overall marketing campaign.

Strategic and tactical pricing

Strategies are concerned with the overall plans for the implementation of policy, while tactics relate to the day-to-day techniques in pricing which can be rapidly altered to suit changing conditions in the marketplace. Thus a *strategy* of discriminatory pricing, involving the setting of different prices to different market groups (e.g. business travellers and holiday travellers) may be introduced, but the actual prices to be charged (APEX, PEX, GIT, ITX fares, etc.) and the ways in which these fares will be adjusted will imply tactical decisions.

One of the strategic decisions which must be taken will be whether to price differentially to different geographic areas. Should the price set be common to all customers, or should it vary to reflect different market demand in the various regions of a country, or between different countries? It may be more costly to sell one's incoming package tour arrangements in the USA, for instance, than in France; or it may be necessary in one country to boost commission levels to agents to secure their support. Long-haul holidays sold in Britain are cheaper on the whole than identical holidays sold in Germany, partly because of higher marketing costs on the Continent and partly because the market will bear higher prices. However, too great a price differential will result in travellers diverting to the UK to pick up their package holidays. Alternatively, should the price be the same to all markets, but adjusted to take into account varying conditions – night flights versus day flights, low season versus high season?

When Billy Butlin launched his first holiday camps, his pricing strategy was 'all-in' pricing; a single price gave his customers access to every entertainment facility in the camp. This meant that there was always plenty to do even in inclement weather, and the strategy proved highly successful. Club Méditerranée was later to build on this model for their successful chain of holiday resorts around the world. The decision to charge a low basic entrance fee and recoup profits through 'add-ons' is a critical one for the tour operators, who choose different approaches. A package tour to China, while having a high basic cost, is often fully comprehensive, including excursions, all meals and even drinks, while a similar tour to the USA may be limited to flight, room and transfers. Each decision must be made on its own merits and reflect market conditions in the host and generating countries. The two destination countries in this example have totally different tourism industry structures, the former being highly centralised and therefore far simpler to organise on a fully comprehensive basis, while costs are extremely low and therefore the package will be seen to be offering good value.

Strategies must be designed to respond to the marketing initiatives of competitors, too. As market leaders, Thomson Holidays became concerned that not only were their competitors waiting for them to launch their brochure before determining prices; some were adjusting prices to undercut Thomsons after the Thomson brochure appeared on the market. They responded by relaunching the brochure with lower prices, and this has now become a well-established routine to the point where relaunches are built into the print run, and a 'second edition' with adjusted prices can be introduced if the market shows signs of flagging at originally published prices, or if the leader is too far out on price. While this significantly adds to print costs, it gives the company much greater flexibility for fine tuning on price.

How should a company respond when challenged on price? The immediate decision to slash prices is not necessarily the best one, and only has the effect of reducing profits for everyone. It may be justifiable where there is evidence of extreme price sensitivity, or where it is thought to be difficult to recapture market share once lost. If, on the other hand, the company has a strong brand image, believes in the quality of its products and has the financial strength to survive a price attack, it may well ride out the threat, or it can counter-attack by improving product quality, or by heavy promotion. With a sufficiently distinctive product, it may even be possible for the company to increase the price, and hence the psychological 'distance' between its own products and those of the competition. In short, there are a variety of solutions, of which price reduction is only one, and the company under attack needs to consider each option carefully.

Beaulieu, the heritage attraction in Hampshire, provides an interesting example of the use of tactical pricing to solve a problem. Its strategy was to charge a high entry price giving access to a wide range of attractions which had involved substantial capital investment. The fear was that the entry cost would be perceived as providing poor value by those unfamiliar with what the attraction had to offer, or the length of time they could expect to spend at the site. The solution was to make little advance information available about the actual cost of entry, and to site the parking area at some distance from the entry kiosk. Customers, having parked and walked as far as the kiosk, would be reluctant to forego a visit at that point because of cost alone, and grudgingly paid up, only to find themselves with much more to see and do than they had anticipated. A survey of visitors leaving the site was then undertaken which found them to be well satisfied with the visit and voting it good value for money.

A contrasting approach is taken by other attractions, where 'off-set' pricing (sometimes known as 'bait pricing') will set a very low entry charge, possibly even a 'loss leader' at below cost, in order to attract visitors, who then find themselves facing extra charges for every event (a common tactic for fairground amusement sites such as the Tivoli, Copenhagen). One interesting example of bait pricing is shown by the hotels in Las Vegas, USA, where prices are extremely reasonable for rooms and food because profits are reaped through gambling on the premises. Fruit machines are to be found in every lobby, public rooms, even around the swimming pools. Scandinavian Seaways has also used Bait Pricing to attract off-season visitors to round voyages on their UK–Denmark service, on the basis that the service will operate anyway (for freight needs) and the additional on-board spend during the 24-hour crossing will enable satisfactory overall profits to be achieved, or will at least provide a substantial contribution to operating costs during the winter.

Discounting tactics

Discounting became a highly controversial topic in the travel industry during the '80s and early '90s. In a market situation where 'money-off' incentives became widespread, where hotel receptionists were given unlimited freedom to adjust prices for late arrivals, where it became common for travel agents to split commissions with their business house clients in order to retain a sale, and where tour operating reservations staff conducted 'auctions' with agents on the telephone for seats on late booking holidays, the idea of a set price for travel services was a fast disappearing concept. This might be seen as an almost inevitable result of deregulation in the industry and the tactical pricing which, for instance, has led to an airline fare structure in which more than a hundred fares can be applied on a single route between two points.

Travel discounts are obviously here to stay. The question is whether they can be controlled, and how far the practice is contributing to the development, or decay, of the industry. Evidence suggests we have moved too far to making the discount the major selling tool, and have chosen to ignore the other tools of marketing.

Marketing theory recognises at least six forms of discounting, although not all these are to be found in the travel and tourism industry.

- **Discounts for cash payment, or early settlement of invoice.** Common in business where credit is normally given.
- **Price reductions for quantity purchases** (bulk discounts). Common in negotiations between tour operators and their suppliers, and proposed for businesses purchasing large numbers of air seats.
- **Trade discounts.** Discounts offered to people in the travel industry for their personal travel.
- **Trade-in allowances.** Only applicable where tangible products are surrendered as part exchange on the sale of a new product.
- **Seasonal discounts.** It is customary to charge lower prices for tourism products purchased 'out of season'.
- **'Distressed stock' and similar discount tactics.** Includes examples such as Advance and 'Late Saver' discounts. The former, by encouraging early bookings, offers two benefits to the company; more precise information on its forward booking situation and (assuming full payment is also made early) the use of prepayment for investment. Late Savers are the equivalent in other businesses of sales, i.e. the clearance of distressed, or unsaleable, stock. This is doubly important in the case of travel, since unsold stock cannot be stored and sold later.

The popularity of late savers among travel

consumers has played an important part in the market's tendency to book travel later in the year, in the hope of securing a bargain. However, apart from advance booking tickets on airlines, the tactic of offering discounts for early bookings is rare, even among tour operators, and there has been little concerted effort by those in the trade to reverse the late booking habits which have developed. Perhaps the most common discount for early booking is to be found in conference bookings, since the decision to hold or abandon the conference must be made well in advance of the event.

There is an important distinction between 'discounting', which is a regular pricing tactic, and 'money-off' offers which accompany special promotions. The use of the latter tactic will be discussed further in Chapter 11.

Clearly, any discounting schemes should only be introduced where there is evidence of price elasticity, i.e. that lower prices will sell the product. In order for discounting tactics to be successful, the discount must be large enough to be seen as a bargain. Here, the concept of the JND ('Just Noticeable Difference') needs to be understood. This is the amount by which a product must be reduced in price in order for it to attract the bargain-hunter. Some firms make it a practice successively to reduce prices until

stock is clear, and this too is a practice which is being introduced experimentally by some tour operators pricing their late savers.

Yet another price tactic is the use of the psychological discount. The firm in this case introduces an artificially high price, with the expectation that this will seldom, if ever, be used. Instead, all markets will be offered attractive 'bargains' against the hypothetical price. In the field of consumer durables, references to 'manufacturer's suggested price' provides a base for retailers to fix their own price. While the practice is less widespread in travel and tourism, it is found in areas such as some hotel printed 'rack rates' from which a wide range of discounted prices are offered. Hotels, and cruise ships, have been able to offer apparent bargains by selling accommodation at the basic price and upgrading clients to superior accommodation without additional charge, while airlines have scope to upgrade clients from economy to higher category seats, subject to availability. This provides apparent bargains, but without any cost to the principals.

The total number of price tactics which can be employed is beyond calculation, and limited only by the initiative of the company introducing them. The pricing tool remains a powerful technique for market manipulation and a means to respond quickly to changing market conditions.

Questions, tasks and issues for discussion

1 Under what conditions is 'meeting the competitor's price' an unsuitable policy for a travel company?

2 Should prices be reduced for *advance* bookings of holidays instead of *late* bookings?
    Prepare a paper for discussion which examines why tour operators have so seldom used the advance booking discount incentive.

3 What should be the pricing policy for a tourist hotel in the Scottish highlands? Explain the relationship between price and market opportunities for the hotel.

4 What lessons can be learned from ILG's collapse in 1991? (Conduct some secondary research to find out why this occurred.)
    Have these lessons yet been learned by the industry?

5 Prepare a report which argues the case against an 'open skies' policy on European air routes.

Exercise

Conduct a random sample street survey to test the sensitivity to price for travel using the new Eurotunnel between England and France, compared with ferry services between Dover and Calais.

Write a report which proposes an appropriate price for:

(a) a round trip passenger ticket by rail between London and Paris, and

(b) a round trip excursion fare for two passengers and car for the tunnel trip only.

7 Marketing communications

After studying this chapter, you should be able to:

- understand the role of communication in marketing
- list the elements of the promotional mix and assess their qualities for communicating
- evaluate alternative strategies for budgeting
- understand what is required to create successful promotional messages
- recognise the importance of personal presentation skills in the travel and tourism industry

Once a product has been created and a price determined for it, the marketing focus switches to promotion. However good a product, it will seldom sell itself. Knowledge about the product has to be *communicated* to the potential customers, either through word of mouth, advertising or some form of display. Furthermore, the company has to decide not only the best means of bringing the product to the attention of the market, but also the best means of physically delivering the product to its customers. In the case of travel and tourism, even though we are not dealing with a tangible product, we still have to find a means of delivering knowledge of our products to customers, and certain tangible items associated with travel – brochures, itineraries, tickets and vouchers and insurance policies, for example. This process of delivery is known as *distribution*, and it involves both the selection of suitable channels for distribution and the physical movement of items associated with the marketing of the product. We will be looking in more detail at the function of distribution in the following chapter, while in this chapter we will be considering issues concerning the communication, or promotion, function.

The communications process

Figure 7.1 explains the process by which an

Fig. 7.1 The communications process

organisation communicates with its target market. The process of communications starts with a source of information – the person, organisation or company with a message to deliver. The source must determine what message to deliver to its target, the receiver. An airline, for instance, may have many different messages which it wants to deliver to the different target markets it serves. To the businessperson, the purpose of the message may be to communicate details of convenient mid-morning flights to European capitals, or information about the airline's outstanding on-time record, while the leisure market will be more interested to hear about free airport parking facilities or new low prices to the main holiday resorts served by the airline.

The *kind* of message we want to deliver will determine the *form* in which the message will appear, i.e. how we will *encode* the message to achieve the greatest likelihood of its being received by our target market. If we have a lot of facts to communicate to our customers, such as a list of cheap fares and their dates of availability, we will probably need to have the message printed, so that our customers can study it at length, absorb it and even tear it out and keep it for future reference.

Encoding means not only determining the best way of getting our message across, but also the most *effective* way given the typical constraints under which the company operates. With un-limited money, it is relatively easy to ensure that every potential customer is made aware of our product; but in the real world, funds are always limited, and we have to ensure a profit at the end of the day. Encoding means putting the message into a form in which it will be clearly understood and absorbed by the target market. We could choose, for instance, to place an advertisement in English in a Continental magazine, designed to attract people to come to England and take one of our tours, but this would hardly be an effective way of getting business. Not only would many non-English speaking Europeans fail to understand our message; we could also anticipate some antagonism from those who do speak the language, on the grounds that we are not making a very serious effort to attract people to our product if we don't put it into our customers' language. If on the other hand we are advertising for a new member of staff who speaks fluent Japanese, to deal with incoming tour clients, it would be highly appropriate to prepare an ad-vertisement in Japanese, even in an English newspaper, to ensure that we won't receive applications that waste our time. We have to design our message for maximum impact.

The next step is to decide which channel we shall use to deliver our message. If we have already decided that it must be a printed message, this partly determines the medium we shall use. We could advertise in magazines or papers read by our target audience, or we could place advertisements in the travel trade press to make travel agents aware of our product's attributes, so that they in turn will recommend our product to their clients. We could also send a newsletter through the mail to agents with the same message, or provide our sales staff with a circular to give to agents during their calls. This latter technique would also give us the added advantage of being able to reinforce our message with a personal selling presentation.

Having in this way settled on our strategy for putting our message across, we sit back and wait for the bookings to start rolling in. Unfortunately, though, all our best efforts can be frustrated if the receiver doesn't *decode* our message. 'Interference' in the communications process can affect the decoding of messages in a number of ways. A big news story breaking in the morning paper on the day of our advertisement could mean that many of our customers fail to notice our message. Our mail shot to travel agents may be ignored because the agent that day has unusual pressure of work and doesn't find time to read 'non-priority' mail. A train derailment could mean that newspapers for one region of the country fail to get through, and nobody in that region gets to see our advertisement. Some of our potential clients may simply not be in the right mood for receiving messages when they see our advertisement, while others may have had a poor recent experience of our service, and are unwilling to read anything positive about the service. A businessman, about to read the message in the newspaper over his morning breakfast, is interrupted by a phone message . . . There are many ways in which interference can prevent our message getting through, and these are frequently beyond our control. Even if the message is received and believed, many potential customers will have forgotten it within a few minutes; clients are bombarded with messages every day of their lives, and only a small percentage are likely to be retained. All we can hope to do is to minimise the loss of our messages by careful initial design of the communications process.

Determining the promotions mix

The Marketing Manager has four distinct ways of communicating the promotional message to the public:

1 By *advertising* the product through a selected medium such as television or the press.
2 By using staff to engage in *personal selling*, either behind the counter, over the phone, or calling on clients as sales representatives.
3 By engaging in *sales promotion* activities, such as window display or exhibitions.

4 By generating *publicity* about the product through public relations activities, such as inviting travel writers to experience the product, in the hope that they will review it favourably in their papers.

It should also be recognised that much communication about products actually takes place by word of mouth recommendation. The benefits of a satisfied customer suggesting your product to another potential customer cannot be over-emphasised. This 'hidden sales force' costs a company nothing, yet it is the most highly effective of all communications modes, since the channel has credibility in the eyes of the potential customer, and will be judged as an objective assessment.

'. . . much communication about products actually takes place by word of mouth recommendation . . .'

Recognition of the importance of influencing those who can in turn influence others to buy new products has led to the concept of the 'two-step flow of communication', in which messages are directed by the company to the opinion leaders in society, rather than to the general public. Opinion leaders include representatives of the mass media as well as those most likely to initially purchase new products. A travel company with a limited promotional budget might be best advised to concentrate its expenditure on influencing travel writers, by providing study visits to view their products at first hand, since a favourable report on television or in the press will have a huge impact on sales. In 1991 Pluckley in Kent, the scene of the successful TV series *The Darling Buds of May*, developed a wholly unexpected tourist market and Brittany, where some of the scenes were shot, received a similar boost in tourist visits from Britain. One TV programme such as this can generate enormous curiosity on the part of viewers, which is translated into a significant rise in visits.

Factors influencing the choice of mix

What determines the mix of these four promotional tools in the marketing plan? In some cases, companies will choose to employ only one of these elements in the mix, while other companies will use a combination of all four. There are no right or wrong answers about such choices, although guidelines based on the following criteria can be helpful.

1 *The nature of the product.* Clearly, it will be difficult to sell a complex or technical product without personal sales advice. Many in the holiday trade would argue that, although resorts are often thought of as homogeneous and interchangeable, a customer actually needs quite a sophisticated level of knowledge to make a decision about what resort or hotel to choose. A brochure can spell out in cold print what kind of beach the resort offers, or the facilities the hotel provides, but more subjective issues are difficult to put across in print. Questions about issues such as the ambience of the resort, the quality of the food served in the hotel, and what kind of fellow holidaymakers the client will encounter in the resort can only properly be answered in a direct face-to-face sales situation, where the salesperson can help to match the customer's needs to the products on offer, to ensure customer satisfaction.

2 *The target* at which the communication is aimed. A decision will be made on the mix of communications directed to the consumer and to the trade.

Communications aimed at the trade employ what is known as a 'push' strategy; that is, the aim of the company is to encourage dealers to stock the product, and to push it to their customers. This will often involve direct selling, supported by trade advertising, or sales promotion techniques such as the payment of bonuses for achieved targets.

A 'pull' strategy, on the other hand, is designed to generate consumer demand for the product, pulling customers into the shops and forcing retailers to stock the product through the sheer level of demand. Here, the emphasis will be on extensive national advertising, with perhaps some sales promotion support. No intelligent retail travel agent can afford to ignore the products of major tour operators such as Thomson or the Owners Abroad group of companies to concentrate on selling smaller companies, because of the sheer popularity of the biggest companies, which would mean turning business away.

3 *The stage in the life cycle* in which the product is to be found. The communications task for a new product is to make customers aware of its existence. This means informative messages, usually carried by mass media advertising, with some sales support, to let as many people as possible know what it is you have to sell, and the product's benefits. Later, as competition for the new product increases, the task will switch to that of persuading the public that your product is the best of those available, calling for greater emphasis on sales promotion. As the product becomes well-established and sales peak, the task will be to remind clients of the product's existence, and encourage them to think of your brand first when shopping. This is achieved by a mix of 'reminder' advertising (perhaps little more than constant repetition of the brand name) and point of sale display material. These tactics will be discussed more fully in subsequent chapters.

4 The *situation* in which the company finds itself in the marketplace. In a highly competitive environment, a company will be under presure to employ many of the same promotion techniques as its major competitors, to ensure that its products are seen by the same consumers. This may require regional adjustment of the communications mix, depending upon the relative strengths and weaknesses of the

company in different areas. This is particularly the case where a company is also selling its products abroad, where both the message conveyed and the channels used to reach the market may be quite different from those used in the home country.

5 The company must determine how it will *budget* for its promotional strategy.

The communications budget

How much should a company spend to promote its products? Theoretically, the answer is simple: it should continue to spend money on promotion until the point is reached where the additional cost of producing and promoting the product becomes greater than the sales revenue it produces; i.e. you keep spending as long as marginal revenue exceeds marginal cost, in economic terms. In practice, this point is not easily ascertained, and the Marketing Manager will fall back on one of several traditional approaches to budget setting.

It is still not uncommon in the travel industry to find expenditure on promotion being determined on an *ad hoc* basis, without any attempt to budget for this in advance. The criterion is, 'what can we afford at present?' and an advertisement is inserted into a local paper as the need (or the finance) arises. While this has the advantage that the company is being seen to respond to changing market conditions, the procedure lacks foresight and planning. It may be that at the point where expenditure is needed to take advantage of an opportunity (a tour operator, for instance, offers a retailer a 50/50 deal to jointly advertise its services), no funds are available. It makes more sense to budget at the beginning of the financial year for anticipated promotional expenditure.

At its least sophisticated, this simply means deciding what it is believed the company can afford to spend in the coming year. This could be based on some percentage of the previous year's sales, or the expected sales in the coming year. The exact percentage to be allocated again tends to be arbitrary. Some managers have fixed ideas about the appropriate proportion of sales to be allocated to promotion; in the travel industry, figures ranging between 1% and 6% are commonly quoted, although many travel agents make no advance commitment for promotional spend whatsoever. If the trend in sales is linear, that is, progressing each year at roughly the same rate of increase, some justification might be found for the principle, although it would need some 'fine tuning' to take into account such changing circumstances as inflation rates, and obviously any major change in marketing, such as the launch of a new product, would call for a total reappraisal of the system.

Without specifically matching promotional funds to objectives, there is also a danger that marketing managers will be tempted to overspend in the early months of the financial year, to avoid any possibility of cutbacks occurring later in the year. When travel businesses face a decline in sales, they tend to look at how costs can be readily pruned, and the communications budget is an easy target when managers are looking to effect savings.

In a highly volatile industry such as travel and tourism, it is in any case problematical to forecast accurately anticipated sales for future years. But a more serious criticism of this method of budgeting is that it suggests that sales should dictate promotion, rather than being the outcome of promotion. One could even argue that if sales are expected to go up by so much next year, why should one invest money for promotion anyway? Availability of funds is only one criterion for determining the budget, and if it becomes the sole criterion there is a danger that promotional opportunities will be missed.

Other firms set budgets on the strength of what their leading competitors are planning to spend. This is seen as safe, in that it will at least reduce promotional competition if all companies spend the same amount. However, there is no reason to suppose that other companies have better means of judging what is an appropriate budget for promotion, and their circumstances are likely to be different anyway. While the expenditure of major companies can be ascertained (the Advertising Statistical Review carries such information), the information may not be available at the time the company's budget is prepared, and in any case most travel companies are small, and are working with comparatively small budgets, details of which are unlikely to be easily available.

It is far better to argue that the promotional budget should be decided on the basis of the sales objectives for the coming year. This technique is known as 'objective-task' budgeting. The company predetermines what it would cost in promotional spend, for example, to increase the level of awareness of its products to 60 per cent of the total market, or to increase sales by 10 per cent, and sets aside a budget sufficient to achieve these aims.

There should be a clear relationship between the size of the budget and the overall size and share of the market at which the product is aimed. Market size and share determine profit expectations, and the promotion plan should be geared to achieving a satisfactory level of sales in that market. This can be most effectively quantified when planning an advertising campaign, and Chapter 9 will illustrate how budgets are related to objectives.

The message objectives

If communications are to be effective, it is critical that they follow clear objectives, and are designed to maximise the achievement of these objectives. This means that we must start by having a very clear idea both about the market's knowledge of the company and its products, and its attitudes towards these. The sort of questions the company must ask itself are:

- 'What proportion of our market are aware of who we are, the products we produce and the benefits they offer?'
- 'What image of the company do our customers have? Is it *specific*, that is to say, does our market share a common view, or is it diffused – do people have different or confused views about what the company is trying to be and to say?'
- 'What image or beliefs about the company or its products do we need to change?'
- 'What have our present goals been aiming to achieve?'

Readers who take a short term view about communications, believing that they have only to do with promoting current opportunities to the market, may feel that this emphasis on image creation is academic, or at best appropriate only to the largest companies. This is not true at all. The image a company is projecting greatly aids the process by which the consumer differentiates one company and its products from another. While a travel agent should certainly include as part of his promotional activities a list of 'late savers' in its shop window, and perhaps advertise such opportunities in the local press, there are also many far-sighted agents who are concerned about their long-term image. This may mean taking a regular column in the local paper with photographs of their staff, drawing the public's attention to the fact that the staff regularly visit resorts abroad to improve their product knowledge. This is part of the process of polishing the image, by building public opinion to see that agent as 'caring', 'expert' and 'personal' in its approach, e.g. if the first names of individual staff members accompany the photos in the advertisements, new and potential clients will become familiar with the name, location and image of the company, and will tend to think of that agent first when booking a holiday.

Consumers must be reached at three different levels by the communications process.

1 At a *cognitive* level, they must be made aware of the product and understand what it can do for them.

2 At an *affective* level they must be made to respond emotionally to the message, to believe it and to be in sympathy with it.

3 The message must affect *behaviour*, by making consumers act on what they have learnt; in short, the consumers must be motivated to buy the product.

These points will remind us of what we learned about the purchasing, or adoption, process in Chapter 4. One model of this is illustrated below:

awareness→interest→evaluation→trial→adoption

Here, awareness represents the cognitive element, interest and evaluation the affective, and trial and adoption the behavioural. The company's aim is not only to get consumers to try the product for the first time, but to convince them that this particular product serves their needs best so that they will buy again either the same product or another product from the same company; in short, to turn the consumer into a loyal user of the company's products.

At any given point in time, individual consumers in the company's total market will have reached different stages in this process of adoption. Some will already purchase the product regularly, others will have tried it for the first time and are still evaluating it, still others will have only just become aware of it, while a number of potential purchasers will have yet to become familiar with it. Each of these buying stages represents a different challenge for the communications team.

The full range of possible objectives in communicating have been well diagnosed by Russell Colley, in his DAGMAR (Defining Advertising Goals for Measuring Advertising Results) model[1]. The value of Colley's approach is that it forces the communications team to define their objectives in terms which can be measured, so that the effectiveness of the communication can be judged. A communication campaign has to be planned to specify what each individual message is designed to achieve, to which stage of the buying process it is directed, and how much is to be spent in achieving it. This will be made clearer in Chapter 9.

In all, Colley identifies some 50 objectives, but for our purposes it is sufficient to list these under three groups of objectives:

* those associated with *informing* clients about the product;
* those designed to *persuade* customers to buy;
* those whose purpose is to *remind* customers of the product or the company.

As we revealed earlier, these different objectives are closely linked to the stage in the life cycle of the product, but there are other criteria, too, which will influence the form of the message.

A package holiday may represent anything from a highly homogeneous programme of sun, sea and sand aimed largely at a mass market, to an escorted cultural tour which is relatively unique in the market and is aimed at a small but discerning clientele who have money and are prepared to spend it on esoteric travel. In the former case, the holiday is being sold in a highly competitive environment where price has become a critical factor; there is little or no brand loyalty, and little to distinguish the product of one company from another. Assuming that the product is already well-established, the task becomes largely one of persuading clients to buy this product rather than those of competitors. In the latter case, we are dealing with a sophisticated market making the choice between a far smaller number of distinctive holidays. Paying perhaps £2000 or more per head, the clients will want a great deal of detail about what they will be getting for their money. Brochure photographs of exotic locations can draw their interest, but alone are

Fig. 7.2 An advertisement aimed at group organisers, emphasising product benefits and price concessions (Courtesy: Heckford Advertising/Metropolitan Borough of Wigan)

unlikely to do the selling job. They must be supported by comprehensive details about the historical and cultural sites to be visited, the background to the accompanying guide-lecturer's expertise, and the size and composition of the group they will be joining for the tour. While some of this information can be conveyed by a good brochure, it is likely to be achieved far more effectively by word of mouth selling, and a knowledgeable travel agent is indispensable in counselling clients about such holidays.

Designing the message

Message design has to take four factors into account:

- the source of the message
- the message appeal
- the channel to be used
- the target audience.

The *source* of the message will be a major factor in establishing its credibility, and it goes without saying that credibility is vital if the communication is to be effective.

A message gains credibility in a number of ways. First, it will be believed if the source is seen as dependable. A recommendation by a close friend or relative, whose judgement we value, will be a strong stimulus to buy, and this is reinforced by person-to-person communication, where the receiver has the opportunity to question the source and elicit more details about the product. If the product information is coming from a stranger, other means must be found to judge its trustworthiness.

If, for example, the person delivering the message is seen as an *expert* on the subject in question, this will greatly add to credibility. A travel writer, commending a holiday on the BBC *Holiday* programme, will be immensely credible both because of their perceived expertise and objectivity and because the message is delivered by the BBC itself (the *Holiday* programme appears to represent an interesting bending of the rules governing advertising on the BBC!).

Trustworthiness can also be achieved by using someonw closely associated with the product.

The use of John Nettles (of *Bergerac* fame) to promote Jersey as a destination for holidays is a neat, if unsurprising, strategy of the Jersey Tourism Committee, adding credibility to the message since the actor is assumed to 'know' the island intimately (see Fig. 7.3). Much destination advertising incorporates some well-known personality who is linked in the public's mind with the destination.

A third way to invest a message with credibility is to ensure that it is *likeable*. A message delivered by someone who is natural, straightforward, or able to inject an element of humour into the delivery, will help to aid its credibility. In a non-tourism context, Victor Kiam's series of advertisements for Remington achieved their objectives because the source proved to be genuine – not an actor playing a role, but a real company president whose business acumen was unquestioned – as well as natural and humorous. The combination of these qualities proved outstandingly successful in creating a memorable series of television ads. One caveat, however: research has shown that there is a danger in making messages too humorous, since the humour can interfere with the learning process. It is the product the advertiser wants to be remembered, not the personality!

Messages can be devised to appeal in two ways to an audience. Firstly, the appeal can be *rational*, using an economic argument to sway the customer. An airline may feature its low prices on key routes, or its punctuality record. Secondly, the appeal may be *emotional*, such as those ads of Singapore Airlines which feature its attractive female cabin staff. Of course, these appeals are not necessarily mutually exclusive. If SIA's objective is to encourage travellers to believe that its stewardesses provide a level of service not found in other airlines, the appeal combines logic and emotion. There are, however dangers in using such sexist advertising in Western countries. We can use emotional benefits such as safety, by playing on fear (although care must be taken not to become counter-productive here; there is a danger that by suggesting one's competitors are unsafe, one may instil a fear of flying in general!). A more subtle approach is reflected in British Airways' message, which

Fig. 7.3 An example of 'personality' advertising directed at the trade (Courtesy Jersey Tourism)

plays on the theme 'the world's favourite airline'.

In the late '80s, Thomas Cook produced a controversial series of television ads in which its aim was to encourage consumers to choose Cooks rather than other travel agents because – it was hinted – only Cooks offered complete financial stability. This 'fear appeal' of losing holidays had strong market impact, although the decision to produce what was tantamount to 'knocking copy' produced many complaints from other agents to ABTA, who ruled that Cooks were casting unjustified doubts and damaging

the business *per se*. There is a danger in such campaigns that the impression left with consumers may be of the total instability of the retail travel business, which could have the effect of increasing direct bookings or last minute bookings.

In considering whether to use rational or emotional arguments in communications, it is worth bearing in mind that rational messages are more likely to appeal to the better-educated consumer than emotional ones.

Promotional messages are sometimes criticised

on the grounds that their arguments are too one-sided. In fairness to the communicator, the aim of commercial messages is to present a company's products in the best possible light. However, in some instances more will be achieved by presenting a more balanced view of the products. This is particularly true when one is dealing with well-educated consumers or where the consumer is potentially hostile to the concept. In the travel world, the hyperbole of the copywriter and past inaccuracies in brochure texts have led to some suspicion about travel brochures in general, although the ABTA Code of Conduct and an increase in control through statutory law have led to marked improvements. However, some travel companies have taken to producing 'objective guides' to resorts and hotels which present a two-sided picture of refreshing honesty, and this has greatly helped to increase their clients' trust in, and loyalty towards, those agents.

Successful communications

We can summarise this introduction to the communications' process by saying that good communications require that a company:

- determines its objectives clearly, and defines these in terms that are measurable
- assigns sufficient funds to the campaign to ensure that the mission can be accomplished
- limits the objectives set, so that the receivers clearly understand the message and remember it
- wherever possible, directs the message to a specific market whose traits and characteristics are known and understood
- designs a message which is short, attention-getting, credible and which reinforces the desired image of the company and its products
- tests all communications before launching the campaign, to ensure that they will be effective.

Huge sums of money are spent by the larger travel companies on promotion. Major campaigns such as those offered by leading airlines, shipping companies, hotel chains or tour operators can cost over £1 million – too much to gamble. The companies must make every effort to ensure that the campaign achieves the sales level, or other target, determined. In the following six chapters, we shall go on to look in detail at each of the communications tools available to marketing organisations, and see how these can be most effectively used.

Personal selling

Travel and tourism is a people business; that is to say, the people who attend to the needs of tourists form an essential ingredient of the product itself. Whether referring to sales staff who are responsible for dealing with customers behind the counter, resort representatives who cater to their needs when they arrive at their destination, or any of the hundreds of staff with whom the customer will come in contact – hotel waiters, barstaff, porters, hotel cleaners, coach drivers or airline cabin crew, all play a major role in ensuring that the total product satisfies the client.

It may be self-evident, but it has to be stressed that service does not mean servility. As a nation, we must learn to take a greater pride in our skills at serving the needs of others. Above all, this means being outgoing or friendly in dealings with tourists at all times: the phrase 'the customer is always right' applies especially to the business of tourism, and irrespective of the long hours of hard work which travel staff are called upon to perform, the customers will always expect them to be friendly and cheerful, on or off duty. In short, *the travel product is indivisible from the staff who deliver it*. If we are buying a television set from a sales assistant who is poorly dressed, unkempt or unfriendly, we may be disappointed, but the reputation of the brand name may still ensure that we go ahead and buy it, if the price is right. With travel, no reduction in price will compensate for an impolite tour guide, a surly coach driver or a slovenly waiter.

Those who intend to work in the travel industry in a role which will in any way bring them into contact with tourists must be willing to present a well turned out appearance, to be patient and helpful, and above all to smile and appear friendly. The way we express ourselves on paper when communicating with clients is also an important element in the travel transaction. Good written communications call for tact, especially when dealing with complaints, attention to detail and the use of correct English; poor grammar and spelling reflect badly on the company employing you, and the effect is compounded as you progress with the company – our inadequate grammar doesn't mysteriously improve when we are promoted!

'Salesmanship' goes much further in the travel business than merely effecting a transaction. Interpersonal communications are part of the 'after sales service' which is provided in all travel products as part of the tourism experience, and when these communications are good they can compensate for many shortcomings which are inevitable in any tourism product, such as poor weather or air traffic delays. As such, they are therefore a vital element in the company's marketing strategies, and adequate training must be built into the marketing plan to ensure that these communications, too, are effective.

The use of social and personal skills

Two types of skill need to be employed when dealing with clients (and with other colleagues); personal skills and interpersonal, or social, skills. Both involve verbal and non-verbal communications, the more important forms of which we shall deal with here.

Personal skills

In the initial encounter with clients, first impressions are crucial. The way a travel clerk, hotel receptionist or resort representative appears and presents him or herself will set the scene for a successful company–client relationship. For this reason many companies impose strict rules on matters of appearance and grooming. Yet we live in an age of freedom that would have been inconceivable even 30 years ago, and do not readily accept restrictions on our right to dress as we please, adopt the hairstyles of our choice, and use

preferred cosmetics. For many the world of employment provides the first challenge to these rights, and tourism employees must learn to adjust to the constraints that the conditions of employment will impose.

At a basic level, this will mean conforming to a style of dress and grooming that the employer requires. Airlines, for example, provide uniforms for their staff and issue guidelines on acceptable grooming standards. In the past they have imposed very rigid rules, insisting that female employees wear make-up, for instance. However, in a recent test case in the USA, Continental Airlines were judged to have acted illegally when they dismissed a female employee with an examplary professional record for refusing to wear make-up. The situation in the UK has not been made clear, but the US case obviously gives cause for careful review.

Needless to say, travel staff coming into close contact with customers must be fastidious about personal hygiene. Regular washing and bathing is essential, together with oral and dental care, avoidance of food which may offend clients, such as garlic or onions, and the use of anti-perspirants being strongly recommended, especially for those engaged in physical work (such as stowing hand baggage in overhead compartments).

Deportment is important, too; we communicate non-verbally as well as verbally, and the way we walk, sit or stand reflects an attitude of mind towards the job. Staff will be expected to look alert and interested in their clients, to avoid slouching when they walk, and to sit upright rather than slumped in a chair. Clothes must always be clean and neatly pressed, as well as suitable for their purpose. The objective of most companies is to present a 'uniform' appearance, to convey a corporate image of the company, and increasingly this means actually wearing a uniform. Hotel, airline and car rental staff, couriers, resort representatives and even travel agents are being asked to adopt uniforms. Even representatives serving in warm climates are having to give up the casual leisure wear that has been customary in order to present a more formal image with skirt and blouse and neckscarf. Of course, in such conditions, it is doubly important that uniforms are washed and pressed regularly.

Jewellery is generally frowned upon, and must be kept to a minimum.

These are all *indirect* and non-verbal communication skills which tell the client something about the company and its employees. Next we will turn attention to *direct* communications skills, both verbal and non-verbal, which involve interaction with clients.

Social skills

A reference was made earlier to the importance attached to friendliness in dealing with clients. Employees must approach customers in a friendly and confident manner. This means a welcoming smile, eye contact, attentiveness and a willingness to listen. When shaking hands, a firm handshake will convey a sense of confidence and responsibility – vital for the client seeking reassurance or help, or opening negotiations to buy a product. The use of the client's name enhances the image of interest and attention (hotel porters are trained to read the labels of incoming guests' baggage, so they can use the client's name as early as possible in the host/guest relationship). The tone of voice is important, too; voices should be well modulated and soothing, especially when dealing with an irate customer. Fortunately, earlier prejudices against regional accents have largely disappeared, but a strident or whining voice grates, and it only requires a little effort to change this.

When handling complaints, the voice should convey concern. Many clients look for a sounding board to work off their anger when they have a legitimate complaint and agreement rather than argument will help to modify their anger. A wronged customer is seeking two things, an apology and a reassurance that action will be taken to investigate the complaint. It costs a company nothing to deliver either.

Attentiveness to the client's needs can be demonstrated by volunteering an interest in them. A resort representative, for instance, can enquire in passing whether clients are enjoying themselves, or a counter clerk can ask a customer browsing through the brochures 'is there any particular kind of holiday you have in mind?' to generate a sales sequence.

In general, we in Britain have far to go to perform at the level of service which many of our foreign competitors offer. This is perhaps the greatest weakness of the British travel product, and it is a salutory experience to observe a professional waiter in, say, Italy or Spain, and compare the quality of service they offer with the general level to be found in this country. This is not to say that there are not many excellent and well trained staff in the UK, of course, and the increasing emphasis on training is steadily improving the picture, at least in the larger companies. In the USA, which is not always thought of as a service-orientated country, the level of control exercised over staff in tourism often astonishes the British observer. Training programmes for Disneyworld, for example, dictate the exact form and level of performance of all employees coming into contact with clients, even down to an obligatory smile and a 'have a nice day' on parting. Whether it is possible, or even desirable, to emulate this example in Britain is debatable, but our concern for our clients must improve in all sectors of the industry.

Above all, our attitude of mind towards service must change, to a pride in one's job and a respect for the client. The use of derisive terms for customers, such as 'punters', is symptomatic of a poor attitude to service which is indefensible if the industry is to become truly professional in its approach.

The sales sequence

We have talked about the vital ingredients – deportment, appearance and facial expression – which give clients initial confidence when dealing with representatives of a company. In this final section on communications, we will go on to look at the sales sequence itself.

While the most common setting for selling is the retail agency, and the examples below will be particularly appropriate to that setting, the principles of the art of selling apply equally in all situations where client and sales staff come face to face, as in the case of resort representatives selling trips or cruising staff selling shore excursions.

The sales sequence requires a sales person to proceed in four steps, by

- establishing *rapport* with clients
- *investigating* client needs
- *presenting* the product to clients
- getting the clients to take action – to *commit* themselves

Rapport

The sales sequence has two aims: to sell the company's products, and to match these products to client needs so as to ensure the client receives satisfaction. In order to meet the latter objective, the initial task for any salesperson is to engage the client in conversation, to gain the client's trust and learn about his or her needs. This process, known as *rapport*, will reveal how open the client is to ideas, and how willing to be sold to. Some customers are suspicious of any attempts to sell them products, preferring a self-selection process. They may see sales staff as ignorant about the products, or 'pushy', but even such clients as these can be put in the right frame of mind to buy from a particular shop if they receive friendly and helpful service.

In order to strike up a conversation with a client, one must avoid the phrase 'can I help you?', common as it is. The phrase simply invites the reply, 'thank you, no, I'm just looking'. A more useful opening to generate discussion would be, 'Do you have a particular kind of holiday in mind?', or, to a customer who has just picked up a brochure, 'that company has a particularly good choice of holidays this year. Were you thinking of a particular destination?'

The good salesperson must be something of a psychologist, judging from clients' facial expressions their frame of mind and reactions to questioning. A customer in a hurry, who appears to know exactly what he or she wants, will not wish to be delayed by your engaging in conversation, but a fast, efficient service accompanied by a friendly smile will encourage the customer to return. Above all, the salesperson should act as naturally as possible. Being yourself will best reassure clients that you are genuine in your desire to help and advise.

Having gained the client's trust, the next step is to *investigate* their needs. Once again it is necessary to ask open questions which elicit full answers, rather than closed questions which call for yes/no replies. The sort of questions the sales staff will need to know include:

- who is travelling, and how many will be in the group?
- when do they wish to travel, and for how long?
- how do they want to travel?
- where do they want to go?
- how much do they expect to pay?

Clients will not necessarily know the answers to all these questions themselves, so one needs to start by asking those that they can reply to easily, and gradually draw out their answers to questions they may not have thought about yet. Some of these answers will be vague to start with ('we had thought about somewhere hot, not too pricey, sometime in the summer') and may become gradually more detailed as the conversation proceeds.

Needs must never be assumed. Clients might say that they don't want to go on a package holiday. There could be many different reasons for this, ranging from a bad experience on earlier packages to a desire for complete flexibility or a wish to escape from the holiday masses. The exact reason for the preference should be known so that the salesperson knows what products to offer – there are, for instance, very flexible IIT (independent inclusive tour) packages where the client would not be 'one of a crowd'. It may be that friends have put them off the idea of packages because of their experiences. In any case, at each stage of the investigation, it is as well to make sure that the needs identified are agreed between the client and the salesperson:

'Let me see, you wanted somewhere quiet and remote, just to lie back and relax, is that right?'
'You did say that you didn't want a large hotel, is that right?'

Presentation

Once a salesperson is satisfied that there is enough information about the client's needs, then they may go to the next step, that of *presentation*. This means presenting the right product to meet the client's needs, and presenting it in a way which will convince the client that that is the product he wants.

Here, the key to success is not only to mention the features of the holiday or other product being sold, but also the benefits to the client:

'I would suggest that you stay in Igls rather than Innsbruck itself. It's quieter at that time of the year, less congested, and offers some very attractive woodland walks, just what you were saying you wanted. There's a small hotel, the Ritter, which is owner-managed and has an unusually friendly and personal atmosphere, ideal for someone like yourself staying alone.'

Obviously, product knowledge is crucial to the success of this stage, but personal experience of the resort itself isn't always necessary; sound knowledge of the brochure material will generally suffice.

Even if the product you are offering is exactly what the client requires, it is always good to offer one or two alternatives; clients like to feel they are being offered a choice. Pick out the benefits of each, but stress that the first choice really seems to meet the client's needs best. Too many alternatives, on the other hand, will lead to confusion, and may delay a sale.

Investigation

One important aspect of the sales sequence which generally arises here is the need to handle objections from the client. Objections may be genuine, based on price, or they may be due to the client being offered insufficient choice. On the other hand, they may be made because the client has an additional need that has not yet been met, and this may require the salesperson returning to the investigation stage to draw out this need. It may also be because the client is not yet ready to buy, and may need more time to consider.

If the product is more expensive than was originally envisaged, the client will need reassurance of the extra benefits to be received and that the product is offering real value for money. This is best achieved by showing the client a product at the price he or she was willing to pay, and comparing the two, pointing out the additional benefits of paying a little more.

Whatever the reason for the objections, it must be identified and countered by matching all the client's needs to a product as closely as is possible to achieve.

Commitment

The final stage in the sequence is to *close the sale*. This means getting the client to take action. There can be several outcomes to a sales sequence. The client may buy the product, either by paying in full or leaving a deposit; they may take an option on it; they may agree to the salesperson calling them later, or agree to call back later, or they may leave the shop without any commitment of any kind. Although ideally the aim of all sales conversations is to close with a sale, this is clearly not possible, and the important thing from the salesperson's point of view is to ensure that the *best possible* outcome is obtained. The customer may want to go home to talk over the product with their partner, but if they leave satisfied that they have received good service, there is a high likelihood that they will return to make the booking. Of course, if they are merely uncertain, the sale may be clinched by going over the benefits once more, and reminding them that it is better to take an option (which does not commit them) to avoid disappointment if the particular holiday they have in mind has been sold by the time they return.

A good salesperson is continually looking for the buying signals emitted by clients: statements such as, 'yes, that sounds good' clearly indicate a desire to buy. Where the signals are not clear, a comment from the salesperson such as, 'would you like me to try and book that for you?' may prompt the client into action. However, clients should never be pushed into a decision; not only will they not buy, they may also determine never to return again.

Finally, remember that the selling job doesn't end when the client has paid. Hopefully, they will become regular customers. Reassurance of your desire to help them at any time with their travel arrangements, and a closing comment such as, 'I know you will be happy with that particular hotel. Do come and tell me about it when you get back' will reinforce the sale and reassure customers that they have made the best possible choice, not only of the product but of the retailer through which they purchased it.

Travel agency design

It is appropriate to close this chapter with a look at travel agency design, since the effective presentation and design of an agency is critical to its acceptance as a location for the purchase of travel by consumers.

It has often been said that travel agents are fortunate. All they need are a shop, some posters and a telephone, and they can set up in business. Of course, it is not as easy as that, and today's competitive climate makes it certain that design of travel agencies will become ever more important to their success.

While it used to be considered that a travel agent need not take premises in the centre of town because customers would seek it out when they required advice, this too is no longer the case. Every high street in the land has its own travel agency and the number of customers they attract is directly related to the position they occupy within the town. Good visibility of the shop, e.g. being on a prominent road junction, may well be a bonus, but the greatest test of any shop site is the number of pedestrians who pass the door. A counting machine and a stopwatch employed at various times during the week will give the best indication of the relative merits of the position when considering new sites. Availability of car parking facilities is also worth exploring and considering, especially in the small town location.

Any retail concern will normally obtain the best site it can afford for a new business, and will then do its best to maximise the use of that site. Similar considerations can be applied to existing agency locations.

Most research into why customers choose one travel agency in preference to another leads one to the conclusion that the most important factors are that it is in a convenient location and that it is noticed. Thus the outside appearance is of critical importance. In increasingly professional high streets, other traders have led the way with crisp, colourful fascias stating their identities, and superb, well-lit and imaginative displays of merchandise to entice the shopper in. A theme is almost always apparent, and the displays are changed frequently to create interest. Travel agents would do well to learn these lessons, especially to forego their 'bargain bazaar' approach, characterised by numerous stickers with conflicting messages.

In terms of layout, all trades now favour open windows which allow a view of what is beyond the window display. They also favour a fairly flat shop front which maximises the space available within.

From the outside, and within, two factors dominate first impressions – colour and light.

Colour

Colour plays a key part in establishing an identity. Different colours are credited with individual values:

- reds convey warmth and vitality
- white is clean, cold and clinical
- greens are considered natural, caring and wholesome
- blues are considered crisp and efficient
- yellow is happy and joyful (though sometimes it can be garish)
- burgundy looks sophisticated
- browns and oranges are comfortable and relaxed.

Above all, to choose a colour will establish a background for all that you want to display. Never forget that it will look very different when 'stocked' with brochures and posters.

Good examples of colour usage are red for Thomas Cook, green for Pickfords, blue for Hogg Robinson and burgundy for American Express.

Thomson Holidays and the Owners Abroad group publish between them some 40 brochures for summer alone, which few agents could afford not to stock. Some agents follow a policy of attempting to restrict sales to companies whose products they know best, while others believe that variety is the major force in what they offer vis-à-vis their competitors. The choice of what to display and sell is referred to as the 'racking policy'.

All travel agents will be quick to agree that these brochures are the most important sales tool. They cost a great deal of money to produce, and supplies are often restricted; yet very often little control is exercised over them. Whatever racking policy is decided upon, the positioning of brochure displays is critical. If they are freely available in the open area of the shop, then certain basic rules will apply. The most effective positions for display will be those close to the door, or opposite the entrance, at around shoulder to eye height. Should the brochures displayed there be the ones you want to attract attention, or the ones that will sell readily anyway? Once a policy has been decided, it should be positively translated into the display facilities (and the related storage capability) in shop design.

Lighting

Light can make or break any scheme. Fluorescent lighting is economical and highly efficient for overall background levels, but is extremely poor for creating impact. Concentration of light in small areas of relative darkness will highlight any goods much more effectively. The intensity will depend upon the method chosen, with tungsten bulbs, spotlight bulbs and quartz halogen low voltage units each improving in effectiveness by degree. Modern lighting deserves expert advice, once the objectives of the shop design have been decided upon.

Lighting also leads into practicalities, for the overall light levels within a shop will affect the environment for both the customer and the workers. High overall light levels are seldom attractive, and they will also interfere with ease of vision on computer screens. The level of light in which staff undertake clerical duties, especially poring over closely packed timetable information must, however, be good.

Within the travel agency, the first impression should be friendly and welcoming, and designed to put customers at ease. It must be clean (and therefore designed to be easy to clean), up-to-date in design and practical to operate. Figures 7.4, 7.5 and 7.6 provide illustrations of travel agency layout design, racking and lighting considerations.

Practicalities

To convert enquiries into bookings will need not only a desk, but also access to telephones, computer VDUs and reference material. These facilities must be to hand and tidily arranged. Consideration must be given to storage and security of money, and it must be decided whether each clerk will have a personal till or whether a central cash desk is to be operated.

Display, demonstration and excitement

Travel is about images of places far away and highly desirable. It is about people enjoying themselves and taking a break from their drab daily routines. Travel agencies should exude some of this excitement of possibilities, but it is very easy for the travel agency to become boring and ineffective. Thus the use of display panels with emotive photographs, dramatic (not 'so what?') posters, video walls and video demonstration players for travel information and even the use of modern computer booking systems, all help to add to the atmosphere of growing excitement.

As with most moods, however, never assume that things happen by accident. The relationship of space and distance is important. Staff positioned too far away from brochure racks will tend to appear to be uncaring. The way in which layouts are thought out will help to provide a tidy appearance, e.g. one must not leave convenient space where new brochure supplies can be dumped by delivery carriers in full view of customers. The shop will need to be comfortably warm in winter and cool in summer. The layout has to be equally effective for customer comfort and staff convenience; no mean task. What is certain is that to do the job well is both important and expensive.

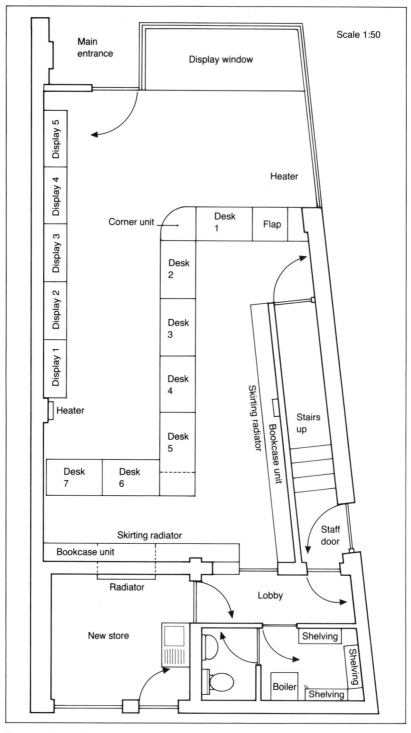

Fig. 7.4 Shop plan for Go-Right Travel

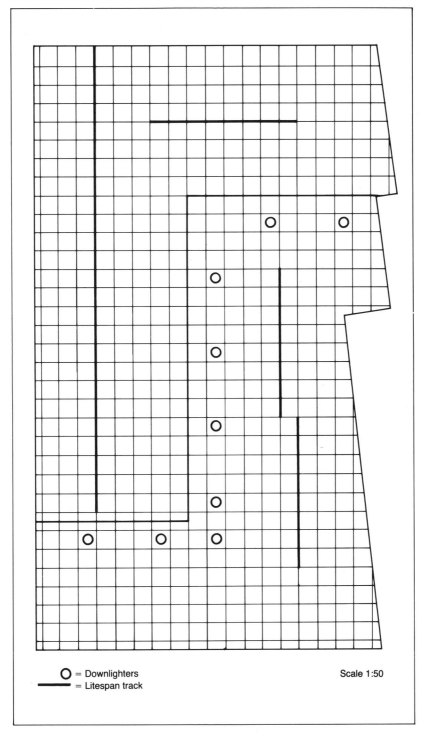

O = Downlighters
= Litespan track

Scale 1:50

Fig. 7.5 Overhead lighting and suspended ceiling for Go-Right Travel shop

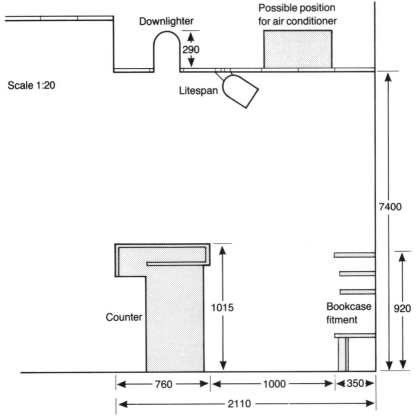

Fig. 7.6 Elevation of interior, showing counter, bookshelves and lighting, Go-Right Travel

Desks or counters?

One debate that has continued for many years is whether desks or counters are the best method for carrying out transactions with the customer. There are divided views, and these can be paraphrased as:

1 *counters*

- do not encourage customers to 'settle in' and stay for longer than necessary
- enable staff (on high stools) to work at the correct height to deal with customers standing up and prevent them feeling dominated by the customer standing above them in a 'superior' position
- provide a security barrier and enable cash to be kept at each position
- provide adequate space below the desk top for either a split level desk with computer screens, etc., tidily built out of view, or for other storage and reference facilities.

2 *desks*

- are more friendly, encouraging customers to sit and chat
- can be set out informally near brochure racks
- are much less expensive in shopfitting terms, as they are able to be deployed without being fixed or specially fitted.

Which policy is chosen is not important, as long as it is implemented well.

The emphasis on corporate design in all areas of business will ensure that the travel agency of the future, if it is to survive as a distributive system, must employ the newest techniques in retailing, and above all must provide the welcoming, attractive and comfortable trading outlet which customers are coming to expect in all shops.

Fig. 7.7 Interior of Excalibur Holidays office, Bournemouth. Note the individual desks, instead of counters, concealed lighting, open plan design and use of plants.

Fig. 7.8 Excalibur Holidays, Bournemouth – modern brochure racking

Questions, tasks and issues for discussion

1 How effective is the communications process in your classroom? From which forms of teaching and through which learning processes do you:
   (a) remember information best?
   (b) acquire skills best?
   What 'interference' occurs to prevent your receiving messages?

2 Discuss the merits of personal selling through travel agents compared with advertising direct to the public, in the promotion of package holidays.

3 Identify one TV programme or film which has influenced you to see or want to see a destination. What exactly was the appeal that motivated you? How best could the resort or area in question be promoted to you to reinforce this motivation?

4 Collect two advertisements which offer contrasting messages, and explain why the appeals are different.

5 Assume the role of a small, independent travel agent, and design a message for an advertisement aimed at counteracting messages from the major multiples which appeal to 'security' and 'price sensitivity'.

Exercise

You have been asked to undertake an appraisal of the effectiveness of communications in a local travel agency. Select any agency of your choice (if you have a student-run agency within your college, you may care to choose this) and, based on the issues discussed in this chapter, observe the effectiveness with which the agency communicates with its market.

Write a report to the manager of the agency which critically assesses each of the criteria you have identified. Include in your report an appraisal of the importance which price plays in the marketing of travel products in the agency, as identified in the products displayed in the windows or within the agency. What other promotional appeals are being used to support sales by the agency?

8 The distribution system

After studying this chapter, you should be able to:

- identify the factors affecting the choice of different distribution systems
- appreciate the role of the travel agent as retailer of travel services
- recognise the importance of design in the retail travel shop
- distinguish between methods of co-operative distribution and evaluate the respective merits of each
- recognise the importance of the sales representative's role in marketing, and understand how this is successfully managed
- understand the function of inventory control in travel and tourism reservations systems

It is convenient to think of distribution as part of the overall communications process, since it involves the selection and operation of channels by which a company communicates its products to its markets. Technically, in marketing theory there are two aspects to distribution. One deals with the distributive channels, the other with the physical delivery of products to those channels, and ultimately to the consumer. The latter process entails the keeping of inventories of goods to balance supply and demand, the warehousing and storage of goods, and the transportation of goods to dealers and customers. However, these latter functions relate largely to the marketing of tangible products, while in the case of travel and tourism, customers are brought to the product rather than the product being delivered to the customer.

We are therefore concerned here with somewhat different aspects of the distribution process. Nevertheless, there are common issues in distributing goods and services. Particularly, tourism requires the establishment of a *reservations system*, both to handle the sales process and in order to act as an inventory control system to balance supply and demand. This reservations system can usefully be thought of as a 'travel distribution system', which is closely linked to the way in which channels are man-

aged, and will be dealt with in this chapter as part of the examination of the role and function of distribution channels.

The prime purpose of distribution channels, however, is to sell a company's products, and for this reason we shall also look at the functions of selling and sales management as part of this chapter.

Channel choice

Before we consider how channels are chosen, let us first make ourselves aware of the options open to a company, when planning its distribution strategy.

A principal, such as an airline, cruise company or hotel, can if it so wishes choose to deal direct with its customers, through intermediaries, or some combination of both. The term 'intermediaries' is used to describe any dealer who acts as a link in the chain of distribution between the company and its customers. Most companies choose to deal through one or more intermediaries. The reason for this is simple; it is cheaper for a company to do so than to set up its own network of retail shops or sell its products direct in any other way. By paying a commission or other agreed form of financial remuneration to their intermediaries, companies buy the use of a distributive network. The system also acts as a convenience to consumers, as they can choose from a range of different products under one roof, instead of having to visit each producer's shop in turn to select their product.

Should an airline decide to sell its flights direct to the public, it must provide a network of shops for the purpose; at least one in every important trading centre in the UK and abroad. Alternatively, it could find other means of selling tickets, such as through automatic vending machines, through telephone bookings or by mail order, but all these offer disadvantages to the customer, and moreover each separate airline will have to set up its own distribution system, duplicating the retailing effort (although some airlines on non-competitive routes would undoubtedly act as representatives for the distribution of other airlines' tickets). The resulting airline shops will have only a limited number of products to sell; flights, and package holidays using that particular airline's services. Customers would be forced to move from shop to shop to compare flights and prices, or to buy other products, such as car hire, associated with their trips.

Multiply this picture by the huge number of different travel principals, and you will begin to understand the enormity of the direct sell problem, and the sheer impracticality of cutting out the intermediary entirely. A few key travel products could well be distributed in this way, if the market is very large, highly concentrated geographically and purchases frequently; or alternatively if the company is very small, but the product is highly specialised, and one which potential customers are prepared to search out. Certain short break and activity holidays are sold in this way.

Many US airlines do have their own retail outlets in major commercial centres in their own country, just as in Britain the level of demand for air tickets can just support a limited number of British Airways (BA) shops in major cities. Most travellers, however, will find it more convenient to book their BA flights through their local travel agencies, which handle 70–80 per cent of the total volume of air tickets. BA must also be careful,

therefore, not to antagonise their travel agencies by expanding their direct sell efforts too forcefully, which would threaten agency support. With low brand loyalty among the flying public, it could be relatively easy for many agents to persuade their clients to switch to other airlines.

Figure 8.1(a) explains the process by which goods and services reach customers through a 'chain of distribution', starting at the producer and ending at the point where the customer accepts 'delivery' of the product. The diagram has been simplified to indicate a typical number of links found in the chain, but in the case of some products, additional intermediaries can extend this chain considerably. Using the analogy of the airline once again, an airline is a producer of a transport product, and is therefore at the start of the 'travel chain of distribution', although the reader should be aware that the product chain actually stretches back through the aircraft manufacturer to the supplier of raw materials for the aircraft.

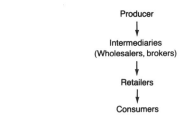

Fig. 8.1(a) The chain of distribution

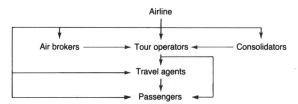

Fig. 8.1(b) Distribution channels for airline seats

An airline sells its seats in a variety of ways. Individual seats can be sold direct to a customer, or they can be sold through a retail travel agent. The airline will also sell seats in bulk through tour operators or 'air brokers'. Tour operators in turn use these seats to create package tours (some argue that in so doing, they are creating new products, and should therefore more correctly be termed 'producers' of products rather than wholesalers), which are then sold either direct or through agents.

Some types of air broker enter the chain at a level between the airline and the tour operator, purchasing large blocks of seats at bulk prices and selling these in turn to operators, while other brokers act as 'consolidators' for airline charter flights, helping tour operators with low load factors to integrate their flights with other operators who are similarly placed. Some of these consolidation seats will find their way onto the market, being sold individually through travel agents to the public as 'late booking saver fares'. Tour operators may themselves off-load unsold seats at 'saver fares' to the public through travel agents or direct. The distribution system for air seats thus becomes quite complex, with seats being sold through a variety of different dealers. This can be seen in Fig. 8.1(b).

An airline operating both scheduled and charter flights will typically use all of these distribution methods to maximise its load factors, but must continually re-evaluate the service provided by each of these links in the chain to ensure that the current system offers the most effective means of reaching customers at the lowers possible cost commensurate with the quality of service required.

Selecting the channel

New companies to the travel and tourism business must determine their strategy for distribution, just as existing companies must re-evaluate it from time to time. There are three key factors which a principal must bear in mind when making this choice:

- cost
- control
- level of service

Cost

Much has been made of the belief that so-called 'direct sell' tour operators can sell their product more cheaply to the public by cutting out the intermediaries. In fact, the issue is not clear-cut.

Certainly, some holidays sold direct are cheaper than identical holidays sold through more traditional channels, but this is not always so, nor is it necessarily the case that the same level of profit is being achieved on the holiday. The critical factor in reducing price is the reduction of cost, and while this may be a factor of lower distribution costs, it may equally be the result of more successful negotiatioins with airlines and hotels, or greater 'muscle' because of the greater number of seats or beds being contracted.

Companies selling their products through retailers have one great advantage over the direct sell operators; most of their costs are variable costs, i.e. distribution costs arise only when a sale is made. A direct sell operator, however, will have the fixed costs of operating the shop whether the public come in to buy the product or not. This means that either the direct sales operator must enjoy a high level of turnover to support the cost of the shop, or the product must be so unique and so certain to find a ready market that the promotional costs are comparatively low. In this respect, the direct sell operator Tjaereborg provides us with an interesting case study, since with a product like mass market package holidays which are fairly homogeneous, the company must invest heavily in promotion at the launch stage, both to bring the product to the public's attention and to persuade them to adopt a novel system of buying it. In addition to a programme of national television advertising, there are heavy direct mail expenses in sending brochures to prospective customers, and the company must provide an exceptional telephone service to ensure that members of the public can get through to the company once their interest is aroused. Any failures here will drive the customer back to the more familiar travel agent.

Great care therefore must be taken to ensure that the information and booking system is capable of supporting the level of demand which it creates. However, once the direct sell company achieves a satisfactory market share, enabling it to reduce marketing costs relative to other costs, its avoidance of intermediaries' commissions will enable it to compete on price with other operators of similar size.

The problems faced by Tjaereborg and other

direct sell companies in getting an established share of the travel market is typical of the problems facing companies seeking new ways of reaching the market. British customers are conservative in their buying habits, and it has been difficult to overcome the strengths of traditional channels. The convenience of the location is a critical factor in the success of the travel agent, just as it is a critical factor in the distribution success of any fast-moving consumer good. But with the low brand loyalty towards travel products, the convenience and accessibility of the retail outlet becomes second only to price in importance for the product's success. This is one aspect of the level of service which a company provides for its clients.

Control

The principal must also consider the degree of control which it can exercise over its distributive outlets, when planning the distribution system. The use of intermediaries necessarily results in some loss of autonomy, although if the principal owns its own retail shops it can exercise a much higher level of control.

There is firstly the loss of personal contact with clients, if the sales function is in the hands of an independent distributive outlet. It becomes more difficult for the company to understand its market, or identify changing market needs, and it is very dependent on receiving regular feedback from dealers or agents who, without a personal vested interest in one company's products, may not keep their ear so close to the ground. A greater problem still for effective marketing is that the travel agent, dealing with many hundreds of products, will be less committed to any one product than would the staff of one's own company. Bonus commissions can be used to provide some incentive, but other companies are offering similar financial rewards to increase sales, and travel agents will have their own priorities in pushing products. In a field where there is so little brand loyalty, this lack of control over distribution is of great concern to principals, especially in the case of companies such as airlines which have massive capital investment in equipment, but very little control over its sale.

It is for this reason that some airlines determine to have their own retail sales shops, even at the expense of higher distribution costs.

Having one's own distributive outlets offers a further advantage: it becomes far easier to co-ordinate the company's marketing activities generally. An airline launching a new route can be certain that the route is featured in the retail shop windows, that brochures are in stock and prominently displayed, that special point-of-sale material is on show, and that the sales staff know the product and bring it to their customers' attention.

Product knowledge among retail agents is a controversial issue among principals. Any company which can convince agents that their staff have intimate and first-hand knowledge of the destinations they feature in their brochures will have a considerable sales advantage over other operators, as the agent will feel more confident in calling that operator's staff to discuss their clients' needs. Similarly, a company retailing its own products, such as Tjaereborg or Portland Holidays, can far more effectively mount a promotional campaign to support their sale, and ensure good co-ordination between all aspects of the promotion. The promotional support any travel agent can give to one product among all those they represent is necessarily limited. Their staff's product knowledge, too, having to be wide enough to know something about all the hundreds of holidays they sell, must equally be more shallow in dealing with any individual company's products.

Intensive versus selective distribution

A medium to large-sized company has a far easier choice of alternatives open to it when planning its distribution strategy than a small company. If the larger company sells products appealing to the mass market, and that market is geographically widely distributed throughout the country, it could be anticipated that the company would normally seek to maximise the number of possible outlets through which its products can be purchased. Such a strategy is termed *intensive distribution*.

Earlier it was pointed out that sales achieved by way of commission paid to travel agents involve a proportionately small fixed cost element of the total transaction costs. However, this should not disguise the fact that establishing a network of dealers does involve a substantial on-going cost to a company. There are over 7000 branches of ABTA travel agents in Britain. Each must receive at least a minimal level of servicing if they are expected to be productive for the company. In addition to supplying brochures, this will mean regular mailings to keep agents informed of new products or changes to existing products; the offer of merchandising assistance and materials such as window displays; providing agents' educationals or other forms of training in product knowledge. Additionally, strong supporting agents will expect a regular call from the company's sales representatives.

All these support services will have to be committed over and above any commissions paid to the agents for sales achieved. Such support is clearly beyond the means of the smaller company. A tour operator expecting to carry, say, 5–6000 passengers in a year could not begin to contemplate a strategy of intensive distribution, since on average less than one booking from each agency will be received. Instead, the operator will opt either to sell products direct or go for some form of *selective distribution* network. If for instance the market is strongly London-based, a certain number of agents located in the Capital may represent the company; if the market is more evenly distributed throughout the country, a strategy of *exclusive* distribution could be employed, by the appointment of a 'sole agency' in each major conurbation.

Hotel representative agencies are also appointed by hotels to represent and market their services, particularly to overseas markets where the hotel may find it difficult to reach the client direct or through travel agents. These hotel representatives receive 'overriding' commissions from the hotels they represent which are sufficient to allow them to accept bookings from travel agents to whom they allow the normal agency commission. Sometimes the contract between hotel and representative will include a clause that the latter will not represent any of the hotel's leading competitors.

The agency relationship and its distribution implications

This is a convenient point at which to explore in more detail the relationship between agents and principals, especially tour operators, and to consider how this relationship affects the distribution issue.

In 1964, the much publicised failure of Fiesta Tours brought a clamour of calls for greater protection of the public in respect of payments for inclusive holidays. The following year saw the first protection scheme which was enacted voluntarily by ABTA – 'Operation Stabiliser'. It provided for a fund to be set up to which both tour operator and agent members would contribute.

To ensure that the fund was not called upon unnecessarily, both classes of members agreed to financial vetting annually. They also committed themselves to a binding agreement whereby ABTA travel agents would sell only ABTA tour operators' holidays, and ABTA tour operators would sell only through ABTA travel agents. Though the protection now provided has been enhanced substantially, the principles enshrined in this agreement have survived to the present day, and have been judged to be in the public interest by the Restrictive Practices Court. The practice, however, will be wound up after 1992, as it conflicts with EC trading policies. The public have recognised the protection so provided and this, combined with mutual trading obligations, has made it difficult for non-members to survive. There are presently few tour operators, and even fewer travel agencies, trading outside the Association's membership.

There are nearly 700 tour operator members of ABTA, and each publish not just one but sometimes as many as 25 different brochures segmenting holidays offered into winter and summer, and into destination, holiday types and activities.

There is no requirement that all tour operator members shall accept bookings from all travel agent members, but there are few who will actually refuse to accept such bookings and pay the 'normal' 10 per cent commission.

It follows that tour operators have a difficult marketing choice to make. They can promote bookings via all ABTA travel agents, or restrict their representation to those they believe will be productive. If they accept bookings from all, then the first occasion upon which they allow commission will establish a consensual relationship whereby, even in the absence of a formal contract, the agent may claim to be recognised and/or appointed by the operator.

If one is to follow a policy of acceptance from all agents, then it makes little sense not to send brochures to them, too. Even one copy for file purposes will absorb over 7000 copies, if sent to the entire membership list. Not one of those is likely to reach the potential buyer. To send a bale of, say, 50 copies per branch immediately establishes a print run of 350 000 copies. The distribution costs will also be substantial, as they are unlikely to cost less than £1 per bale, and could cost considerably more, dependent upon weight or size.

If every tour operator followed this policy, then the travel agent would be deluged with brochures. The display area is unlikely to provide more than some 100 spaces (facings), and might have, say, 1000 brochures to promote. No member of the staff could conceivably become expert in all the information in brochures, and thus the value of their advice (based on knowledge) would also weaken.

It is certain that the agent is unlikely to have adequate display space to maximise the effect of all the brochures in stock. It follows that those featured will almost certainly fit industry norms, such as the ability to fit the racks. An unusual shape or size will affect its chance of being promoted. A 'clever' heading in a position other than at the top of the page will probably mean that in an overlapped display it simply isn't seen.

This may seem an unlikely scenario, but it is not. An agency cleared out its brochure store and found no less than 100 brands of travel brochures in stock that it neither desired to represent nor had ordered. The cost of production, distribution and storage were prodigious, and yet not one penny of this expenditure was justifiable, as all went to pulp.

Thus one of the first parameters to establish is how the brochures are to be distributed.

Availability and suitability of distributors

It is one thing for a company to determine whom it would like to represent it. It is quite another to get the positive support of the retailers concerned. Because of the limited amount of shelf space available to display brochures, agencies will be highly selective about the range of products they will sell and the companies they will represent. Even the largest premises will be unlikely to have racking space for more than 300 brochures, and by the time that 'preferred operators' have been displayed (major companies' brochures, and those paying bonus commissions which receive the approval of management), this will considerably reduce any space that might be available for new products coming onto the market, or those of small companies, however attractive they may be. Even when the agencies are keen to adopt the new product, there must be a good match between the agent's catchment area and market, and the company's intended market. To some extent, the image of the producer needs to be reflected in the image of the distributor.

The suitability of the retailer is also determined by the level of service they will provide for their customers. Convenience of a local outlet to the intended market is only one attribute of service; the times at which the outlet is open to the public is no less important. Some agencies have experimented with late night bookings on one evening each week, others have opened during the peak booking season on Sundays in order to handle customer enquiries. Notwithstanding the antagonism with which agents have greeted the gradual introduction of more flexible working hours, the ability to book holidays outside the normal hours of opening has been helpful to consumers and may help to combat the threat of direct bookings made via home computers, which is now a real possibility. In areas such as city centres where a lot of travel bookings are made during office workers' lunchtimes, agents are learning to become more flexible by providing part-time staff during the peak lunch periods to cater for the extra demand.

Technology in distribution is making a major impact, as increasingly tour operators are expecting agents to deal with reservations direct through their on-line computer system. If agents are unprepared to invest in computer technology, they lose out in the ability to offer clients fast access to information. What is more, the facility to telephone to make bookings is being withdrawn by the larger tour operators, making it impossible for non-computerised agents to represent these operators. Equally, non-computerised tour operators are finding it difficult to compete against high technology reservations systems, with agents increasingly preferring to deal through the on-line reservations systems of the better-equipped principals.

As long as agents continue to provide the level of service which their customers want – good product knowledge, objective advice, and convenient location and opening hours – and as long as these services can be provided at a cost competitive with other distribution systems, the travel agent will continue to flourish.

The travel agent as distributive system

As we have seen, the agent's role in the distributive system is to provide a convenient location for the travelling public to seek out information about travel, to make reservations and to buy their tickets; and to do this at a cost which is comparable with other forms of distribution. The proximity of location to the market has always been the principal factor in the success of a travel agent. A street level shop in or close to the high street is essential, even at the expense of the higher costs which the shop must bear. However, since a travel agent's stock is composed entirely of brochures, less space is required

than in most other forms of retail outlet, and costs can be held down by sacrificing square footage. This does mean that the travel agent must measure success in terms of turnover per square footage, and consequently shops are designed today for a fast throughput of clients, even though the product might in some cases (e.g. cruising and long-haul holidays) be thought to need the care and attention of a professional counselling service.

A characteristic of agency operations over the past few years has been the low margins of profitability which most have achieved, as an outcome of the intense competition between tour operating companies, which has made package holidays relatively cheap against other goods and services. This has been exacerbated by the introduction of late booking discounts, greatly reducing the average turnover per booking. Without a commensurate increase in levels of commission to compensate for this decline, agents have had to push for higher throughput, and thus turnover, per branch and per staff member employed, in order to survive. At the same time, the decline in retail profitability had little effect on the growth in numbers of travel agencies. In the four years between 1983 and 1987, the number of ABTA travel agencies increased by 30 per cent to nearly 7000 outlets. By the end of 1989 it had reached almost 8000. Only in 1990 did numbers show any signs of falling, with some 300 fewer agencies at the close of the year.

Historically, when increases in commission levels have been negotiated, this has usually resulted in expansion of the number of retail outlets, rather than in increased profitability of the existing units, making principals reluctant to consider raising the commission paid to agents as a means to achieve higher levels of service to their customers.

Small independent agencies have witnessed a phenomenal growth in large travel agency chains during the latter part of the 1980s. This so-called 'march of the multiples' has resulted in the six biggest chains controlling over a quarter of all agencies and, it is often said, something like half of all the business transacted. For the first time, power is moving from the principals to the distributive sector in the travel industry, with chains being able to negotiate increases in commission for the higher levels of sales they achieve. At the same time, their greater capital resources have enabled them to invest heavily in computer systems for their reservations, accounting and management information needs, widening the advantages they enjoy over their smaller competitors. Their higher market profile resulting from national television advertising coverage, and a willingness to offer booking incentives, especially discounts, threaten the survival of small agencies. Additionally, many independent agents must pay cash for trans-actions, while most multiples have credit agreements with all their major suppliers, easing their cash flow position.

These developments have forced the smaller agents to re-think their role in order to survive. Since the small agent cannot compete on price, it must adopt alternative strategies to compete. Three possible solutions include:

- More aggressive sales techniques.
- Developing 'exclusive distribution' contracts, to represent the smaller, specialist tour operators whom the larger chains are reluctant to support.
- Providing a superior professional service with informed recommendations rather than merely retailing whatever the consumer asks for.

In the past, travel agencies have been seen largely as 'order takers' – a convenient point for the purchase of travel arrangements – but competition has now forced a reappraisal of the role, and agents are placing greater emphasis on the ability of their staff to sell, to establish rapport with their clients, and to offer a superior level of product knowledge, so that clients actively seek them out to receive advice, particularly for the independent, tailor-made travel arrangements that provide greater earning potential than the standard package holidays.

Co-operative distribution systems

Consortia

One means by which agents, and principals, can market themselves more effectively is through becoming part of a co-operative marketing venture. The consortium is now a characteristic development in joint travel and tourism marketing, allowing organisations to unite for marketing purposes while retaining their financial independence. Consortia are now prominent in the marketing of tourist attractions, hotels, and retail travel agents.

The consortium provides a means by which individual companies with common, but not competing, interests can join together for mutual benefit. Perhaps the most common benefit is the publication of a joint brochure. A group of tourist attractions, such as ABLE (Association of Bath and District Leisure Enterprises) or DATA (Devon Area Tourist Association) can in this way afford to produce thousands of brochures for extensive distribution to hotels, restaurants, tourist information centres, libraries and other sources where holidaymakers in the area are likely to ask for information.

With each member's facilities listed at proportionate cost, an attraction can gain far wider circulation and publicity than would be the case if each company were to produce and distribute its own brochure. Groups of stately homes, heritage sites and small hotels have similarly banded together to publicise their products nationally and internationally.

While the production of a joint brochure is the most common benefit to be found in consortia, there are many other benefits to be achieved in a marketing consortium. In the case of travel agency consortia, a major benefit is the negotiation of higher rates of commission for group members. A number of agents coming together within a region can equal the sales power of a major multiple in the same region, and can therefore gain substantial bonus commissions for targeted sales. One such consortium, Woodside Management Systems (with headquarters in the USA) has built up an international network of business travel agents

Fig. 8.2 Co-operative promotion: Bath's ABLE consortium of tourist attractions brings together over 30 local attractions in a joint brochure

to negotiate lower prices for hotel accommodation and other travel products for its members.

A consortium can also reduce its members' operating costs by offering opportunities for bulk purchase of supplies such as stationery, computers, and services such as window dressing, while hoteliers gain from the economies of scale inherent in the bulk purchase of food, drinks and other hotel supplies purchased through a central buying organisation.

Hotel consortia in particular have developed common themes as part of the consortia marketing policy; for example, hotels have formed *group marketing consortia* with themes of historic interest, common price categories or similar standards, such as star ratings, while *area marketing consortia* such as Torquay Leisure Hotels have been formed to promote the sale of hotel rooms in the same geographical region of the country. Marketing consortia provide the added benefit for hotels of enabling each to act as an agent of the other hotels in the chain, providing an international distribution network. In this way the smaller hotels are capable of competing with the larger chains, although the superior reservations procedures of the latter, usually with advanced computer reservations systems, still give the large organisations a lead at present.

One other advantage of the consortium is that it provides the means to recruit management expertise on a scale unthinkable for the small company acting alone. Travel agents and small hotels can for the first time employ centralised accounting, legal assistance, staff training, as well as marketing expertise for consortium members. Other small tourism units are just beginning to recognise the scope which consortia offer, and sectors such as farm holiday operators are forming groups to integrate their marketing.

While the benefits of consortia are self-evident, readers should be aware that the operation of consortia is not without its problems. One is the result of the autonomy of each individual company within the consortia. Determining the financial contributiion of each member to the consortium's common fund is one such issue; should this be in proportion to the turnover each achieves? Should the amount of space in the brochure be equal for all members, or variable according to the number of products each company offers, or the relative size of each member? Hotel consortia, for instance, generally determine their contribution according to the number of beds in each unit. Then some means by which pages will be allocated in the brochure must be agreed. Members prefer to have their products listed in the opening pages, since the consumer is more likely to notice the first pages than those towards the back of a brochure. Should members therefore pay proportionately more for the early pages in a brochure than those occurring later? Equally important, how is the consortium to be managed? Generally speaking, in the early years of a new consortium, members take it in turns to appoint someone from their management to administer the consortium's affairs, although as time progresses, and the success of the consortium becomes more assured, a small secretariat is usually formed.

Franchises

A second means by which an organisation can expand its system of distribution rapidly is by *franchising*. This is an arrangement under which a business (whether principal or distributor), known as the franchisor, grants an organisation (the franchisee) the right to use the company's name and market its products in exchange for a financial consideration – usually some form of 'royalty', or percentage of turnover. In most cases the rights are exclusive within a district, so that the franchisee becomes the sole distributor of the product in the area. The franchisee will also usually pay an initial sum to the franchisor to cover various 'set-up' costs, which can include help with site planning, practical advice in setting up the business, and staff training. The franchisee will also agree to conform to the terms of the contract, such as purchasing raw materials or products exclusively from the franchisor, and maintaining clearly defined standards of quality.

While there are a number of different ways in which a franchisor may operate, the most common benefits which the franchisee gains are the rights to sell an established brand name product, and the centralised marketing support provided by the franchisor. In turn, the franchisor gains by the rapid expansion of sites operating under one name, and a fast-accumulating central fund with which a national or international advertising campaign can be launched. This campaign creates brand awareness and a ready demand for the product, which leads to further demand for franchises by those eager to start up in business by themselves at reduced risk. Since

franchisees are their own bosses, they can also be relied upon to work harder to ensure the success of the organisation.

The franchise concept is not a new one – indeed, its origins go back over 200 years to the breweries' 'tied house' system, under which an inn or pub is licensed to sell the ales and beers of that brewer only – still a common practice in Britain today. However, the modern franchise was introduced on a major scale in the USA some 20 years ago, and has become particularly prevalent in the expansion of the fast food business (Kentucky Fried Chicken, McDonalds, Pizza Hut, Spud-U-Like).

The travel and tourism industry has been in the forefront in franchising developments in Britain, as well as elsewhere. Apart from catering institutions, hotels, camping grounds, car hire and travel agencies have all launched successful franchise operations. Hotel chains such as Holiday Inns achieved enormous growth in the 1960s and 70s with their operating franchises around the world, and in the '80s car hire franchising led to the expansion of companies such as Budget Rent-a-Car, as well as Hertz and Avis. Although attempts to franchise travel agencies in Britain go back to the 1960s, these and other initial attempts to franchise the travel business failed. A number of reasons can be put forward to explain this failure. In the first place, a successful franchise must have a name with strong drawing power, as well as offering a unique product. The franchising of a travel agency offered no product or price advantages, nor did the possession of a franchise in itself guarantee an IATA appointment or other principals' approval.

Exaggerated claims were often made about potential profits that could be expected, while the training or other back-up marketing facilities did not materialise. In a business such as travel where the product is highly specialised, lack of adequate training for staff is fatal. Even promises of exclusivity were sometimes broken. All too often, in order to get franchisee support, the franchisors were tempted to appoint anyone with the money to pay, regardless of their business acumen, with the result that standards were inconsistent and quality suffered.

An additional legal hurdle to the franchising of retail travel was the fact that at that time, commissions could not be split between an agency and another organisation, and the payment of royalties was in itself a form of split commission. Not until the freedom to discount and to split commission in the 1980s did the door become fully open to travel agency franchising, with the now defunct Exchange Travel group the first to introduce it. One attraction of that franchise was the accounting back-up provided by their head office, which relieved branch managers of many administrative tasks and allowed them to concentrate on marketing. However, by that point the narrow profits being achieved by agents and the additional turnover required to pay the 1 per cent management service fee made the venture questionable. The collapse of Exchange in 1990 (for reasons still being assessed at the time of writing) terminated Britain's first serious effort to franchise retail travel.

Building links with the retail agent

Although the two examples given above indicate ways in which agents themselves can unite to form more effective sales units, the 'manufacturer' of travel products will be chiefly concerned with finding ways in which they can provide the most effective support to retail agents to maximise their own sales.

In order to see how this can be achieved, first let us examine the relationship between the travel agent and the principals. The agent's main role, as we have seen earlier, is to provide a convenient outlet for travellers to enquire about, and book, their travel arrangements. In exchange for this service, the agent receives commissioin, varying between 7 and 10 per cent of the travel revenue, from the principal. It is now increasingly common for principals to pay higher rates of commission to agents meeting set sales targets, as a means of increasing their commitment to selling, since agents purchase no advance stock and show little brand loyalty to principals. It is therefore pertinent to ask what other factors, apart from higher financial remuneration, will encourage an agent to support one principal rather than another.

The answer to this is more complex than is at first apparent. Certainly, agents will take account of opportunities to increase profits through increased commissions, but if this were the only criterion, every principal would be forced into a commission war with their competitors. Furthermore, a decision taken by the management of an agency to rack a company's brochures is only the first step for the principal, who must also ensure that the staff of that agency actively push their products.

Market share is clearly a factor here. All agents who succeed in gaining appointments will sell the products of all of the six or so leading tour operators, since not to do so would be tantamount to commercial suicide. Even here, though, one company's products may be more actively sold than another's, notwithstanding comparable levels of commission. The determinants in this 'trade-off' can be listed as:

- **the image of the company and its perceived stability**: there must be no danger or rumours that the company is headed for collapse.
- **the match between the company's products and the client's needs**: most agents see that it is in their own interests to satisfy their customers.
- **the reliability of the company** in such issues as overbooking, consolidations, delivery of tickets, and communications. Thus, if an agent frequently finds it difficult to get through to the reservations department of one particular company on the telephone, they may switch to another company which proves easier to reach. The significance of computer reservations systems in easing this communications process will be further discussed later in this chapter.
- **agency staff product knowledge**: there is no substitute for personal experience gained by sales staff, in encouraging them to sell hotels or destinations, and enabling them to be more convincing in doing so.
- **co-operative promotion programmes**: many companies will actively support travel agents in their sales efforts by paying 50 per cent of

the costs of special promotional events run by agents, or add contributions to specific advertising programmes. These joint promotions enhance the image of both organisations in the other's eyes. To the agent, it shows a willingness to support their efforts to sell, while it reveals to a principal that the agent is more than merely an order taker, and is actively selling the company's products.

- **the personal relations** generated between a principal's sales representative or other staff and the agency counter staff. This factor must never be underestimated. For many agents, the sales rep *is* the company he or she represents, and their personality is a significant factor influencing agency support, both in terms of recollection and recommendation. For a small specialist company, the role becomes even more significant, since the principal's aim will be to get the agent to think of their company first when handling enquiries.

- **the relative ease with which transactions can be completed**: time is money to an agent. If procedures are too complicated, and especially where the total value of the sale is small, the amount of work in which the agent becomes involved will cost more than the relative commission earned. A study undertaken by Upminster Travel examined the relative profitability of the various travel services sold by the company. It was concluded that the sale of rail, cross-channel ferry and domestic air tickets were subsidised by the profits achieved by selling package tours, shipping and long-haul air bookings. Many agents subsequently have chosen not to deal with coach and rail bookings because of the relatively small commissions paid. Some services, such as hotels, require agents to claim their commission after clients have used the facilities. This is not only an onerous procedure, but it also slows the agent's cash flow. Agents are also reluctant to deal with hotels which are without booking offices or representative agencies in the country, since telexes, faxes or telephone bookings abroad boost booking costs.

- **the sale of domestic holidays**: many agents have been reluctant to deal with UK domestic package holidays, either believing that commissions are inadequate or that booking procedures are too complex. However, the increase in short break holidays in Britain, coupled with the aggressive marketing of packages by companies such as Rainbow Holidays and the tourist boards' efforts to integrate commission-paying holidays into single comprehensive brochures have all gone a long way to making the products more acceptable to agents.

- **the availability of credit terms**: most principals allow a measure of credit to their better supporting agents. The small, less well-established independent agents are therefore doubly disadvantaged, in that they not only find it difficult to negotiate higher commissions but are also required to pay cash for transactions. Managing cash flow is a critical issue for agents, and its successful management can increase profits substantially, while the absence of credit is a major operating drawback.

- **credit cards**: many agents have resisted accepting credit cards for the purchase of travel, since the agency costs of 1–2 per cent make further inroads into already slim profit margins. The widespread phasing-in of EFTPOS (Electronic Fund Transfer at Point of Sale) which is now underway allows clients' bank accounts to be debited immediately and funds transferred to the principals' accounts. Cards such as Switch and Barclay's Connect, with which agents are reluctantly having to come to terms, have the effect of further reducing the cash flow of non-credit intermediaries.

Two other factors should perhaps be mentioned here. Patriotism is hard to measure, but does play a role in some agency recommendations, where air travel or cruising is concerned. An agent may well recommend a British product, where other things are equal. The recovery of British Airways' fortunes during the '80s has undoubtedly been aided by the goodwill of the British public and agents. On a regional scale, a similar attitude towards local companies can be detected among agencies, an attitude which is not merely a result of commercial interest. A local tour operator will often be on closer personal terms with travel agents in the area and will derive goodwill from being part of the local community.

Based on an assessment of these points, and an organisation's relative strengths and weakneses in each area, principals can develop distribution strategies within the overall marketing plan to improve their standing with agents in one or more of these directions.

It will also be helpful for principals to be aware of each agent's policies regarding the racking of brochures. Each agent or chain of agents determines its individual policies as to what products it will sell and what brochures it will display. Many will also have clear guidelines about how the brochures of the various companies represented will be displayed. Thomas Cook's approach is not untypical, in their designating four categories of tour operator product:

1 Those on the 'winners' list', roughly the top 20 operators in size;
2 'Recommended' operators, roughly the next 35 in size;
3 'Authorised' operators, those which the company is prepared to sell;
4 Non-authorised operators.

Those companies on any agent's winners' list will automatically receive full agency support, those in the second category more limited support, while policy for those in the third category may be to sell but not display brochures, although a file copy of the company's brochure may be kept in the office.

Clearly, such a policy is demand-led. Other companies may delegate space for local operators, for companies in which they have a specialist interest (for instance, car ferry companies' brochures will be prominently featured by travel services offered by the RAC) and any companies for which special commission deals have been negotiated, or with which jointly sponsored promotions have been arranged.

This selection and categorisation also operates in reverse, with principals grading their distributors according to the level of sales they achieve. As in all businesses, the 'Pareto Principle' applies, in that a small proportion of agents tend to produce the bulk of the business for any company's total sales. Typical ratios would result in 20 per cent of retail distributors making 80 per cent of the bookings.

It is this feature of distribution which determines a company's policy regarding agency support. Companies could, justifiably, decide to support only those agents providing them with a reasonable level of bookings. This will reduce distribution costs, but it will inhibit the maximisation of sales, especially in its tendency to discourage new, or marginal, agents from selling the company's products. With the current emphasis on expanding market share, tour operators in particular are keen to receive all the bookings they can get, with the result that agents are categorised into bands based on turnover achieved. This will determine how much support the principal gives the agent.

One operator, a specialist medium-sized company, has used the following grading system for its agents. While the number of bookings will vary according to the total number of passengers carried by the company, the principle is common to most operators and other travel companies:

category	definition
P	Preferred multiple, with substantial number of bookings achieved each year
AA	Agency with at least 12 bookings
A	Agency with minimum of 6 bookings
B	Agency with 2 bookings each year
C	Agency making at least one booking
D	Agency failing to make any bookings
Z	Agency without bookings but demonstrating some potential

'Preferred multiples' will generally be supported with bonus commissions for targets achieved, based on some percentage increase over their performance in the previous year. They are also likely to receive offers of 50/50 promotional help, a regular cycle of calls by sales representatives, full merchandising service such as window display material, a regular mailing of information in the company's newsletter, invitations to brochure launches in the region and offers to attend educationals to experience the company's package tours. Those in lower categories will have reduced levels of support, to a point where those in the lowest category may be given only an office copy of the company's brochure and minimal support in other directions. This still enables the agency to 'prove itself' and be offered increased support when bookings are received.

The principal must also exercise control over the number of brochures distributed to agents. A watch must be maintained on the ratio of bookings to brochures. This ratio can vary widely, with some agents achieving bookings for every three brochures they give out, and others perhaps making only one booking in 20 brochures. A high ratio of brochures to bookings is indicative either of poor sales techniques, with little attempt being made to do more than distribute brochures in response to enquiries, or lack of control over brochure orders given to principals – junior agency staff may be given the task of re-ordering brochures without any clear idea of actual numbers needed, resulting in a high wastage rate at the end of the year.

John MacNeill, then Managing Director of Thomson Holidays, once pinpointed seven characteristics by which a principal could identify the efficient travel agent. These are listed below as a useful checklist for those considering making agency appointments:

- The agent will have a viewdata reservations system in use;
- Staff will have enough product knowledge to satisfy their more demanding clients;
- The agency shows evidence of efficiency in reducing its costs;
- The agent operates a well planned policy of selective brochure racking;
- Its management have the ability to recognise booking patterns and trends over time;
- The agency actively sells, using its initiative to tap the local market;

- Helpful feedback is provided to its principals regarding the local marketplace.

The role of the sales representative

A principal's sales representatives play a crucial role in the relationship between the company and its agents, since the 'local rep' will be the main, and sometimes the only, point of contact between the two. In spite of this, there is a tendency among principals to reduce this function in the organisation or seek other means of communicating with their agents. This is due to the comparatively high cost of keeping sales reps on the road. It can cost upwards of £25 000 per annum to maintain a sales rep, including travel expenses. However, there is arguably no more effective way of building links with retailers, and it is perhaps signficant that while principals have been searching for alternative methods of servicing their distributive outlets, travel agents themselves have begun to employ their own external sales reps to call on businesses and other organisations to increase sales, often using part-time staff paid on commission to generate such business.

'. . . the representative's most valuable service . . . is to act as a troubleshooter'

However, most principals continue to employ a field sales force, whose task is to develop existing business and generate new business, by making regular calls on retail agencies and by calling direct on businesses (in the case of transport and accommodation principals) or organisations likely to offer the prospect of group travel bookings. By this means, travel agents are kept regularly informed about product development in the company, and are offered merchandising help and advice on any promotions they might wish to make featuring the company's products. However, undoubtedly the representative's most valuable service, in the eyes of many agents, is to act as a 'troubleshooter' to solve problems. Knowing them personally, agency managers will call them first if they have a problem, or they need, for example, to clear a fully booked flight for valued customers. The rep's own personality, and his or her ability to help in these circumstances will play an important part in the development of the agent's image of the company.

Although, with the proliferation of computerised reservations systems, most companies today will have up-to-date information about sales achieved by agents in each product category, the sales rep is still the best person to advise the company on agency potential, to determine what level of support each agent should receive, and to recommend specific counter staff for agents' educationals.

Reps have a responsibility to get to know personally each agency manager and member of the counter sales staff on whom they call. They must be thoroughly familiar not only with their own company and its products, but those of their leading competitors and their relative prices. They should have clear objectives to achieve on each visit, to ensure that it is cost-effective.

Attitudes towards the visit of sales reps differ considerably between agents. While most prefer to see a company representative at some point during the year, they may resent 'cold calls' made without prior appointment, and some object to giving up their time to dealing with the many different representatives who call on them. The rep therefore has to ascertain the views of each travel agency manager towards their visit, using considerable tact, picking convenient times for visiting and determining whether an agent is interested primarily in learning about the company's products, exchanging social and trade gossip, or keeping the visit as brief as possible and merely noting that the principal is expressing an interest in them.

In the past, reps were frequently used to deliver the principal's brochures, but this is now more cheaply undertaken by professional carriers, usually employed by the printers. Some attempts have been made by tour operators to publicise their brochure launches by the use of so-called 'merchandisers', whose function is to deliver brochures to agents while getting maximum press coverage. However, these teams are usually employed *ad hoc* and have little knowledge about the company or its products, and therefore in no sense serve as representatives of the principal.

Two other means are also increasingly used to communicate with agents. These are:

- the telephone sales force
- the external sales team.

Telephone contact has become an increasingly common means by which principals keep in touch with their agents. Many of the functions common to sales reps can be conveniently undertaken by making a telephone call periodically from head office. At very least this has the effect of considerably reducing sales calls, and therefore costs. However, some airlines and other organisations have switched entirely to the use of the telephone to maintain agency contact, with some consequent loss of personal contact between agency and principal. This is symptomatic of the pressure on companies to reduce their marketing costs as competition increases.

Employment of an external sales team to service companies is also finding favour as another means of cost reduction. TWA is an example of an airline pursuing this policy. Under this scheme, a contract is drawn up with an external agency which provides a team of knowledgeable sales staff to call on the company's agents and generally represent the company's interests. Members of the sales force are frequently people with prior experience of repping with travel companies, and are therefore well acquainted with the industry, so only minimum training is needed to up-date them on the company's own products. Costs are reduced because these teams may also represent a number of other travel products (generally non-competitive in nature) at the same time, when they call on agents. The cost of each individual agency call is therefore divided between several principals. While undoubtedly reducing distribution costs, it can be argued that the system fails to establish either a unique image for the company or a genuine relationship between principal and agent, since these intermediaries are not direct employees of the company. Moreover, the level of control which can be exercised over the sales force is reduced. Nevertheless, for the smaller principal with a limited budget for sales representation, this can provide a solution to the need to service the retail agent.

The management of the sales representatives

Whether company policy is to employ its own sales force or to buy in the use of an outside team, the Sales Manager's role starts with the need to set objectives for the team. This will include establishing the tasks they are to undertake, and setting any targets which they are to achieve. However, many of their tasks will not be directly revenue-generating. As we have seen, sales staff have a servicing function, building good relations with the travel agents and with businesses, grading agency potential, gathering feedback from agents about market trends, providing merchandising assistance, and generally acting as a source of reference for agents. Reps will play a key role in the annual brochure launch presentations (see Chapter 11 on sales promotion), helping to organise regional functions and participating in them. However, where an outside sales force is employed, the objectives are likely to be less ambitious.

Based on objectives given to the sales force, its size can be determined. This requires four steps:

1 Totalling the number of customer contacts to be made, whether agencies or other sources of potential business, and dividing these into categories according to the level of service each is to receive.

2 Deciding how often each category is to be visited, and what other forms of support the sales staff are to provide.
3 Totalling the number of sales calls required and assessing time allowances for other activities.
4 Establishing the number of sales staff to be employed in order for these duties to be performed, and dividing their responsibilities into geographic regions.

In the case of a large company, this could mean employing a sales team of perhaps 20–30 people. Obviously, a much smaller company cannot afford to offer the same direct representation, and must reduce the call frequency or employ an outside sales team. A further drawback to employment in a smaller company is that there is less opportunity to establish a career structure for sales reps. Larger companies will enable reps to be promoted to District, Regional or Area Sales Managers, perhaps going on to Controller of Sales or Sales Director, whereas in a small company the sales rep may report direct to the General Manager, and may indeed have less autonomy in determining the budget spend than is the case with a larger organisation.

However, smaller companies do off-set some of these disadvantages by providing more flexible employment for their sales reps. Often, in the case of tour operators, staff will work as overseas resort representatives during the summer season, and will be brought home during the winter either to call on agents as sales reps or to complement the reservations staff during the busy booking season which traditionally follows the Christmas holidays. This has led to full-time employment for many formerly seasonal staff, which has improved staff quality and ensured that sales staff have excellent product knowledge through direct personal experience.

Other tasks of the Sales Manager are to determine scales of remuneration and conditions of work for the sales team, and plan their training. These functions are likely to be undertaken in conjunction with other members of staff in a large company, such as the Personnel Officer and Training Officer. However, the Sales Manager alone has direct responsibility to motivate staff, direct them and monitor their performances. We will examine these latter functions briefly here.

It is wise to give sales reps as much autonomy as possible and minimise direct supervision. Greater individual control over their job leads to greater job satisfaction for the reps, who will give better performance as a result. Sales reps will require a period of induction training, to give them a background on the company and its products, sales methods and record keeping, and other procedures specific to the company; they will also require up-dating from time to time as procedures or products change. Although more commonly found in the larger organisations, training manuals given to new staff can play a helpful role, providing they are kept up-to-date, so a loose-leaf manual is probably best for this purpose. Record keeping is one means by which the sales rep will communicate with the Sales Manager, but this should be complemented by a regular pattern of meetings to exchange feedback. Reps are frequently separated from the events in their head offices for long periods while on the road, and can become divorced from events taking place at the head office unless a regular programme of meetings is organised for them. For the most part, however, contact is maintained through the use of report forms which are completed by the sales reps each week.

The report form provides the basis for the schedule of visits planned by the reps each week. A typical report form will come in three-sheet self-carbon format, in which sheet 1 outlines the weekly plan, indicating to the Sales Manager the planned schedule of calls for the coming week. These are sent in advance to the Sales Manager, who will then know where to find the reps should any of them be needed urgently. Sheet 2, the weekly check sheet, includes the information from sheet 1 together with comments by the sales rep on the outcome of each visit. Explanations are given for any changes to the programme that had to be made during the week. This is mailed to the Sales Manager at the end of the week's cycle of calls. The rep retains the third copy, with all this information, for his or her own records.

In this way the Sales manager is kept fully informed of events in the field, and in the same way, any sales leads received at head office need to be passed quickly to the sales rep in the area for prompt action, within an agreed time scale. Details of any new agency appointments must be passed quickly to the reps, since a new agent is highly motivated to generate business for principals and will benefit from early encouragement. Leads followed up by the rep are reported back on the weekly report forms, with an assessment of the potential for business. New agents or potential sources for business will be given the rep's name and contact address.

Most travel companies' reservations systems are now computerised, giving the Sales Manager access to a vast amount of statistical data regarding sales by area, agency and period. This will give Sales Managers details of revenue within the responsibility of each rep, enabling comparisons to be made between targeted and actual sales performance, and indicating trends over time. These figures must be regularly disseminated to the reps in the field, so that they have access to full information on their own performance and that of their agents. At the same time, reps must receive up-to-date information on other promotions under way or planned by the company, and the organisation's overall marketing plans, so that promotion efforts can be effectively co-ordinated. Discussions should take place between the Sales Manager and the reps themelves when agency sales targets are determined each year, particularly if these are to be linked with bonus commissions. Finally, the travel expenses incurred by reps must be monitored by the manager. While these are generally predetermined as part of the overall sales budget, they need to be reviewed from time to time, not only because costs change but also because a company should not inhibit the potential for increased business by too tightly controlling a rep's expenses. A sales rep over budget on expenses should not be criticised if these expenses have resulted in a comparable increase in sales as a result of the rep's efforts.

Inventory control

In the long-term, the Marketing Manager's task is to manage demand; that is, to achieve a balance between supply and demand. This is not easy in the travel business, where demand differs seasonally; is difficult to predict, being affected by political as well as economic circumstances; and where resources are finite, so that, for example, a popular destination or tourist site cannot accommodate all who are interested in visiting it, or access may have to be limited due to ecological damage caused by excessive demand.

In the short-term, the Marketing Manager may employ any of three techniques to control demand without changing supply:

- *prices* can be raised or lowered to influence demand
- a *waitlist* can be built up
- a system of *forward booking* can be introduced.

The last technique leads to the formation of a reservations system, which is a key element in the travel distribution system.

Reservations systems

Reservations systems are used in most forms of transport and accommodation, and in booking theatre tickets and package tours. These services cannot easily increase their supply in the short-term. There are also limited reservations systems in operation for some other services used by tourists, such as up-market restaurants, campsites during peak season, and popular museum exhibitions (especially for group visits). Arguably, reservations systems could also be more widely used to control demand at other tourist facilities such as beaches (which become unattractive if unlimited access is permitted) and ski slopes (where long queues can form during periods of high demand).

Reservations systems also enable organisations whose resources are *not* finite to forecast future demand more accurately and arrange to expand supply. Thus, inclusive tour companies can negotiate for more airplane seats and hotel rooms during the peak season at those destinations which, while not full, have shown indications of being more popular than was first forecast. Advance reservations have also made possible pricing structures such as the Advance Purchase

Excursion fares (APEX) on airlines, which enable the airline operators to predict more accurately their future patterns of demand and load factors. Above all, reservations permit principals to maximise their load factors (or occupancy rates), by repricing or by repackaging, or in some cases by switching customers from products experiencing excess demand to those where demand is light.

The criteria for a reservations system, whether it be manually or computer operated, are that it is capable of displaying availability, can register bookings as they are made, and can effect cancellations and redisplay the cancelled booking for resale. The cost must be kept low as a proportion of total service charges, whether to travel agents or to the general public (if access is direct). Access should be easy and user-friendly, i.e. simple to understand and to operate.

Reservations systems can be organised in one of three ways:

1 A manual system in which entries are made into diaries or other record books. A common practice among tour operators is to hang huge charts of hotels and airline seats on the walls of the reservations department, with staff entering bookings with erasable marking pens. Bookings are then expunged as cancellations are received. Other operators have used a system of colour-coded discs hung on pegs, or cards stored in slots, on the charts, which can be removed if cancellations occur.

With this form of reservations system, travel agents telephone their bookings through to a reservations clerk, who registers options, or makes bookings, over the phone, by removing discs or cards, subject to deposits received by mail. These systems are, however, declining in use.

2 Reservations are held in the principal's computer system. Agents telephone the reservations clerk, who consults the computer and offers bookings over the phone, again normally subject to receipt of deposits by mail within a period of seven days.

3 The principal operates an entirely automated computer reservations system. Agents access the computer live ('on-line') by means of a VDU

(visual display unit) in their offices, and can take options, or make a booking, without the intercession of any member of the principal's staff.

Both manual and computerised reservations systems may provide for *overbooking*, whereby more units (seats, hotel beds or whatever) can be sold than can be supplied. Although widely condemned (and under certain circumstances illegal), principals argue that overbooking is a necessary distributive technique to allow for the 'no-shows' which are common practice in travel, especially where business travel is concerned. Business people have been in the habit of making several return flight reservations if they are uncertain about when their business dealings will be completed. The alternative would be for companies such as airlines to settle for lower overall load factors, with a commensurate increase in prices to the consumer. Attempts to introduce the payment of deposits or cancellation fees have proved inoperable in the past, and the overbooking system has become a fact of life to which the travelling public have become accustomed, within the bounds of 'acceptable risk'. However, where overbooking becomes too extensive, as has occasionally happened in the case of hotel bookings on package tours abroad, other control mechanisms come into force, such as the intercession of government agencies or threats of action from bodies such as TOSG (The Tour Operators' Study Group, consisting of leading members of the inclusive tour business in Britain). Tour operators themselves can no longer legally claim exemption for responsibility for overbooking by others, and therefore have to resolve overbooking problems for their clients as they arise.

The cost of using different reservations systems is a major consideration for travel agents, who seek to reduce their overheads. Most reservations for the products of small companies are still made by telephone, with reservations clerks who become well known to travel agency staff. However, for this system to be effective, the agent must be able to obtain a connection quickly with the principal. If an agent experiences difficulty in getting through to the reservations department, or if calls are 'queued' at busy times, leading to high telephone bills, there will be a marked reluctance to use the services of that company unless no suitable alternatives exist. Principals can reduce agents' overheads through the use of 'Freefone' (0800) calls in which the agent is not billed for the cost of the call; or by using a system in which telephone charges are billed at the local call cost only for long distance calls.

Computerised reservations systems

The major development over the past few years has been the rapid switch to computerised reservations systems providing on-line reservations facilities to agents. At one time, the installation of such systems was costly, and only principals carrying many thousands of customers each year could consider their installation, but continuing falls in the price of computer software and hardware have now made it possible for much smaller principals to consider automated reservations systems. Thomson Holidays' introduction of their TOPS system in the '80s, a low cost, user friendly and extremely reliable reservations system, enabled that company to increase sales substantially and establish a huge lead over the rest of the inclusive tour business. Their later decision to abandon telephone sales entirely for their summer holiday programme points the way to future developments and the need for *all* agents to be linked by VDU to principals' computer systems in order to survive.

In the airline world, the rapid development of computer reservations systems provided a new tool for the Marketing Manager. Originally seen merely as a method of controlling huge inventory speedily and efficiently, it soon became apparent that the way in which information was made available could radically improve sales potential.

In the USA there were a number of systems, each of which grew out of an internal inventory control system for the airline itself. Originally the agent, or the client, was required to telephone a reservations clerk who would operate the Visual Display Unit (VDU) and respond with the answers required. The speed of the system in responding to the enquiry, and the amount of information given, soon became a critical factor, with the travel agent often calling the airline with the most efficient booking system, rather than one with the flight most likely to suit the client.

Airlines then realised that not only would there be huge staff cost savings if agents were given their own VDUs and access to the system, but they would also become more committed to that airline, particularly if it assisted them in other ways, such as ticketing, invoicing and financial controls.

From the agent's point of view, however, there was the nightmare prospect of having several VDUs in the office, each dedicated only to the provision of information and processing for one concern.

Two approaches developed. In the USA, the *single access* philosophy meant that all information, irrespective of the carrier to be used, became available from the computer system of the chosen airline. Anti-trust legislation has now made it necessary for the airline to supply information without bias, and it must list flights between a pair of airports in strict timetable order, rather than listing its own flights first.

Two airlines have been at the forefront of development (United Airlines with the Apollo system, and American Airlines with the Sabre system), and now both offer competitive and extremely comprehensive systems that can deal with many additional travel components, as well as the air ticket transaction, e.g. hotels, car hire, resort information, weather and entertainment details. They are also capable of printing tickets, itineraries and invoices, and coping with accountancy functions. A third American competitor has appeared in the shape of Worldspan, introduced by TWA and linking with Delta Airline's system and those of the Canadian airlines.

The alternative approach, which was favoured in the UK, was to establish a multi-access system, known as Travicom. Financed principally by British Airways, this set out to operate a totally unbiased system on behalf of all the major scheduled carriers. The enquiries generated by a travel agency's VDU were directed to a central computer which acted as a switchcentre and a translation device. The message was then con-

nected to any one of some 30 airlines throughout the world and an immediate reply sought. The system's major drawback was that the reservation, once made, was stored in that distant computer core, rather than at one central point. This made paper back-up essential at the agency, and delayed the introduction of the paperless office.

In 1987 both Sabre and Apollo became available in Europe for the first time. British Airways saw the need to operate on a larger scale and reached agreement with other major carriers, initially within Europe, to commission a totally new system which could operate on a global scale. This system, Galileo, has merged with the US Apollo system, to reinforce the global strength of this organisation. Travicom users and technology have been absorbed into the new system progressively.

Lufthansa and Air France have also set up a different but parallel system, codenamed Amadeus, with similar objectives, which is headquartered in Munich and already gaining the support of agents on the Continent. Battle is now joined to see which of these global reservations systems will become the market leader.

Reservations technology is advancing at such a pace that a discussion of the merits of current systems has little place in a textbook such as this. Suffice it to say that these developments will have profound effects on future distribution strategies, not least in terms of extending direct marketing opportunities. Airline tickets can be purchased in some countries from machines at airports, and this system is easily extended to the use of EFTPOS to pay for the ticket. Such expansion in direct selling, which threatens to cut out the retail agent, must be a further cause for concern among agents.

Future directions

Apart from computer technology, other new factors are beginning to shape the future of distributive systems. The practice of 'networking' between travel companies is leading to expansion in potential new distribution systems. Tourist Information Centres (TICs), for example, are increasingly acting as commercial booking agents for travel and tourism products, especially for the sale of bedroom accommodation. In Britain, Etna is a computerised information and booking system in use in TICs for the booking of hotel beds. The trend to integration in the travel industry, which will allow tourism principals to exercise greater control over the distribution systems through their ownership of retail agencies, is another direction which must concern the independent agent.

Reciprocal referrals between hotels, links between hotels and airlines, and between hotels and car hire companies, all provide alternative routes for the sale of travel products which can be further exploited. Finally, the concept of 'net bulk purchasing', by which travel agents actually purchase in advance travel products and are responsible for selling them, offers a new means of retailing, and a threat to the smaller agent who will be less able to fund this type of investment or stand the risk it implies. While this concept has not developed to any great extent yet in the travel industry, there is no doubt that principals will give it more serious consideration in the future, in their efforts to find new means of distributing their products.

Questions, tasks and issues for discussion

1 Examine the feasibility of British Airways extending direct sell travel shops and reducing their reliance on travel agents as distribution outlets. Would this be a wise decision (a) immediately, and (b) in the next five to ten years?

2 Computer technology is a fast moving subject. Prepare a paper which updates the latest developments in computers as they affect the distribution of travel products. What conclusions would you draw about the place of technology in travel distribution by the year 2000?

3 How effective are travel agency consortia? Could they become more powerful in retail travel?

4 Examine present practices in the distribution of theatre and concert tickets, and suggest ways in which their distribution might be improved.

Exercise

You have been commissioned by a firm of consultants to solicit the views of travel agents in your area on the role of sales representatives. You have been asked specifically to find out what agents require of both airline and tour operator representatives, and how satisfied they are with the services provided by these representatives.

Plan a research programme which will involve interviews with selected agents in the area, and collect data. Based on the results of your investigations, draw up a short manual for the use of **either** an airline representative **or** a tour operator's representative, which will provide new employees in this role with some guidelines in their dealings with agency managers and counter staff.

9 Tourism advertising

After studying this chapter, you should be able to:

- understand the purpose of advertising
- know how to create effective advertisements
- appreciate the role of the advertising agent
- understand the factors behind choice of media
- recognise the need to plan for promotional budgets

In the context of this book there are three main areas of advertising, namely advertising by the principal to the consumer, advertising by the agent to the consumer, and advertising by the principal to the agent.

Advertising in tourism is similar to advertising for any other medium. It essentially follows the AIDA principle of:

- attract *Attention*
- create *Interest*
- foster *Desire*
- inspire *Action*

It can, and often does, follow this pattern stage by stage. A good example in another field has been the programme of privatisation launches of British utilities such as British Gas and the water and electricity companies. To attract *attention* advertisements are placed (especially on television) which may be less notable for their promise than for their bizarre attention-getting qualities. Having created awareness, *interest* is created by an invitation to receive information that has been especially prepared to convert curiosity into a readiness to consider a proposition that will follow. *Desire* is fostered by a combination of public relations activity surrounding the prospects for the launch and the likelihood of profit. *Action* is inspired by sending application forms or publishing them in the newspapers, but may be encouraged further by advertisements reminding the consumer of the closing date of the offer.

Such a neat example is rarely available in travel and tourism, but it is apparent that most advertisements in this field are traditionally limited to the first two criteria, possible using desire as a motivant. Sometimes the process is more simply described as 'to remind, to inform and to persuade'.

Expenditure

Inevitably the real problem is the amount of money available in an industry where margins are traditionally low, and where public relations activity is more common because of the ease with which interest can be created by journalists, resulting from the offer of free facilities to them.

Above and below the line

One of the most used phrases about advertising expenditure is 'above the line' or its corollary 'below the line'.

It is unlikely that costs will be limited to the actual spend in the newspapers or other media. When budgeting, it is normal for all costs directly attributable to the campaign to be referred to as 'above the line', whereas ancillary costs, e.g. in the example above, the costs of producing and mailing information on the company to be floated, are deemed to be 'below the line'.

Advertising agencies

Paying the piper

Just as the public are encouraged to use the services of a travel agent and are promised that it will cost no more than booking direct (with a few notable exceptions), advertisers are likely to use an advertising agent to create, design, prepare and place the campaign. One benefit is that an advertising agency will have access to statistical information from major market research programmes that are not readily or economically available to the advertiser.

Traditionally, the basis of employment has been the premise that whereas the customer would pay in full for each £100 of space in the press or on TV, the advertising agent will pay only £85. The advertising agent will, however, become the principal in the transaction and be expected to pay the media owner even if the eventual client defaults or becomes unable to pay. This margin actually establishes a 17.65 per cent mark-up on the spend by the advertising agent. It has become common practice for this margin also to be added to any other work that an agency commissions on behalf of a client, such as related point-of-sale displays, promotional videos, etc. Inevitably, all rules are made to be broken and dependent upon the size of the business transacted, individual deals may be done.

The principle applies just as much to small as large advertisers, and even a local travel agent may find that in return for placing a regular series of advertisements in a local newspaper via an advertising agent he or she will be able to have the layout and designs created professionally, instead of being set up in boring type in an uninspired fashion (compare the layouts illustrated in Figs. 9.1 and 9.2). Though fortunately becoming less common, the type of layout shown in Fig. 9.1 is referred to disparagingly as a 'tombstone' advertisement.

Fig. 9.2 Advertisement B: Example of imaginative layout

Fig. 9.1 Advertisement A: Example of unimaginative 'tombstone style' layout

Advertising effectiveness

Advertising in itself is a product and like any other product its effectiveness must be decided by a number of factors. Some of the most significant will be:

- the idea chosen and the medium in which it is to be promoted

- the number of people to whom it is promoted and the frequency of repetition
- competition from others at the time of the campaign
- the timing of the campaign in relation to the buying pattern

All too often those responsible for advertising budgets dry up in terms of creativity. Sometimes, in order to maintain annual appropriations, they will place the advertisements in a half-hearted way, lacking in original thought. If this is blamed upon lack of budget it is an excuse for waste, for a boring advertisement is sure to fail the first two criteria − attention and interest.

Sadly this is sometimes seen in the advertising of National Tourist Offices who, faced with inadequate budgets, try to satisfy too many interests and impress few. A series of slide photographs on TV, with an end caption of 'Surprising Germany', surprised no-one. Italy obtained its first appropriation in many years and instead of catching attention by promoting some unique aspect of the country, produced 'Italy Has Everything' advertisements − hardly believable or attention-getting.

In contrast, the Swedish Tourist Office were winners of the CIMTIG/TTG (Chartered Institute of Marketing Travel Industry Group/Travel Trade Gazette) awards in this category for a memorable advertisement on television in which a moose puppet told of Sweden's virtues in a sing-song voice that combined clear English and yet a sound of Sweden.

The CIMTIG/TTG awards scheme has for many years promoted better understanding of what makes for good advertising in the industry. TV, radio, newspaper, magazines and other media are included and awards are made to those responsible for the best creative work each year. Experts then comment about their good and bad points at the presentation ceremony.

Media choice

However good an advertisement may be intellectually, it would be wasted in a dark room and the medium, or media, chosen in which to display it will be a central point in making it work. Local travel agents' budgets may run to the use of local newspapers, local radio and possibly to local or regional publications. In considering what is best, they must weigh not only the price but also the advantages and disadvantages carefully.

Publications:
- how many copies are produced and distributed?
- of these, how many are distributed in the catchment area?
- is there any evidence of their being read by more than one person?
- are they wanted or unwanted, i.e. paid for, or free sheets?
- how frequently are they published and how long is their effective life?
- is the publication considered highbrow or lowbrow?
- is colour or spot colour available?
- what is the reproduction method and quality like?
- can the position of the advertisement be controlled?

TV or radio:
- how many listeners can one expect on average?
- is it possible to choose the days and times and relate them to a relevant programme?
- what proportion of the listeners/viewers live within the catchment area?
- are customers likely to be attracted from a wider area than would otherwise use your services?

Publications

For the advertiser on a larger scale there are many more opportunities and thus a wider choice of questions to be answered. The question of demographic segmentation will become much more important. The cost of reaching each thousand readers in itself may be less important than the likelihood of those readers being target clients, e.g. when advertising cruises it is not sufficient to assume that they are an expensive commodity and that sales are more likely to emanate through the columns of *The Times*. It could well be that *The Times'* readers would be more likely to purchase highbrow trips up the Nile to see the Temples of Abu Simbel than readers of the *Sun*.

Conversely, for a Mediterranean cruise there may well be more *Sun* readers per pound spent on advertisements who are able and willing to afford the trip than there are *Times* readers.

The International Publishing Corporation (IPC) have done considerable research into the pattern of purchasing holidays. They contend that the woman has a more than average effect upon holiday choice, thus they promote the value of advertising in their weekly and monthly women's magazines as a high priority for sellers of holidays. They also analyse readership profiles for each magazine in the group so that advertisers can choose the one that best fits the profile of targeted consumers.

Television and radio

That television is effective as a medium is obvious. Equally understood is the fact that it is extremely expensive and can be quickly forgotten. Because of the costs involved in screening, major advertisers employ the very best creative talents to devise, produce and test their schemes. All of this further increases the budget necessary if your advertisement is to rate alongside the excellence of others. Furthermore, having produced a superb advertisement, it would be foolish not to use it frequently, preferably at the peak times for your target audience.

As a medium, television is outside the range of all but the largest travel and tourism concerns. By contrast commercial radio is often much more local in its coverage and requires much less investment in production costs. Imagination is the key to effectiveness, as listeners are not limited to what they see on a screen. It is a particularly effective medium for tactical messages as production is rapid. Whereas television is generally limited to large concerns, radio can be used by local travel agencies and for regional promotions.

When budgets are large, the complexity of choice is much greater but fortunately a great deal of information and advice based upon research is available. A wise advertiser will use the expertise available in defining media requirements.

Frequency

Whatever the medium, and however good an advertisement may be, its effectiveness increases upon repetition, even if this sometimes seems to be *ad nauseum*. To spend a large amount of money on the creation of an excellent campaign and not to repeat it often is a waste. A really good campaign will be worth repeating year after year, subject only to amendment and up-dating.

Competition

As Chapter 2 makes clear, there are three marketing strategies that lead to commercial success, namely:

- low cost leadership – selling cheaper than your competitors
- differentiation – creating a high added value, a desire for your product in preference to that of your competitor
- focus – specialisation to a substantial degree that makes your product difficult to copy and unique

Competition from others makes it essential that your advertising campaign is robust and it is unlikely to be so unless it achieves one of these criteria.

A *price platform* is fragile, and low cost leadership is always vulnerable. To simply claim 'we're cheapest' is difficult to maintain when a price war results in each firm deliberately undercutting its main competitors. Eventually prices will drop to a level that is impossible to sustain and it is the nerve, or wealth, of each competitor which will determine who survives, rather than the merits of the product, or the management quality of the company. There is an inherent belief by the public that cheapness in itself leads to poor quality, and thus a disbelief in claims for quality allied to low price.

Differentiation is the path chosen by most brand leaders in any industry. The fact that cellulose tape became known as 'Sellotape' and that vacuum cleaners are referred to as 'Hoovers' is a great credit to the originators. Kellogg's Corn Flakes, Nescafé, Heinz Baked Beans and other top selling products never promote price, but the reputation that they have built up for product reliability. They exploit this with advertising that builds upon their standing. They become natural *first choice brands* against which all competitors are judged. This inherent quality is referred to as 'added value' and it can be increased by advertising. It is, however, a quality that does not come easily or quickly and which can be easily lost if production standards fall and consumer expectations are not realised.

This technique can be used by a local travel agent who concentrates on the experience of staff and their ability to advise more competently than competitors. On a larger scale, a memorable campaign by Thomson Holidays built their reputation for reliability by depicting their quality controllers as serious business men (typified by city suits and bowler hats). In both cases the advertisements are about the quality of service provided rather than about the product itself.

Focus is about specialisation. It might be concentration on a new product, or upon virtues that are unique to a company. It is much more difficult to quickly copy a campaign that is based upon a true marketing advantage that has been planned, such as 'All of our villas have private swimming pools', or 'We have trained baby patrollers at each of the hotels marked', or 'Every cabin has shower and toilet'. As explained elsewhere, assessment of unfulfilled customer needs is an integral part of a marketing plan and enables selling advantages to be established which are unique to the company concerned.

Timing of the campaign

If you had an unlimited budget, you might wish to advertise throughout the year. Inevitably, however, judgement has to be exercised about

when the most effective time will be. Tour operators traditionally published brochures well before Christmas for the next summer season and hoped that the expectancy amongst past customers plus a little help from public relations would carry them through to Christmas. Little money would be spent prior to Christmas as it would be unlikely to divert thought from Christmas goods anyway. As soon as the turkey was cut, advertising on TV and in weekend papers would deluge the potential customer.

'Tour operators traditionally published brochures well before Christmas . . .'

Unfortunately, booking patterns changed and whereas it was traditional for the majority to reserve places in January or February, many will now wait until a short period before departure to book. Advertising in the early period might help to reverse this trend with resultant cash flow and forecasting advantages, but it flies in the face of a marketing principle – that of giving the customers what they want, rather than what you want to sell them. It follows that persuading customers to commit themselves early needs a substantially larger budget and some extremely persuasive reasons.

Conversely, unsold holidays and travel facilities are a prime example of 'perishable goods' for they have no value whatsoever after departure. Anything paid for them must be better than nothing and the way in which late booking opportunities are promoted can greatly affect the fortunes of any company. If they become too attractive, however, then they will impact upon the willingness of others to pay the full price and commit themselves early. A very substantial part of the travel industry's advertising budget is now reserved for this 'tactical advertising', normally offering remaining holidays at knockdown prices.

Who advertises?

Another feature detected has been the tendency for advertising to be placed by substantial national travel agency chains in place of the tour operators. This undoubtedly reflects their changed bargaining power, as it relates to additional commission paid to them for achieving high growth. It is a normal feature of the retailer/supplier relationship that the efficient large scale seller of goods in the high street will be able to influence what is provided and to demand terms far beyond those available to the independent. Increasingly it can be expected that brand loyalty will become more the province of the retailer than the supplier and that advertising will play a significant role in this transfer of power.

Cost justification

One thing that is certain is that no business actually wants to advertise, to give a proportion of sales revenue to a media owner. Thus it will need to be convinced of the benefits to the business before taking space. If this is so then the corollary also applies, that the effects should be measured afterwards.

On a small scale this is difficult unless the product advertised is a specific one, for which sales would have been unlikely otherwise. Two examples of this in a travel agency context are shown in Figs. 9.3 and 9.4. Both advertisements demonstrate the importance of price in making offers, but neither are actually based on price alone.

The 'Early Bird Ski Savers' advertisement was placed in July, very early, and at a time when only enthusiasts normally book. In order to

Fig. 9.3 Advertisement C: Emphasising Price Benefit

Fig. 9.4 Advertisement D: Emphasising Price Benefit

obtain their first preferences they pay the highest prices. This travel agency had not transacted many ski sales previously. By making a clear discounted offer they managed to attract not only many skiers who had previously booked direct, but also a worthwhile number of group bookings for whom early booking was essential to obtain rooms together. The result was a measurable increase of 400 per cent over the bookings received for the whole of the previous year, up to the closing date. Such bookings, which would have been relatively simple to transact with first choices still generally available, gave a greater cash flow benefit and helped in achieving volume bonuses.

After building up expertise in negotiating air fares to Australasia for clients of the agency, it was decided to advertise outside their natural catchment area. The air fares used as 'lead-in' prices were attractive and resulted from negotiations with second-line carriers, but in addition a special '£50 Free Insurance' offer was made in respect of full tariff fares. Either way sales were predicted, and proved to be, substantial in net profit terms. By keeping a record of enquiries received from addresses outside the catchment area it was possible to relate the actual cost of advertisements and net benefit each week.

A common practice is for travel agents to obtain 50/50 support from tour operators and other principals, whereby they benefit from professionally produced advertisement layouts describing the particular company's wares, and into which they slot their own identity. This is said to extend the benefits of the national advertiser's campaign onto the agency by association. Sometimes it looks as if agents get a raw deal, as their proportion of the space is rarely more than 20 per cent. The benefits are invariably difficult to measure.

For a large scale advertiser, particularly if carrying out a brand identity campaign rather than one related to a specific product, the success can be judged in two ways. First, the results will show in the statistical analysis of bookings or enquiries received. Secondly, it can be tested by 'before' and 'after' market research of brand awareness, particularly as regards products or brochures that a potential customer would 'definitely consider' before making a purchase.

A quite remarkable example of cost justification is demonstrated by Hoseasons, a leading tour operator whose business is based upon pre-eminence in the letting of waterway craft on the Norfolk Broads and in other areas of the UK. Their range of products increased immensely during the '80s and they now market a wide range of self-catering accommodation as well as boats, both within the British Isles and in Europe. Hoseasons estimate that around two-thirds of their customers each year are either previous users of their services or contact them as a result of recommendations. In order to encourage this sector they follow them up with direct mail. This leaves around a third of their million plus customers whose bookings are derived as a result of advertising or PR activities.

Traditionally, advertisements for boats and self-catering in the UK have been in small spaces in a variety of newspapers and magazines, especially at weekends, in the *Radio Times* and *TV Times*, and in the publications of the English Tourist Board. With a multiplicity of media it is very difficult to guess at individual effectiveness and this could lead to the advertising budget getting totally out of control. It is thus central to their success that they can compare effectiveness of their advertisement spend, and this covers around 1000 insertions each year, ranging from small circulation specialist magazines to national publications and television advertising.

They do it by asking all enquirers to define which advertisement caused them to make contact. This information is logged, as is similar data requested on each booking form received. It is then possible not only to see what brings the most enquiries, but which advertisements result in the best conversions.

Thanks to a sophisticated computer system they are able to compare such aspects as:

- the publication chosen
- the style of the advertisement
- the date of publication
- the space cost
- the replies received
  – by telephone

– by post
– through other sources.

They are able to establish a cost per reply analysis which is extremely accurate and gives guidance to future policy making. It also enables them to test the success, not only of general advertising themes, but the more specific product-led or tactical messages too.

premises, or to select those areas which it is believed will be most productive. Unlike direct mail, it is not possible to personalise the message, but it can be a very effective way of seeking out the 90 per cent who probably do not use the services of the business. This has been widely used as a method of distributing discount vouchers which can only be redeemed through a given outlet. A particularly successful group

Fig. 9.5 A British Airways/Lunn Poly joint advertisement using a 'split image' to maximise impact: a CIMTIG award-winning advertisement
(Courtesy Lunn Poly)

Door-to-door distribution

If direct mail is the logical quality route for communication to selected customers and/or potential customers (see Chapter 12), door-to-door distribution is its much less expensive counterpart. Particularly for a local travel agent, it can be extremely effective to either cover all households within a given distance of the

used to produce their own annual newspaper, supported by advertising from principals, and then distributed this on a door-to-door basis throughout the catchment area of all its branches.

Posters

One aspect of advertising widely used in the travel business is that of posters. There are some remarkable successes such as the English Riviera posters of the 1986 and 1987 seasons which relied heavily on their artistic quality and were widely displayed in the London Underground stations, but generally posters are used more as POS (Point Of Sale) advertising within travel agencies. Good quality full colour printing on large sheets is expensive, and yet the majority rarely are displayed. Posters are probably at their most cost-effective when used as a medium to distribute display matter for a tactical theme to be used by agents and then discarded.

One of the greatest problems of posters as a medium for selling to the customer is that it is extremely difficult to measure success. It probably needs a very large scale campaign to have real impact. Used by travel agents occasionally within their own locality, on buses, railway stations, etc., the results have normally been poor.

Planning advertising

Few businesses are in a start-up situation and most will have previous practice and expenditure with which to compare when creating an advertising plan for the next season, year, or other period. Having established a current level of expenditure each element needs to be examined to ensure that it was justified, using the best information available. Whatever expenditure is then confirmed should be considered an inherent cost in the selling of that product, for too often advertising is seen merely as something to be taken out of available profit margins. In reality, advertising is as much a component of selling a holiday as is the brochure or airline ticket.

Against this background a view will undoubtedly be taken as to the adequacy of the overall spend, whether new products or services justify additional funds, and whether new policies need to be implemented. In respect of the forecast period a timetable will need to be considered, as will the target audience and thus the media to be incorporated. Some flexibility needs to be retained for unforeseen situations and tactical requirements, but an overall plan will be much more likely to achieve the objectives chosen than will *ad hoc* decisions taken throughout the year.

The following examples give an indication of how this might work in practice for a local travel agent:

Overall spend established at .75% of a £2.2m turnover=£16 500

The three main objectives are:

- maximising business from existing customers
  - method - by direct mail
  - budget £5000
- improving firm's reputation and profile
  - method - by weekly advertisement in local paid newspaper
  - budget 52×£100=£5200
- reaching all residents of the area
  - method - by monthly tactical advertisement in free sheet
  - budget 12×£400=£4800

Thus there is a figure of £1560 for contingencies to which may be added any funds promised by principals for joint promotions.

Once the budget is established then it is sensible to establish a plan which anticipates which products are to be featured at what times of the year and by which medium.

Questions, tasks and issues for discussion

1 Discuss present travel advertising for coach services and for British Rail. What are the objectives of each? How far are the advertisements competing for the same markets?

2 Prepare short notes on the Go-Right Travel ads which appear in this chapter. Suggest how you might change these to improve their appeal to customers.

3 Collect any examples of direct mail letters received by you, your friends or neighbours. Analyse their strengths and weaknesses in the light of comments made in this chapter.

4 Collect six travel advertisements, and prepare a report which:
   (a) identifies the objective of the message
   (b) suggests the market(s) at which the ads are aimed
   (c) evaluates the extent to which the ads achieve their objectives.

5 Which travel advertisements do members of your group recall seeing within the last six months on television? Analyse what it was about the ads that made them memorable.

Exercise

Assume you are Advertising Manager for a specialist tour operator which, *inter alia*, offers a series of short break and main fishing holiday packages in Britain. The holidays attract some 4000 anglers a year, at an average cost of £95 for the short break holidays (which account for 70% of all the packages) and £170 for the longer packages.

In the past, the company has used a rule of thumb which allowed 3% of the annual turnover to be spent on press advertisements.

Draw up a draft campaign for press advertising, indicating the media you will use, and the form the advertisements will take.

NB It will help to have access to a recent copy of BRAD (British Rate and Data) for up-to-date advertising costs in the different media.

10 The travel brochure

After studying this chapter, you should be able to:

- understand the importance of the travel brochure as a marketing tool
- recognise the regulatory and other constraints affecting brochure production
- identify design and print needs from the perspective of the consumer, the distributor and the printer
- understand the implications of brochure distribution

The role of the travel brochure

The travel brochure is probably the most important single item in the planning of tourism marketing. Whatever the product being promoted, it is likely that a brochure of some sort will be used. A hotel will need a prospectus; a resort area – a guide or directory; an airline – a timetable booklet, and the holiday company will undoubtedly use a brochure to offer its holidays.

The various travel brochures occupy subtly different roles and the importance placed upon them in each instance reflects the priority they occupy in the plans of the concern they promote. Because the role of the holiday company's brochure is the most significant, this chapter will devote itself mainly to that aspect.

It could be said that the very issuance of a travel brochure is the distinction between travel agents and tour operators. When ABTA defined the difference between members they decided that tour operators were

'those who advertise and offer holidays for sale'.

Legal requirements make it essential for anyone in a substantial way of business to describe what is offered in some detail. The practical realities of this call for a brochure to be produced.

The need for accuracy

Because it sets out the principal's promise there is an absolute need to ensure that the description is accurate. The Trade Descriptions Act (1968), the Unfair Contract Terms Act (1977) and other consumer legislation have changed the nature of the offence of giving inaccurate details. Formerly considered to be a minor misdemeanour, a civil matter which could give rise to claims for compensation, it is now classified as a criminal act which may also result in prosecution and punishment. No-one would justify knowingly issuing incorrect information but slovenly compilation itself has become a serious offence. Even the justification that one did not have knowledge of a change of circumstances is unacceptable as a defence.

The laws place enormous burdens upon the travel company, resort or promoter of any tourist facility. No longer can they rely upon the previous year's definition or tried and tested photographs in their library without checking that each and every fact is still correct. The tree that stands in front of a hotel may well have grown until it obscures the promised sea view from some of the rooms. Woe betide the tour operator who assumes that all similar rooms have such a view if the complainant's is now obscured.

One effect of these laws is to make literature less interesting, more coldly factual, and sadly, less helpful. Tour operators especially will avoid illustrative prose to describe a facility that may conceivably not be available or where different judgement is possible. Better say nothing than be pilloried is the dictum. To give one example, the facilities at a hotel that could help a disabled traveller will often be ignored rather than risk a possibility that they could be inadequate, e.g. 'wheelchair accessible' could well be true for the majority of wheelchairs, but what if the wheelchair is of a non-standard size?

Similarly, travel agents are now necessarily wary of keeping and/or handing out resort or country pamphlets, in case they have become out-of-date in some respect which could result in their being prosecuted for giving wrong information in connection with the transaction. Is your literature correct, honest and wholly truthful? – must be the acid test. This is not an unreasonable requirement but it does have drawbacks that were probably not envisaged when the legislation was drawn up.

Further regulatory requirements

ABTA has played a crucial role in regulating the sale of travel products in the UK. Tour operators and travel agents who are members of ABTA have agreed to abide by that organisation's Guidelines and Codes of Conduct, which offer clear directives, including those relating to information which must be contained in brochures.

However, at the time of writing, substantial changes are taking place, as a result of proposed legislation within the European Community, which will affect the extent to which ABTA will exercise control over the industry in the UK. Indeed, the changes may threaten the very existence of ABTA in its current form.

Following publication of the Package Holiday Directive issued by the European Commission in 1990, the UK Government published in July 1991 a Green Paper which makes clear that the licensing of tour operators will become a function of government agencies. The obligation to belong to ABTA in order to trade (the so-called 'Stabiliser' rule) will no longer be enforced. Regulations regarding a tour operator's relations with its clients will be tightened, and clauses excluding responsibility or stating that the operator acts only as an agent of the supplier abroad will no longer be valid. Additional care in the accuracy of brochure statements will have to be taken. How this new legislation will affect travel agencies is not yet clear. What can be certain, however, is that control over what agents, as well as tour operators, can say and do will be stricter than the already clear guidelines provided by ABTA.

All of this, of course, necessary as it is for the protection of the tourist, does little to help promote the idea of the holiday dream. Thus the brochure planner has to consider how to incorporate all necessary information in a clear and concise way, without detracting from the presentation of what is being sold. A modicum of legal training or, at least, access to legal advice will also benefit the planner.

Style and layout

Every company strives for its brochure to be distinctive and attractive. This publication is the only tangible evidence that the consumer has of the company's promises, unique benefits, financial and management strengths, and its style.

One might say that travel is a 'fashion industry' and that as fashions change it is necessary to restyle not only the product but also the description of it. Conversely the statutory and other requirements make it difficult to do so.

Logical progression has created a standard approach whereby most travel brochures now follow a pattern of three sections:

- introduction pages
- contents pages
- 'extro' or exit pages.

The introduction establishes the company's style, makes statements about policies and commercial practices, promotes unique selling points and 'bargain' offers and, hopefully (though not always) contains an index.

The contents pages are almost always arranged in sections defined by destination country. Most companies lead with their strongest destination but it is not unknown for the first to be a resort that they wish to emphasise for other reasons.

For touring holidays Cosmos established a winning formula of high quality colour reproduction: descriptive titles for each tour; simple masthead route maps; a day-by-day itinerary; plus three photographs, respectively featuring a place, a tourist attraction and people on holiday. Imitation is said to be the sincerest form of flattery and Cosmos's founder, George Jackman, recognised the many compliments paid to him.

Similarly for air holidays, winning ways have been developed and much copied. The large number of holidays sold as well as the wide variety of competition has led to many different styles. Undoubtedly the most successful has been Thomson's Summer Sun layout with larger photographs of hotels (the main distinctive feature of otherwise similar summer holidays) combined with rather less words but with price grids featuring a huge choice of flights, departure points, durations and dates. Simply to accommodate these grids on the page is an act of skill. Attempting to make the result understandable and still visually attractive requires abilities approaching genius.

The third section (jargon phrase 'extro', being the opposite of 'intro') contains details of booking conditions, extraneous information, insurance schemes and all the other 'small print' aspects required by law and by regulatory bodies. The booking form is normally on the back cover or one of the last pages but should not (according to the ABTA Code of Conduct) be printed on the back of booking conditions or other contractual information which the customer should keep.

Brochure covers

The design of the brochure cover is possibly the most important aspect in persuading the customer to consider any product. The choice of design is a difficult one for there are many possibilities, such as:

- a spectacularly attractive photograph of a typical destination

- an attractive holiday situation
- a markedly different cover from one's competitors
- a pictorial amalgam of the contents
- a statement of what is contained or of sales features.

Each policy has its supporters. Long-haul holiday brochures tend to feature a photograph of some idyllic faraway destination. Most Mediterranean holiday brochures favour the happy or glamorous beach scene. Many comprehensive larger brochures hedge their bets with an amalgam of pictures.

Two examples of different approaches were the original Wings brochure which ignored colour photography and for many years stood out on the racks as the blue and white striped brochure, with nothing other than the company logo to relieve the simplicity. In complete contrast was the Carousel brochure with a frenetic cartoon holiday scene.

In recent years bold statements about special offers and product features have dominated many designs. Cosmos, for example, dropped the pictorial representation altogether and devoted their cover to the offers, displayed in heavy, easily readable type.

Whatever design style is chosen it is wise to ensure that it is relevant to the contents, not merely attractive in itself. Many companies have made covers so appealing that customers have taken a copy even when they have had no intention of buying anything remotely like the contents.

One aspect of design that should never be forgotten is that brochure space in travel agencies is always limited. The result is that many are overlapped on the racks. Those that are identified or titled in a place that is easily covered will lose their impact.

Design and print

It is quite certain that a few brochures are still designed by amateurs, and they stand out like sore thumbs among the professional offerings. If these companies are successful it is despite their brochures, not because of them.

Designing a brochure is a highly skilled art needing an exact specification of the intentions, features and statutory provisions necessary. From these the designer can make a 'rough' for approval by the client. A professional design house will have modern technology available, including the ability to simulate photographs by computer.

The number of pages is important in itself. Multiples of four are inevitable for a folded sheet printed on both sides produces four 'pages'. According to the print run envisaged it may be possible to make substantial economies by utilising the maximum amount of space on each sheet or roll of paper. Rarely will cut sheets be used that equate to the eventual page size. It is probably that large sheets that incorporate 4, 8, 16, or more pages will be printed at one time, but with really large runs the relationship between several huge rolls of paper fed simultaneously

will need to be reflected in the pagination and the layout chosen.

The page size will relate not only to design considerations, but also to the method of printing chosen. Normally standard ISO (International Standards Organisation) paper sizes will result in the greatest economies in cutting paper. The system was introduced into Britain in the early 1970s and replaced earlier 'Imperial' sizes. Inevitably, some printers still have older equipment but ISO is now the dominant system.

The system has been developed to be practical and economical. The concept is based upon a square metre of paper arranged in such a way that paper is cut so that the relationship between the two sides remains constant when folded (try it out). Thus each 'A' size is exactly half of its next larger counterpart, from 'AO' which uses a square metre of paper down to A6, which is around the size of a postcard.

The fact that the *shape* is common to whatever 'A' size is chosen makes it much easier for design purposes, as reductions and increases in size can be scaled easily. For large scale posters and wall charts there is also a 'B' series of larger sizes.

Related to the standard paper sizes there are also standard envelope sizes. Generally the prefix 'C' is added to the paper size, e.g. C4 for paper size A4, or C5 if you fold the sheet of paper in half before insertion.

Virtually all brochures are now produced in 'A4 size (210 × 297mm) and, as a result, display areas are normally designed to fit this requirement too. Woe betide the holiday company that decides to produce a 'king size' brochure that will neither fit the brochure racks nor go into the envelopes that an agent has in stock. Even a few millimetres can make all the difference.

An interestingly different brochure was produced by Tjaereborg during their first few years in the UK. As they did not sell through agents they did not need to follow the established pattern. For printing reasons they chose the normal size but printed 'landscape' format rather than 'portrait', i.e. long side at the top. In 1985 they changed over to the conventional style and lost an aspect of originality. The reason was that they had reduced the thickness of paper to minimise postal charges (very important to a

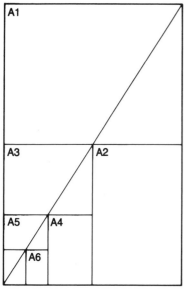

Size	Millimetres	Approx. inches
A0	841 × 1189	33⅛ × 46¾
A1	594 × 841	23⅜ × 33⅛
A2	420 × 594	16⅛ × 23⅜
A3	297 × 420	11¾ × 16⅛
A4	210 × 297	8¼ × 11¾
A5	148 × 210	5⅞ × 8¼
A6	105 × 148	4⅛ × 5⅞

Fig. 10.1 'A' series paper sizes

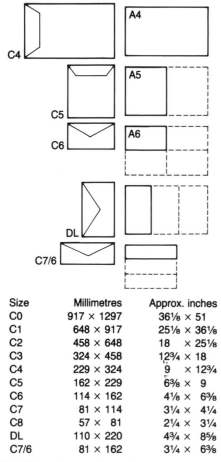

Size	Millimetres	Approx. inches
C0	917 × 1297	36⅛ × 51
C1	648 × 917	25⅛ × 36⅛
C2	458 × 648	18 × 25⅛
C3	324 × 458	12¾ × 18
C4	229 × 324	9 × 12¾
C5	162 × 229	6⅜ × 9
C6	114 × 162	4⅛ × 6⅜
C7	81 × 114	3¼ × 4¼
C8	57 × 81	2¼ × 3¼
DL	110 × 220	4¾ × 8⅝
C7/6	81 × 162	3¼ × 6⅜

Fig. 10.2 'C' series envelope sizes

direct sell company) and the pages flopped badly in the wide format.

The paper thickness and type is an important factor. If there are many pages you will wish to reduce the weight by using thinner paper. Often this will mean using a different heavier paper for the cover to prevent floppiness. If the brochure contains few pages, then extra weight will be less important and the 'feel' may be improved by using heavier than average paper.

Matt finish paper will give a certain style to a well designed publication, especially if full colour is not to be used. Art finished paper (shiny) is, however, essential if high quality colour reproduction is to be the aim. Within art paper, the heavier the weight, the better the reproduction is likely to be. High quality but lightweight art paper is a relatively recent

development and tends to be expensive.

When ordering your brochure it is, therefore, necessary not only to talk about the quality of the printing process but also about paper. It is a critical matter to see that the chosen printer not only has the capability you need but also access to adequate stocks of the correct paper at the exact time of your print run.

The printing process to be chosen will largely depend upon the number of copies to be printed and the colour requirement. There are almost as many processes as there are paper types but most modern ones are based upon photographically reproduced images and a lithographic or webb-offset printing machine. It is worthwhile getting to know the advantages and disadvantages of each method and some time spent at your printers will pay off in preventing difficulties caused by using an inappropriate specification.

When it comes to pictures there are some basic rules too. Photographs should be high in contrasts. Colour pictures should be taken on transparency film on as large a film format as possible (roll film 120 size preferred − 57mm square). The camera should have an excellent lens. If really necessary, 35mm photographs can be used but they should always be originals and not duplicates to ensure reasonable colour and detail.

When all has been put together you must decide upon whether a proof is to be provided or not. It is possible, but very expensive, to set up the exact process and produce a few samples. Normally black and white photocopies are made of the laid out type matter, possibly supplemented by colour prints made photographically.

Corrections should be made at an early stage: remember that printers only correct their own mistakes free. The type matter is first set up in the column format to be used and proofed as 'galley prints'. The corrections have to be made at this time, before incorporation into the page layouts. There is a British Standard (5261C:1976) regarding proof correction instructions, see Appendix 3. Any corrections to the copy, such as grammatical errors that are spotted after the original type has been set, are considered 'author's corrections' and are charged as a supplementary cost.

Segmentation of the market

The most important dichotomy which faces large holiday companies is whether to address different parts of the market with separate and different brochures and/or brands, or whether to include all in one massive authoritative publication.

If a company is known for its expertise in providing summer beach holidays, will it be regarded as expert or even competent if it decides to branch out into coach tours, or into city holidays or fly cruises?

There is no doubt that some customers like to deal with those that they feel are able to provide a personal, caring and expert service. Others may believe that financial strength simply brings better value and that buying from a larger concern is preferable.

The larger the brochure is, the more pages are irrelevant to the eventual purchaser and the greater is the cost of distribution. By contrast, several smaller brochures each covering merely a segment (perhaps defined by destination, but also possibly by holiday type, price or activity), will not reach so large a group of potential purchasers. Similarly if the company's offerings for a segment are not contained in the brochure picked up it might be assumed that they do not undertake the type of holiday required and the booking will be placed with a competitor.

In the end, costs dictate policy, and it is easy to see why. To quote a recent example, one major company produced no less than four million copies of their summer sun brochure, at a cost of 80p per copy, while their much smaller Lakes and Mountains brochure cost only 15p. Naturally the proportion of costs relating to design can be written off more easily on the longer run, but the special brochure undoubtedly paid off for this easily defined holiday type (see Fig. 10.3).

Different approaches inevitably develop as a response to the problem. Some companies put everything into one brochure. Others, such as Thomson Holidays, prefer to segment by holiday type. To give one example in detail of the range of brochures produced by a major operator, Fig. 10.4(a) lists the summer and winter brochures produced by the Owners Abroad

	Summer Sun (%)	Lakes & Mountains (%)
Design/artwork	12	30
Paper	48	35
Print	40	35
	100	100

Fig. 10.3 Comparative percentages of cost for summer brochures

Summer	Winter
Falcon Flights	Falcon Flights
Falcon Corsica	Falcon Far and Wide
Falcon Family	People Like Us
Falcon Summersun	Ski Falcon
Falcon Greece and Turkey	Martyn Holidays
Falcon Florida/Far and Wide	Sunward Holidays
Falcon Resorts	Falcon Resorts
Twenties Holidays	Sovereign Wintersun
Enterprise Summersun	Sovereign Cities
Enterprise Lakes & Mountains	Enterprise Wintersun
Enterprise Florida	Enterprise Ski
Enterprise Sol	Go Morocco
Sovereign Sunshine	Go Canaries
Sovereign Cities	Go Ski
Sovereign Golf	Ski Whizz
Go Greek	
Go Turkey	
Go Kenya	
Go Morocco	
Martyn Greece	
Martyn Madeira Year Book	
Martyn Canaries	
Martyn Algarve –	
Private Villas with Pools	
Martyn Portugal	
Sunward Holidays	
Just Turkey	
Villas Italia	
Falcon Sailing	
Small World	
Flairfares	

Fig. 10.4(a) Brochures produced by the Owners Abroad Group

group, Britain's second largest tour operating company.

There is no right or wrong way. What is important is that the marketing executive considers all the merits and demerits of each

All the holidays under the sun.

WITHIN OUR RANGE YOU'LL FIND THE HOLIDAY FOR EVERY DISAPPOINTED ILG CUSTOMER. WE HAVE THE BEST MATCH FOR DESTINATIONS, ACCOMMODATION, PRICES AND DATES.

ALL THE COMPARATIVE INFORMATION IS IN YOUR 'BIG BLUE BOOK'   OR CALL UP TOFS ON ISTEL 41#, FASTRAK FAL OR PRESTEL *TOFS#.

Fig. 10.4(b) Owners Abroad Group brochures 1991
(Courtesy Owners Abroad)

possibility and formulates a clearly understood policy.

Evolution problems

Increasingly there seems a 'sameness' about travel brochures. The brightest creative brains pour huge amounts of effort into trying to make a brochure distinctive and especially attractive. Yet they know that a new formula will be copied quickly if successful. Statutory requirements have to be satisfied; computer logic has to be obeyed (for the booking form at least), and cost justifications have to be considered.

Imagine a small operator creating an attractive Villa & Apartment brochure. He will be proud of the finest properties and will be tempted to give them most space and best photographic coverage. Initially this will pay off and bookings will 'overflow' to less exceptional properties when the first choice has been sold. Year by year

as the programme becomes more successful, the range of properties will expand. Similarly, and because of the increased number of customers, the number of brochures printed will also grow. Even with economies of scale the brochure cost per booking will inevitably rise. More importantly, the cost per page in the brochure will need to be related to the goods on sale there. However nice an individual villa may be, there will normally be only one. How much better, it might be said, for an apartment to be featured, particularly if it is one of many similar apartments, which are less expensive and easier to sell.

One major company with a programme of villas and apartments followed this road until they produced a brochure with a picture of a villa on the front cover and yet otherwise had only apartments inside. Their product lacked distinction and profits slid into oblivion.

Similar problems regularly occur when small allocations of rooms at popular hotels can no longer justify the cost of the brochure space and have to be replaced by less interesting but more substantial allocations in larger establishments. Owners of the hotels prefer not to be beholden to any one travel company and soon a variety of competitors are offering much the same holiday. Customers quickly spot price differences and the company taking the least profit sells out first.

There is also an implication that the company offers better value throughout its brochure. The customer who cannot obtain his first choice may prefer to change in the belief that, if more is to be paid, the 'cheaper company' will offer him greater satisfaction for the few pounds extra being demanded, whereas the 'more expensive company' is simply overcharging. In practice a sophisticated 'switch selling' technique may be taking place with the cheaper company having only a few rooms at the comparative hotel but many more at hotels that are not being shared.

Whatever pricing policy is followed, the highly competitive nature of the market means that prices are forced down to very low levels of profit. Thus tour operators are faced with a dichotomy. Either they take on huge commitments to fill hotels that they reserve for themselves and keep as exclusive offers (where they can control margins more easily), or they take small batches of rooms at a selection of hotels shared with others and face keen price competition.

As hotels have grown larger (over 1000 beds is not uncommon) the chance of exclusivity has receded. Unique advantages are more difficult to justify and price has become an ever more important factor in consumer choice. This places even greater emphasis upon the need for the brochure to create an individuality and character for the company and its products – no simple task.

Successful brochures

It is interesting to take a trip down memory lane and to examine the most successful brochures of each era. They were frequently those which anticipated the next change in consumer demand, but reduction in relative costs has always been a strong motivator in an elastic marketplace.

Early Horizon marketing stressed middle-class respectability when the inclusive holiday was rather an unknown quantity. The introduction within the brochure was by the much-respected Lord Douglas of Kirtleside (then retired Chairman of BEA, the European part of what is now British Airways).

Cosmos' coach tours anticipated the pent-up demand of 'average' Britons to be able to enjoy the sights of Europe at prices they could afford, in an age when foreign travel had been restricted to the rich or to those in uniform. The brochures featured exceptionally high quality colour photographs of tourist attractions at a time when printing was, generally, of a poor standard.

Universal Sky Tours made holidays by air financially accessible to many for the first time. They then improved the quality with such original features as reserved seats on their Britannia Aircraft. Their brochure covers were emblazoned with low prices and new features.

In Everyman Holidays, Sir Henry Lunn Ltd introduced segmentation by promising noticeably cheaper family holidays in parallel with their mainstream product. They stated categorically that the hotels were simpler and that the flights were at less convenient times, i.e. during the midweek period at night. For those that could accept these constraints, lower prices were available. Another area of potential sales was opened up.

Price alone has not been the only arbiter. Kuoni have established dominance in the long-haul market as it has progressively expanded. Swiss Travel Service have consistently offered a caring personal product to a high price country. Through specialisation and excellence both have recorded exceptional financial results. Their brochures have been designed to appeal to a more sophisticated clientele and prices are given much less emphasis.

For all the success stories, there have been failures too. Most were those who believed that yesterday's successful formula was adequate for tomorrow's market and who failed to recognise the fast-changing nature of demand. Even one year can produce a huge shift of consumer purchasing as compared with its predecessor. Brochures that do not reflect changing demands soon become tired and ineffective. When you realise that the brochure for next season normally goes to press before the current similar season has truly got under way, you can understand the need for a crystal ball in the office of the marketing manager and the brochure planner.

Getting the brochure to the prospective customer

Customers who seek information on an intended holiday have a variety of ways in which to obtain holiday brochures. If they know the company with which they are likely to travel they can contact them direct. If reacting to a television advertisement, a telephone number for a central response company will have been supplied. Most likely, however, customers will visit a travel agent.

In most travel agencies the brochure racks will be easily accessible and piled high with the offerings of competing companies. In some the display may reflect company policy regarding commission agreements (some tour operators may pay more), customer satisfaction or simply the manager's preference. It is likely that the prime positions, e.g. at eye level, close to the door, will also reflect the policy adopted.

Probably the sales staff will wish to discuss requirements and direct the customer to the most appropriate choice. In reality this rarely happens and the first arbiter of customer choice will be the attractiveness of the brochure and/or a recognition of the tour operator's name.

Selection can be extremely subjective. The cover picture may well set the scene for consideration of a brochure. Often it has little relevance to the contents. Sometimes a specialist company will make their brochure cover so attractive that they run out of brochures early. They may take few bookings because the contents are not what the customer actually sought or were relatively expensive when most choice was still available.

Timing of distribution is also important. Inevitably the first brochures tend to be published by the market leaders who feel strong enough to set the price levels for the coming season. They launch with a blaze of publicity and create a consumer demand for brochures, even if only for curiosity's sake. Smaller companies may be tempted to ride along on the crest of that wave. All too frequently they find that their brochure is picked up as a comparison though it is not relevant to the consumer's actual desires. One such company found that the result of coming out early was that their entire year's print order was distributed and 'lost' by October in respect of the following summer. A reprint and doubled distribution costs were incurred as a result.

Equally disastrous is to advertise heavily and not to have adequate stocks available. Consumers are notoriously fickle and, having got them to the travel agent to obtain a brochure, you may be assured that they will not leave empty handed when so much choice is available.

The booking process

When someone decides to take a holiday the normal first reaction is to seek additional information on the probable choice. Even now there is inadequate research available as to whether hotel, destination, holiday company or simply price is the prime criterion in the progression from initial thoughts to actual commitment.

The first decisions will probably be:

- whether or not to go abroad
- whether or not to travel independently.

Consciously or unconsciously they will also include:

- whether or not to fly.

In the case of independent overseas travel the information requirement may be for car ferry or airline information. The literature for these companies might be considered merely as a means of disseminating factual information and the brochure requirement thought to be for concise details of timetables and fares only. A closer look at the realities shows that this is not so.

Car ferry companies are in fierce competition for customers. Their brochures clearly show this: they set out not just the facts but the competitive advantages of each shipping line. They give details of a wide variety of incentives to travel at unpopular times designed to reduce the peaking of demand and to mop up under used capacity in off season.

Similarly, the airlines no longer enjoy monopolies on most routes. The element of competition makes it increasingly important that they also promote their competitive plus points. Full colour A4 brochures are often issued by airlines.

If the brochure is important to carriers it is *essential* to tour operators. One only has to look on the shelves of a travel agency to appreciate how vast is the selection of holidays, all competing for the consumer's attention.

Brochures in a video age?

The first purpose of a travel brochure is to describe a facility being offered. How much better can that be done with movement and greater use of pictures? The video now presents both new challenges and opportunities to travel companies.

Travel companies have commissioned a variety of video cassette programmes that give in-depth information about particular holiday areas or types. Some travel agencies have established libraries of such cassettes that can either be used in the travel shop or taken home on loan so that the whole family can see them.

Unlike the brochure, it is possible to update the cassette and to re-issue it at any time in the season.

Whether potential customers are really interested in going to an agent to see 'more television' is a question that will be answered only by time and experience. There is a widely-held view that people use travel agents mainly to obtain opinion and helpful advice to verify their prior decision. If this is the main role it is doubtful how much they will be interested in video, however skilfully presented. Perhaps an even more interesting development is just around the corner. It is said that one videodisk could contain photographic images of every hotel on offer in every ABTA tour operator's programme for a complete season.

With a growing tendency towards independence and later bookings one can see a diminishing role for brochures that attempt to predict customer desires so long in advance. The combination of a database that contains all the flights currently available, and another with accommodation availability would present the agent with the capability of mixing and matching the facilities required by a customer. Having achieved the best possible combination, the result could be displayed on a screen for the customer along with a picture of the hotel. The customer could then be given an appropriate printout of the information relevant to their individual booking only, together with any amendments that have occurred and a print of the photograph of the hotel.

Such a development is not far away in terms of computer capability. If it catches on, the days of the travel brochure as a means of selling inclusive holidays are numbered.

Questions, tasks and issues for discussion

1 Are brochures issued by the mass market tour operators designed to maximise clarity of understanding about the products and their prices? Examine three major brochures and identify factors which support your view.

2 'A genuinely consumer orientated brochure would tell the truth about destinations, warts and all'.
Discuss this point of view in small groups, looking at both sides of the question.

3 Working in groups, prepare a rough draft of artwork for the design of the cover of a package holiday brochure for a company whose aims are:
   (a) to communicate the brand name effectively, and
   (b) to stand out against other brochures in an agency rack

4 Are the legal or quasi-legal regulations governing the content of brochures adequate for consumer protection, or should they be tightened up? Take the role of an OFT officer whose task is to consider this question, and prepare a short report identifying any area where you think controls are currently inadequate.

Exercise

Select two current package holiday brochures which are directed at separate markets, and evaluate their success in terms of the issues discussed in this chapter.

At what market are they aimed? How successfully do they fulfil their objectives? What theme and image do they convey, and how do they communicate this? Consider issues of style, layout, clarity of booking conditions, quality of paper, etc.

11 Sales promotion for travel and tourism

After studying this chapter, you should be able to:

- distinguish between different sales promotion activities
- understand their use to achieve differing objectives
- be aware of the stages in campaign planning for promotions
- understand how to evaluate the effectiveness of campaigns
- appreciate the role of exhibitions, workshops and presentations in the travel industry

The nature of sales promotion

As we have explained in Chapter 9, advertising is technically referred to as 'above the line' promotion, and all other forms of promotion are therefore deemed to be 'below the line'. However, the division between the two is not always clear cut. Window display, for example, is one of the *merchandising techniques*, that is to say, techniques designed to promote products at the point of sale (POS). Although it could be argued that travel agencies' windows are used to advertise products such as current bargain offers for flights and holidays, window display is still generally treated as a form of below the line promotion.

Most members of the travel industry are familiar with advertising and its uses, but are less confident in the use of sales promotion techniques. This is unfortunate, since there are so many forms of sales promotion which can be undertaken, limited only by the imagination of the marketing staff. However, they must be used with caution, since not all sales promotion is suitable for all forms of product.

Sales promotion activities are *attention getters*, since their objective is to achieve immediate sales impact. However, if this is achieved through money-off or bargain offers, this can have the effect of demeaning the inherent value of the product, suggesting that the seller is anxious to unload his products. Ronnie Corbett's joke that he remembered an event because it was the week Allied Carpets were not having a sale carried an important message for the marketer: that too much emphasis on 'deals' will degrade the product in the consumers' eyes and at the same time undermine profit levels.

When planning promotional strategies, it is best to think of sales promotion as complementary to advertising. In very few instances is it appropriate to use one or other of the communications techniques alone in the marketing plan, even though they may serve different objectives. Each has its place in the overall plan. Often, advertising is seen as the main tool to achieve long-term objectives, such as building the corporate image of the organisation and its products, while sales promotion is used to achieve short-term objectives such as clearing current stock. In fact, making such a clear differentiation is too simple. A travel agent's window display can be used to build a long-term image of the company as much as to sell current products. What is important is that the sales promotion and advertising objectives do not conflict, but rather reinforce one another. If, for instance, the advertising objectives aim to create an image of quality and service for the company, this can be undermined by sales promotion objectives focusing on price bargains.

As sales promotion is designed to appeal particularly to those customers who are price-sensitive, such techniques tend to attract buyers who have little brand loyalty. It follows therefore, that in those areas of travel where brand loyalty is a feature, such as certain cruise markets and holiday centre operators, sales promotion will be a useful tool if it is aimed at present clientele to attract more business from the existing market instead of trying to encourage brand switching from other companies. In other industries such as FMCGs (Fast Moving Consumer Goods) there are powerful sales promotion techniques to encourage brand switching, such as free samples to attract trial. With travel there is less opportunity for such techniques (although it should be noted that efforts to sell timeshare apartments in Spain have been accompanied by free trips by air to see the accommodation). We must remember, though, that with less expensive products, in travel as in other businesses, sales promotion using bargain offers can gain many uncommitted consumers. Entrance tickets to theme parks, museums and similar tourist attractions, all make extensive use of vouchers to increase their 'gate'.

While it would be true to say that part of today's emphasis on sales promotion in the marketing plan arises from over-use of advertising as a communications tool in the past, another factor is the increased competition in the travel industry, which has caused marketing managers to consider more carefully the use of all methods of communication available to them. Co-operative merchandising in particular, between agents and principals, has been extensively used to increase sales and to generate more agency commission. It also has the attraction of being easily understood and measured in its effectiveness, since it aims for an immediate boost to turnover, while not all advertising is so easily assessed.

The techniques of sales promotion

Before we examine how the techniques are employed, it will be helpful to identify the various tools in the sales promotion 'armoury'. These can be categorised as techniques aimed at the *consumer*, those directed at *retailers or dealers*, and those aimed at *the company's own staff*, such as sales representatives or counter sales staff. The list that follows is not intended to be exhaustive (there are many hundreds of techniques which can be used), but it will cover those more commonly used and which are appropriate for application in the travel and tourism industry.

1 Directed at a company's staff:

- incentives (financial, travel, etc.)
- bonuses
- contests and competitions.

2 Directed at dealers/retailers:

- 'give-aways' (pens, ashtrays, calendars, diaries, etc. usually bearing the principal's name)
- contests
- trade exhibitions
- product/brochure launches (presentations, buffets, etc.)
- direct mail (letters, circulars, etc.)
- joint promotion schemes (financial, organisational help).

3 Directed at consumers (either through retailers or direct):

- point of sale (POS) material (window display, wall display, posters, counter cards, brochure racks, etc.)
- sales literature
- direct mail
- free samples
- 'give-aways' (e.g. flight bags) and 'self-liquidating offers' (products promoting the company's name, and sold at cost price by the company)
- competitions
- low interest financing
- money-off vouchers
- purchase privilege plans (e.g. 'twofers' – whereby two are charged the price of one for entrance)
- joint promotions with non-travel companies (e.g. cheap weekends in London through the collection of washing powder vouchers).

Fig. 11.1(a) Effective 'reminder' promotion: Jersey Tourism's crocus promotion (Courtesy Jersey Tourism)

Fig. 11.1(b) The crocuses bloom on the agent's desk; a constant reminder of the product they promote.

It will be appreciated from a glance at this list that the scope for new ideas in sales promotion is almost unlimited. Travel companies offer a huge range of give-aways to their clients, including flight bags, carrier bags, wallets for tickets and foreign exchange, and passport covers. Hotels offer a steadily increasing range of useful facilities to their guests, including shoeshine cloths, 'first aid' sewing kits, shower caps and shampoo. Additionally, VIP clients might receive fruit or flowers in their room.

While most of these promotional tools are designed to do no more than create goodwill among clients and provide a sense of 'added value' to the product, they will often also have an underlying purpose; that of ensuring the company or its products are remembered. Therefore the most successful give-aways to be presented to the travel agent are those which will

be considered attractive or useful enough to be put on display in the office. Ashtrays, paperweights and calendars serve this purpose very well. Lists of useful telephone numbers which an agent might want to keep in sight next to his desk will ensure that the principal's name is kept prominently displayed throughout the year, and aid recall. From this we can see that such sales promotion aids serve similar purposes to advertising – they can be used to remind, to inform and to persuade (customers to buy and retailers to sell).

Where the product is sold through retailers, the marketing manager can adopt one of two courses of action. One method is to aim the promotion at the consumer directly, in order to build brand awareness and create a demand which will pull people into the shops to buy the product. For this reason, the technique is known as 'pull strategy', with the customer pulled into the shop by the effects of the promotion. In effect, the client is pre-sold. Retailers will be persuaded to stock the product through the level of demand they experience. Alternatively, sales promotion is geared to *merchandising* activities, which are designed to persuade the retailer to stock the product and help him to sell it. This is termed 'push strategy', with promotion aimed to attract customer sales at the point of sale.

A new tour operator seeking to develop a market will be unlikely to be able to afford the national advertising which a pull strategy would call for, but could succesfully develop a push strategy by selecting key retailers and helping them, through 50/50 joint promotional expenditure, to sell to their customers.

Co-operative promotions with non-travel companies are proving a popular way of reaching the travel public. Travel can be offered as an incentive to purchase other goods or services, or consumer durables can be offered to those booking holidays. Specially priced package tours have been offered as an incentive to purchase FMCGs, while British Rail teamed up with Boots to provide free rail travel against purchases in the store. Hoteliers have promoted short break holidays in this way, while other examples of successful joint promotions include cross-channel ferry companies and manufacturers of alcoholic drinks. Vouchers, redeemable for travel arrangements, have been successfully used as staff incentives in many large companies, particularly as rewards for the achievement of sales targets. Travel has been found to be a greater incentive than straight financial compensation in motivating staff.

Most retail promotion activities have tended in recent years to focus on price appeal. Thomas Cook, for instance, offered three forms of sales promotion based on price, and one more novel technique:

- a 'price promise' in which Cooks agreed to match the price of any holidays they sold which could be purchased more cheaply elsewhere
- a 'trading charter', with a money-back guarantee to their clients who purchased the

products of any tour operator which failed
- a formal guarantee to match the customers' need with a particular holiday
- a 'business travel challenge' in which companies could submit to Cooks details of their expenditure on staff business travel booked through other agents over a three month period. Cooks would then estimate what savings could have been achieved had the bookings been made through them.

Planning the sales promotion

As with any marketing activity, the establishment of a promotional campaign requires careful advance planning. The stages by which such planning is undertaken is shown in Fig. 11.2.

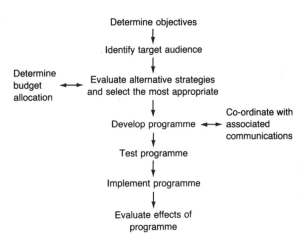

Fig. 11.2 Stages in the organisation of a sales promotion campaign

Once again we need to be clear what our objectives are before we prepare the programme. It is not sufficient to define these in the broadest terms, such as 'increase our winter sports programme sales by 10 per cent'. We must also indicate whether our objective is to attract new buyers or to increase sales to present buyers, since different promotions will be called for in each case.

The target audience will be either our own sales force, our retail agents, or the consumers themselves, depending on whether a push or pull strategy is determined upon. It may be appropriate to aim at more than one of these audiences in the promotional plan.

Before considering what methods to use to influence the market, the company should be in possession of as many facts as possible which might affect the decision. Obviously, the question of the product itself, its nature and quality must be considered. If the image of the product has always been one of quality, what form should the promotion take that will not demean it in the eyes of the target audience? A promotion undertaken jointly with a company that markets a well-established premium product (executive car, up-market alcoholic drink) will enhance the image of the travel company. However, all companies like to believe that theirs is a quality product. It is important that the company first identifies through research what image the firm actually enjoys.

Strategically, it can be useful to take into account the forms of sales promotion which the firm's competitors employ. It may be thought desirable to compete head-on with a competitor by emulating the methods they have used to attract new business, while in other cases it might be better to distance the product from its competitors by deliberately introducing a very different form of promotional strategy.

Strategies will vary according to both the nature of the product and the stage in the product life cycle (PLC). At the launch stage, it will be the intention to build awareness of the new product, and this is best achieved in the case of travel by focusing on advertising and public relations activities, supported by a smaller proportion of the budget spent on sales promotion. This could entail direct mailings to key addresses, or incentives to retailers. On the other hand, a new museum may have different artefacts on display, but to many potential visitors it may be seen as just another museum, and it will be competing for business from local holidaymakers with all other museums and attractions in the area. While local advertising is used to draw attention to the product, co-operative voucher schemes may be introduced to provide discounts for entry to two or more attractions.

As markets for products become saturated in later stages of the PLC, promotional stimuli may have to be increased to draw second or third time visitors, pending product innovation. The use of 'twofer' tickets to increase sales in theatres towards the end of a show's life cycle is an example of promotion used to boost sales.

As with all forms of communication, decisions on the selection of techniques will be based on which combination of these can be best expected to achieve the desired objectives in the most cost-effective manner. If a money-off deal is being considered for a tourist attraction, marketing staff must decide how many of these discounted tickets are to be offered, to whom, and at what reduction in normal price. Means must be sought of ensuring that those willing to pay full price will not be seduced into paying lower entry prices, and the total cost of the programme and increase in revenue expected must be estimated. The programme cost will be not just the loss in normal entrance price, but also the cost of communicating the offer to the public. Against this, one must weigh the benefits of increased entry numbers, and probable increased spend on facilities at the attraction. The final figure must then be compared with other promotional techniques under consideration, to judge the best package.

In setting up the programme, a decision must be taken on when to start the campaign, how long it is to last, and exactly how it is to be delivered. There must be sufficient 'lead time', i.e. time available to introduce the programme, which in some forms of promotion (such as co-operative ventures involving on-pack coupons in consumer goods) can take months of planning. If the duration of the campaign is too short, there may not be time for it to become effective, while if it is allowed to run for too long, it not only loses its impact, but may affect the company's image and annual profitability.

The promotion is developed in the context of the overall promotional mix, so that the time scale and activities tie in with any other communications activities. A major promotional campaign may include advertising support, sales calls by sales representatives, and publicity (an innovative campaign could, for example, get coverage in the trade press, or even in the local press).

Fig. 11.3 Sales promotions involving special offers (a & b: Courtesy Thomas Cook; c: courtesy AT Mays the Travel Agents)

If the campaign is to operate on a large scale and involve substantial investment, it is wise to test its effectiveness in advance, wherever that is possible. Market research can be used to question a cross-section of a potential market on sensitivity towards different prices for a product, or the degree of preference between money-off offers and other forms of promotion. The following could represent the line of questioning to be employed:

A 'How willing would you be to purchase a ticket to this attraction at a price of £3.50?'

very willing ☐
quite willing ☐
uncertain ☐
unlikely ☐
very unlikely ☐

B 'If this ticket were to be made available at a discount, how likely would you be to buy it at a price of . . .

	£3.00?	£2.75?	£2.50?
very likely	☐	☐	☐
quite likely	☐	☐	☐
uncertain	☐	☐	☐
quite unlikely	☐	☐	☐
very unlikely	☐	☐	☐

C 'If you were planning to visit this attraction, with a regular entrance price of £3.50, would you rather have the offer of:
(a) a discount of £1.50, or
(b) a second ticket free, to use either for yourself for a return visit, or for a friend or relative to accompany you?'

discount ☐
second ticket free ☐
both equally suitable ☐
don't know ☐

An alternative to this form of research is to conduct an experiment with different forms of sales promotion for a limited time, to judge which is most effective. A direct mailing, circulation of brochures to local hotels with money-off vouchers, and an advertisement in a local paper carrying a money-off coupon could each be judged for effectiveness over a given period of time, prior to a full-scale launch. One must take care, however, that other factors do not account

for any change experienced in turnover. Where possible, these activities, in 'experimental areas' are compared with the results in 'control areas', regions where no campaigns have been mounted, since sales increases may be the result of factors other than the promotion itself. If the increase in turnover is proportionate in all regions, the effect of the campaign itself is likely to have been minimal.

Evaluating the impact of promotion

There are a number of ways in which the effectiveness of the company's sales promotion efforts can be judged. It is, of course, relatively simple to measure the effectiveness of money-off offers where these are given against vouchers or coupons clipped from advertisements, returned from direct mail shots or redeemed following any other form of distribution. Equally, competitions for consumers or for retailers can be judged from the numbers of entries they attract. Most sales promotions of this kind are designed to generate immediate sales and are judged in those terms. A comparison is then made between the level of sales achieved before the promotion and after it. However, the objective may have been to 'clear current stock' (i.e. to sell off unsold holidays) which may not increase the overall level of sales. Reduced price offers may simply encourage early booking by clients who would have been prepared to pay normal prices later in the year, rather than attracting new customers who would not otherwise have booked a holiday. If the intention was to clear unsold stock in this way, all well and good; but if this unwittingly leads to a slump in later sales and overall reduction in turnover, the campaign can hardly be deemed to have been successful. This can be illustrated in Fig. 11.4.

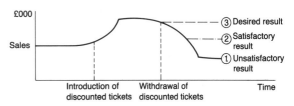

Fig. 11.4 Sales resulting from a sales promotion campaign at a tourist attraction

A return to sales at level 2 following the promotion will be satisfactory, since the promotion will have had the effect of increasing sales during the period of the campaign without subsequent losses. But the company may have aimed to attract a larger market through increased awareness, with resulting sales at level 1. If the actual result is a fall to level 3 for the balance of the season, the campaign's objectives will not have been realised.

However, a sales promotion should not be judged only in terms of its success at generating sales in the short term, and its success in achieving other objectives should be likewise measured.

Let's take the example of a travel agency window display – an area of unrealised potential for many agents. If it is designed to bring people into the shop to purchase a holiday, a simple count of enquiries and bookings resulting from the products on display is easy to keep. But a window is also designed to attract passers-by to notice and remember the agency and what it sells. It is rarely tested for its effectiveness in achieving this, however. An hour spent observing passers-by and their behaviour in front of the window can be illuminating. How many of those passing glance at the window? How many actually stop to take in the contents? What are they actually looking at in the window – bargain offers or special displays for long-haul travel?

Surveys can be carried out locally, before and after campaigns, to measure increases in awareness of the agency, or changes in the company's perceived image. In the same way, visitors to a tourist attraction can be questioned on leaving, so that patterns of purchase behaviour can be compared between those who took advantage of a promotional offer and those who didn't.

Unfortunately, it has to be accepted that not all promotions lend themselves to easy means of measurement. Dealer or consumer 'give-aways' are designed to build long-term goodwill and recognition, and their impact is much harder to assess. Finally, it should be borne in mind that the best way to evaluate any tactic is to see how it compares with other sales promotion tactics in

its effects. A business must experiment over time with different forms of promotion and learn to judge which seems to work most effectively. Any one technique employed continuously, however, will pall, and a variation in the tactics employed is likely to have greatest impact.

At this point, we will deal with some of the more common methods of sales promotion in use in the travel industry.

Exhibitions

Exhibitions play an important role in the travel industry, providing opportunities for buyers and sellers of travel products to meet and do business. Some, like the World Travel Market (WTM) in London, and the International Tourism Exchange in Berlin, have become of international significance.

Three types of exhibition can be identified:

1 Those aimed at the public.
2 Those aimed at the trade.
3 Those which are private and to which entrance is gained by invitation only.

Events such as the WTM, which is only open to the trade, feature prominently in the travel trade calendar, and their function is as much social as commercial, giving members of the industry an opportunity to see and be seen. Few major companies can afford not to be represented at the show, which covers all sectors of the trade: incoming, domestic and outbound tourism. Retail agents have the chance to enhance their product knowledge, while it provides national and local tourist offices with a rare opportunity to publicly demonstrate their product, the country or region they represent, through the medium of film, wine tasting, national costume, ethnic dancing and other associated forms of entertainment. The importance of the show will also ensure that it receives a good press coverage. However, it is undoubtedly the opportunities for personal contact that the trade welcomes most. Often, trade symposia or meetings will be organised to discuss current topics of interest, running concurrently with the exhibition, to take advantage of the presence of so many key figures in the trade.

Against these benefits, it has to be said that exhibitions are costly to stage, and to participate in. In addition to rental costs based on square footage occupied by stands, there are set-up costs for equipment, hospitality and literature costs, and other incidentals to be considered. The competition for status among larger companies means renting larger stands than are strictly needed, and at the most prominent sites, for which premium prices can be commanded by the organisers. Sales staff are tied up while participating in the show, and other marketing staff must be employed in planning and organising the event (a major show can involve year-round planning.) In spite of all the planning, attendance figures can disappoint at many unproven travel exhibitions, while even with a good attendance it is not always easy to measure benefits against costs. For this reason, participants may well treat the event as a public relations exercise rather than a sales promotion.

However, the marketing objective is to make any such ventures as cost-effective as possible. Every attempt should be made to weigh up the cost of reaching and influencing consumers through the medium of the exhibition compared with other means. Participants should obtain in advance an analysis of attendance figures for previous years or audience survey data if published. New exhibitions may only be able to provide calculated guesswork about attendance expectation, which is often wildly optimistic. Some estimate should also be made about the proportion of the audience likely to be interested in visiting a particular stand (something approaching 40 per cent is the Audience Interest Factor for national exhibitions) and an estimate can be made of the cost of reaching that market compared with attempts to communicate with them through other means.

An average salesperson can deal with 12–15 enquiries in an hour, on average, and each salesperson will need about 50 sq ft to accommodate visitors. An estimate of the size of the stand can then be made based on the number of sales staff required to answer enquiries and the space required for display material. This does provide a rule of thumb for the space to be rented, although taking no account of the demands for 'space status' for individual companies. A small cubicle for dealing privately with important visitors to the stand is also recommended.

Some preliminary planning can help to ensure a successful exhibition stand. It is not sufficient merely to staff the stand. Those working on the stand should be well versed in the firm's products, well trained in sales techniques and equally at home dealing with clients and with trade enquiries. Good clients of the company could be sent advance tickets and a map of the exhibition and stand. Adequate supplies of literature should be available, but some control should be exercised over their distribution to ensure brochures are taken by people with a genuine interest in the product rather than children with an avid interest in collecting anything on display! All visitors to the stand should be welcomed, and an attempt made to explore their interests. Potential sales leads should be recorded on stand cards or in a visitors' book, for subsequent follow-up. One must never lose sight of the principal purpose of the exhibition, which is to sell travel.

The travel workshop

One other type of exhibition deserves separate mention here, due to its importance in the travel industry. The travel workshop is strictly speaking not so much an exhibition as a forum for trade buyers and sellers of travel products to come together and negotiate business. British travel workshops are often organised under the sponsorship of the National Tourist Boards, with venues in the UK and overseas, in centres wherever there are sufficient numbers of prospective tourists to Britain. Typical sites for BTA workshops would include New York, Chicago, Los Angeles, Sydney and Frankfurt. Some workshops have particular themes such as coaching holidays, or a regional emphasis, such as tourism in South West England. Suppliers with an interest in incoming tourists, such as hoteliers, coach companies and ground handling agents, arrange to rent desk space in the workshop, which normally runs for between one and three days. Tour operators and others from the tourist generating countries can in this way conveniently meet their suppliers of tourism services under one roof (often without having to travel far from their own home ground) and can negotiate with them for the following season's tour programme requirements – beds, transfer services, excursion programmes etc. This is one of the most cost-effective means of organising the production of package tours.

Making presentations

The dictionary defines a presentation as an 'act of introducing or bringing to notice'. The presentation is widely used in the travel industry to introduce a company's programme to retail travel agents, although these in turn can run their own presentations for clients, to bring a particular range of holidays to the public's notice. The major tour operators generally organise presentations to agents throughout the country when launching their new programme of holidays for the year.

This will typically take the form of a reception, perhaps a buffet meal, and a formal talk about the new programme or product, given by senior members of the sales force. The approach is typically low key, since it is aimed at young agency counter staff, and the emphasis is on personal contact and a 'fun evening', although it also provides an excellent opportunity for sales staff of the principal to meet agency counter staff at first hand and obtain feedback about the market.

Effective presentations call for good visual promotion: flip charts, overhead projectors or other forms of instructional aids should be used to accompany the formal talk, and it is customary to demonstrate the product with videos, a tape-slide presentation or film. The largest principals mount highly impressive shows, usually in up to half a dozen different centres around the UK, using a tape-slide dissolve unit (or multi-dissolve unit), stereo sound, stroboscopic lights or even laser beams. This can mean a promotional budget running into thousands of pounds.

Planning and organisation

If a presentation is being made to potential consumers, the aim will be both to generate direct bookings and to build goodwill among the clientele, or potential clientele, of the company. It is therefore well worth taking a little effort with the planning and organisation of the event, to maximise the prospects of its success.

First, the venue and date for the presentation must be carefully chosen. Even with the best intentions and with good decorative effects, the local hall can be a depressing venue for such an event, and can depress the image of the company. Better a conference room at a good quality hotel or at a purpose-built conference centre, which will be comfortable, well decorated and geared to meet the company's requirements. Arrangements for booking these facilities have to be made well in advance to ensure their availability. The company should also make sure there are adequate parking facilities and good public transport to the venue.

'Dates should avoid any clashes'

An evening meeting will attract more people than a daytime event, especially if the aim is to attract working people to a public presentation. Couples usually consult each other in the arrangement of holiday bookings, so the sale must be made to both partners. Wherever possible, dates should avoid any clashes with local or national events. For example, a presentation designed to attract the public would be unlikely to have succeeded if it had been scheduled to occur at the time the England vs Germany 1990 World Cup was being broadcast.

Entry should always be by ticket invitation, to control numbers (this is vital where food and drink have been laid on) and tickets should be checked at the door. Announcements of the event can be made through a direct mailing to clients, and an invitation to the local paper to others to apply for tickets (with the possible chance of arranging some editorial coverage in the paper alongside your advertisement).

If drinks are to be served, it is sensible to provide not more than one glass before the formal talk – you want your audience to be receptive to the sales talk!

Where a film evening is arranged, it is advisable to run not more than two films, and total running time should not exceed about 20 minutes; the span of attention of many audiences is limited, however good the film! Whoever is responsible for giving the presentation should ensure that they have seen the film in advance, and that the right one has been delivered. All mechanical and electrical equipment should be in good working order, but it still makes good sense to carry spare parts that might be useful – adaptor plugs, new bulbs for overhead projectors, etc. – especially if there is any doubt about the reliability of the venue itself to cater for emergencies. Arrangements must be agreed in advance for lighting controls, with someone present to help dim lights for films, OHPs, etc.

Presenter and staff should be at the venue well in advance of the start, to allow ample time to check on, or arrange for, directional signs, and to ensure the room is decorated with appropriate travel material. A 'publicity pack' of travel material should be placed on each seat in the auditorium. Adequate cloakroom and toilet facilities must be available near to the auditorium, and clearly signposted.

All members of staff present should have name badges, large anough to read, with first name *and surname* (a customer may want to write to you one day!) When guests arrive, they should be greeted by a member of staff and given a drink to help 'break the ice'; background music can also be useful as an ice-breaker when people arrive and mingle, especially in a large gathering.

Where the objective is to encourage sales, the company should make it as easy as possible to make a booking. Sales desks can be available and staffed after the presentation to deal with further enquiries. Prepaid reply cards can be inserted in the publicity packs for more information.

Above all, one should exploit whatever opportunities arise for publicity associated with the event. Photographs can be taken during the evening, and sent to the local or trade press with a covering press release, which may gain a few valuable column inches in the local press (especially if local personalities are invited to the event).

The cost of events of this kind can be reduced for smaller companies such as travel agents by linking together with other companies to make a joint presentation. Many tour operators are willing to pay 50 per cent of the costs of mounting an agency presentation to the public, if they are convinced that it will be productive, and they may also contribute staff to talk at the event. However, they may wish to ensure that only their company is represented at the event, so the agent will be wiser to focus on a single principal's products, if seeking support. On the other hand, where a destination is to be promoted, the national tourist board of the country, or a carrier operating to that country, may be willing to support an agent in a joint promotion. Such sharing of costs will ensure that the promotional budget is stretched to gain maximum cost-effectiveness.

Questions, tasks and issues for discussion

1 T-shirts are often used as a medium to promote a message for travel companies. Identify two or three T-shirt campaigns which have caught your imagination, and explain why you think they are good at getting their message across.

Create and design a T-shirt slogan for a tour operator of your choice, indicating your objectives.

2 The range of accessories available from one supplier which can be personalised to carry the name of the principal includes:

address books, attaché cases, bottle openers, business card files, calculators, calendars, clocks, cocktail trays, conference folders, cutlery, desk diaries, flight bags, leatherware (wallets, etc.), lighters, magnifiers, paperweights, pens, pencils, pen watches, rulers, silver trays, tankards, tape measures, ties, and umbrellas.

Discuss the merits of these different 'give-aways', and suggest which you would adopt if you were responsible for promotions in a tour operating company.

3 Study different brochure racks in local travel agencies (there are many different designs in use). Describe how they differ in function and in customer appeal. Which do you think best, and why?

4 Which is it better to spend a limited promotional budget on: sales promotion activities or advertising? Justify your decision.

Exercise

At the next World Travel Market, draw up a programme to assess the effectiveness of the stands (each member of the group or class to select one stand to study). Evaluate:

(a) the effectiveness of the stand, its design and display.
(b) how good the stand staff are at welcoming visitors to the stand and dealing with their enquiries.

12 Direct marketing: theory and practice

After studying this chapter, you should be able to:

- recognise and distinguish between the various forms of direct marketing
- recognise the benefits which direct marketing offers over other forms of marketing communication
- understand, through the application of basic principles and drawing on examples of successful techniques used in the industry, how each form of direct marketing can be successfully applied
- mount a successful direct mail campaign
- recognise the benefits of the computer database as an aid to direct marketing

What is direct marketing?

All marketing activity by a manufacturer is ultimately directed at the consumer. Most such activity is designed to create a demand for a product to be supplied through whatever are the traditional channels used by the industry concerned. Kelloggs create a demand for their cornflakes through television advertising, but they do not feel it necesary to tell you where you can purchase your next packet.

Direct Marketing is a term used in many different ways. It can be defined as the use of non-personal media or telesales to introduce products to consumers and encourage their purchase direct from the company concerned. The most common techniques in use are:

- mail order
- direct response advertising
- direct mail.

Mail order

Mail order marketing generally makes use of catalogues from which consumers can order products direct, either through the mail or in some cases through direct outlets of the company. An extension of this form of marketing is 'party selling' – perhaps best associated in the public's mind with Tupperware kitchen ware, which is sold through a social gathering in the representative's or a friend's home, using catalogues and/or direct demonstration of the product.

Direct response advertising

Direct response advertising involves placing advertisements in the media which encourage consumers to reply direct to the supplier, often using a suitable coupon clipped from a newspaper or magazine advertisement. As these coupons can be coded according to the paper in which the advertisement appears, it is easy for the company to measure the success of each advertisement. A travel advertisement which makes use of this technique, actually providing a tear-off miniature leaflet which can be returned without postage charges ('Freepost') to the company, is illustrated in Fig. 12. 1.

The technique of direct response advertising can be an effective one, providing that the

Fig. 12.1 Brittany Ferries advertisement carrying a direct response voucher

(Courtesy Brittany Ferries)

product is both well-established and its benefits clearly understood.

Direct mail

Direct mail is the technique whereby a company communicates directly with its potential customers by mail, in order to put across a sales message. The technique has the considerable advantage that letters can be personalised, and target markets clearly identified, so that customers can be expected to be reasonably interested in the product. Wastage is in this way minimised. The process has been greatly aided in recent years by the introduction of computer databases which can pinpoint specific target markets and provide comprehensive lists of names and addresses. Databases such as those offered by Acorn are based on the national census data, and identify potential customers by residential area and lifestyle.

Apart from these well-established techniques, there is a growing number of new forms of direct marketing, such as telemarketing (or telesales) – the use of the telephone to sell products, either using local telephone directories to 'cold call', or using pre-screened lists of prospective customers.

Advances in technology are now providing other means of reaching target markets, such as direct response TV selling, personal computer selling and even fax sales – contacting clients through their fax machine.

Some see these techniques merely as an unpleasant intrusion into people's personal lives, resenting the increase in unwanted 'junk mail' or the invasion of privacy resulting from the use of personal telephone lines to increase sales. Direct marketers, however, are using these new methods to cut out traditional intermediaries and in so doing, are reducing their selling costs. The result is a wide range of profitable business opportunities for those who dare to be different.

Primarily we shall be examining here the use of these techniques to cut travel industry intermediaries – in this case usually the travel agent. However, in many cases, the techniques described will have potential applications for others too; direct mail principles, for instance, will equally apply to travel agents corresponding with their clients.

Direct sell holidays: the case of Tjaereborg

One famous arrival in the ex-UK holiday market was that of the Danish tour operator Tjaereborg in 1977. They were a totally new company to the UK, though well-established in the sale of holidays in Scandinavia. Although a major operator in these territories, unlike traditional British companies they sold their holiday products direct to the public, possibly originally because in their home territory travel agents were few and far between. Whatever the reason, they had built up a considerable expertise in the necessary techniques, and their arrival was greatly feared by the travel trade in the UK. Their advertising 'promise' was that by purchasing direct from them the consumer could 'save' the cost of the travel agent. Old-established tour operators feared being undercut and seemed to believe Tjaereborg's claims, judging by their frightened reactions. Travel agents, too, became agitated, feeling that their livelihoods were under threat.

Of course it is possible to sell any product by a different method than that adopted by the majority of the suppliers in a given market. The reason for the existence of any distribution channel, however, is because the consumer wants it; because he or she likes to purchase their products in a particular way. Clothing is sold in many different ways. Though direct sell catalogue companies exist, selling either to the customer (for example, Next), or through an agent, (for example, Marshall Ward), most buyers still prefer to visit shops. So it is with travel. After more than a decade of marketing effort by Tjaereborg and others it is likely that the proportion of 'direct-sell' overseas holidays in the mass market has stabilised at around 10 per cent of the total – hardly a cause for concern.

The most important truism to remember is that every method of marketing has its own inherent costs. Tjaereborg could indeed cut out the cost of the travel agent's commission, but in so doing incurred other costs such as a heavier advertising spend. In particular they were less able to sell off at short notice those remaining seats on their flights to those browsing for last minute opportunities.

Among the most famous exponents of the techniques of selling direct to the customer was Christian Bran, who offers the formulae for success. He does not claim that they are ones of cutting cost, indeed he even describes how it is possible to reduce the appeal of quality products by charging too little for them. His advice on determining the suitability of the direct selling philosophy for a given product is that the company must be certain that it has enough money available to succeed with its promotions. Failing this, it may be wasting its resources and skill in attempting to sell direct. He goes on to suggest that when a company is new to a field, the cost of selling direct is likely to be higher than using the established channels of distribution. Unless the company has an exeptionally good product, they will need a higher than normal margin of profit to succeed in the venture. Once the company has built up a regular clientele, the position may become easier.

Many businesses in the tourism industry rely almost entirely upon selling direct. They range from the small bed and breakfast establishments, through visitor attractions and specialist tour operators, to large scale holiday centres like Center Parcs. A glance at the weekend press advertisements for holidays will convince readers that many travel companies rely almost entirely upon direct responses, rather than distribution through the travel agency network.

Problems in the expansion of direct marketing

Most success stories in direct marketing are those of highly individual concerns supplying a limited number of distinctive products to an eager market. Current fashion is a particularly strong motivator, especially if good public relations coverage can be achieved, such as through a feature in the weekend colour supplements about a new or different concept. There are countless examples of firms that have been successful on a small scale, but have then upped their product supply substantially, resulting in their being unable to maintain the individual character and quality of the product. By flooding the market, they find that their sales techniques cannot keep pace.

Some years ago British Airways purchased Martin Rooks, a leading name in direct sell foreign holidays. The firm had been run by the Rooks family, initially to specialise in holidays for railway workers who had free pass facilities for the travel tickets, but who had fairly small incomes and low budgets. From this, Martin Rooks branched out into air holidays, based upon the simple principle that by budgeting tightly the firm could afford to operate a limited number of holidays at a set mark-up per holiday, unrelated to the holiday cost. It meant that the more expensive holidays were particularly attractive when compared with competitors, something that was soon discovered by more people than the railwaymen at whom the product had been originally aimed. The company spent very little on advertising, appointed no agents, and relied heavily upon its reputation for such low prices that, should you miss the publication of its

brochure, all its holidays would be sold out. Every year the first 'on-sale' day was marked by long queues outside its offices in Victoria, partly assisted by press comment about the remarkably low prices offered. Little was ever left unsold for long.

When British Airways purchased this small highly successful firm one of its first moves was to increase volumes hugely. The established formula ceased to work and heavy advertising expenditure was incurred to sell the excess holidays. Profits slumped. Eventually it was sold along with other British Airways holiday companies and still exists under Owners Abroad Group management as a sister concern to Tjaereborg, whose original Danish owners have withdrawn from the UK market.

Gardeners' Delight: a success story in direct marketing

A good example of successful direct marketing is that provided by Gardeners' Delight Holidays, operated by JAR Services. In the early part of 1991, as this text was in preparation, the travel industry was experiencing an unprecedented slump due to the dual effects of the Gulf War and a severe economic recession. Despite this, owner John Ramsbotham was still able to claim an exceptionally heavy booking season.

John and Jane Ramsbotham started the firm in 1978, when he was manager in a group of business travel agencies, as a hobby enterprise which combined his own travel expertise and his wife's knowledge of gardens. They are now both fully occupied in operating around 20 tours annually (including some overseas) to a pattern that has proved successful (see brochure, Fig. 12.2).

Most trips use high quality city centre hotels which are able to offer large enough allocations of good quality rooms at weekends, and at competitive prices. They claim to average around 39 passengers per trip and are content with this number, as many of the purchasers travel alone and like to be able to sit on their own in the coach when they choose so to do. Right from the outset the holidays were designed to give the 'guests', as they are known, something to do in the evenings, with gardening speakers of repute attending some of the nights. In addition many of the holidays

A CELEBRATION OF

ENGLISH GARDENS

AUTUMN FLOWERS

Friday 21st September

1990

A weekend break for flower arrangers
including a morning visit to the
N.A.F.A.S. Festival
Demonstration by Sheila MacQueen
Candlelit dinner at Newstead Abbey

Fig. 12.2 Direct mail brochure for Gardeners' Delight Holidays (Courtesy: JAR Services)

are accompanied by expert gardeners, together with one or both of the founders.

Quality is a keynote, and a fully inclusive programme includes transfers from the arrival station to the commencement point, often carried out by the owner of the company personally. All admission fees to places visited, generous amounts of wine with dinner, and daily newspapers are also supplied. Similarly, every effort is made to give a same day service to brochure requests, bookings and confirmations.

Each year they produce a new set of holidays with virtually no repetition, as repeat bookings by their satisfied customers is a strong feature of this business. John scorns his own inbuilt antennae developed over many years' experience in saying that 'with such a small programme there is no question of test marketing – it either works or it doesn't'. (In reality his test marketing is carried out by sending his new ideas out to an established customer list and inviting them to book.)

The most important source of new business is from old customers, and these are carefully followed up as a first priority, not only with each year's new brochure, but also accompanied by a Christmas card personally signed by John, Jane and the garden expert 'host' who accompanied the previous year's tour purchased by that customer. Outgoing publicity to attract additional business and to replace those who do not re-book is limited to judicious press releases to garden journals and gardening writers, which achieve good results. The company also takes a stand at the Royal Horticultural Society shows in November and in January. Apart from this, a few simple advertisements are placed in gardening magazines (see Fig. 12.3), emphasising the expertise of the hosts. The budget is planned in advance, and is very small.

GARDENERS' DELIGHT **HOLIDAYS**

FLOWER ARRANGING BREAKS WITH GARDEN VISITS

29th May Marsham Court Hotel, Bournemouth
with Sheila Macqueen demonstrating. Visit NAFAS, Furzey, Exbury etc.

21st Sept. Metropole Hotel, Llandrindod Wells
with Brian Halliday as host. Visit well known and private Border gardens.

Fully inclusive: coach from London if required.
3 star hotels - all rooms en-suite, lunches, wine with dinner etc.
Free 44 page brochure on these and other leisure breaks with a difference from:

J.A.R. SERVICES (14th Year)
Garden House, 45 Church Road, Saxilby
Lincoln LN1 2HH Tel. (0522) 703773 (24hrs)

Fig. 12.3 Advertisement for Gardeners' Delight Holidays (Courtesy: JAR Services)

John and Jane now enjoy a 'lifestyle business' which enables them to carry out creative activity, to be self-sufficient, and to derive considerable personal satisfaction through customer contact. It is unlikely that they will ever become wealthy, since it is almost impossible to replicate the care and attention they put in to enable the scale to be increased beyond what they can cope with personally. There are many such businesses in tourism, and every one that gives good service to the customer and supports its promoters adequately should be regarded as a success.

Off the page selling: the case of Jules Verne

A quite remarkable travel group is named after the famous author of *Around the World in Eighty Days*, Jules Verne. Its founder, Philip Morrell, has crossed many seemingly impossible barriers in making adventurous holidays available to a small but sophisticated sector of holidaymakers. Opening up China, treks across the Himalayas, re-creating the great train journeys across Russia, cruising on Egyptian riverboats, air tours of East Africa by Catalina flying boats: these and many other exotic ideas are everyday fare for this company. In addition, a sister company, Serenissima Travel, specialises in cultural holidays featuring art, music and history.

A noteworthy development by this group has been the use of 'off-the-page selling' whereby full page advertisements featuring sumptuous use of colour pictures are taken in the weekend quality newspaper supplements. This enables them to produce wordy descriptions, normally of just one tour, almost in the style of an editorial. The newspaper page becomes the brochure itself, presenting its selling points to the unsuspecting buyers over a leisurely weekend breakfast, rather than waiting for them to go out to obtain information based on some half-formed holiday idea. That the method has been successful is evidenced by its expansion into additional publications, for full page colour advertisements in national newspapers are one of the most expensive forms of printed advertising. The customer, once attracted to these relatively highly-priced products, can be assiduously maintained upon the companies' mailing lists for introduction to new products and opportunities in the future. The principle is similar to that of John and Jane Ramsbotham's follow-up of satisfied customers.

Direct contact and direct mail

In round terms, some 60 million people live in the UK. Each year around 40 million holidays are taken, of which 20 million are taken overseas; eight or nine million of these are package holidays. The exact figures differ each year, and the serious student will need to examine the latest statistics from government agencies and other sources to establish trends. In addition it must be remembered that, while the proportion who take no holiday at all sticks stubbornly at around 30 per cent (probably the elderly and disadvantaged groups within the population), the number who take more than one holiday each year is increasing, as indeed is the number of holidays taken by the majority.

Trying to reach this huge market is difficult, and can be wasteful unless care is taken to reach those most likely to buy. A famous saying, 'I know that half of my advertising budget is wasted – but I don't know which half', illustrates the fact that any form of published advertisement will always have a high wastage factor in reaching out to people who will never be purchasers of a particular product.

Marketing distinguishes between the 'shotgun' approach, which scatters advertising messages widely in the hope that some of it will reach an interested audience, and the 'rifle' approach, which selects specific target audiences to address. This latter approach will heighten the possibility of success, and contacting potential clients directly through mail or other means is more likely to achieve such success.

Most advertising is designed to get the interest of the consumer. Strengthening the 'brand' and adding value to it also have their place and these have been described in Chapter 5. Once having established contact, the business should capitalise upon the interest expressed.

Another factor to be considered is the coverage achieved by any medium chosen for one's advertisements. It might seem simple to consider the case of local advertising by a travel agent, but in reality only about a third of the homes in a given area normally purchase a local paper; many do so only for specific items such as the classified advertisements, and the births and deaths announcements. It may, therefore, be considered beneficial to create one's own medium for reaching the customer. Saga, the retired people's specialist operator, runs a very highly regarded magazine dealing with matters that are of interest to that age group. This acts as a regular sales brochure for the company.

A well known travel agency group decided that it could improve its local coverage substantially by producing its own 'free sheet'. The agency operated in seven closely linked towns, in a densely populated part of the country. The agency group explored the situation and found that there were more local newspapers than the number of towns, each with a substantial wastage of coverage outside the natural 'catchment' area which the travel agency had defined from close examination of its client records. Additionally, there were the usual 'free sheet' advertising newspapers. Though these appeared to give greater coverage, as they were delivered to every house in the defined circulation area, it was also known that their readership was poorer than that of purchased papers, which were considered to be 'wanted'.

By examination of the techniques of the free sheets it was soon apparent that a formula for costing could easily be established. A minimum size of newspaper had to be achieved to appear credible. This was set at eight pages of tabloid size. Travel is a colourful subject and yet few local papers offered colour facilities. The special edition was to have colour photographs on at least the outside pages and the centre spread. The editorial content would all be about travel opportunities, and in particular would feature staff of the travel agency branches and their travels in the previous year, to establish their knowledge and experience in the minds of the readers. A formula of:

- one third of space to be devoted to editorial matter
- one third of space to photographs
- one third of space to advertisements by travel companies

gave a more generous proportion to reading matter which would interest the customer than could ever be achieved in local newspapers.

The criteria and objectives of the special newspaper were communicated to all major travel companies that the travel agency group represented, and they were invited to advertise, sharing the cost of advertisements equally with the agency. Careful budgeting provided a contribution to the travel agency's origination costs, as well as to the print and distribution costs. Effectively this doubled the advertising budget that could be provided by the agency itself.

The free sheet grew year by year and eventually was being produced with 16 pages and distributed to 100 000 homes. Conceived as a once-a-year boost to the agency's standing and reputation, it became a recognised vehicle for information on new products for the coming season, for details of special trips from the area, and for travel orientated competitions for the readers (as an aid to their remembering the advertisements), with major prizes sponsored by the advertisers. The agency group outpaced a growing list of local competitors and retained the highest sales levels against its competitors in all the towns where it traded. The group chose what it wanted to say and defined to whom it sent its message. In this case its objective was to achieve blanket (i.e. total) coverage in the locality, an objective that it met successfully.

Using databases

Once having established contact, preferably defined by a sale, any well run business can now maintain relevant data on that customer inexpensively by the use of computer techniques, as we discussed earlier in this chapter. The equipment needed has plummeted in price in recent years, while the capabilities of even the simplest systems now make it possible to compile seemingly individual letters to each customer.

The more personal any communication becomes, the more effective it is likely to be. At one end of the scale it is easy simply to place an advertisement in a publication produced by others, but at the other end, the single individually-compiled sales letter, personally addressed and describing why a specific proposition is appropriate to the addressee, will have strong sales appeal. Between these two extremes are a myriad of other possibilities, and the initiative of the direct marketer will be tested by the way the customer responds.

Direct marketing for destinations

The proposition need not only be for a product, such as a particular holiday; or a service, such as that of a travel agency, but may also include promoting a destination itself.

The Tunisian National Tourist Office

In the Spring of 1989 the newly appointed Director of the Tunisian National Tourist Office in London was faced with disappointing sales for his country in the coming season. His budget was limited and, though a small consumer advertising campaign had been planned around Easter to arouse the public's interest in holidays to Tunisia, he was also aware that too few of the 30 000 or so travel agency staff employed by the 7000 travel agencies in the UK were really conscious of the opportunities his country's resorts presented. This was hardly surprising, for the whole of North Africa counted for only 0.73 per cent of air holidays taken in that year. It follows naturally that if less than one in a hundred customers is likely to choose Tunisia, staff of travel agencies are hardly likely to devote too much time and effort to improving their own knowledge of the travel destination.

Thus the Director saw increasing the awareness of travel agency sales staff of his country as a major first step. At his disposal he had a small but enthusiastic team at the office to answer enquiries and to give promotional assistance; he had a newly-published colour brochure giving information on the main holiday features of the country, and he had a new video cassette which also described the resorts.

With the help of an outside consultant, a scheme was devised to undertake a series of mailings to every travel agency in the UK in an attempt to capture their attention. In the first instance humour and local colour were to be established by a pun on the theme. A package was sent out which contained a box of best quality dates from Tunisia, for the travel agency staff to share. The date palm had been used in previous advertising, and it was here used as a visual anchor to promote the theme of 'You Have A Date With Tunisia'.

A facsimile letter followed, produced simply on an office word processor and personally addressed by the Director 'Dear Travel Agent', and signed by him (see Fig. 12.4). This set out the five main sales features of Tunisian holidays, then:

- gave details of the video that was available on request
- described a competition for travel agency staff to go on a 'dream trip' to Tunisia themselves
- offered low price holiday opportunities to travel staff in the early season (to get better product knowledge)
- gave prior notice of study tours for staff in the Autumn
- offered promotional help upon request.

Enclosed with the mailing were simple-to-complete postcard entry forms so that each member of the travel agency could enter the 'dream trip' competition after reading the relevant brochures (see Fig. 12.5); a request postcard for a copy of the video; and a list of the names and addresses of all holiday companies publishing brochures to Tunisia, from which the travel agency could sell. The items were enclosed in a specially constructed box carrying an attractive label bearing the date palm symbol and an instruction to 'Open Immediately', to distinguish it from packets of brochures that might languish in the agency before being opened.

The response of competition entries and video requests confirmed that the contents were well-received and that Tunisia received high profile attention in the valuable Easter booking period.

The creative quality of this campaign was in marked contrast with competitor countries, and helped Tunisia to return good results in a difficult season.

Some guidelines for good direct mail letters

The previous section will have emphasised the importance of letters being directed personally, by name and by appropriate business title, if relevant. This will ensure that the letter gets to the right person, and makes it more likely to be read. Many people believe that using the name again in the text reinforces the message, but although this can be achieved with most mail-merge software programs, the technique can appear contrived.

There is inevitably a trade-off between cost and quality, but generally cost savings are counter-productive if the mail is well directed. A fast dot matrix printer will enable many more letters to

TUNISIA
THE MEDITERRANEAN HOLIDAY THAT'S NEVER OUT OF SEASON

March 1989

Dear Travel Agent,

YOU HAVE A DATE WITH TUNISIA

Dates are just one of the many things of which Tunisia is
proud and we hope you will enjoy our gift whilst you think
about Tunisia for a few moments.

For the holidaymaker we offer a variety of plus points.

- sophisticated hotels and resorts
- superb food
- sports galore from golf to windsurfing and
  horseriding
- the best beaches in the Mediterranean, and
- the magic of the Sahara desert and its oases

It is no wonder that our advertising has featured the
theme:

'WHY JUST HAVE ONE HOLIDAY WHEN YOU CAN GO TO TUNISIA ?'

We know that 1989 is a difficult year and we are doing our
best to help you sell our holidays. We are now running a
national and regional press campaign which is intended to
highlight the remarkably low prices at which your customers
can purchase a dream holiday in our varied country.

In order that you can see for yourself just what we have to
offer we are also undertaking a number of initiatives aimed
at supporting you, our valued travel agent partner.

YOUR DATE WITH OUR NEW VIDEO

Those travel agents who we know have video facilities, are
being sent a copy of the new unbiased video 'Tunisia - Dream
Holiday Destination' produced by Travid. This will help you
and all of your colleagues in the office to appreciate the
range of facilities we have to offer.

The Tunisian National Tourist Office   7a Stafford Street, London, W1X 4EQ
Travel Enquiries: 01-499 2234, Administration 01-629 0858 , Fax: 01-495 3321
Prestel Tunisia Information 344 220

Director: Kader Chelbi

**Fig. 12.4 Front page of direct mail shot to travel agents
from the Tunisian National Tourist Office**

be produced in a given time than will a daisy
wheel or laser printer, but will they make the
letters appear more like 'junk mail'? Brown
envelopes are cheaper, but they imply penny-
pinching economies. Window envelopes may
seem less desirable than plain ones, but a
personally addressed letter in a window looks
better than an envelope with a label, and it is
difficult to type individual envelopes with
anything but the most sophisticated equipment.

The *content* of the letter itself is obviously of
critical importance. The aim of the text will be to:

- capture attention with a headline that
  intrigues
- start by stating how the reader will benefit
- describe what is offered and demonstrate the
  product's benefits
- fully detail the offer being made
- explain what the reader needs to do next, i.e.
  how to purchase the product.

A direct mail letter is one type of promotion

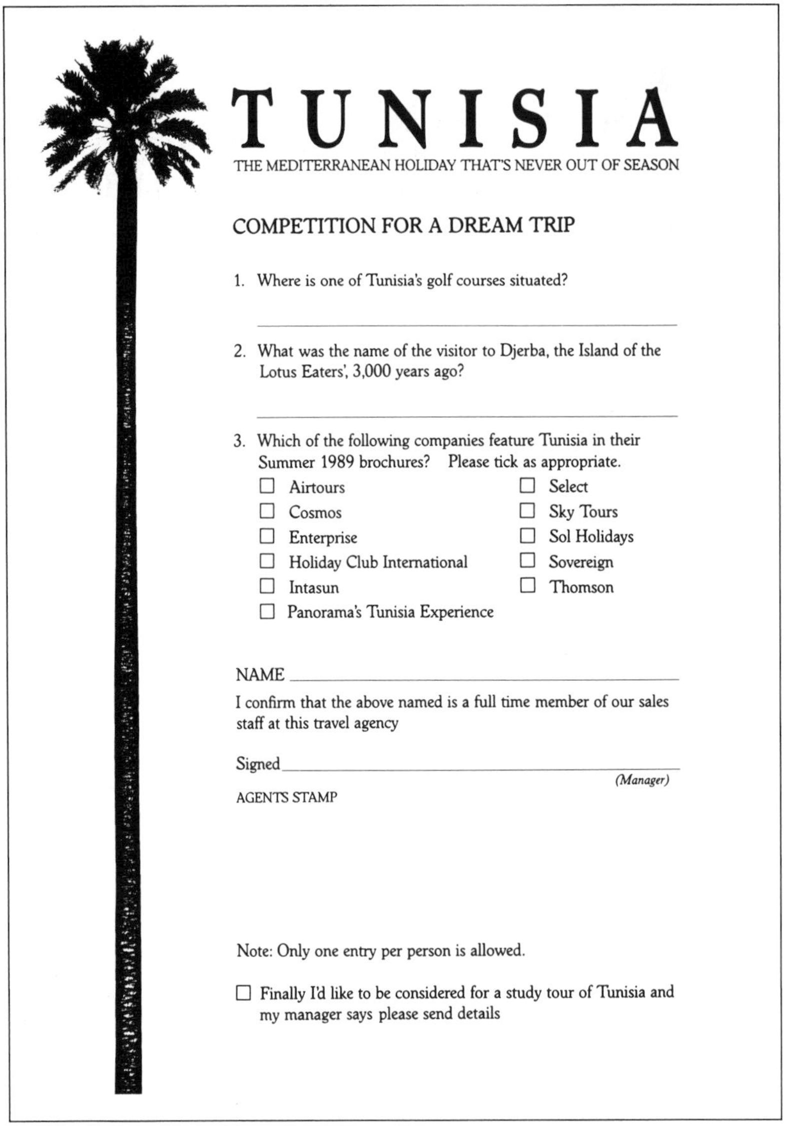

TUNISIA

THE MEDITERRANEAN HOLIDAY THAT'S NEVER OUT OF SEASON

COMPETITION FOR A DREAM TRIP

1. Where is one of Tunisia's golf courses situated?

_____

2. What was the name of the visitor to Djerba, the Island of the Lotus Eaters', 3,000 years ago?

_____

3. Which of the following companies feature Tunisia in their Summer 1989 brochures? Please tick as appropriate.

☐ Airtours   ☐ Select
☐ Cosmos   ☐ Sky Tours
☐ Enterprise   ☐ Sol Holidays
☐ Holiday Club International   ☐ Sovereign
☐ Intasun   ☐ Thomson
☐ Panorama's Tunisia Experience

NAME _____

I confirm that the above named is a full time member of our sales staff at this travel agency

Signed _____

(Manager)

AGENTS STAMP

Note: Only one entry per person is allowed.

☐ Finally I'd like to be considered for a study tour of Tunisia and my manager says please send details

Fig. 12.5 Competition entry for travel agents accompanying the mailshot sent out by the Tunisian National Tourist Office

where brevity is not necessarily the best technique. To be effective, the text must capture the reader's attention and get their interest. The text should be written in good, simple (and correct!) English, preferably in relatively short, punchy sentences. Many of the leaders in this field use devices such as indented paragraphs, emboldened or underlined words for emphasis or clarity, and add apparent afterthoughts in postscripts.

If inviting a response by mail, then it is essential to encourage action by making it _easy to reply_. An order form or reply card should serve this purpose. A simple printed, addressed envelope will help to increase replies, but still better is a reply-paid envelope or a 'freepost' facility where the cost is met by the promoter (at a small premium on the number of replies received). Most effective of all is actually to put a stamp on the envelope – many people seem to feel guilty

Tŷ Brunel 2 Ffordd Fitzalan
Caerdydd CF2 1UY

Brunel House 2 Fitzalan Road
Cardiff CF2 1UY

(0222) 499909
Telex 497269
Fax 495031

BWRDD CROESO CYMRU
WALES TOURIST BOARD

Miss B G Anderson
8 Tryfan Road
Bristol
BS8 4YA

WHAT DO YOU WANT FROM A
BARGAIN BREAK?

Dear Miss Anderson,

As you've previously expressed an interest in our GREAT LITTLE BREAKS in Wales, I thought you might like a copy of our new brochure.

WALKING?

A typical example of a weekend's walking holiday – two nights at a delightful countryside hotel in the "Heart of Wales." With a variety of guided long and short walks in the locality. Includes room, breakfast and evening meal.

£41 PER PERSON

To receive your free copy, just complete and return the enclosed reply-paid card right away. I'll be happy to send you your brochure by return.

You'll find it's packed full of great ideas for a few days away.

Whatever you want from a bargain break away, you'll find it in Wales.

Perhaps you just want a quiet weekend in the country and a little fresh air. Or, maybe, you'd prefer an active weekend of windsurfing, golfing, fishing or pony trekking.

Our GREAT LITTLE BREAKS will cater for all tastes. Giving you that well-earned rest from your usual routine. Providing a refreshing

Fig. 12.6 A successful direct mail campaign which attracted a 30 per cent response (Courtesy: Wales Tourist Board)

WINDSURFING?

A two night windsurfing break in a self-catering bungalow for 4 on the Pembrokeshire Coast. Including hire of equipment.

£21·50 PER PERSON

Spring and Autumn are the perfect time for walking or pony trekking. And in Winter you can still enjoy the wild beauty of the Welsh countryside and come back to the welcoming warmth of your hotel lounge for the evening.

So, regardless of the time of year a few days in Wales can always provide a pleasant break.

Send for your GREAT LITTLE BREAKS brochure now.

Just complete and post back the reply-paid card now to claim your free full-colour brochure.

It will have full details of how you can book your GREAT LITTLE BREAK. Do it today and you could be spending a few days in Wales in just a few weeks' time. I hope to hear from you soon.

Yours sincerely,

WYN MEARS
UK Marketing Director

PS. Please do us the favour of answering the few questions you'll find on the brochure request card. This will help us to provide you with an even better service in the future.

WHATEVER YOU WANT, IT'S HERE
322 SPECIAL OFFERS TO HELP YOU GET AWAY

SEND FOR YOUR GREAT LITTLE BREAKS BROCHURE TODAY

Fig. 12.6 (continued)

about the waste if they don't send it back.

One highly successful promotion undertaken by the Wales Tourist Board, which attracted a 30 per cent response, was a direct mail campaign to promote short breaks in Wales (see Fig. 12.6). The campaign incorporated many of the key points identified here, and was also well illustrated with suitable promotional material.

Questions, tasks and issues for discussion

1 Collect any examples of direct mail letters received by you, your friends or neighbours. Identify the benefits offered by the products being sold, and analyse the strengths and weaknesses of the letters in the light of comments appearing in this chapter.

2 Discuss with your friends how happy or otherwise they are, or would be, to receive telesales messages at home. Does it depend upon the product being offered? How might the sales pitch be modified to make it less offensive to listeners?

3 If you were drawing up a mailing list in order to send out a direct mail letter to people living in your immediate neighbourhood, how would you describe the 'market profile' of the typical resident in the neighbourhood? What kinds of products would be likely to prove attractive to these people?

Exercise

Using the market profile identified above in question 3, imagine you are a marketing assistant with a package holiday company offering the kind of holiday in which some of your neighbours would be interested. Prepare a direct mail letter to be sent out to these neighbours, and accompany this with a short note identifying:

- the punchy headline and any other attention-getting techniques you have used
- the product benefits you are stressing
- how you are encouraging the recipients to take action
- what material you would plan to include with the mailing.

13 Public relations and its use in the tourism industry

After studying this chapter, you should be able to:

- compare the benefits of a public relations campaign with other forms of communication
- identify the role of the PRO and the functions of PR
- understand how PR campaigns are mounted
- evaluate alternative approaches to gaining publicity
- appreciate the importance of measuring the success of all promotional techniques

David Ogilvy, of the advertising agency Ogilvy Benson and Mather and one of Britain's greatest exponents of advertising, once declared to an audience in New York composed of senior travel industry staff that he would choose to spend $250 000 on public relations before he spent a penny on travel advertising. His aim was to highlight the importance of an area of communications that was all too easily overlooked by those in the industry, and to make clear that in his view PR actually produced better value for money than the more traditional avenues for promotion.

One reason why PR has tended to take a lesser role in the communications mix is that it is even more difficult to quantify the benefits of PR expenditure than of other forms of promotion. Another reason is that the uses of the technique and what can be achieved are less well understood by the industry. Nonetheless, there are some notable examples of entrepreneurs who have recognised its power and used it – Richard Branson of Virgin Atlantic Airways springs immediately to mind. There are, however, dangers associated with the overuse of the medium, and too high a public profile can attract unwelcome publicity, as Branson would be the first to admit.

PR: its definition, characteristics and role

PR is best defined as a set of communications techniques which are designed to create and maintain favourable relations between an organisation and its publics. The last word is deliberately used in the plural, since an organisation actually has to deal with several different publics, of which its consumers are only one. Companies will want to build good relations with their shareholders, with suppliers, distribution channels, and, where pertinent, with unions. External bodies such as trade and professional associations and local chambers of commerce are other organisations which a company might wish to influence, while opinion leaders such as members of parliament, travel writers, and hotel and restaurant guide publishers are yet more groups with which the organisation must maintain good relations. Finally, companies will wish to be on good terms with their neighbours, and will want to be seen as part of the local community and to support local activities.

Characteristics

The need for PR has arisen with the growth in size of organisations. The resultant lessening of personal contact between a firm and its customers led to criticism of impersonality, a belief that big corporations had become 'faceless' and 'uncaring'. Some observers such as Robert Townsend[1] believed that the answer was to scrap the PR departments and get back to personal relations again, but it is questionable how far this is practicable once a company has grown to become a major corporation. A few years ago, all tour operators handled their reservations systems manually, and specific staff were assigned to handle bookings from agents over the telephone. Retailers were on first name terms with individual staff members, and knew whom to call when they had a problem. This close relationship eased criticisms of the company in other directions. The movement to on-line computer reservations systems, coupled with a reduction in agency calls by sales representatives, depersonalised the company for agents, who found it easier to find fault with the company. Customers, too, grew alienated from the businesses with which they dealt, and organisations were set up to safeguard consumer interests and to lobby for better consumer protection. The Air Transport Users' Committee is just one such body in the travel industry which has been established to look after the interests of the travelling public.

Role

Because of the importance of travel and tourism as a service industry, the reputation of a travel company's products hinges on the quality of its staff, and the attitude of that staff to the company's customers. When a company is carrying in excess of a million passengers abroad each year, it has to make greater and greater efforts to retain a friendly and personal image. PR can play a role in supporting and publicising that image, although its creation must still lie with other marketing staff, whose role is to train and to maintain quality control.

As with other communications techniques, public relations plays a part in informing and reminding customers about the company and its products, in order to generate an attitude towards the company favouring the purchase of its products. In generating information, however, the PR message has to be seen as accurate and unbiased, while still reflecting the needs and interests of the company – a considerable challenge for the public relations officer! This objectivity is essential if PR is to do its job effectively. However, it is the media that will determine what appears before the public. Since the aim is to ensure credibility, PR messages, with their perceived objectivity, are more convincing than advertising and in the long run are likely to have a greater impact on sales, if a far more subtle one. This, however, underlines the fact that public relations is essentially a weapon for long-term, rather than immediate, impact on a company's markets. Since consumers are becoming increasingly sophisticated, and hence more immune to the messages carried by advertising, the role of PR in an organisation is doubly important.

Lest readers feel that PR concerns only the largest companies, it should be clearly understood that there is a role for it in any organisation, however small. Small companies, too, need the goodwill of the local community and a strong reputation to generate sales, and this can be aided by the application of simple techniques, as we shall see.

In addition to creating favourable publicity for the company, PR is helpful in diminishing the impact of unfavourable publicity. The travel industry has more than its fair share of this, and there are some in the industry who feel that the media are only concerned to report the negative events, focusing on disasters such as overbooking, air traffic controllers' strikes, aircraft near-misses, coach crashes and the collapse of tour operating companies. Many of these events are beyond the control of individual companies, but the impact of negative publicity will affect them anyway and must be tackled.

There is a misconception in some circles that PR's role is to 'paper over the cracks' which result from poor management or product faults. No amount of publicity will help a company which does not seek to correct underlying problems. PR must be used as an adjunct to good marketing practice, not as a substitute for it.

Five distinct activities are associated with the role of public relations:

1 Press relations. This requires the company to maintain a close working relationship with press journalists and others associated with the media, with the aim of generating favourable publicity at every available opportunity.
2 Product publicity. This involves the implementation of tactics designed to bring products to the attention of the public, whether through the use of the media, or in some other manner.
3 Corporate publicity. Concerns efforts to publicise the firm itself, either internally or externally, in order to create a favourable image.
4 Lobbying. Involves activities designed to promote a cause. A firm may, for instance, support plans for legislation or regulation, such as airlines' attempts to gain legislation for more night flights out of London airports; or a lobby may be mounted to defeat a proposal for legislation, such as the European Community plans for certification of travel agents. While lobbying is generally concerned with governmental or local authority issues, it could also be mounted to influence trade regulation, such as a move to defeat ABTA's proposals to increase bonding requirements.
5 Counselling. The Public Relations Officer has the task of counselling management about public issues and identifying developments, both internal and external to the firm, which could influence a company's image. The PRO will then recommend a plan of action to counter any unfavourable developments. Thus the PR department has a monitoring and research function also.

The organisation of public relations

It will be appreciated that while some of the above activities are directly associated with the marketing function, others are only peripheral to it, in the sense that their overall objective will enhance the company's sales opportunities. For this reason, in large organisations some PR activities may be carried out in the marketing department, while others are conducted quite separately, at a senior level. One carrier, for instance, employed a PRO as Assistant to the Managing Director, with all corporate publicity conducted directly under the supervision of the Managing Director. In such a situation, the PRO becomes a highly influential figure within the organisation, while technically still a member of 'staff' rather than 'line' management.

A difficulty in large companies, where marketing and PR functions are separated, is that the priorities of the two become distinct, although both are concerned with external relations. Where the PR function is not a responsibility of the marketing staff, suspicion of its activities is aroused, since marketing is only concerned with product enhancement. The wider perspectives of the company's interests are of less concern. PR staff, for their part, tend to take the view that marketing staff, with their concern for the customer, may overlook the company's social responsibilities to the community at large, and believe that PR considerations should play a greater role in product decisions.

By way of example, let us take the case of a major tour operator seeking new destinations for its market. The marketing staff will be principally interested in the attraction of the resort to the company's clients, be concerned that the new resort has the right facilities, will be accessible at a price which the company is willing to pay, and that the tourist authorities in the area are supportive. They will be less concerned with issues such as the impact on the local community of the new development, or the political consequences of an intention to file for an increase in flights from regional airports, which might need careful handling. Marketing staff might feel that the use of so-called 'personality girls' to merchandise the launch of a new programme will gain them plenty of press coverage, but PR might urge against the portrayal of women in this role, predicting a backlash against such a sexist approach.

In the USA, PR staff are playing a much greater role in marketing decisions, in areas of product policy, pricing, packaging and promotions, as American corporations become more sensitive to their social responsibilities. PR is now exerting considerable influence on British marketing, as companies seek to understand and respond to the changing attitudes and needs of the buying public.

The Public Relations Officer

Larger companies will employ their own Public Relations Officer, although small to medium-sized companies are more likely to use the services of an outside PR consultancy. PROs usually have a media/communications, rather than marketing, background. In fact, they tend to be former journalists, with good press contacts and an intimate knowledge of media operations. This means they will also have good communications skills. It is their contacts which are valued most highly, though, since they will help to gain increased media coverage for the company.

Where PR activities are intermittent and *ad hoc*, it will be much cheaper for a company to employ a firm of public relations consultants to handle campaigns. External PR companies provide an excellent service, having broad ranging experience of many businesses and good contacts to exploit. Their sole drawback is their distance from the day-to-day activities of the company, so they must rely on being well briefed by a member of the company in order to do an effective job.

Mounting a PR campaign

Favourable publicity for a company doesn't just happen; it has to be planned and programmed. Those responsible for PR must *create* news, as well as exploiting opportunities that arise to make news. A publicity campaign should form part of the overall marketing plans for the year, as part of the communications mix.

As a starting point to the campaign, the PR staff must know who the organisation's publics are, and what their present attitudes towards the organisation and its products are, so that there

is knowledge of what needs to be done. While market research should already have a picture of the firm's consumers or potential consumers, additional research will probably be needed to establish the attitudes of other publics, such as staff and shareholders. This will provide an overall picture of the strengths and weaknesses of the company in its public affairs, which will allow a set of objectives to be drawn up for the PR campaign. As with all plans, objectives should be stated in a form which is measurable, e.g. to raise awareness of the company's social commitment among the local community from a present 20 per cent to 40 per cent within one year.

The next step is to determine the strategies and tactics which are best suited to achieve these aims, and to decide what budget will be required to undertake the campaign. In the case of PR, the implementation of a campaign may last much longer than the usual one year marketing plan before targets are achieved. Changing attitudes and opinions through PR is a slow process, and a corporate campaign could last as long as five years. Finally, the success or otherwise of the campaign must be monitored. In a campaign lasting several years, this monitoring should take place during the campaign as well as after it, to evaluate its growing effectiveness; some fine-tuning to the campaign, such as tactical adjustments, may be needed in the intervening period.

Gaining publicity

Let us assume the objective is to generate publicity to develop a favourable attitude towards a local travel agency. How is this best achieved? The first task of an agent is to ensure that the local catchment area is aware of the agency's existence, and of the products it provides. PR can support the advertising and sales promotion activities of the company by, for example, publicising the opening of the offices. New shops and offices open all the time, so in itself this is hardly newsworthy for the local press. It will be the task of the PRO to make the event newsworthy, in order to attract visitors and gain media coverage. Offering free drinks will bring people through the door, but using a well-known personality (perhaps local, and with some connection to the world of travel and tourism, such as a travel writer) is more likely to gain coverage. It must always be borne in mind that what is newsworthy for the company is not necessarily of interest to the press, and an agency opening will have to contend with many other local events for coverage. Something really attention-getting is needed; something which will draw the public's attention, and that of the media too. The important thing about publicity, though, is that it feeds on new ideas all the time, and the agent must continually be thinking up new gimmicks to gain attention.

After the opening, the agent must find ways of keeping the name in front of the public. Some agents have been able to establish themselves with the local press or radio station as the 'gurus' of travel, who are called upon to be interviewed whenever something newsworthy occurs in the industry. This is particularly valuable for long-term image building (it helps if the proprietor's name is the same as that of the company, since the company name will probably not receive a mention!) Participation at local fairs, providing raffle prizes at fund-raising events or charities, sponsoring an entrant for a local hot-air balloon race, all offer chances for building community links and generating local goodwill.

A firm can build on the particular strengths of its own staff to gain additional press coverage. One agent employed a counter clerk with excellent skiing skills. This not only enabled the agent to build up a specialist expertise in winter sports holidays, but also gained some useful column inches in the local press. Another well-established agency proprietor is known in the trade and the local community for his enthusiasm for golf, losing no opportunity to publicise his links with golfing personalities, and participating in golf tournaments at home and abroad which get good press coverage. Key names in the retail world, in their role as spokespersons for ABTA, have become well-known faces to hundreds of thousands of TV viewers through their appearances on interview programmes or travel programmes. There is a 'caveat' on guesting on television, however. Television is still largely a medium for entertainment, and the role calls for a special kind of talent in presenting oneself effectively on camera.

Press relations

Developing and maintaining links with the press and other media is a critical task of the PRO, who will also need to be on first name terms with prominent travel writers if representing a major principal. It is to the PRO as 'spokesperson' for the organisation that the media will turn to get information about the company, and the PRO's skills involve the ability to be both tactful and frank when dealing with them.

If the organisation plans to announce some prominent event, such as a takeover, or the establishment of a new trading division, this may be sufficiently newsworthy to merit calling a press conference. This will entail invitations to travel journalists and other representatives from the trade, national and local media to attend a meeting at which senior executives will announce details of the new plans. A *press reception* will include provision of food and drink (some form of hospitality is normal for all press conferences). The conference itself is usually presaged with a *press release*, or news release, which is the principal method of communicating to the media information about the company which is thought newsworthy. The press release is a brief summary of the news which the company wishes to publicise, and generally occupies one side, or at most two, of A4 stationery. News releases are always well presented on special letterhead paper which gives the name and address of the company, a contact name (usually that of the PRO) and both home and work phone numbers, as a PRO must be contactable 24 hours a day if journalists want further information. Companies devise their own titles for letterheads, usually a phrase such as 'News from . . .' (Fig. 13.1 offers part of a typical example of a press release).

Since the press release is the company's main form of communication with the media, it is important that it exemplifies the quality and efficiency of the organisation. It must be well printed, or duplicated (today a word processor

Portland Holidays

MEDIA INFORMATION

Date: 27 August, 1991
Ref: DGPR/PH S92

DEMAND FOR QUALITY HOLIDAYS

Holidaymakers are demanding value for money and spurning cheap packages which offer low standards.

That was the message today from Charles Pollard, Managing Director of Portland Holidays, the UK's biggest direct-booking company, who predicted steady growth in the popularity of inclusive foreign travel after a drop of around 20 per cent during the past three years.

During Summer 1992, he said that inclusive foreign holidays were expected to total around eight million and that quality and consistency of standards rather than low prices would be the major selling point.

"What today's holidaymakers are looking for is to be able to book with confidence - knowing they'll get the holiday they've paid for with a guarantee of value for money," said Mr Pollard.

"Direct-booking will always represent especially good value because clients go direct to the tour operator rather than paying travel agents' commission. Direct-booking is bound to increase in popularity as people take more holidays and become more selective in their choice. Nowadays our clients know exactly what they want when they phone. We have found that they prefer to deal with an expert who has first-hand knowledge of their chosen resort," he added.

-ends-

For further information please contact:
Charles Pollard/Claire Wilson, Portland Holidays: 071-380 0281
or Sarah Gibbins/Gina Lamb, Fleet PR: 071-630 9483.

Portland Holidays Ltd, 218 Great Portland Street, LONDON W1N 5HG

Fig. 13.1 A press release from Portland Holidays
This produced editorial in many regional newspapers,
including those in Swindon, York, Manchester, Swansea,
Belfast, Huddersfield and Wolverhampton. (Courtesy:
Doug Goodman Public Relations)

is often used) on quality paper incorporating the organisation's logo in the heading. The text needs as much care as any advertising copy, since the material may well be used verbatim by a newspaper's busy editing staff, and if succinct and well-written, the copy has a much greater chance of being used. Copy should be double spaced, with wide margins. As with direct mail letters, the opening sentence needs to be an attention getter, conveying the main theme of the message. Information must be accurate, and of course newsworthy; not a company 'plug' which editors will immediately see for what it is and discard. If it is essential to continue onto a second side, the word 'MORE . . .' should appear at the foot of the page. The text should be carefully proof-read for grammatical or spelling errors before posting.

Sometimes it is appropriate to use photographs to accompany the press release. In any case, media representatives may contact the company for photos of staff, etc., so that a small photographic library should be kept for publicity purposes. Good quality black and white prints (not negatives) should be filed. Information about the photos should not be written on the back, but a title and brief description of what the photo portrays should be typed on a separate sheet of paper, fastened with adhesive tape to the bottom of the photo, and folded behind it.

Feature articles

Sometimes an opportunity arises to prepare a 'feature article' on travel and tourism. An example is the Guest Writer's column in *Travel Trade Gazette*, and often local newspapers invite contributions on a travel theme. Feature articles are easiest to arrange with local papers in conjunction with a commitment to advertise in the same edition. Some 'advertising features' such as this almost cross the borders between publicity and promotion, becoming a thinly veiled plug for the company's products. Nonetheless, the material must be newsworthy – a topical issue of interest to readers, for instance – if it is to be used.

Press facility visits

One other function falls within the domain of the public relations department. This is the *press facility visit*. This is organised in a similar fashion to the travel agents' educational visit, which will be discussed a little later in the chapter. Its purpose is to invite media representatives – travel writers, journalists or correspondents from TV and radio – to visit a particular attraction or destination, or to use the services of a particular travel company, in the hope that the trip will receive a favourable commentary in the media. This can be a two-edged sword, since it invites opportunity for critical comment, too. The

strategy is widely used, however, by national or regional tourist offices, air and sea carriers, and tour operators, since a favourable press will have a huge impact on bookings. Principals may also invite correspondents from programmes such as *Holiday* or *Travel Show* to film their product; this again, if favourable, will generate substantial business for the region or company concerned. Occasional opportunities arise for plays or films to be made on location in areas or sites that will attract tourism. Films such as the James Bond series, and television programmes such as *The Lotus Eaters*, *Who pays the Ferryman?* and *The Aphrodite Inheritance* all generated interest in visits to the Mediterranean regions in which they were filmed in the '70s and early '80s, while the film version of *Hamlet* starring Mel Gibson set in Dunnottar Castle, Scotland and *The Darling Buds of May* filmed in Pluckley, Kent both helped to generate domestic tourism to those regions in the '90s.

Sponsorship

Sponsorship is a further means of achieving publicity for the name of a company. An organisation might sponsor the publication of a book or film about the history of the company or the industry, which could not be commercially viable without subsidy. Many long-established companies in the travel industry, such as shipping companies, have used this means of sponsorship. Other companies might choose to sponsor an academic text on travel and tourism, as British Caledonian did in the case of Alan Beaver's textbook *Mind your own Travel Business*. Alternatively, a documentary film might be produced on some subject concerning tourism.

More altruistic forms of sponsorship include financial support for the arts – theatre, fine art, concerts, festivals – and sporting events. The attraction of this form of publicity is that it generates goodwill, while costs can be set against taxes, and suitable activities for sponsorship can be found to fit any organisation's purse. Travel companies have sponsored educational study trips for students, or even sponsored staff for educational courses, as a gesture to generate goodwill among employees.

Local goodwill

Apart from sponsoring events in the local community, there are many other ways in which a company can get local goodwill. A retail agent in particular is highly dependent upon good relations with locals, since the catchment area exclusively provides the clients, so it is important to keep the name in front of the public. Events such as anniversaries of the company's founding can be used as a theme for generating news, organising contests and competitions, or mounting exhibitions. One agent saw an opportunity to build goodwill with the local school by offering to provide out-of-date brochures for geography assignments. This simultaneously solved the problem of getting rid of unwanted brochures and preventing the racks being depleted of current brochures.

Contact with shareholders of large companies is usually maintained through the annual report, except where crises emerge such as take-over bids, at which time a hastily mounted corporate advertising campaign aimed at shareholders may have to be mounted to counter the bid. Such campaigns are organised in consultation with management and the advertising agency.

Annual reports have become much more than simply a means of reporting performance to shareholders or would-be shareholders. Reports are now glossy and attractive, designed to create a sense of pride; travel companies, such as Singapore Airlines, have received international acclaim for the quality of their annual reports, which have a readership extending well beyond the shareholders themselves.

Sometimes the 'public' to be influenced are the law makers. If legislation is planned which is thought to be contrary to interests of the company, a campaign may be launched to persuade MPs to abandon the plans for legislation, or to sway public opinion against it. Such a campaign could be mounted by an individual company, but it is more likely to be taken up by the trade body. The usual vehicle for 'lobbying' is the direct mail letter, or an advertisement may be placed to encourage the travelling public to write to their MPs to protest.

Internal goodwill

Internally, too, there are publics to be wooed. Here, the aim may be to improve staff morale, or staff management relations, and in doing so reduce staff turnover or increase productivity.

In a large company, this will mean establishing a campaign just as is done with external publics. A common means of communication in the large travel firm is the *house journal*, an internal magazine of news and views about the company and its staff. While some of these journals are excellent, many are put together with insufficient time and effort to achieve the aims of good public relations, becoming little more than an in-house joke.

Corporate identity

The public relations department is usually involved in the introduction or modification of the company's corporate livery. The development of a 'house style' is an important element in an organisation's communications strategy, designed to support a particular image of the organisation. The logotype, or logo as it is more commonly known, is a symbol, name or combination of these forming a design which will instantly communicate the company and its image to the public. In the travel industry, this 'instant communication' takes on added significance, since the logo will appear on vehicles such as coaches, aircraft, ships and trains, as well as on stationery and shopfronts. It must therefore be instantly recognisable on the sides of fast moving vehicles as well as under adverse conditions such as poor weather or failing light. Above all, once adopted, the logo should be standardised and appear identically on every form of communication used by the company. If the company wishes to project a modern, dynamic image, the design should be modern, too. Care must be taken, though, not to produce a design which will date quickly. Design fads, for all their contemporary appeal, soon date and will need frequent up-dating – an expensive undertaking and one where the benefits of a recognisable logo may be lost. Note the huge sums expended by British Telecom to change

Fig. 13.2 The Thomas Cook logo in use on shop fronts,
coaches and stationery (Courtesy: Thomas Cook)

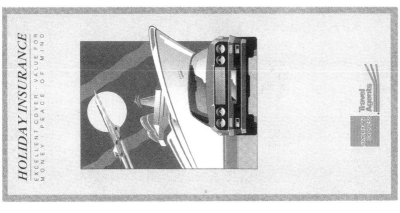

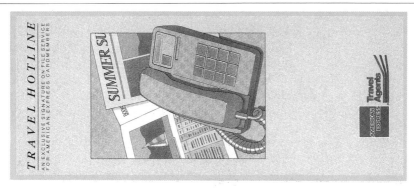

Fig. 13.3 Corporate identity: the American Express logo and corporate image in use in a series of publications (Courtesy: American Express)

their livery and logo in the early '90s – and the adverse response to it expressed by Telecom consumers.

Thomas Cook was obliged to reappraise its livery a few years ago, as it had neither a recognisable logo nor a standardised company name. The company appeared under various guises around the world, including Thomas Cook and Son, Thos Cook and Wagons Lits/Cook. In the 1970s, the decision was taken to standardise the name and incorporate this into a new logo. For the travel division, a bright pillar-box red was chosen for maximum impact, while a more sedate silver grey was selected for the financial services. The result of the redesign was a new, exciting and immediately recognisable insignia on vehicles, stationery and travel shops.

Reputation

Public relations techniques are also used to help develop and maintain the organisation's reputation with suppliers, distributors and colleagues in the industry. Membership of a professional body is one means by which individuals can exert influence through the building up of a circle of contacts. Travel companies are generally pleased to support staff who volunteer to serve on ABTA committees, and may pay subscriptions for staff who qualify for membership in the Institute of Travel and Tourism, or the Tourism Society, the HCIMA (Hotel Catering and Institutional Management Association) or the Chartered Institute of Transport. Even membership in Skål, the association of travel executives, which is ostensibly designed as a social club, provides a forum for contacts and the strengthening of influence among colleagues in the trade on a local basis, and for this reason some companies are willing to underwrite members' subscriptions.

The travel agents' educational visit

There can be little doubt that a travel agent who personally knows a destination is more likely to sell it with enthusiasm. There is no stronger force in a selling conversation with a customer than *personal* experience.

One of the authors paid a visit a short while ago to an agency which was fortunate in having a well-travelled proprietor, and overheard the following conversation. An elderly couple had visited several travel agencies in their prosperous seaside town. In each they had sought advice regarding a possible trip to Hong Kong and how to balance the duration and the contents. 'Young Man' said one, 'we would like your advice, though we appreciate that you won't have been there.' He was able to reply truthfully that not only had he been born in Hong King but had recently been back there, also visiting Beijing (Peking) on a side trip – something he thoroughly recommended them to do. All other agents visited were forgotten and a sale was swiftly made, and for a much greater sum than originally envisaged.

Although the example given may be unusual, as well as fortuitous, knowledge of nearer and more frequently demanded destinations is a basic stock-in-trade for any travel agent, but one that is all too often absent. Indeed, many agents appear to take the view that it is their right always to take their own holidays in the most exclusive and least commercialised destinations.

Some national tourist offices have recognised the importance of encouraging the maximum number of travel agency 'familiarisation visits', as a means of marketing their country. They therefore regularly assist in the organisation and sponsorship of such visits. Malta is a good example of this practice.

Following independence in 1964, Malta had a long period of estrangement from Britain, with whom close ties had previously existed. Factually, tourism from the UK had halved during a period of growth for Mediterranean holidays. The only way to rebuild numbers was seen to be by offering low prices that were directly competitive with nearer destinations. Whereas many Spanish destinations were only two hours from British Airports, Malta was three. This had an obvious effect on costs and to remain competitive meant effectively discounting the local costs substantially, through the offering of a lower 'tour operators' exchange rate. In the longer term, however, it was soon seen that Malta had to justify higher prices by offering something different. Higher prices also meant that higher quality would be demanded, and Government policies moved towards encouragement of the best in hotels and other facilities.

One problem to be overcome was that Malta's perceived quality in the eyes of past visitors was not always good. It was, therefore, decided to embark upon a policy of facilitating as many travel agents' visits as possible in order that they could see the improvements for themselves. Careful planning was needed to determine the best time for such visits, when there would be unsold seats on aircraft undertaking regular services, and yet when the weather would be kindly too. All major tour operators with programmes to the island were invited to participate in hosting the visitors and showing off their wares, but within strictly controlled criteria. Visitors were to be generously hosted, given little free time (these were working trips not holiday substitutes), and shown a range of the unique facilities that Malta offered to emphasise how different it was to other rivals for clients' attention. As well as seeing hotels, visits were included to historic sites and churches, as well as to the ubiquitous high tech disco.

This pattern has now been repeated several times with around a thousand travel agency staff benefiting. All have had to make applications to go, to ensure that they wanted to visit Malta, rather than being pressed by management to do so. All have paid to go to ensure commitment, even though the sum has been nominal and employers have been asked to fund it. Returning agents expressed delight about what they had experienced and promised to recommend Malta in future. The formula has thus proved successful in the most important way possible, a visible growth in the size and quality of Malta's tourism against falling levels elsewhere.

Though this pattern of major visits (probably 200 or more agents at one time) has been used by other destinations, more common are small group visits organised by individual tour operators responding to identified gaps in their future sales charts. Sadly, these are often less

**Your Invitation To Attend
A Celebration Of Malta's Tourism
Especially Arranged For
British Travel Agents**

Arranged By
THE NATIONAL TOURISM
ORGANISATION OF MALTA

In Conjunction With
AIR EUROPE, AIR MALTA,
BRITISH ISLAND AIRWAYS
And With The Co-operation Of
Leading Tour Operators Who Feature Malta
Plus A Combination Of Malta's Tourism Providers

Fig. 13.4 A national tourist office invitation to a travel agents' educational (Courtesy: National Tourism Organisation of Malta)

objective, sometimes being mere excuses for sales executives to entertain favourite agents. Even this, though, will have a beneficial rub-off in cementing relationships between supplier and seller concerns.

Progressive agency managements try to plan the attendance of staff on visits that will result in a commercial benefit in the future, but it is also recognised that the provision of fully paid educational opportunities is one of the perks of a fairly low paid job and, as such, a means of promoting staff loyalty. While it can be seen to be a training opportunity, the educational visit will probably remain tax exempt. However, if the system is abused it is clear that the tax authorities will disallow the benefit.

It is important that preparation, organisation of the event itself, and any follow-up, should be

Fig. 13.5 Agents enjoying an educational in Malta

faultless, and this does not happen by chance. The organiser needs to establish exactly who is eligible, considering the following points:

- which agencies are eligible for an invitation
- at what level and status of staff the programme is to be aimed. This will usually mean those actively working as salespeople
- whether those who have been before to that destination are eligible
- what age range is preferred
- whether more than one person can come from the same agency
- how long they should have been working in an agency
- whether, if named invitations are to be issued, substitutes will be accepted.

In addition, it will be sensible to arrange to have adequate information on file such as:

- home emergency contacts

- whether a smoker or non-smoker (for rooming purposes)
- whether the agency requires specific information or specially arranged visits to a particular property or facility, such as a golf course for golfing promoters
- details of the agency's local paper for any publicity shots taken during the trip and copy about the visit.

Before setting out it can be useful to obtain the participants' views on what he or she thinks they will see, in order to be able later to compare these with a similar questionnaire completed after their return. It is fairly certain that whatever the views expressed may be, they will represent a microcosm of the opinions of potential clients and may give suitable information for use in later promotional campaigns.

It is also worthwhile attempting to get the agreement of one of the trade press to cover the visit, to maximise the publicity benefits within the trade.

Hopefully, the participant's employers will also require a report on the visit, in the employee's own words, that can be circulated to other members of staff, thereby establishing the existence of relative expertise within the agency, as well as giving sales pointers. It is sensible also to furnish the participant with a certificate to display within the agency to publicise that he or she has 'successfully undertaken a study tour of' the destination concerned.

'Before setting out, it can be useful to obtain the participant's views on what he or she thinks they will see . . .'

Handling unfavourable publicity

Having discussed ways in which favourable publicity can be generated, some reference must also be made to dealing with the inevitable unfavourable publicity that will arise from time to time. Negative publicity can develop at both the macro and micro levels. At a macro level, the impact of strikes or go slows by air traffic controllers or customs officers can create enormous disruptions to travellers, which the media are not slow to exploit. At a micro level the company can be affected by such diverse problems as fires in hotels with locked emergency exits, dangerous hotel lifts, and faulty gas heaters causing asphyxiation in self-catering facilities, to say nothing of major disasters such as aircraft

crashes or the extensively reported accidental sinking of the Townsend Thoresen ferry at Zeebrugge in 1987. Quite apart from disasters of this magnitude, many minor problems arise with which PR must deal. Rumours of redundancy or takeovers can affect staff morale, resulting in the loss of key members of the company through resignation at a crucial time, while a CAA refusal to grant an ATOL, or a request from ABTA for a company's bond to be increased, may sow seeds of doubt in the minds of the travelling public or within the trade, which can undermine the company's reputation and lead to its collapse.

It may be thought that the PRO has a thankless task in having to help 'pick up the pieces' after such events; but their close relationship with the media makes their role invaluable when crises such as these occur. In a situation where a major crisis has occurred, successful PR will depend upon three things:

- the PRO must be well briefed and in full possession of the facts. A good working relationship with a frank and trusting management is essential if this is to be achieved.
- PROs must in turn be as frank as possible with the media. An obvious attempt to cover up will be seized upon by journalists, which will threaten the whole future relationship between the two parties.
- PROs must act fast, taking the initiative in calling the press and other media to a press conference to announce details of the event, rather than waiting to respond to media pressure. Fast action helps to dispel rumours which may paint a worse picture of the crisis than exists in reality.

Townsend Thoresen's public relations in handling the Zeebrugge disaster was a model of fast and frank action which kept the media fully informed, and the company's willingness quickly to accept blame took a great deal of the heat out of a volatile situation. There was no attempt at a 'cover-up', and management appeared anxious to see a thorough airing of the circumstances giving rise to the sinking.

A less critical, but nevertheless important, PR issue was the regeneration of British Airways as an efficient and profitable airline prior to its privatisation in 1987. The company was overstaffed and inefficient compared with its leading competitors, and suffered a poor public image. The necessary rundown of staff as a prelude to improving productivity worsened already weak morale within the company. A public relations campaign was launched both through a corporate advertising campaign aimed at the public to communicate the new image and the changed nature of the company, while a major internal campaign was launched to retrain staff to improve levels of service and restore their pride in the company. A major element in this campaign involved a one-day presentation 'A Day in the Life of British Airways' with staff from all over the world flown in to participate. The programme provided an opportunity for staff from all levels within the company to meet and learn more about each other's role. The exercise was a highly expensive, but extremely effective, example of good internal PR.

Evaluating campaign results

At the beginning of this chapter it was pointed out that evaluating PR campaigns is often more difficult than evaluating the success of other forms of communication, since PR has long-term objectives and these are often qualitative in nature. However, many PR exercises are measurable, providing targets are established initially determining what the campaign is to achieve. One means of measuring PR success is through the measurement of media *exposure*. An analysis of press cuttings, for instance, will enable the company to measure the number of column inches of publicity received during the period of the PR campaign. Press clipping services are provided by PR agencies, if the company hasn't the resources to undertake this themselves. Depending upon the media carrying the coverage, an estimate can be made of the audience reached through these reports, and some comparison made of the comparative costs if this coverage had had to be purchased commercially for advertising. While such tools of measurement are helpful, they provide no measure of the impact of the exposure, or whether goodwill, or recall of the company, would have been more effectively achieved through paid advertisements. Nevertheless, coverage in PR campaigns can be gained at very small cost to the company, and offers a valuable contribution to the overall communications process.

It will also be helpful to attempt some measure of the company's leading competitors, since this will give an indication of the relative success of the two organisations' PR departments.

A more accurate means of measuring PR effectiveness, if more expensive, is through the implementation of a programme of research to check changes in awareness, understanding or attitude. This will require surveys to be carried out before, after and sometimes during campaigns, which can be conducted among a sample of national consumers, among members of the local community, or among the firm's distributors. However, clearly national surveys, involving sampling opinion of 1500–2000 randomly selected respondents, are beyond the resources of all but the largest travel companies, or the public sector.

Within the company, figures on staff turnover can offer pointers on levels of job satisfaction, but must be supported by staff interviews to ascertain reasons for departure.

Finally, the impact of any campaign can be measured in terms of increased sales and profits. It may be difficult to be certain that increases are the result of any PR activities, or what proportion of the increases can be ascribed to PR compared with other communications campaigns of the company. Allowances must be made for external influences on market growth, and increases must be compared with comparative figures achieved by the company's competitors. At best, measurement will be inaccurate, but it will give some indication of the effectiveness of the PR department's activities, and help to justify the budget allocated to this function.

Questions, tasks and issues for discussion

1 This task will include a role play between two people, one of whom will take the role of spokesperson for a coach company which has just suffered the loss of a vehicle en route from the South of France, killing three and injuring 11 British passengers. The second person will take the role of a TV reporter interviewing the spokesperson about the crash (if this can be conducted on CCTV for later playback, so much the better). The media have heard rumours that the coach driver fell asleep at the wheel, after having had to curtail his rest hours in France, due to late arrival at the site on the outbound journey.

2 Write a press release designed to publicise the forthcoming launch of a new series of package tours to the Maldives, Mauritius and Madagascar which combine beach and activity (snorkeling, etc.) holidays.

3 Identify the key issues which go to make a successful educational visit for travel agents. Now carry out a small scale survey among agency counter staff who have been on an educational visit, in order to judge how well organised their visits were. Write a brief summary of your conclusions and recommendations.

Exercise

Taking any notable crisis which has affected one travel business during the past two years, plan a PR campaign to handle it.

14 Marketing control

After studying this chapter, you should be able to:

- recognise the importance of control mechanisms in the marketing plan
- distinguish between different methods of control
- implement simple control procedures in marketing

Control in the marketing process

The marketing function in a business is part of the *business system*. That is to say that certain *inputs* into the business, such as labour, money and enterprise together create a *process* which is designed to produce an end-product for consumers. This end-product is the organisation's *output*. A system can be defined as an input, a process and an output, and the objective of good management is to ensure that the input and process is subject to constant monitoring to ensure that the output is the right product, at the right price, in the right place at the right time – a classic definition of good marketing practice. The key word here is *monitoring*; the process which is designed to provide feedback on the effectiveness and efficiency of the system, to control it, and where necessary to change it. This can be illustrated in Fig. 14.1.

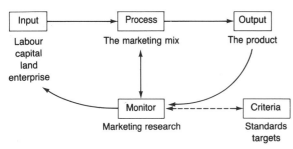

Fig. 14.1 The monitoring and control system

In this chapter we will look at the role of the monitoring procedures which are designed to

control the marketing system. All along we have stressed that planning is an essential part of the marketing process, but the plan will only be as good as the control to which it is subject. Plans are not carved on tablets of stone; they have to be adjusted constantly in the light of changing circumstances, as the company reacts to market forces.

Marketing is carried out in an organisation in three stages:

1 *Pre-action.* At this stage, activities associated with planning for action have to be undertaken. This includes the development of an information system, and a programme of planned market research. Marketing objectives are established, and strategies devised to achieve objectives. Forecasts are drawn up based on the strategies to be implemented.

2 *Action.* At this stage, the marketing plan is implemented. This brings into play the co-ordinating role of the marketing manager, who must ensure that the channels of communication are integrated within the department, so that promotional activities serve a common aim. The co-ordinator must also make certain that where other departments are contributing to the marketing plan, these commitments are met, and on time. Day-to-day activities undertaken as part of the plan will be regularly reviewed and adjusted as necessary.

3 *Post-action.* At this final stage, the marketing manager has the responsibility of reviewing the plan in its entirety, both to see whether targets are being achieved and to see if ways can be

found to further improve the performance of the department. It is this element of the control function which we will be examining in this chapter.

Although control is a key management function, it should not become a responsibility which exercises too much of a marketing manager's time. The objective of good management is to build a marketing control system which is self-correcting, as far as possible. This is achieved by good information systems, the use of management by objectives and the delegation of authority to take corrective action in day-to-day operational activities. Staff within the department need to be aware of what is expected of them as individuals, how they are performing, and to whom they are accountable. It is by no means unusual in a large travel company to find staff unclear about their accountability, or staff who are accountable to more than one member of management, each setting different priorities and having different expectations of their staff.

It is equally important that staff not only know their responsibilities but are also given power to regulate their activities, even at the most junior level. A member of a travel agent's counter staff given responsibility for racking brochures must know, for example, what the agency's policy is for racking brochures, procedures for ordering and re-ordering brochures, what action to take when brochures are refused by a principal or out-of-stock at the principal's. The clerk must be given full responsibility for maintenance of adequate stock, and control over the stockroom so that brochures are placed in an orderly system and can be found quickly when needed. With such a system, the manager should seldom have to intervene, and occasional spot checks or an end-of-season survey to ensure old stock is being cleared is all that is needed to maintain effective control.

At least three different forms of control can be identified in a control system:

1 *Performance control*, which is concerned with adherence to the marketing plan;
2 *Efficiency control*, concerned with finding means of reducing cost or to make the organisation more efficient in its operation;
3 *Strategic control*, in which the objective is to see whether the business is maximising its marketing opportunities within the overall organisational objectives and policies.

Each of these will be examined in the light of travel and tourism practice.

Performance control

This is designed to make sure the organisation meets its set targets. The normal targets identified in the marketing plan will include issues such as:

- turnover
- profitability
- market share
- return on investment
- quality
- consumer attitudes.

The extent to which these targets are being met can be monitored on a daily or weekly basis, and control is therefore dependent upon a regular flow of information which will indicate performance variance coming to those responsible for corrective action. These members of staff must ascertain why the deviance is occurring and whether action can be taken to bring it back into line with forecasts.

Actual identification of variance is a largely mechanical process, but correcting it calls for management skills, both in interpreting data and in the suitable deployment of resources. Here the manager must distinguish between controllable factors, and those outside the control of the business which will require readjustment of the forecast or the marketing plan. Let us say that the sale of in-coming tours to Britain from the United States has declined, and is failing to reach the targets set. This may be accounted for entirely by changing economic or political circumstances, such as the drop in US visitors to Europe resulting from a combination of the Gulf War, threats of Arab and IRA terrorist activity, and a recession at home in 1991, or fluctuating exchange rates between the two countries.

Nevertheless, it is important that the decline in the company's bookings is compared with those of other businesses handling in-coming American traffic, since it may be that internal factors account for part of the deviance. Assuming the organisation's performance is broadly in line with that of the total market, the marketing plan will require adjustment, so that targets are less dependent on US traffic in the coming year. The marketing manager will also want to look at the original objectives, and determine whether they were realistic. A close look will be taken of the controllable elements in the marketing plan; is the structure of the department designed to get the results sought in the marketing plan, for example? What factors in the marketing mix require to be changed to achieve the targets set?

Remedial action to bring performance back on target needs to be taken quickly, but not so quickly as to reflect a panic response to a temporary aberration, which may be self-correcting. At the time of the 1987 election, for example, overseas tour bookings from Britain fell sharply, leading to a rapid slashing of prices on forthcoming tours. While response is needed to clear current stock, in the long-term price reductions may not be needed, and in this case the market picked up after the election. Price reductions through the season led to a serious fall in seasonal margins.

In looking at profitability control, the organisation will be concerned not just with overall profitability but also with the profitability of each 'profit centre', or product range. A tour operator will be observing its profitability on each programme operated, just as a travel agent should examine its profitability for each type of travel service it sells. Harry Chandler's study, referred to earlier, is an interesting and unusual example of an attempt to estimate and control costs through accurate measurement of the labour associated with booking each type of travel service. Although undertaken some years ago, this study remains one of the most interesting examples of an attempt to control marketing costs in a retail agency, and appears in Table 3(a) and (b).

A travel agent needs to consider the profitability of his business by market segment, too. How does the profitability of the agency's leisure sales compare with that of the business house sales, for instance? Many agents are keen to seek more business house traffic because it is seen as relatively stable and with large companies

Table 3(a) Costs of servicing travel products in a retail agency

Type of traffic	% of total business	No. of pax per booking	Turnover per booking	Commission rate %	Revenue per booking	Labour Index	Commission per unit of labour
Package tours	36	2.8	205	11	22.55	24.8	90.9 p
Air long haul	20	1.7	343	7	24.00	41.0	58.5 p
Shipping	11	2.6	550	8	44.00	101.0	43.5 p
Air short haul	23	1.2	70	7.5	5.25	16.2	32.4 p
Air domestic/cross channel	7	2.1	40	7.5	3.00	21.0	14.3 p
Shipping cross channel	*	3.0	40	7.5	3.00	*	*
Continental rail	1.6	1.6	35	7.0	2.45	25.2	10.0 p
British Rail	1.3	1.3	12	7.0	.84	13.8	6.0 p

*shows figures not available in 1973

Notes

1 This exercise was first undertaken by Harry Chandler in 1969, based on 100 files for each type of traffic in the company records of Upminster Travel Ltd. The exercise has not been repeated since 1973.

2 The findings in 1969 suggested that package tours and air long haul were profitable, shipping was marginally profitable, and that other services were unprofitable and were being subsidised. Changes by 1973 suggest that air short haul had by then become marginally profitable, but other services were still being subsidised.

3 Shipping cross channel did not appear as a separate classification in 1969.

Table 3(b) Labour index

Labour index
Assessment of the labour involved in processing the average booking of each type of traffic. This covers phone calls, letters, forms, itineraries, and tickets from *acceptance* of booking, but not before.
Col 1 = standard letters (SL)
Col 2 = printed forms (FM) – includes invoices,
      confirmations, remittance advices
Col 3 = phone calls (PH)
Col 4 = dictated letters (DL)
Col 5 = itineraries (IT)
Col 6 = ticket issuance (TKT)

	SL×2	FM×3	PH×3	LD×10	IT×10	TKT	Labour index
Shipping							
No. of items	1.8	6.0	7.8	4.3	0.3	1	
Labour units	2	3	3	10	10	10	
	3.6	18.0	23.4	43.0	3.0	10	101.0
Air long haul							
No. of items	-	2.1	3.9	0.6	0.7	1	
Labour units		3	3	10	10	10	
		6.3	11.7	6.0	7.0	10	41.0

	SL×2	FM×3	PH×3	LD×10	IT×10	TKT	Labour index
Continental rail							
No. of items	0.3	2.3	1.9	0.2	0.4	1	
Labour units	2	3	3	10	10	6	
	0.6	6.9	5.7	2.0	4.0	6	25.2
Package tours							
No. of items	0.3	3.2	2.2	0.5	-	1	
Labour units	2	3	3	10		3	
	0.6	9.6	6.6	5.0		3	24.8
Air domestic/cross channel							
No. of items	-	2.2	2.8	-	-	1	
Labour units		3	3			6	
		6.6	8.4			6	21.0
Air short haul							
No. of items	-	1.5	1.9			1	
Labour units		3	3			6	
		4.5	5.7			6	16.2
British rail							
No. of items	2.1	1.5				1	
Labour units	3	3				3	
	6.3	4.5				3	13.8

(Courtesy: Harry Chandler, Chandler's World Travel)

can involve many thousands of pounds turnover each year. However, it is a highly competitive business, and may require the offer of a discount to win the contract. Average commissions from principals are lower for business travel than for package tours, and businesses settle their accounts after travel, rather than before. This can mean an agent waiting for several months to be paid. A careful assessment of the value of this account may lead to the conclusion that it is not worth retaining.

Quality control

Measuring quality and ensuring quality is maintained is a relatively simple matter in the production of durable goods; these can be inspected, rejected if below standard, and some tolerance agreed for the proportion falling below standard. Maintaining quality control over a product such as tourism is far less straightforward. Uncontrollable factors such as weather exert a considerable influence over the perceived quality of a tourism service.

Tour operators pay close attention to the requirement that their products live up to their descriptions in their brochures, because this is required by law. Few, however, establish acceptable tolerances for levels of complaints, although this is a measure of quality control. Yet this is easily established, since complaints can be measured through letters of complaint received by the company, or complaints made to the resort representatives, which can be easily recorded. The use of questionnaires is less effective in monitoring complaints, as most questionnaires used require only that clients list their levels of satisfaction or dissatisfaction with the product – there is insufficient information to take action to correct a situation if a high level of complaints is registered. One needs to know *exactly* what is wrong with the service, and what *action* is needed to correct the situation. Suggestion boxes can provide a good picture of consumer dissatisfaction, as can debriefing of staff such as resort representatives at the end of a season.

It is all too easy to believe that if levels of complaint are low, all is well with the company. In fact, there may be a high level of 'disguised dissatisfaction' with the company. British holidaymakers are noted for their vociferous complaints to resort representatives on the first day of their holidays. A good rep is able to placate the client who, however, returns home with a simmering dissatisfaction, leading the customer to book with another company in the following year. Consequently the level of repeat bookings must also be taken into account in measuring quality control.

Financial control

It is not only the financial controller who will be concerned that departments keep within their budgets. While the budget itself is designed to exercise an automatic control over the operations of the business, the marketing department must constantly check that sales, promotion and other expenses remain within the agreed limits. However, too tight control can lead to missed marketing opportunities. The marketing plan must not become a straightjacket.

The use of ratios to determine marketing mix expenditure is a common means of judging performance, but can be misleading if it is based on what 'the average company in the industry' is achieving. While it is common to determine that a fixed proportion of turnover be allocated to promotion, the earlier discussion on communications budgets will have made it clear that spend will need to vary according to the established objectives of the marketing plan. In a time of falling sales, too often the control mechanisms go into operation to cut promotional spend where it might be more appropriate to increase it, to generate more sales.

Changing circumstances can also result in a particular product carrying too high a proportion of the company's overheads. Let us say that fuel prices have been increased. This could lead to a disproportionately large fall in long-haul tour bookings, which will require some readjustment to the allocation of overheads to those programmes.

Efficiency control

If performance control has indicated a weakness in some aspect of the organisation's marketing, analysis will be needed to determine whether the marketing activities or the structure of the department need to be changed in some way to make the marketing more efficient. Even if marketing targets are being met, sheer pressures of competition between principals or between retailers require that ways be constantly sought to reduce costs without impairing efficiency. This means constant re-evaluation of the marketing mix. All means of measuring success must be taken into account, not merely levels of turnover.

Reviewing the organisational structure of the department might mean considering whether sales should be separated from marketing and given its own head; or whether the department has grown to a point where it is worth introducing a marketing controller to co-ordinate activities in the department. Should the marketing functions become increasingly centralised, as has happened in certain large hotel chains, or should they be more decentralised, as other chains have done? Does the administrative structure facilitate the marketing function, or does it hinder it? Above all, is the quality of the staff up to the standard required?

This last question is a crucial one for the travel and tourism industry. In most sectors of the industry, the belief remains that profit levels do not allow better salaries to be paid, and therefore better staff cannot be recruited. However, performance standards do vary between companies, and different management styles are a major contribution to these variations. Are staff being properly trained in marketing techniques? Are they being promoted beyond their capabilities? Are they adequately motivated? What does the manager know about levels of satisfaction among the staff? How are the staff managed – by sanctions, rewards, or, simplest of all but surprisingly rare, by thanking them for a job well done? Frequent examples can be shown of small companies in travel (employing between 20 and 50 members of staff) where the manager seldom meets or greets his staff, but nevertheless expects them to give of their best for the company. Measures of staff turnover and levels of staff satisfaction are important methods of judging the efficiency of the organisation with respect to staff. It it not sufficient simply to *count* the proportion of staff leaving the company; managers must know for what *reasons* the staff are leaving.

Even with a good workforce and organisation, the communications mix must be monitored constantly to compare the relative performance of different promotional tactics and seek ways of making these more cost-effective. Some of these on-going monitoring processes have already been more fully described in Chapter 10, dealing with promotional techniques. Such procedures are an integral part of the control system.

Since the travel brochure is such a critical element in the promotional mix, a company should regularly monitor its brochures by soliciting consumer and retailer views about its brochures compared with those of the competition. Tests of awareness and recall must be carried out, and sales representatives calling on travel agents will be required to report which brochures are racked and where.

The Sales Manager will monitor the ratio of sales to cost of sales, both for his or her own sales force and for the company's retail agents. Identification of more productive distribution outlets will determine future levels of support and should permit analysis of the relative performance of national multiples versus independent agents and small chains. Results of joint promotional schemes will be assessed, as will the effect of different incentives provided to retailers.

Carriers are seeking to employ new technology in their drive for cost-efficiency. The introduction of ticket printing machines at some airports internationally is one means by which they are responding to the need to improve cost control.

Strategic control

From time to time it becomes necessary to look at the total process by which strategic marketing is undertaken in the company, in order to judge whether the organisation is taking advantage of the marketing opportunities open to it. This will require senior staff from outside the department to consider the extent of market orientation of the department and of the company as a whole, how well organised it is to spot opportunities when they occur and exploit them, and how well the organisation plans its strategies. No travel business today can afford to rest on its laurels; markets change rapidly, and complacency over present occupancy levels, load factors or bookings can quickly change to concern as new challenges emerge to face the company.

Management will want to review the effectiveness of its internal, as well as its external, communications. Do the staff share common objectives, and are they working towards a common aim? How well do other departments co-operate with the marketing staff to meet their needs? These are important questions which relate to the operating efficiency of the company as a whole. Where there are divisions of the company on separate sites, or staff are employed far from Head Office, communications can easily suffer. One of the most common management problems in tour operating is the failure to communicate, and above all the failure to establish common aims between Head Office staff and staff in the field, such as area managers and resort representatives. Head Office staff making field visits may not even take the time to meet their field representatives; yet it is the resort representative who is closest to the company's clients, knows their problems and can best offer suggestions for the improvement of services.

If a serious weakness is found in some aspect of the organisation's marketing, a full marketing audit may be commissioned. This generally means bringing in outside consultants to undertake a systematic investigation into every aspect of the company's marketing operation.

Where responsibility is delegated, as is the case in large organisations, control is easier to exercise in one sense because a system of checks and balances is introduced by assigning individual responsibility and accountability. A very small company, where management is vested in a single individual who takes on total responsibility for marketing, as well as general management of the company's day-to-day affairs, will be less likely, and less willing, to build in a system of control. It is this aspect of marketing management which poses the greatest threat to the many small units which still make up the bulk of companies operating in the travel and tourism industry, and which are today struggling to survive in the face of the more professional marketing management of the large corporations.

Questions, tasks and issues for discussion

1 What levels of control do travel agents actually exercise at the pre-action, action and post-action stages of marketing?

2 Should control over racking policy, window display and other merchandising activities of a 'major multiple' travel agency chain be exercised by Head Office, or by the individual branches? What arguments would you offer in favour of each of these approaches?

3 The aim in controlling sales reps is to achieve a balance between giving them total autonomy to do their jobs properly, and ensuring their performance is monitored adequately. How will a good sales manager tackle this problem?

Exercise

As part of the year's current marketing plan for a tour operator, develop a programme of quality control, giving details of how this will be measured, and what standards will be imposed.

Part 2 Case studies

Case study 1
The marketing of a tourist attraction:
Mr Bowler's Business, Bath

(Prepared with the help of Ron Deamer and Russell Frears, Connexions, Bath)

Background

Mr Bowler's Business is an industrial heritage museum situated in Bath, Avon. The origins of the museum go back to 1978, when the museum was established to conserve and display the works and contents of the firm of J.B. Bowler. The firm manufactured aerated waters, as well as operating a brass foundry, engineering works, locksmiths and other sundry business interests. The firm was founded in 1872, and closed in 1969, at which point the premises were demolished. However, in the hundred years of its operation, the proprietors never threw anything away, amassing a huge collection of tools, machines, bottles and papers that provided a unique heritage of more than a century of business operations. In all, the collection comprises more than 40 000 objects and 50 000 documents. This collection was purchased in 1969, with the intention of finding a suitable building to form the basis for a museum.

The establishment of the museum

In 1978, with conservation as the major motive, a group of enthusiasts established the Bath Industrial Heritage Trust, and registered as a charity. With the aid of significant grants from private trusts and the public sector, among which were grants from the City Council and the Science Museum, London, the Trust was able to lease and convert the Camden Works building, a City-owned property built in 1777 as a Real Tennis court, which was later to become in turn a school, a malthouse, a soap works and a packing case factory. The building was rented from the City at a subsidised rent, and the

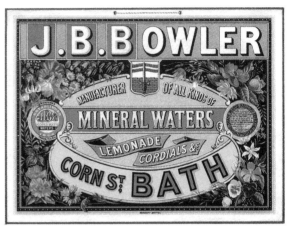

Original showcard of the business of J B Bowler (1895)
(Courtesy: Bath Industrial Heritage Centre)

Council also advanced a small annual grant. The site, however, has drawbacks, in that it is some minutes' walk north of the city centre and the major attractions of Bath, and in a direction in which visitors would not normally choose to take a walk. Bath has a number of prominent attractions which will always have the tourists' priority, and because so many are day visitors, often spending a relatively short time in the city, it will be difficult to attract these casual tourists to the museum. Bath is a notoriously difficult city in which to find car parking space, and the museum itself has no parking facilities, either for coaches or cars. Although there is a bus bay nearby for coaches to drop off passengers, parking is not permitted on adjacent roads, so the casual visitor coming by car has a very real problem in reaching the site. Further, signposting is presently inadequate, although the City Council has now agreed to provide a cast-iron and gold-lettered tourist sign within the city centre.

A number of entire rooms from the Bowler Business were reconstructed within the museum, including the heavy machine shop, ironmongers' shop, brass foundry, finishing shop, office and entire aerated water manufactory. The museum also accommodates two other permanent attractions: an exhibition tracing the history of Bath Stone, and a cabinet maker's workshop.

The museum is registered with the Area Museums Council who may, subject to their being satisfied that their stringent criteria are met, provide a proportion of the funding necessary for the conservation and cataloguing of documents.

In 1988, the Trust became a company limited by guarantee, which gave the organisation scope to attract shareholders with the financial motivation and expertise to give a new thrust and direction to the project.

Marketing the original museum

The museum is run by a group of eight of the Trust's members, who were appointed to the Council of Management, and include the museum's Curator. The operating policy was to at least break even, which the Trust estimated would be achieved with a throughput of 30 000 visitors a year. However, largely through budget limitations which made promotion difficult, the build-up to these figures was slow. More worrying, however, was the slump in admissions in the mid-'80s. Poor and inaccurate recording, which failed to distinguish between paid and unpaid admissions, makes it difficult to obtain exact figures, but overall attendances between 1983 and 1989 are estimated as follows (accurate recording of figures is available only from 1989):

1983	13 000 –	14 000
1984	12 000 –	13 000
1985	10 000 –	11 000
1986	7 500 –	8 500
1987	7 500 –	8 500
1988	9 500 –	10 000
1989	9 600	

While customer profile research has been limited, it has been estimated by observation that typically some 25 per cent of paid admissions are children, while adult groups form a very small proportion of the total attendance. A small-scale survey of just over 100 visitors was undertaken during the summer months of 1985, which indicated that 20 per cent of visitors were from abroad, and 34 per cent from London and the South East. Nearly all visitors were travelling independently, and the number of children attending was low. Very few of the visitors lived locally, but while it is accepted that the level of local awareness of the museum is still not as strong as it might be, the market profile is believed to have changed dramatically since 1985, with fewer overseas visitors and a considerable increase in the number of local visitors.

Staffing

A normal staff complement comprises three full-time staff (curator/manager, deputy curator/archivist, and cataloguer); up to seven part-time employees (often students, employed during the peak summer season); and a pool of volunteers who take on the role of guides within the museum. Full-time staff will often help out part-timers during busy periods, covering the shop and ticket office, or serving in the cafe.

Operating evaluation

By 1988, it was clear that without a radical overhaul in its operations, the museum faced an uncertain future. The museum had always been heavily dependent upon donations, which from the outset were double the revenue achieved through admissions. However, revenue decline in the second half of the '80s meant that it was becoming increasingly dependent on this source of funding. Apart from a long-term (15 year) interest free loan from a private source, the museum also had an overdraft, and the bank was showing concern. It was recognised at that point that a major reappraisal of the museum's finances and operations would be necessary. The Council of Management estimated that they would need to treble the number of visitor admissions if they were to operate efficiently and survive in the long-term. Deciding that an objective evaluation was required, they called in a management consultant in November 1989.

The product

Following the consultant's report, a number of improvements, both in refurbishment and in stock, have been made to the facilities offered on site. Apart from the displays already referred to, the museum offers three further sources of revenue: a cafe, shop, and a meeting room/exhibition area suitable for hiring out. Entry to the shop and cafe is possible without purchasing an admission ticket, and in fact the cafe could benefit from being the sole outlet for snacks in the immediate vicinity. It has not yet been possible to assess whether these separate revenue-producing areas are individually profitable.

The marketing plan

The consultant's report, which appeared in February 1990, agreed with the assessment of the management that a realistic target of 30 000 visitors should be established, based on what was estimated to be a reasonable proportion of the admissions to the nearby attraction, the Bath Assembly Rooms and Museum of Costume, which by 1989 were attracting some 250 000 visitors per annum.

The 30 000 visitors were estimated in the report to break down as follows:

%
45 adults
20 children
15 senior citizens and other discounted
   segments
20 groups (including educational)

It was also agreed that there was a need to raise awareness among the local population of Bath, and that there was substantial opportunity for development of the educational visit market, in spite of the impact of the Educational Reform Act (the proportion of school parties has, in fact, risen

recently to around 25 per cent of total annual visitors).

The image of the museum

The report made clear that there was a need to reposition the museum in the eyes of the public, and that a name change would be necessary to achieve this. The museum's attractions appeal to two types of market; the serious industrial archeologist, for whom the 'museum' concept is important, and the visitor seeking an entertaining experience, for whom the 'heritage centre/tourist attraction' concept is paramount. The original title of the attraction, Camden Works: The Museum of Bath at Work, failed to generate enthusiasm among the mass tourist market, which would be essential if the target figures were to be reached. The Bath Industrial Heritage Centre, the later title, although appropriate for the specialist visitor, similarly failed to motivate the mass visitor. A number of alternative titles were discussed, but the decision was made finally to retitle the museum Mr Bowler's Business, while retaining the earlier Bath Industrial Heritage Centre title as a sub-title designed to attract the serious visitor. The new title was seen as catchy and intriguing, while still managing to retain connotations of the firm's social and industrial history within the City.

Pricing policy

The consultant's report had suggested a rack rate of £2.50. After consideration, however, the Council of Management decided that this would be out of line with other attractions within the area, as well as representing a doubling of the previous entry charge. Rack rates of other attractions in the area at the time were:

	£
No 1 Royal Crescent	2.00
Pump Room/Roman Baths	2.70
American Museum	3.50

The decision was made to charge £2.00 for adults, £1.75 for discounted (senior citizen, etc.) tickets, £1.00 for children (free under 5), and to offer a 10 per cent discount to adult groups of 20 or more. Group leaders such as teachers are, of course, admitted free when accompanying children paying the group entry charges. Other discounts of 10 per cent were offered to holders of open top bus tour tickets, and through the medium of couponing in Avon County Council's 'Around Avon' booklet (one free child with every full admission). Distribution of discounted vouchers would, it was decided, play an important part in future promotional campaigns.

In 1991, the decision was taken to put up the entry charge to £2.50. This had the effect of increasing revenue with very little drop-off in attendance, and has helped to cover the increase in costs experienced by the museum in 1991.

The communications campaign

An assessment of the origin of school parties revealed that many were coming from substantial distances away: London, Surrey, Sussex, Dorset, Essex, Berkshire, with enquiries being received from as far afield as France. Visits were often arranged as part of an educational study trip, with schoolchildren staying at local hostels. It was decided that a more aggressive effort to reach schools in the immediate region would be made, and a direct mail campaign was carried out, directed at schools in Avon.

The Trust was fortunate in being able to secure, through their connections locally, the services of a part-time voluntary fund raiser, who also undertook to attract local companies to use the meeting and conference facilities. The management also intends to take advantage of the unique siting of the cafe in the area, promoting this to local firms for light snack lunches. Additional revenue was to be attracted through the shop by advertising specific products as Christmas gifts, in the local newspaper.

A very small budget had been allocated to promotion in 1990. This was spent as follows:

	%
printing 150 000 leaflets	62.5
leaflet distribution	12.25
local press advertising	21.5
co-operative promotion	3.75
	100.00

Approximately half the leaflets were used in two direct mail campaigns, accompanying the *Bath Star* and *Bath Advertiser* newspapers. These offered 20 per cent discounts, using colour-coded stickers, on presentation of the leaflet at the ticket office. Blue sticker leaflets were delivered at the start of the main school holidays to an area of Bath with a high number of young families, while leaflets with red stickers were distributed after the holidays, in September, to a wealthier area of the city comprising largely older residents. Although the take-up on the offer was small, there is evidence, based on the growing number of Bath residents visiting the museum later, that it was successful in creating local awareness of the attraction. The balance of those leaflets distributed were delivered by hand to Tourist Information Centres in the area, and to all hotels and guest houses in the *Bath Accommodation Guide*.

The leaflet itself proved to be controversial in design. Captioned 'Enjoy Mr Bowler's One and Only Many Flavoured Soda Fountain', it aimed to attract visitors to the aerated water manufactory and cafe, but the concept of a soda fountain was new to many visitors, while the more serious side of the display material was largely ignored. It was later accepted that a new A4 leaflet would be needed for 1991.

The 1990 leaflet appeared too late to take advantage of the trade's traditional 'leaflet swaps'. These take place before Easter, and provide opportunities for the trade to exchange one another's leaflets. Those in which the museum would expect to participate would include the West Country Tourist Board's workshop at Shepton Mallet and the North Wiltshire Tourism Association's Chippenham meeting. Hoteliers and others can use this opportunity to pick up leaflets for their own racks, while members of the public are also invited to many of these meetings, and may themselves pick up leaflets which interest them.

Advertising was largely limited to press advertisements in papers reaching residents within one hour's driving time of the City. However, some advertising space was also taken in coaching trade newspapers and the *Coach Driver's Yearbook*. Also falling within this part of

Original brochure for Mr Bowler's Business (Courtesy: Bath Industrial Heritage Centre)

New brochure for Mr Bowler's Business (Courtesy: Bath Industrial Heritage Centre)

the budget is a regular Newsletter, produced quarterly in runs of at least 350 copies, and a special leaflet aimed at schools promotion. Special teachers' packs are available at commercial cost. A number of more extensive pieces of literature dealing with the displays are also produced and sold at commercial prices within the shop.

The major collaborative promotion involves membership in ABLE (Association of Bath and District Leisure Enterprises), a consortium of some 32 local visitor attractions which produces 500 000 leaflets a year. The museum has also co-operated with advertising agency promotions in supermarkets, offering one free entry for one paying visitor, against the sale of such popular products as Kia-Ora fruit juices, hair colourants and Mars Bars.

Public relations

Public relations have been restricted to small-scale projects to date. The museum holds an Open Week for residents once a year (in common with other Bath attractions), in which local residents can gain entry free, and local trade associations such as the Bath Hotels and Restaurants Association or ABLE are encouraged to hold meetings on the site. Local hoteliers and restaurateurs are invited to take tea at the museum, and the curator will address local

NEWSLETTER NUMBER 8   WINTER 1990

A MERRY CHRISTMAS AND A HAPPY NEW YEAR

BRIGHT FUTURE FOR MR BOWLER'S BUSINESS

The higher profile presented by the Centre through the creation of 'Mr Bowler's Business' is already showing encouraging signs of success. The scheme has been running only since the latter part of June but during this short period the Centre has received a steady flow of visitors already exceeding last year's figure of 9,000 whilst nearly every tourist attraction in the area has seen a reduction in the number of visitors since the beginning of the year!

The new shop and cafe has generated higher income and the range of merchandise and the variety of light refreshments available is constantly being reviewed to satisfy the visitors demands.

A new promotional leaflet has been produced aimed at the school party market. It has already been circulated to 300 schools and Teacher's Centres within a 30 mile radius of Bath. The newsletter-style leaflet informs teachers of the range of educational material available at the Centre and offers a reduction for groups who book to visit during the winter - a traditionally quiet time. In the New Year, schools in Bath will be sent the leaflet plus a questionnaire prepared with the assistance of Professor Joseph Black, to discover how best the Centre can assist with the new GCSE Design and Technology Curriculum.

The Centre is fortunate in having secured the services of Colin Awmack, previously of BEMA, to assist with fund raising. He has already been successful in obtaining grant from Herman Miller UK Limited and is currently sending appeals to industrial companies in and around Bath. We feel sure that his enthusiasm for the project will undoubtedly result in a greater interest by companies in the work of the Centre, which we hope will result in generous gifts in cash or kind.

We still need more visitors during the winter months so please tell all your friends and relations to see this unique collection - and ask them to become Friends!

RAFFLE

There is still time to purchase a ticket for the raffle! The prize is one of the charming handmade Victorian-style dolls that are on sale in the shop. 'Emily' with long dark ringlets and pale pink dress and bonnet normally retails for £26.00 but for only 20p (or 6 tickets for £1.00) you could be the proud owner of 'Emily' just in time for Christmas. The draw takes place on Monday 17th December so if you are interested in buying a ticket please contact the Centre by Sunday 16th December at the latest.

Good Luck!

CHRISTMAS SHOPPING
AT MR BOWLER'S EMPORIUM

Hand-Crafted Victorian Style Dolls	from £25.00
Elsenham Traditional Comestibles	from £2.25
Old Fashioned Candy Sticks	at 10p each
Antique Style Pot-pourri Dishes and Photoframes	from £2.95
Old Fashioned Toys	from £1.95
Rainbow Coloured Marbles	from 7p each

MR BOWLER'S BUSINESS
at the Bath Industrial Heritage Centre
Julian Road, Bath
OPEN DAILY 10am – 4pm until 23rd December

Newsletter of the Bath Industrial Heritage Centre

groups such as branches of the Townswomen's Guild.

As yet, no budget has been established for a programme of market research, but it is recognised that this is an area requiring investment in the future.

In spite of the recession experienced in 1990, attendance increased to 11 300, and the management felt that a reassessment of visitor numbers would be realistic in 1991, adjusting their target to 22 000. At the time of writing it is unclear whether this can be achieved, although 8000 had been admitted in the first six months of the year, prior to the peak summer months.

An assessment of the average spend per visitor in the shop and cafe, together with revenue achieved through average entry charges, gave the management team an overall estimate of revenue which, together with donations actually pledged for the coming year, enabled them to estimate total income and fix the promotional budget at 7.5 per cent.

The members of the Trust recognise that they have a long way to go, but remain confident that they can survive and prosper. Their particular strength is the authenticity and uniqueness of their collection, which is unparalleled in Britain. Their principal weakness is undoubtedly the need to make their product better known both locally and nationally, and, restricted by a small budget, this is a process which takes a long time.

By 1991, both the shop and cafe were open full-time, and this had boosted revenue. Along with the increase in admissions, the future of the museum is looking rosier than would have been forecast two years earlier, but the target of 30 000 is still some way off.

(This case study appears with the kind permission of the Bath Industrial Heritage Trust Ltd.)

Case study 2
The launch of a special event:
Garden Festival Wales, Ebbw Vale 1992

(Prepared with the help of Ceri Thomas, Marketing manager, Garden Festival Wales)

Background to the study

Garden Festival Wales is the last of five planned National Garden Festivals held in Britain, initiated by the Department of the Environment. Former festivals were held at:

Liverpool	1984
Stoke-on-Trent	1986
Glasgow	1988
Gateshead	1990

'Gryff' – the character used as a logo for Garden Festival Wales

The aims of the garden festivals were to help to change the image of economically depressed regions, to speed up the process of land reclamation, to secure long-term economic wealth and job creation opportunities within the site, to assist the local community through post-festival after-use of land, and to provide training for future long-term employment in the region. Garden Festival Wales was specifically designed to project a new image for the South Wales

The alternative logo
(Courtesy: Garden Festival Wales)

valleys, acting as a catalyst for the wider creation of economic wealth and job opportunities.

Festivals were required to recover their costs, and therefore have sought to attract large numbers of tourists. Stoke-on-Trent, which recorded the fewest visitors of the first four festivals, nevertheless achieved a gate of 2.2 million during its five months of operation, while Gateshead, in spite of the recession, achieved 3.2 million. Attendances at Liverpool matched those of Gateshead, while Glasgow's Festival, sited in the city centre, achieved 4.2 million visitors. These attendance figures can be considered very satisfactory, considering the poor summer weather that accompanied several of the festivals.

The product

Garden Festival Wales is a £60M project, constructed on a 185-acre site (including five acres of water) just south of Ebbw Vale. Some one and a half million trees, plants and shrubs will be planted on the site, making this the most authentic garden setting of all the festivals to date. Ninety-six acres will be retained as permanent landscaping on completion of the festival, and the remainder of the site will be occupied by light industry and residential accommodation.

There are three themed areas within the site, representing the past ('Land of our Fathers'), present ('Wales Celebrates') and future ('Journey into the Future'), together with adventure playgrounds, high quality theme rides, a unique 'sky shuttle', a restored Welsh hill farm and an energy-efficient housing development. There are a number of unusual attractions on site, among them the 'GWR' – 'Gryff's Wonderful Roadtrain' – offering free rides around the site, a free pet care centre, a funicular railway, and artistic features planned as integral attractions, with designers, sculptors and artists working together in teams to design different areas of the site.

Five thousand hours of activities and events will be mounted throughout the Festival to provide added interest and to encourage repeat visits, including spectacular floral shows planned by a team of innovative Dutch designers.

The character Gryff (see p. 216) which has been developed as the mascot for the festival, appears both on and off-site, and also offers important opportunities for merchandising.

Major funding for the event came from Blaenau Gwent Borough Council and Gwent County Council, with additional funding coming from the Government (through the Welsh Office) and the European Regional Development Fund. The festival organisers sought substantial sponsorship from the private sector, and at the time of writing had already achieved £7M of their £9M target, the largest individual contributor being the McDonald's family eating chain, which will operate a temporary fast food outlet on site – the only one outside the USA.

The festival site offers a number of important advantages over previous sites. It is the first to be held in southern Britain, with a catchment area for day trips that extends to the West Midlands, South West, and London and the Home Counties; and it is the first to be held in a valley site with mature woodlands, providing a more authentic setting for woodlands gardens.

Marketing strategy

Although Garden Festival Wales extends over a period of five months, as a 'one-off' event it has to create instant awareness and interest in the marketplace. What is more, the product has to be right *from the moment it opens*; there is no time to improve it, or to right wrongs in the following season. The opening date cannot be delayed or postponed, as with some other types of attraction, should the builders fall behind in construction. There are implications for pricing in this situation; it is difficult to justify providing cheap or discounted tickets in the hope of stimulating the market and generating more full tariff tickets later, for example.

To take advantage of the interest in sustainable tourism and ecologically-sound development, the site is designed as a promotional platform for environmental issues. The organisers have retained Friends of the Earth as advisors to ensure this; all publicity material is printed on recycled paper, to give one example.

The market

The market for garden festivals is extremely diverse, with something for everyone, although naturally certain target markets, such as garden lovers, will show a keener interest than others. The organisers expect a total of two million visitors, drawn from within a catchment area of 2–3 hours' travelling time, and comprising 48 per cent day trippers, 22 per cent from the local conurbation, 24 per cent domestic tourists, 5 per cent educational groups, and 1 per cent from overseas. Visitor numbers broken down by expected means of transport are, 75 per cent by car, 20 per cent by coach and 5 per cent by other

GARDEN FESTIVAL WALES

EVENT of the DECADE

Only SEEING is BELIEVING

Garden Festival Wales
Gŵyl Gerddi Cymru
Eblw Vale 92

MAY 1st to OCTOBER 4th 1992

Suggested Itineraries for Coach and Tour Operators Visiting Garden Festival Wales

Garden Festival Wales
Gŵyl Gerddi Cymru
Eblw Vale 92

Garden Festival Wales
Gŵyl Gerddi Cymru
Eblw Vale 92

KEEPING A WELCOME IN THE HILLSIDES

A UNIQUE HOSPITALITY OPPORTUNITY

CROESO!

Merchandising material for Garden Festival Wales

means. (There is no railhead available, but a rail–coach link will be established, and a number of scheduled services will operate to the site during the period of the festival.) Coach group business, which to a large extent will be pre-booked, is an important element in the booking pattern, since it is less weather-dependent (although the developers have given considerable thought to the need to provide adequate undercover attractions for wet-weather days).

Average daily attendance is expected of between 9400 and 10 800, with an absolute peak of over 29 000 on key days.

Income and pricing

Apart from admissions at the gate, revenue will be achieved through:

- catering on site
- the sale of plants and other garden items
- the sale of other goods and services
- rides on site
- merchandising, especially associated with the Gryff character.

The decision was taken not to charge for car parking. Apart from regular entry tickets, there will be the normal discount tickets, for example, for senior citizens and young people, group discounts and season tickets. An effort has been made to sell season tickets in advance of the opening by offering early booking discounts:

£30 for the first 5000 sold, then £35 until the end of September 1991, £40 until December and £45 from January 1992 onwards.

At the time of writing, early indications are that the tactic of discounting advance sale tickets is paying off, the first 5000 being sold well before the cut-off date.

Pre-launch marketing activities

Garden Festival Wales is supported by £7.9 million worth of promotional spend, made up of its own marketing budget, co-operative ventures with contributors, sponsors and the travel trade, and Wales Tourist Board promotional activities

which will be heavily themed in support of the Garden Festival throughout 1992.

The major concern of the organisers, in the promotion leading up to the opening, is to create awareness of the event, through direct mail and public relations activity. Educational groups have been pinpointed as a significant potential market, and three educational resource packs, linked to the National Curriculum and relating to humanities and environmental resources issues, have been developed and mailed to 13 000 schools within three hours' driving time, under sponsorship from McDonalds. Over 15 000 advance tickets were sold to Saga Holidays, the tour operator specialising in packages for the older market. An arrangement was concluded with the Automobile Association for a special offer in the AA Bonus Book (two-thirds of the AA's 7.3 million members live within the catchment area of the festival).

Direct mailings are also being undertaken to coach operators and horticultural associations, and sales calls are being made on special interest groups and coach operators, while special efforts are being made to reach the German, Irish, Dutch and French markets through these methods and through consumer shows, trade fairs and exhibitions.

Anneka Rice is featured in a 'Countdown to opening' promotion, publicised in quarterly newsletters in the lead up to opening, while roadshows in the area are involving the local community and inviting people, especially teachers, to come and learn about developments. The festival organisers run a fleet of four-wheel-drive vehicles to provide tours of the site under construction for coach operators, tour operators and other influential individuals in the travel industry, as well as for representatives from the media, sponsors and contributors. A specially constructed viewing platform has been built near the site from which passing motorists can obtain an overview of the construction activities.

Summary

This case study has been concerned with the pre-launch activities associated with a special event.

Festival News

ISSUE 5   MAY 1st 1991

MAY DAY SPECIAL EDITION

ANNEKA CHALLENGES GARDEN FESTIVAL WALES

Anneka Rice today starts the countdown to the 1992 National Garden Festival with the unveiling of a giant clock. With exactly 366 days to go before the gates open Anneka has challenged Garden Festival Wales to be bigger and better than all the others.

At 10.00am on Friday 1st May, 1992 the twenty-two week spectacular opens its doors to the public. It will be a five month long extravaganza – a showcase for the very best in leisure and entertainment, offering fun and pleasure for everyone whether they are eight or eighty. And it will all take place in a fabulous garden setting against the backdrop of the mountains of the South Wales Valleys.

The whole of the Festival will be themed to reflect the past, present and future of Wales. Land of Our Fathers will

Anneka Rice challenges Garden Festival Wales to be bigger and better than all the others.

be rich in images, all reflecting the historical wealth of Wales. This includes castles, a major exhibition called "The Tree of Time", which charts the history of Blaenau Gwent Borough Council and Gwent County Council and gardens of sculpture. There will also be poetry and crafts as well as major retail and catering outlets including a McDonald's restaurant.

The heart of the Festival will be Wales Celebrates. Here, perhaps, more than anywhere else in the Festival the visitor will witness a horticultural Festival of Excellence. Extravagant bedding displays will compete with enchanting and bizarre theme gardens. Horticultural Halls will play host to a regular programme of Horticultural Spectaculars – displays of flowers unlike anything seen before in this country.

Travelling around the different levels of the site will be made easier with the regular land train or the mountain railway. Journey into the Future offers strange and exciting glimpses of the 21st century. The Hoover exhibit reveals the normally hidden world of household dirt, a mythical beast stalks the hillside and the joys of a healthy body are extolled in a hi-tec health exhibition.

All of this plus exciting rides and a whole programme of events – A Festival of Festivals involving music, dance, drama, literature, sport, crafts and visual arts celebrated through twenty two themed weeks. So whether you fancy Christmas in August, buckets and spades by the mountains, romance or mystery, the Far East or the Celtic Connection – it will all be there.

One visit just will not be enough!

With just one year to go before the doors open to the public, work continues at a cracking pace and each day sees new developments on the 142 acre site.

Many of the Festival's major features are taking shape and are clearly visible from the Festival's public Viewing Platform near Waunlwyd Community Centre signposted off the A4046.

Directly opposite the platform the 40 metre high waterfall is almost ready to plunge into the man-made lake below. To the far right are the car parks which will take over 3,000 vehicles.

A bridge will be built across the A4046 which

will bring the anticipated 2 million visitors to the Entrance building. As soon as they enter the Festival their senses will be bombarded with the sights and sounds of exhibitions, gardens, craftsmen and entertainers. The Boulevard leads them onto the Emporium – home to retailers and caterers offering every conceivable treat; from McDonald's fast food to Sidoli's dreamy ice-cream, the juice of apples in the Bulmers Cider Garden or fresh oranges from Sunjuice.

Artistic endeavour has not been overlooked and the Gorsedd Circle is the first of the feats of artistry that form an integral part of the Festival's design. The Wave Wall snakes through Land of Our Fathers to the lake; a craftsman-built dry stone wall incorporating techniques from all over Wales. The framework for the Hanging Gardens clings to the hillside and from here visitors will be able to view spectacular floral displays from the raised walkways.

In the heart of the Festival is the lake. 5 million gallons of water will be needed to fill it. Here visitors will pause to visit the Oriental Pavilion or the Churches Centre at the Southern End before climbing the Stairway to the Stars and up into the Journey Into the Future.

FESTIVAL OF FESTIVALS

Just as artistic works have been integrated into the overall design so have the Events. A large outdoor arena will offer sports and concerts, the Lakeside and Rainbow theatres will have everything from community plays, male voice choirs, masterclasses, mini-Shakespeare, rock concerts, string quartets and opera. Each week will see a different theme incorporating the very best in music, drama, literature, sports, crafts and visual arts.

Kicking off with a "Celtic Connection" week starting on May 2, the Festival's cosmopolitan theme continues in the Caribbean for "Totally Tropical" fun, looks in on the USA for their independence day celebrations and continues to the Far East for "The Orient Expressed".

Children have their own themed events. Three Schools Weeks will make education FUN while nine days of "Kids Biz" in August will give youngsters plenty of opportunity to let off summer holiday steam. And what about Christmas in August?

157 days of Festival Frolics – you would be mad to miss it!

157 DAYS – ALL THIS CAN BE YOURS WITH A GARDEN FESTIVAL WALES SEASON TICKET

Television personality Anneka Rice became the first recipient of a Garden Festival Wales season ticket when she unveiled the Festival's Countdown Clock.

It did not take her long to recognise the excellent value of the ticket which has proved so popular at previous Garden Festivals. A Garden Festival Wales season ticket gives unlimited access to the 1992 National Garden Festival – 157 days or nearly 1,500 hours. It represents substantial savings for people particularly those who live locally – paying

for itself after the fourth visit.

The first 5,000 tickets will be issued at just £30 for adults. There will be a special opening offer of £89 for a family season ticket (two adults and two children). The price will then increase up until the opening day when it will reach £45 – so the earlier you buy the more you save.

All tickets will carry the photograph of the holder and ticket application forms are available from Garden Festival Wales, Festival House, Victoria, Ebbw Vale, Gwent, NP3 6UF. Tel. (0495) 305545.

INSIDE THIS ISSUE

PAGES 2 & 3
Garden Festival Wales – the vision

PAGE 4
The Biggest Classroom in Britain

An issue of the newsletter published in the lead up to the opening of the Garden Festival Wales

Consequently it is not proposed to examine the marketing plan after the opening of the site in May 1992. The aim is to point up the importance of advance publicity and maximum effective spend to create awareness and a 'buying frame of mind' among the target market, influencing the opinion leaders in the trade, selling in advance wherever possible and, in short, leaving nothing to chance to ensure the success of the venture once the site is open.

Case study 3
Marketing for market dominance in retail travel: Bakers Dolphin Travel

(Prepared with the help of Kevin Abbey, Managing Director, and Gail Izzard, Marketing Manager, Bakers Dolphin Holidays and World Travel)

Background

Bakers Dolphin Travel was formed by the purchase of two West Country travel agencies, Baker's Travel and Dolphin Travel, in 1984. Dolphin Travel had been founded in the early 1970s, a single retail shop in a Bristol suburb which survived throughout the 1970s virtually unchanged until the proprietor took on a partner who had been associated with another well-established West Country chain of agents, and who had a strong marketing orientation and an established reputation in the trade.

The company immediately engaged in a programme of expansion and heavy advertising, gaining a strong profile in the area and increasing turnover in the space of 12 months from £150 000 to over £2 000 000. It became the first agency chain in the area to offer inducements to gain market share, by providing free transfers to the local airport. By the early 1980s it had become the leading independent chain in the region, particularly for the sale of package holidays.

The merger resulted from the desire of Baker's Travel to expand further in Bristol, as previously their strength lay in the West Country's market towns. Dolphin Travel at the same time wished to expand outside of Bristol. Both companies recognised the benefits of uniting instead of competing. A second factor was the wish of Dolphin's founder to retire, leaving the company relatively undercapitalised – a problem not shared by Baker's Travel, which had been in existence since 1898. The merger of the two transformed the company into by far the largest and strongest chain in the area. Today, with its Head Office split between Bristol and Weston-super-Mare, and with 36 branches, it employs over 250 staff. Apart from retail travel, the company operates its own coaches and organises specialist package tour programmes.

The problem

Retail trading in travel has become increasingly unprofitable. Costs are rising, while discounting and efforts by tour operators to reduce prices for holidays have led to lower average revenues. Profits are possible only through a combination of tight control over cost and heavy investment in marketing, in order to push sales and increase productivity. By 1990/91, a combination of circumstances had led to exceptionally difficult market conditions for the retail trade. The UK had entered a serious recession, leading to rising unemployment, especially among those market segments (ABC1s) most prone to take holidays abroad. The Gulf War at the beginning of 1991 compounded what had already been foreseen as a difficult year, and the market slumped. Mass market package tour demand fell by some 40 per cent, while increasing inflation was putting pressure on costs.

At Bakers Dolphin, profit levels had slumped in spite of increasing revenue, as indicated below:

	1988 £	1989 £	1990 £
Turnover	23 000 000	30 000 000	38 000 000
Profit:	304 000	164 000	73 000

However, these figures conceal substantial reinvestment in the form of expansion in branch offices and refurbishment, which is an area of high priority for the company. The underlying picture was of a healthy company which, given the trading situation, was performing better than average, as evidenced by a rise in turnover and the ability to fund expansion out of profits without borrowing.

Company policy

The company plans for the long-term as well as the short-term, believing that most travel agency proprietors take too much out of their company at the expense of investing for the future. Bakers Dolphin operate a rolling programme of refurbishment and on-going in-house staff training. It is also policy to invest four per cent of turnover in promotion, a relatively high proportion for retail travel agencies.

Product policy

Recognising that the major multiple travel agencies severely limited the range of products racked, particularly those of tour operators, the company aimed to stock the widest possible choice of brochures. Shops were designed with a high number of facings (rack spaces), which generally exceeded those of competitors – even the multiples. However, a change in policy was recently forced on the company by the growing tendency among larger operators to brand their various products, producing a separate brochure for each, and in this way commanding an increasing proportion of existing rack space.

Bakers Dolphin now segment their shops according to the markets they serve, and broadly grade their branches into four categories:

1 three 'up-market' premium shops
2 the 'quality mass market' shops
3 the 'general mass market' shops
4 six 'Holiday Warehouse' branches

The last of these are low cost shops designed to provide fast, 'frill-free' service and high productivity. Sales are discounted subject to the purchase of travel insurance (a high profit sector for the agent). Staff in the Holiday Warehouses tend to be younger (keeping down salary levels), and expensive marketing ploys such as attractive windows displays are avoided. The average discount on sales is 3½ per cent, although the ability to negotiate higher commissions against achieved targets with some operators helps to increase earnings.

Brochures are racked in the four categories of shop according to the grade of customer served, the commercial arrangements made with principals, and any other circumstances which would require different treatment for a specific shop. Branch managers have little autonomy in their racking decisions, since agencies seeking the best trading terms with their suppliers must ensure the best possible sales in all branches. This means increasingly centralised decision-taking in marketing, as in other areas of retail management.

A key 'product' in a travel agency is the quality of staff employed. Salaries are in general poor, compared with other sectors of the retail trade, and staff turnover is attributed largely to those leaving the industry, rather than those moving to other companies in the travel business. The comparatively low staff turnover experienced by the company is ascribed to good personnel management, which pays particular attention to the morale of every member of staff. Members of staff are on first name terms at all levels, and counter staff receive personal letters from the Managing Director on their birthdays or other special occasions.

Staff can achieve higher salaries against targets set on a monthly basis. Performance is reviewed on a regular basis, where the Managing Director meets with his staff, hiring a nightclub or similar venue for the evening. Following a sales briefing, rewards are given to 'Top Dog' achievers. A special award is given to 'Superdog of the Year'. These 'Top Dog' nights originated when only five staff were employed, but are continued as good morale boosters, and have even on occasions extended to chartering a plane to fly all staff to Cardiff for an evening out.

Organising for marketing effectiveness

Due to the size of the company, economies of scale in marketing can be achieved, with a strong centralised marketing force under one of the two joint managing directors (see below).

Managing Director ——— Managing Director
(Marketing/Personnel)   (Administration)

Marketing   Sales   Sales
Manager   Development   Support
                 Manager   Manager

Marketing
Assistant

Bakers Dolphin marketing force

Company image

The company sets great store by a uniform company image and strong 'branding', especially in support of their own products. This is achieved by bold, imaginative use of colour in their offices – a livery of yellow and blue, with strong emerald green carpeting – which is carried through to the stationery, coach bodywork and name badges. A recent redesign has led to modificatioin of the logo, introducing a 'luggage label and suitcase' theme (see below).

Redesigned Bakers Dolphin logo

Examples of co-operative advertising between Bakers Dolphin and tour operators

Niche marketing strategy

In the face of widespread discounting by some multiple travel agents, the company decided to concentrate on certain sectors of the business, avoiding price wars which they recognised they couldn't win. This has led to their focusing on high price holidays and certain identifiable products such as cruising, Far Away holidays and the over-55 market.

Another identified niche is to provide the best level of service possible for late bookings in the mass market package holiday business. This is achieved by arranging for two members of staff to access the CRSs of all the major tour operators within the coming four weeks in order to draw up a list of best price holidays. This reduces the workload of other staff, improves productivity and simultaneously sorts out the 'time wasting' customers who are always looking for the unobtainable bargain – a feature of the market which has become a major problem for retail travel agencies. The company also holds regular evenings devoted to specific long-haul destinations, inviting up to a thousand potential clients.

Much advertising is collaborative, with costs being shared with principals, and focuses on specific niche markets. A typical campaign carried out in 1991 is featured below.

The $100 marketing campaign

The aim of this campaign was to build up demand for specific long-haul destinations and types of holiday seen as least likely to be affected by the Gulf War. The strategy was to offer a new incentive of $100 cash for every booking – an offer thought to be unique to anything previously offered by the trade. The offer was made in a way which was designed to ensure that the public saw it as equal to any deals being offered by other agents, while not actually representing a 'discount', as straight discounting was against company policy. The target market was potential holidaymakers to North America, Australia, New Zealand and the Caribbean, with the major focus being on the USA, which the company had been targeting for several years. This destination was

also seen as one of the safest in the world during and following the Gulf War, while the exchange rate of the £ against the $ (at that point 1:2) was an additional factor encouraging promotion.

The budget for the campaign, launched in January 1991, was as follows:

Activity	Budget £
1 *TV*	
30 10-second spots at £300	9 000
production costs	1 200
2 *Press*	
Bristol Evening Post	
Thursday 10 Jan (full page) }	
Friday 18 Jan (half page) }	2 800
Bristol Journal	
Friday 11 Jan (full page)	1 500
Regional Press (five journals, half page in each)	1 500
Production costs for all press	1 000
3 *Leaflet drops*	
A total of over 240 000 leaflets were delivered to selected addresses by postcode throughout the West Country where Bakers Dolphin had offices. Costs were:	
Printing	4 100
Production	500
Distribution	2 100
4 *Further promotion*	
This included brochure racking cards with holders, window displays and associated material, brochure stickers and inducement leaflets, at a further cost of:	8 278
Total budget	31 978

Evaluation of the campaign

With a redeemable offer tied to the campaign, it was possible to measure accurately the effectiveness of the campaign. It proved to be one of the most effective run by the company. Notwithstanding the problems created by the Gulf War and the recession, the campaign

**Promotional material for the Bakers Dolphin $100
campaign (Courtesy: Bakers Dolphin Holidays and World
Travel)**

generated £626 000 in turnover, an increase of 30 per cent over the same period in the previous year. Furthermore, profits achieved actually increased because the cost of the incentive was actually lower than normal incentives offered. The perceived value, to the target market, of the $100 campaign was higher than the actual cost to the company, while the favourable exchange rate also helped by holding down the cost of the offer.

Summary

The company feels well prepared to survive in the difficult trading conditions of the '90s. The

1991 slump forced them to curtail some of their activities in a cost-cutting exercise which was seen as essential to survive in the short-run. This led to reductions in in-house and specialised training, and staff entertaining. It is perhaps significant, however, that the marketing budget in itself was not cut back as severely as most other budgets, and the company's philosophy is to market itself out of the slump and into increased profitability, through effective product positioning and market awareness programmes.

Case study 4
Marketing management in the public sector: sustainable tourism and the case of Konstanz, Germany

(Prepared with the help of Petra Meyer, Deputy General Manager, Tourist Information Konstanz GmbH, and Prof Dr Jörn W Mundt, Berufsakademie Ravensburg, Germany)

An aerial view of Konstanz and Lake Konstanz (Courtesy: Tourist Information Konstanz)

Background

Konstanz, or Constance, lies on the western side of the Bodensee (Lake Constance in English), where the lake drains into the River Rhine. The lake's borders are shared between Germany, Switzerland and Austria, with some 158km of shoreline in Germany.

Konstanz was founded on the site of a Roman fort. The central mediaeval part of the city,

The Council House, Konstanz, built in 1388 and the Zeppelin Memorial, built in 1938 (Courtesy: Tourist Information Konstanz)

directly adjacent to the shore, survives largely intact to this day. The city hosted the only Ecclesiastical Council held on German soil, between 1414 and 1418, and the Council building, which was erected in 1388 as a warehouse and saw the election of a new pope in 1417, remains one of the major attractions. The Romanesque-Gothic basilica, in which the sessions of the Council took place, dominates the old episcopal town.

Modern-day Konstanz, with a population of 75 000, is the centre of one of the most attractive holiday regions in Germany, attracting 200 000 overnight visitors in 1990, and accounting for 486 000 bednights. With an average stay of only 2.4 nights, Konstanz is a typical destination for city trips, but the bulk of visitors are day trippers. This is partly accounted for by the city's vicinity

to popular holiday regions, but also reflects the fact that the island of Mainau, owned by the Swedish Count Bernadotte, with tropical plants and a regular programme of cultural events, attracts some two million day visitors annually.

The problem

Konstanz suffers from serious congestion, resulting mainly from its seasonality as a destination. While a considerable number of visitors travel to the city and to Mainau by ship, using the Lake as access, nevertheless the majority continue to arrive by private car. The resulting congestion is not only a nuisance to the area's residents, but poses an environmental threat to the nature preservation site in the area, the *Wollmatinger Ried*, a marshland which features vast fields of reeds forming the habitat of many threatened species of animals and plants that depend on an unpolluted environment.

The season runs from April to October, but peaks in July and August. Some of this seasonality is self-created, however, with the international *Seenachtsfest*, an event featuring cultural and entertainment activities held jointly by Konstanz and the adjacent Swiss town of Kreuzlingen. This event is held every second Saturday in August, and culminates in a spectacular fireworks display, attracting some 150 000 visitors, of which two-thirds go to Konstanz. In

Fireworks at the Seenachtsfest, Konstanz (Courtesy: Tourist Information Konstanz)

addition to the congestion caused by private cars travelling to the festival, further problems are caused by noise, litter and unsocial behaviour, especially heavy drinking, which poses a security threat to locals and visitors alike.

Although the city benefits from high annual occupancy rates in the hotels (over 50 per cent throughout the year and virtually 100 per cent occupancy during the season), this has led to a drop in perceived value for money, and there is now a fear that unsatisfactory experiences will lead to low repeat visits and negative word-of-mouth recommendation. Although limited to only some of the hotels, the authorities fear that the image of the city as a whole is suffering. High hotel prices are also inhibiting younger visitors, who are recognised as the tourists of tomorrow.

Until 1989, relations between tourism suppliers and the city's tourist office were poor. This resulted partly from the failure of the local authority to recognise the significance of tourism within the local economy. The attitude towards the tourist office was that the benefits achieved from tourism did not justify the money they were spending. The result was that the tourist office did not get the backing of the authorities in their plans for tourist development within the city.

Strategies

In order to improve relations between the local suppliers and the city's tourist office, it was decided to form a private limited liability company to take over the running of the tourist office. The philosophy behind this move was to integrate local business into the decision-making process, in marketing Konstanz. Shareholders in the new tourist office are active members of the association of hoteliers and pub and restaurant owners (*Wirtekreis Konstanz*), of the association of retailers (*Treffpunkt Konstanz*), and of the *Fremdenverkehrsverein*, the traditional local body in Germany representing the travel industry's interests. The city council (*Stadtrat*) retains the majority of shares in the new company, which is not expected to break-even on costs, in order to cover deficits and to retain a measure of control over its activities.

The principal benefit achieved by the new organisation is to remove the tourist office from the bureaucratic administrative machinery of local government and thereby enhance flexibility in operating, marketing-orientation and cost control, in order to minimise subsidies. The incorporation of the successful municipal *Klausenhorn* lakeside campsite into the new company has boosted income. In 1990, its first year of operation, the new tourist office was able to cut its expenditure by 10 per cent.

The second strategy was to reduce seasonality. The new tourist office has concentrated on creating off-season packages designed to form a new image of the city as a worthwhile off-season and winter destination. Traditional advertising has been dropped, while promotion has concentrated on brochures and press releases, which have achieved good coverge in the general press.

A characteristic of the new packages is the emphasis they place on the use of public transport access, including charter buses, while those insisting on the use of private transport are encouraged to make use of bicycles. This environmentally friendly programme involves the tourist office in co-operation with the municipal authorities, who are responsible for local bus and ferry services; with the island of Mainau; and with the White Fleet company (owned by German Railways) which offers two days' unlimited use of local transport, including excursion boats to the island of Mainau and either ferries or excursion boats to the thousand-year-old city of Meersburg opposite Konstanz. Purchasers receive a guided tour of the mediaeval town and an information pack, which is offered in an attractive and practical cotton bag. Most brochures are printed on recycled, environmentally friendly paper.

To limit the use of private cars, advertising for the *Seenachtsfest* is undertaken only in locations which have convenient access to Konstanz by train. The campaign is supported by special train fares which include the entrance fee to the festival. Extra trains are put on, and tour arrangements within the destination are included to reduce traffic and noise.

The 'sustainable tourism' theme is further enhanced by a requirement that all suppliers for the programme use only environmentally friendly materials, and reduce their packaging to the minimum. An attempt has been made to reduce alcohol misuse by broader offers of non-alcoholic beverages. Finally, the fireworks on the German side of the border now focus on visual effects rather than 'big bangs'.

To increase visitor satisfaction, hotels experiencing high incidents of complaint will neither be incorporated into the packages nor recommended to other tour operators. Members of the public making enquiries for accommodation at the tourist office will only be offered such hotels as a last resort.

The tourist office is attempting to tackle the problem of cheap accommodation for the youth market by considering extending the existing youth hostel and/or the establishment of a young people's hotel, in co-operation with the neighbouring Swiss town of Kreuzlingen.

To improve cost-effectiveness in marketing the city, the co-operating partners, the Konstanz Tourist Office, the Regional Tourist Board, the island of Mainau and the White Fleet operators take it in turns to visit the German trade fairs, representing the interests of their partners as well as their own services. Promotions at trade fairs abroad involve similar co-operation with the city of Lindau, the International Lake Constance Association (IBV) and the island of Mainau. Further co-operation was achieved in 1991, with the formatioin of INTABO, an association of organisations providing convention facilities in the Lake Constance area. Partners are from the three surrounding countries, and include the Konstanz Tourist Office.

The new marketing strategy recognises that marketing the city of Konstanz must involve the promotion of the *region as a whole*, with the co-operation of all interested parties; the *identification* of market segments, ranging from holidaymakers to businesspeople, for whom appropriate offers must be tailored; and achieving this within a framework of *sustainable tourism* to heighten the satisfaction of visitors and local inhabitants alike.

Case study 5
Study of an award-winning advertising campaign: The London Zoo

(Prepared with the help of Angela Horsman, Marketing Director, Zoo Operations Ltd.)

Background

The London Zoological Society was founded in 1826, and over the years became a popular venue for visitors of all kinds, in particular couples with young children. However, the popularity of zoos waned after its high peak at the beginning of the 1950s, when London Zoo attracted over three million visitors. In recent years, attendance has been a little over one million annually, as shown below:

Year	Attendance (000s)
1973	2045
1981	1053
1982	1027
1987	1304
1988	1326
1989	1182
1990	1195

The decline is common to most British zoos, and is in part the result of a failure to innovate or refurbish for a long period of time. The problem has been compounded by the substantial growth in the number of rival tourist attractions established in the UK during the past few years, while a growing anti-zoo movement also contributed to the movement away from visiting zoos.

London Zoo in particular suffers from poor access by public transport, while many other rival attractions can attract the day visitor to the country by providing good car parking facilities. Nevertheless, the zoo still manages to persuade 35 per cent of its market to arrive by public transport, and offers a total of 2000 car parking spaces in the immediate vicinity.

Only Chessington among the zoos has been able to reverse this general decline, by investing substantially in new types of attraction on site, and in effect turning the zoo into a leisure park.

In 1988, the London Zoo came under new management, and a new company, Zoo Operations, was formed – designed to upgrade facilities and to market the zoo more effectively. The zoo's shopping and catering facilities were assessed as below standard, and were upgraded; a new, quality, gift shop was introduced, along with a number of new catering facilities ranging from fast food outlets to the top of the range Raffles Restaurant, with a Singaporean decor. Staff were equipped with new uniforms. These innovations resulted in a 21 per cent increase (in real terms) in the average spend per head between 1988 and 1990. Currently, revenue is received in the following proportions:

	%
Admissions	55
Catering	25
Retail shops	20

Apart from these sources of revenue, there are minor contributory revenues through the zoo's 'Lifewatch' membership and animal adoption schemes.

Objectives of the 1990 campaign

Earlier qualitative research had shown that many potential visitors had an outdated image of the zoo, as an attraction reminiscent of a Victorian menagerie crowded with school parties. Few were convinced that it represented the opportunity for 'a good day out'. On the AIDA model, consumer interest had to be raised, and potential visitors convinced that they would gain satisfaction from a unique and worthwhile experience. In short, the message was to convey to the target market that a day at London Zoo would be interesting, fun and provide lots of things to do.

Advertising strategy

The core market for the zoo had been determined through earlier research as being mainly mass market (with a slight up-market bias), and largely females between the ages of 20 and 45, with children, and living between one and two hours' travelling time of the zoo. A campaign was devised in March 1990 to reposition the zoo for these markets, and to persuade them to pay a visit. The campaign was to run from Easter to the end of August, and television was selected as the most appropriate medium for disseminating this message, being able to achieve a high impact and rapid coverage of the target market.

The advertising agency, Lowe Howard-Spink, in collaboration with the Zoo's Marketing Director, Angela Horsman, established the product benefits as:

• the opportunity to see a wide variety of unusual animals at close quarters

'Creature Comforts' – television advertisement for London Zoo (Courtesy: London Zoo)

- the interaction that takes place between visitors and the animals
- the combined educational and entertainment value of a visit.

The advertisement was prepared in two formats, a full 30 second and a 10 second edit, delivered in the ratio of 1:2. A humorous theme was adopted, employing the punchline 'if you don't know your aardvark from your emu, visit London Zoo'. The advertisement featured clay animated animals with unusual sounding (but authentic) names. The company responsible, Aardman Animations, later gained an Oscar in Hollywood for this work, as Best Animated Film. The commercial, *Creature Comforts*, proved to be a huge success, capturing the imagination of the potential visitors, especially young children.

The zoo team were well aware of the peak visiting days and decision to visit patterns, which enabled them to be very selective in placing the advertisements, 'cherry picking' the best air time and thus maximising the effectiveness of the ads at times of normally high attendance. The promotional budget was limited to some 22p per visitor, less than half that of many rival attractions, and consequently had to be effective. The campaign ran from Easter, supporting the peak Easter holiday days, the May Bank Holiday weekends, peak weekends in July and August and the weekend of August Bank Holiday (see below).

The key TV advertising campaign was supported by a number of other promotions, including limited newspaper, magazine and bus shelter advertising, the publication of a regular newsletter and a programme of study visits for key 'gatekeepers' (or Ambassadors in the Zoo's parlance), including London taxi drivers, members of the British Incoming Tour Operators Association (BITOA), Blue Badge guides, coach and waterbus operators and other members of the travel trade.

The budget for this schedule of promotional and PR activities was broken down as follows:

	%
advertising	60
promotional literature	12
familiarisation visits, exhibitions, etc.	12
joint promotions and incentives	5
other public relations	4
marketing research	3.5
educational	2.5

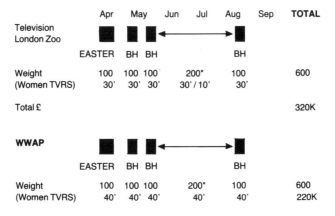

MEDIA LAYDOWN 1990

	Apr	May	Jun	Jul	Aug	Sep	TOTAL
Television London Zoo	■	■	■	◄——————►	■		
	EASTER	BH	BH		BH		
Weight (Women TVRS)	100 30'	100 30'	100 30'	200* 30'/10'	100 30'		600
Total £							320K

	Apr	May	Jun	Jul	Aug	Sep	TOTAL
WWAP	■	■	■	◄——————►	■		
	EASTER	BH	BH		BH		
Weight (Women TVRS)	100 40'	100 40'	100 40'	200* 40'	100 40'		600 220K

* Targeted at remaining "top 10" days
BH = Bank Holiday

The media campaign run by London Zoo in 1990 (Courtesy: London Zoo)

Research methodology

Market research was undertaken before and during the advertising campaign to track awareness of the campaign and its success in influencing visits. All surveys were conducted on visitors at the zoo, based on randomly selected personally interviewed respondents. The research schedule ran as follows:

Stage I	pre-test	24, 25, 27 March
	post test	14, 15, 16 April
Stage II	pre-test	19, 20, 22 May
	post test	26, 27, 28 May
Stage III	pre-test	14, 15, 16 July
	post test	25, 26, 27 August

100 respondents were interviewed on each of the above dates. The resulting data was later weighted on the basis of the known attendance figures for the day.

Evaluation of the campaign

Before the start of the campaign, leaflets and brochures were recalled as the major source of awareness (40 per cent), followed by posters on the underground (forming part of the 1988 campaign). Television registered only 12 per cent awareness. Following the Easter 1990 campaign, awarenes of television ads rose to 86 per cent. Similarly, while before the May Bank Holiday TV awareness had dropped to only 32 per cent, it rose again following a further burst of advertising to 70 per cent. A further market research survey in mid-July revealed a 35 per cent awareness of TV advertising, and this rose to 57 per cent in the final burst of advertising in August. (See below for full details.) Visitors were also asked whether advertising had affected their decision to visit. In the case of the August Bank Holiday advertising burst, 13 per cent had been influenced to visit by the advertisements.

Conclusion

The campaign aimed to increase awareness, not of the zoo – it had already been established that this was not an issue – but of the *benefits* which the zoo could offer a selected target market. The success of this advertising campaign is evidenced by the substantial growth in awareness of these attributes.

Similarly, the increase in visitor attendance over the period of the campaign can be directly

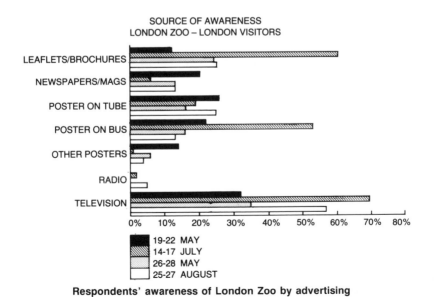

Respondents' awareness of London Zoo by advertising medium

LIFE*WATCH*

Every living thing is our concern

GET INVOLVED IN WILDLIFE CONSERVATION

JOIN LIFEWATCH TODAY!

LONDON ZOO
& WHIPSNADE

A leaflet published by London Zoo to raise public awareness of its campaign

ascribed, through the research evidence, to the effectiveness of the featured campaign. Undoubtedly, the theme of the campaign, and the choice of humour of a type appealing to both adult and child, were major factors in catching the public's attention and affecting long-term attitudes. Unfortunately for the Zoo, the appeal of the plasticine figures was so great that it led to its emulation, in a remarkably similar campaign, by the electricity companies, whose spend dwarfed the Zoo budget, and it was decided that the campaign should be withdrawn. By this point, however, the Zoo had started to achieve widespread publicity about the threat of impending closure on the existing site and dispersal of the animals. The effects of the media coverage of this threat led, in 1991, to the best attendance figures for 30 years, during the crucial May Bank Holiday period.

In 1992, the Zoo suffered several well-publicised crises, culminating in substantial management reorganisation and the establishment of new objectives linked primarily to conservation. While the results of the policy change will reduce the scope of the Zoo's activities, and its overall size, considerably, it is hoped that these moves will ensure its long-term survival. Whatever the future may bring, however, the success of this individual advertising campaign will remain undiminished. As an example of a humorous campaign generating an exceptional level of awareness as well as generating sales, the case study remains an outstanding example of successful tourism advertising.

Case study 6
Promoting short breaks:
the case of Best Western Hotels

(Prepared with the help of David Curtis-Brignell, Director of Marketing and Sales, Best Western Hotels, and Chapman Thornton Belgrove Garrett, advertising agents.)

Background

The Best Western Hotel chain is the biggest consortium of hotels in the world, with 200 hotels in the UK alone. The consortium is made up of independent, largely owner-managed hotels which have formed an association in order to gain mutual marketing benefits.

Unlike other hotel consortia, Best Western does not recruit members at a common price level or other shared characteristic. In the USA, the consortium's reputation is for budget accommodation, while in the UK, member hotels range from one star to four star properties.

The advantage the consortium enjoys is in its product *range*, in that it can offer a hotel to suit the needs of all markets. In this respect, the organisation sees itself as the equal or superior of any of its leading competitors. However, there are inevitable drawbacks to this heterogeneous grouping of hotels, as the range of different properties and locations inevitably results in their enjoying different peaks and troughs in demand, posing a greater challenge for group marketing.

Research has shown that brand awareness of the hotel is strong among members of the public, but not as strong as would be expected of a company accommodating some 2.5 million guests a year within the UK alone. This is due in large part to the failure of individual hotels to help create a corporate brand image. Indeed, many guests staying at Best Western Hotels are unaware that the hotel is a member of the consortium. The group is considering a number of strategies to help to overcome this, including greater use of corporate signs externally and in reception areas, and enforcement of logos on items in bedrooms. However, advertising remains one of the most effective means of getting the corporate image across to the market.

In recent years, the consortium has made strenuous efforts to raise corporate awareness and to generate mass response among the public by the use of both colour and mono press advertising. Targets have generally been the ABC1 consumer leisure market, with more limited campaigns aiming to reach the meeting and conference buyer, and the travel agent. Campaigns have been limited to the national press and magazines, with some excursions into direct mail. The need for direct response, and budget restrictions, have ruled out the use of outdoor advertising, radio or television, although expansion into these media is being considered for the future.

Creative strategy in the colour advertising campaign is designed to present an image of quality, linked with the individuality of the hotels featured, while at the same time stressing that the hotels are typical of other members of the chain. A similar strategy has been followed in the USA, where individual properties are used to describe attributes which typify the Best Western Hotel.

The campaign for the short break market

Over the lifetime of the present marketing plan, running from 1991 to 1994, a number of key objectives have been identified. Among these is the aim to increase the company's market share of Getaway Breaks and holidays. This objective will provide the focus for the present case study.

Getaway Breaks is Best Western's leisure brand, and has become a highly successful programme since it was launched a few years ago. At the time of writing, it has become established as number four in the travel agents' preferred product list of short break operators, and in the 1990 NOP Hotel Guest Survey it was the fourth-most-used product for leisure guests, behind three of the Forte group products.

The short break market in the UK, using hotels, motels or guest houses, was estimated to be worth some £688 million in 1989, while Best Western's Getaway market share was estimated at the end of 1990 at around £12 million. The Getaway programme is marketed both direct to the public and through travel agents. In the latter case, the chain makes strenuous efforts to ensure that racking space for the Getaway brochure is made available in the multiples' offices, and that established targets are met. The chain is keen to gain travel agency support, and developed an innovative advertisement in the trade press, in which a sachet of pot-pourri was attached as a thank you for agents' sales efforts (see opposite).

Direct sales resulting from advertising have shown substantial growth each year. In 1989, 34 per cent of respondents, selected in a survey of consumers replying to advertisements, had made a booking, with 85 per cent of these booking direct with the hotels. In 1990, although the response rate remained the same at 34 per cent, direct bookings rose to 92.5 per cent of the total. The survey also revealed that 30 per cent of respondents intended to take the same number of short breaks in the following year (1991), and 63 per cent planned to take more breaks.

Media planning in 1991

A series of quality image advertisements were planned for early 1991 to promote the short break product, with an emotive copy which emphasised the diversity of locations and properties within the chain (see p. 240). Full colour advertisements appeared in the *Sunday Express* magazine and *You* magazine, with mono advertisements in a range of supporting media, with the aim of attracting direct response enquiries, mainly for spring breaks. Details of the media schedule appear in:

Medium	Inserts	Dates	Budget (£)
1 Consumer response			
Sunday Express magazine (colour)	1	FEB 24	23 500
You magazine (colour)	3	MAR 3, 17 APR 7	60 000
National Trust Magazine (mono)	3	FEB, MAY, SEP	6 600
ETB Holiday Planner – *Readers' Digest* (colour)	1	JAN	2 560
Daily Telegraph magazine (mono)	1	JAN 26	1 200
English Heritage (mono)	1	MAR 15	423
Jewish Chronicle (mono)	1	FEB 8	277
M&S Magazine (mono)	1	APR	2 777
Readers' Digest (mono)	1	APR	3 200
Seasons (mono)	1	MAR	397
Daily Mail (mono)	1	MAR	1 050
2 Scotland Plus			
Daily Telegraph (mono)	1	FEB 9	FREE*
Daily Express (mono)	1	Feb 16	1 800
3 Scottish Tourist Board (annuals)			
STB Adventure and Special Interest	1	FEB/MAR	280
STB Short Breaks in Scotland	1	FEB	1 650
STB Where to Stay	1	JAN	1 154
Total budget:			106 868

(*replacement for fault by the medium in earlier advertising campaign)

Media schedule for Getaway Breaks

The total spend represented some 59 per cent of the budget for the year allocated to these three types of advertising. The schedule does not include parallel advertising spend directed at the business market, or at the UK and overseas travel trade.

THANK YOU.

For helping Best Western become the world's number one hotel organisation.

For working with us to make Best Western Getaway Breaks into a runaway success.

And for pointing so many customers towards our 200 independently-run inns, country houses, castles, city-centre and seaside hotels.

We show our appreciation by guaranteeing you full agent's commission on all Getaway Breaks, even when they are booked direct with us.

Now we would like you to accept this little sachet of Best Western pot-pourri for the office.

As a constant reminder of the sweet smell of success.

Vine House, 143 London Road, Kingston-upon-Thames, Surrey KT2 6NA.

STANDARDS NOT STANDARDISATION

An advertisement targeting travel agents (Courtesy: Chapman Thornton Belgrove Garratt)

**An advertisement for Best Western Getaway Breaks
(Courtesy: Chapman Thornton Belgrove Garratt)**

Evaluation

The colour advertisements have been widely praised for their effective message, and have resulted in a substantial increase in direct bookings. Below is provided an analysis of the effectiveness of advertisements, and the cost per response, based on results up to 13 March 1991. The campaign resulted in the achieved short break bookings being the highest ever for Best Western in the UK, for the period in question.

Publication	Insert Date	Telephone Responses	Coupons	Total	Cost per Response
Sunday Express magazine	24 FEB	319	1 134	1 453	16.17
You magazine	3 MAR	657	1 446	2 103	9.51
National Trust	FEB	67	98	165	12.72
ETB Holiday Planner (*Readers' Digest*)	JAN	43	413	456	5.61
Telegraph magazine	26 JAN	260	3 777	4 037	0.29
Jewish Chronicle	8 FEB	3	5	8	34.66
English Heritage	MAR	26	75	101	4.19

Best Western Hotels advertising generated response analysis as at 13 March 1991

Case study 7
Co-operative marketing of river tourism: boating holidays in the Anjou Region, France

(Prepared with the help of Professors Philippe Violier and Jacqueline Clais, ESTHUA, University of Angers.)

Background

As in Britain, French waterways provide excellent opportunities for leisure and boating activities, and 'fluvial tourism', as it is known in France, has become an important form of holidaymaking in that country, both for the domestic and foreign markets.

One of the most attractive areas for this activity is the Maine basin, which is part of the Loire River system lying in western France, some 100km inland from the sea. The 'Pays des Trois Rivières' (three rivers region) provides some 300km of unrivalled rural waterways, including the three principal rivers, the Mayenne (and its tributary the Oudon), Sarthe and Loire (the last not presently navigable, but there are long-term development plans to make it so). The varied landscape of the region, together with the attractions of historic towns in the vicinity – Angers, le Mans and Laval – and its situation on the border of the chateaux country, make this an attractive and easily accessible destination for Parisian holidaymakers; there are motorway and TGV high speed trains to all three of these towns.

Fluvial tourism marketing

Navigation on the rivers is restricted to those holding official permits. Although there is still scope for substantial expansion in commercial leisure boating, at present 11 houseboat rental companies operate in the region, with a total of 194 craft. The largest base has as many as 42 craft, the smallest only six. In addition, five of the companies operate a total of nine barges, but this form of activity is as yet little developed.

The eleven companies market their services in two distinct ways. Firstly, marketing is undertaken through the public sector interdepartmental syndicate of the Maine Basin, the SIBM, whose head office is in Angers. This body was created in 1979 and is charged with the promotion and coordination of the whole of the Maine Basin's tourist activities. It is financed by the regional authorities of the Pays de Loire and the three departments (Mayenne, Sarthe and Maine et Loire). The organisation operates a centralised reservations system selling to French tourists through a joint brochure which features all the houseboat rental companies. This brochure has a print run of 40 000 copies, of which 20 000 are disseminated in France, 15 000 in Germany and the balance in Switzerland. The German and Swiss markets are tapped through specialist tour operators (STB in the case of Germany, and Arcatour in Switzerland).

In France, the SIBM is present at several shows in Paris (salon Nautique, salon du Plein Air), this region accounting for 30 per cent of the total market. Stands are also taken at fairs in Bordeaux and Strasbourg. This promotion is complemented by advertising in *Indicateur Bertrand, Evasion* (a free magazine distributed at motorway tollbooths in the west and southwest of France), and the *Guide du Tourisme Fluvial en France*. The SIBM also welcomes French and foreign journalists on educationals. Finally, brand loyalty is secured

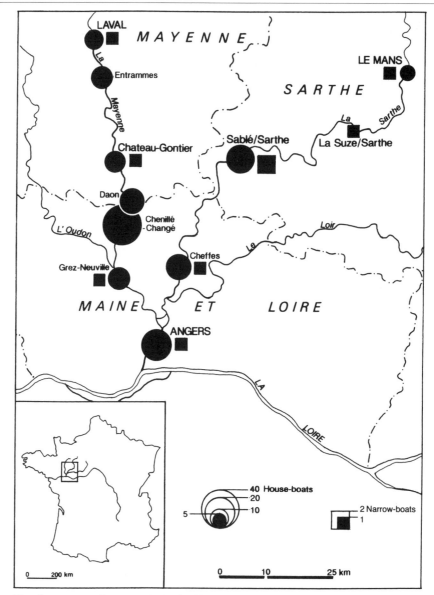

River boat companies operating in the Maine basin, France

through direct mail campaigns to previous clients.

The reservations system in 1990 booked 96 boat-weeks for French clientele, while STB and Arcatour were responsible for 151 boat-weeks and 33 boat-weeks respectively. In all, the central reservations system is responsible for some 10–15 per cent of bookings handled during the year.

The SIBM has been able to make substantial increases in the sale of holidays to the foreign markets over the past decade. Foreign bookings now account for some 65 per cent of the total bookings, compared with only 35 per cent in 1984. There has been a particularly dramatic increase in the proportion of German bookings, which now represent over 50 per cent of all foreign bookings, compared with only 25 per cent in 1984. River cruising represents a leading product in the marketing plan of the Regional Committee for Tourism (CRT) in its efforts to promote to the German market. On the other hand, the British market remains largely untapped, with sales concentrated almost entirely in the hands of a single British operator with an Angers office which markets its (British-owned) boats independently.

Apart from sales through the central reservations system of the SIBM, all the boat rental companies produce their own brochures and sell directly to the French market, through advertisements in the media, or through travel agents. However, this form of promotion comes second only to that of word-of-mouth promotion. The small size of these companies makes it impossible to finance participation in trade shows, apart from the Boat Show, and this role is left very much in the hands of the SIBM.

The alternative marketing approach is adopted by the largest and oldest-established of the boat rental companies. These seek to form links direct with foreign tour operators, rather than through the SIBM. In some cases these rental companies unite either locally or nationally in order to sell their services to tour operators; to give one example, a boat company in Mayenne has formed a partnership with similar companies in Sarthe and Aquitaine. National consortia provide particular advantages for the small boat rental company, not only in allowing these to cut marketing costs through the production of joint publicity material, but also by being able to provide a fleet of craft throughout the country on a scale that will interest the mass market operator. Finally, the consortium brand name will ensure loyalty and repeat business throughout the entire network of navigable rivers and waterways, as research has shown that keen amateur sailors tend to select this form of holiday repeatedly.

The promotional campaign of Mayenne Navigation

One boat rental company, Mayenne Navigation, operates two river bases, one in Entrammes along the Mayenne, and the other in Rohan, in central Brittany. The company was founded only in 1985, opening its second base at Entrammes in 1990. Though only recently formed, it has an aggressive marketing approach, and apart from

sales through the SIBM it is now tapping the British market through the Hoseasons Holidays consortium and the tour operator 'Sunselect'. It also belongs to the consortium 'France Passion Plaisance', a group of seven companies with 13 bases in France and Belgium. This consortium publishes a brochure in six languages, and places emphasis on consistent standards and quality control. The brochure is circulated through 18 foreign tour operators: four each in Germany and Belgium, three in Spain, two each in Holland and Austria, and one each in Italy, Switzerland and Great Britain. These operators receive between 15–20 per cent commissions, and access the reservations system via Minitel computer, which provides them with a monthly update of their bookings on screen. Finally, direct marketing is undertaken through advertising in the French specialist journal *Fluvial*. In 1991, this was carried out in two separate activities: an advertisement on the back cover, which has consistently generated up to ten enquiries a day, and a contest, with a first prize of a week's boat rental. This promotion has enabled the company to develop a customer database which will be tapped for direct mail promotion in the low season.

Thus it will be recognised that small boat companies face a choice of strategies in collaborating with others to market their product. They can join a consortium which sets out to market fluvial tourism on a geographical basis, or one which unites a network of different boating companies throughout France. Experience of customer behaviour will identify the most profitable approach. River-cruising enthusiasts enjoy changing places and landscapes, but the network within the Maine basin allows several weeks' rental. Some suggest that the SIBM should focus exclusively on functions of planning and 'animation', leaving commercial marketing to the individual companies; but the small size of most of these companies hinders the opportunity to reach their potential markets, and we have seen that an established body such as the SIBM, acting on behalf of many small companies, can deliver an effective marketing message.

Appendix 1 Sources of tourism research data

The following is a short list of principal sources of data which are relevant to travel and tourism research:

A *International Tourism Statistics*
CAB International
  – World Travel and Tourism Review
Economist Intelligence Unit (EIU)
  – International Tourism Quarterly (ITQ)
  – Special reports on tourism
  – Travel and Tourism in the Single European Market (Ed. Storey, A) 1990
Euromonitor
  – World Travel Market
Europa Yearbook
  – A World Survey
European Community (EC)
  – Basic Statistics of the Community
  – General Statistics Bulletin
International Air Transport Association (IATA)
  – World Air Traffic Statistics
International Civil Aviation Organisation (ICAO)
  – Civil Aviation Statistics of the World
  – Digest of Statistics
Organisation for Economic Cooperation and Development (OECD)
  – International Tourism and Tourism Policy in OECD Member Countries
United Nations
  – Statistical Yearbook
  – Monthly Bulletin of Statistics
World Tourism Organisation (WTO)
  – Current Travel and Tourism Indicators
  – Economic Review of World Tourism
  – Tourism Departures and Main Destinations
  – Yearbook of Tourism Statistics

B *National Statistics*
Applied Leisure Marketing
  – Leisure Destination Survey: Holiday/Short break series
    Motivation and behaviour of British Leisure Visitors in the UK 1989
  – Daytrips from Home series 1989
  – Destination Market Overview 1989

British Tourist Authority (BTA)
  – Annual Report
  – British National Travel Survey
  – Digest of Tourist Statistics
  – UK Tourism Survey
Civil Aviation Authority
  – Statistics
Economist Intelligence Unit
  – Travel and Tourism Analyst
Employment, Department of
  – International Passenger Survey (IPS)
    The main results are summarised in the Business Monitor MQ6
  – Overseas Travel and Tourism (Quarterly)
English Tourist Board (ETB)
  – Annual Report
  – English Heritage Monitor (annual)
  – The English Hotel Occupancy Survey (annual)
  – Insights: The Tourism Marketing Intelligence Service
  – Overseas Visitor Survey 1990
  – Regional Fact Sheets (for the Regional Tourist Boards)
  – Sightseeing in 19- (annual)
  – Tourism Intelligence Quarterly
  – Visits to Tourist Attractions (annual)
Harvest Information Services
  – Airlines 1990
  – Hotels 1990
  – Travel Agents 1990
Jordan & Sons
  – Britain's Tour and Travel Industry 1990
  – The British Hotel Industry 1988
Keynote Reports
  – Airlines 1986
  – Cross Channel Ferries 1987
  – Travel Agents and Overseas Tour Operators 1987
Market Assessment Reports
  – Development of the UK Tourism Market to 1993 1990
Mintel Reports
  – The British on Holiday at Home
  – Holidays

Scottish Tourist Board
- Annual Report
The Tourism Society
- The Tourism Industry 1990/91
Transport, Department of
- National Travel Survey (NTS)
- Transport Statistics in Great Britain
Wales Tourist Board
- Annual Report

In addition to the above statistics which focus on travel and tourism, there are a number of other statistical publications which may include travel and tourism statistics, or are pertinent to tourism. These include:
Bank of England Quarterly Bulletin
Central Statistical office (CSO)

- Annual Abstract of Statistics
- National Income and Expenditure ('Blue Book')
- Regional Trends
- Social Trends
- Economic Trends
- Monthly Digest of Statistics
Employment, Department of
- Family Expenditure Survey
- General Household Survey
Information Division, The Treasury
- Economic Progress Report
National Institute Economic Review
Trade and Industry (DTI), Department of
- British Business Weekly

Appendix 2

Proof-reading marks

There are standard correction marks, as follows:

Text	Marginal mark	Meaning
One thing is quite certain and that is that few brochures are any longer designed by amateurs.	c/	Insert 'c'
There are some and they STAnd out like sore thumbs among the professional offerings. If the companies concerned are are successful it is despite their brochures, not because of them.	≠/	Change to lower case
		Delete word
	⊗/	Wrong typeface
Designing a brochure is a highly skilled art needing an exact specification of the intentions, features and statutory provisions necessary. From these the designer can make a 'rough' for approval by his client. a professional design house will have amazing modern technology available even including the ability to simulate photographs by computer	⊗/	Damaged characters on print supplied
		Delete and close up
	≡/	Change to capital
	Y	Insert space
	⊙/	Insert full stop
The number pages of is important in itself. According to the print run envisaged it may be possible to make substantial economies by utilising the maximum amount of space on each sheet or roll of paper.		Transpose words
		Start new paragraph
	[/	Take over to next line
	2/	
Rarely will cut sheets be used that equate to the eventual page size. It is possible that large sheets that incorporate 4, 8, 16, or more pages will be printed at one time, but with really large runs the relationship between several huge rolls of paper fed simultaneously will need to be reflected in hte pagination and the layout chosen.	⊥/	Push down or remove blemish
	=/	Correct alignment
	⊏	Cancel indent
	T/	Reduce space between words
The page size will relate not	✓	Leave unchanged

References

Chapter 1
1. T Levitt, *Marketing Myopia*, Harvard Business Review July/August 1960, pp 45–56

Chapter 2
1. P Kotler, *Marketing Management, Analysis, Planning and Control*, Hemel Hempstead, Prentice Hall, 7th Ed. 1991

Chapter 3
1. Economist Intelligence Unit, *Choosing Holiday Destinations: the Impact of Exchange Rates and Inflation*, London, EIU 1987

Chapter 4
1. A Maslow, *Motivation and Personality*, London, Harper and Row, 1984
2. J A Howard & J N Seth, *The Theory of Buyer Behaviour*, New York, John Wiley, 1969
3. S Plog, *Why Destination Areas Rise and Fall in Popularity*, paper presented to the Southern California Chapter of the Travel Research Association, 10 Oct 1972
4. P Pearce, *The Social Psychology of Tourist Behaviour*, Oxford, Pergamon, 1982

5. Heart of England Tourist Board, *Tourism in the Heart of England: a Strategy for Growth*, HETB 1985

Chapter 6
1. *Marketing*, 'Discretion Plays a Bigger Part', 13 August 1987
2. A Rogers, *Pricing in the Hotel Industry*, Oxford Polytechnic, 1974

Chapter 7
1. I R Colley, *Defining Advertising Goals for Measured Advertising Results*, New York, Association of National Advertisers, 1961

Chapter 12
1. C Brann, *Cost Effective Direct Marketing by Mail, Telephone and Direct Response Advertising*, Cirencester, Collectors' Books, 1984

Chapter 13
1. R Townsend, *Up the Organisation: How to stop the Corporation stifling People and strangling Profits*, London, Coronet, 1971

Bibliography

Ashworth, G J & Goodall, B, *Marketing Tourism Places*, London, Routledge, 1990

Ashworth, G & Tunbridge, J, *The Tourist-Historic city*, London, Belhaven Press, 1990

Bishop, J, *Travel Marketing*, New Romney, Bailey Bros and Swinfen, 1981

Brann, C, *Cost Effective Direct Marketing by Mail, Telephone and Direct Response Advertising*, Cirencester, Collectors Books, 1984

British Tourist Authority, *First Impressions: Reception of Overseas Visitors' Enquiry*, London, BTA 1986

British Tourist Authority, *Gaining Your Share of an 8 Billion Market*, (including market guides to 27 countries), London, BTA, 1990

British Tourist Authority, *The Independent Hotel: a Guide to Overseas Marketing*, London, BTA 1977

Buttle, F, *Hotel and Food Service Marketing*, London, Holt Rhinehart 1986

Campbell-Smith, G, *Marketing of the Meal Experience – a Fundamental Approach*, Guildford, University of Surrey 1967

Coltman, M, *Tourism Marketing*, New York, Van Nostrand Reinhold, 1989

Cooper, C & Latham, J, *The Market for Educational Visits to Tourism Attractions*, Poole, Dorset Institute of H.E. 1985

Cross, D, *Please Follow Me – The Practical Tourist Guide's Handbook*, Salisbury, Wessexplore/ETB 4th Ed 1991

Doswell, R & Gamble, P R, *Marketing and Planning Hotels and Tourism Projects*, London, Barrie & Jenkins 1979

English Tourist Board, *The Future for England's Smaller Seaside Resorts*, London, ETB 1991

English Tourist Board, *Report of the Working Party to Review Tourist Information Centre Services and Support Policies*, London, ETB 1981

English Tourist Board, *The VFR Market: Marketing Opportunities and Guidance*, London, ETB 1988

Foster, D, *Sales and Marketing for the Travel Professional*, London, McGraw-Hill 1991

Gartrell, R, *Destination Marketing for Convention and Visitors' Bureaus*, Dubuque, Iowa, Kendall Hunt 1989

Getz, D, *Festivals, Special Events and Tourism*, New York, Van Nostrand Reinhold 1990

Goodall, B & Ashworth, G, *Marketing in the Tourism Industry – The Promotion of Destination Regions*, Beckenham, Croom Helm 1988

Greene, M, *Marketing Hotels into the 90s*, London, Heinemann 1987

Hawkins, D E, Shafer, E L & Rovelstad, J M, (Eds), *Tourism Marketing and Management Issues*, Washington DC, George Washington University, 1980

Hotel and Catering Industry Training Board, *Marketing for Independent Hoteliers*, Wembley, Middx, HICTB, n.d.

Hotel and Catering Industry Training Board, *Marketing for Publicans*, Wembley, Middx, HCITB 1982

King, B & Hyde, G, *Tourism Marketing in Australia*, Melbourne, Hospitality Press, 1989

Kotas, R, (Ed) *Market Orientation in the Hotel and Catering Industry*, Guildford, Surrey University Press 1975

Kotler, P, *Marketing management: Analysis, Planning and Control*, Hemel Hempstead, Prentice Hall International 7th Ed 1991

Lanquar, R & Hollier, R, *Le Marketing Touristique*, Paris, Presses Univ de France 1981

Laws, E, *Tourism Marketing: Service and Quality Management Perspectives*, Cheltenham, Stanley Thornes, 1991

Lickorish, L, Bodlender, J, Jefferson, A & Jenkins, C L, *Developing Tourism Destinations: Policies and Perspectives*, London, Longman 1991

Lickorish, L J & Jefferson, A, *Marketing Tourism*, London, Longman 1988

MacSweeney, E F, *Public Relations and Publicity for Hotels and Restaurants*, London, Barrie & Jenkins 1970

Middleton, V, *Marketing in Travel and Tourism*, Oxford, Heinemann 1988

Morrison, A, *Hospitality and Travel Marketing*, Albany, NY, Delmar 1989

Moutinho, L, *Consumer Behaviour in Tourism*, Management Bibliographies and Reviews, Vol 12 No 3, MCB University Press 1986

Nykiel, R A, *Marketing in the Hospitality Industry*, (2nd Ed) New York, Van Nostrand Reinhold 1989

Reid, R, *Hospitality Marketing Management*, (2nd Ed) New York, Van Nostrand Reinhold 1989

Reilly, R, *Travel and Tourism Marketing Techniques*, Albany NY, Delmar 1980

Ritchie, J & Goeldner, C, (Eds) *Travel, Tourism and Hospitality Research: a Handbook for Managers*, New York, John Wiley 1987

Schmoll, G A, *Tourism Promotion*, London, Tourism

International Press 1977

Shaw, S, *Airline Marketing and Management*, London, Pitman 1990

Shepherd, J W, *Marketing Practice in the Hotel and Catering Industry*, London, Batsford 1982

Sumner, J R, *Improve your Marketing Techniques – a Guide for Hotel Managers and Caterers*, London, Northwood Books 1982

Taneja, N K, Airline Planning: Corporate, Financial and Marketing, USA, Lexington Books 1982

Tourism and Recreation Research Unit, *Recreatiion Site Survey Manual: Methods and Techniques for Conducting Visitor Surveys*, London, E & F N Spon 1983

Vladimir, A, *The Complete Travel Marketing Handbook*, Lincolnwood, Illinois, NTC Business Books 1988

Wahab, S, Crampon, L & Rothfield, L, *Tourism Marketing*, London, Tourism International Press 1976

Witt, S & Moutinho, L, *Tourism Marketing and Management Handbook*, Hemel Hempstead, Prentice Hall 1989

Wood, M, (Ed) *Tourism Marketing for the Small Business*, London, English Tourist Board 1980

Index

ABLE, 124
ABTA, 16, 34, 90, 104, 121, 123, 149
  Code of Conduct, 8, 86, 105, 149, 150
Accor Hotels, 67
ACORN databases, 172
Advertising, 138–46
Advertising agencies, 139
Advertising Statistical Review, 100
AGB, 34, 35
AIDA, 55, 59, 138
Airtours, 88
Air Transport Users' Committee, 9, 87, 185
AMADEUS Computer Reservations System,
  136
American Airlines, 136
American Express, 66, 110
Annals of Tourism Research, 34
APEX fares, 134
APOLLO Computer Reservations System, 136
Austrotours, 67
Avis Rent-a-car, 126

BAA, 34
Barclays 'Connect' card, 128
BCG Matrix, 21
Beaulieu, 92–3
Beaver, Alan, 190
Benefits, product, 5
Bran, Christian, 173
Branding, 65–9
Branson, Richard, 65, 184
Break-even analysis, 83
Britannia Airways, 10
British Airways, 10, 58, 103–4, 118, 128, 136,
  155, 174, 197–8
British Rail, 162
British Tourist Authority (BTA), 9, 10, 33, 34,
  51, 76, 167
Brochures, 148–57
Budget Rent-a-car, 126
Bus and Coach Council, 34
Butlin, Sir Billy, 74, 92

Carousel Holidays, 150
Center Parcs, 174
Chartered Institute of Marketing, 4, 86, 140
Chartered Institute of Transport, 194
CIT, 4
Civil Aviation Authority (CAA), 33, 34
Clovelly, 8
Club, The, 56
Club Méditerranée, 92
Colley, R, 101
Computer Reservations Systems, 135–6
Concorde, 74, 80
Consortia, 124–6
Consumer Marketing, 9
Consumers' Association, 9, 87
Cook, Thomas, 66, 68, 89, 104, 110 129, 162,
  194
Coper, Hans, 79
Corporate identity, 191–4
Cosmos Holidays, 66, 67, 150, 155
Cross-elasticity of demand, 16
Cunard Line, 67, 70
Cycling for Softies, 53

DAGMAR, 101
Databases, 177
Delphi forecasting, 24
Delta Airlines, 136
Design, travel agency, 110–15
Devon Area Tourist Association (DATA), 124
Digest of Statistics, 7
Direct mail, 172–3, 176–7
Direct marketing, 171–83
Direct response advertising, 171–2
Direct sell holidays, 173–4
Discounting, 93–4
Disneyworld, 107
Distribution, 117–37
Douglas of Kirtleside, Lord, 155

Eagle Airlines, 65
Economist Intelligence Unit (EIU), 34, 46
Eco-tourism, 8

Educational study-trips, 194–6
Elasticity of demand, 16
English Tourist Board, 24, 34, 144
EFTPOS, 128, 136
European Community Directive on Package
    Holidays (1990), 149
Everyman Holidays, 155
Exchange Travel, 127

Fast Moving Consumer Goods (FMCG), ix,
    66, 160, 162
Fiesta Tours, 121
Forecasting, 22–4, 85
Forte Hotels, 67, 75
Franchising, 68, 126–7
Freefone, 135
Frequent Flyer Programme, 57

GALILEO Computer Reservations System,
    136
Gardeners' Delight Holidays, 174–5
Gibraltar, 59
Global Holidays, 67
Green tourism, 8
Greyhound Bus, 36
Gross National Product (GNP), 50
Gulf War, 10, 22

Heart of England Tourist Board, 60
Henley Centre, 85
Hertz Rent-a-car, 126
Hilton Hotels, 67, 68, 69
Holiday Inn Hotels, 66, 68, 74–5, 126
Holiday Which?, 9
Hoseasons Holidays, 144
Hotel, Catering and Institutional Management
    Association (HCIMA), 194
Howard and Sheth, 54

Industrial marketing, 9
Institute of Travel and Tourism (ITT), 194
Intention to purchase surveys, 24, 34
International Airline Passengers' Association
    (IAPA), 9
International Air Transport Association
    (IATA), 91
International Broadcasting Association (IBA),
    86

International Tourism Exchange, Berlin, 166
IPC Magazines, 60, 141
Irish Tourist Board, 56

Jersey, 59, 103
Jersey Tourism Committee, 103
Jorvik, 89

Kiam, Victor, 103
Kotler, P, 28
Kuoni Holidays, 155

Laker, Sir Freddie, 65
Levitt, T, 4, 63
Lewis, John, 89
Lufthansa Airlines, 136

MacNeill, John, 130
Malta Tourist Office, 194–5
Marginal costing, 83
Market focus, 20–1
Market gap analysis, 74
Market research brief, 36
Market segmentation, 55, 60–1, 153–4
Marketing,
    budgets, 25–6, 99–100, 138
    communications, 96–115
    control, 200–6
    history, 5
    Information System, 31–2, 33
    mix, 28–9
    organisation, 3, 4
    orientation, 26–8
    planning, 13–29
    research, 30–47
Maslow, A, 50, 56, 57
MEAL, 34
Monopolies and Mergers Commission (MMC),
    86, 88

National Consumers' Council, 87

Office of Fair Trading (OFT), 16, 87, 90, 91
Ogilvy, David, 184
Olympic Games, 90
Olympic Holidays, 67
Operation Stabiliser, 121
Orient Express, 65
Overbooking, 135

Owners Abroad, 15, 66, 88, 99, 110, 153, 174

P&O Line, 66, 70
Package Holiday Directive, European
    Community (1990), 149
Panel interviews, 36, 46
Panorama Holidays, 60
Paris Travel, 67
Pareto Principle, 129
Pearce, P, 58
Peer groups, 53
Perpignan, 6
Pickfords Travel, 110
Plog, Stanley, 56
Point of Sale merchandising (POS), 146, 159
Polperro, 8
Portland Holidays, 70, 120
Press relations, 188–90
Price elasticity of demand, 80
Price leadership, 20
Price Marking (Bargain Offers) Order (1979),
    86
Price Marking (Food and Drink on Premises)
    Order (1979), 86
Pricing policy, 79–94
Product differentiation, 20, 63–4
Product launches, 73–4
Product Life Cycle (PLC), 70–2, 88, 99, 163
Product-orientation, 3, 4, 5
Product policy, 62–77
Product screening, 75–6
Push and Pull strategies, 91, 98–9

Qualitative research, 45–6
Quantitative research, 45–6
Questionnaire design, 40–5

Rainbow Holidays, 128
Rank Organisation, 27
Reference groups, 53
Remington Razors, 103
Reservations systems, 117, 134–7
Restrictive Practices Court, 121
Return on investment (ROI), 87–8
Rooks, Martin, 174

SABRE Computer Reservations System, 136
Saga Holidays, 56
St Tropez, 53

Sales management, 132–3
Sales promotion, 159–69
Sales representatives, 130–2
Sales sequence, 107–10
Sampling, 37–40
Scandinavian Seaways, 93
Secondary research, 32
Selling, 105–10
Serenissima Holidays, 65, 69
Services, nature of, 10–11
Singapore Airlines, 103
Skal Club, 194
Social marketing, 9
Socio-economic groups, 52
Sponsorship, 190
STATS MR, 34
Substitutability, 16
Sunair Holidays, 69
Swedish Tourist Office, 140
Swissair, 67
Swiss Travel Service, 155
Switch cards, 128
SWOT analysis, 17–18

TATR (Travel and Tourism Research), 34
Tesco Supermarkets, 64
Thomson Holidays, 20, 26, 40, 46, 64, 66,
    67–8, 69, 70, 88, 92, 99, 110, 130, 135,
    142, 150, 153
Time-variable demand, 11
Tivoli Gardens, 93
Tjaereborg Holidays, 27, 69, 119, 120, 151–2,
    173–4
Torquay Leisure Hotels, 125
Tour Operators' Study Group (TOSG), 135
Tourism Management, 34
Tourism (Sleeping Accommodation Price
    Display) Order (1977), 86
Tourism Society, 34, 194
Townsend, Robert, 185
Townsend Thoresen Ferries, 197
Trade Descriptions Act (1968), 6, 148
Travel Trade Gazette, 190
Travicom Computer Reservations System, 136
TUI (Touristik Union International), 20
Tunisian National Tourist Board, 178
TWA, 131, 136
Twenties Holidays, 64

Unfair Contract Terms Act (1977), 148
Unique Selling Proposition, 64
United Airlines, 136
Universal Skytours, 155
Upminster Travel, 128

Verne, Jules Holidays, 68, 176
Virgin Airways, 65, 184

Wales Tourist Board,183
Wings Holidays, 150
Woodside Management Systems, 124–5
Worldspan Computer Reservations System, 136
World Travel Market, 166

Yugoslavia, 17
Yugotours, 67